THE STORY OF MANKIND

ETERNITY

THE STORY OF
MANKIND

BY

HENDRIK WILLEM
van LOON

LIVERIGHT
New York   London

Library of Congress Cataloging in Publication Data
Van Loon, Hendrik Willem, 1882–1944.
    The story of mankind.

    Includes index.
    Summary: This classic history, first published in 1921 and winner of the first Newbery Medal,
was illustrated in pen and ink by the author. This version has incorporated recent events to make
it an up-to-date world history.
    1. World history—Juvenile literature.   [1. World history]   I. Title.
D21.V3   1984   909   83-27566

ISBN 0-87140-156-8

Liveright Publishing Corporation
500 Fifth Avenue, New York, N.Y. 10110
W. W. Norton & Company Ltd.
10 Coptic Street, London WC1A 1PU

    4 5 6 7 8 9 0

To JIMMIE

"What is the use of a book without pictures?" said Alice.

PUBLISHERS' NOTE CONCERNING
THE UPDATED EDITION

The current edition has been brought up to date with the addition of a new concluding chapter by Professor John Merriman of Yale University and a number of new illustrations (appearing on pages 563, 565, 568, 571, 574, and 590) by Adam Simon. The publishers wish to express their deep gratitude to Professor Merriman and Mr. Simon.

In 1972 the publishers also updated the book with the assistance of Dr. Edward C. Prehn, Professor Paul Sears of Yale University, and Professor Edwin C. Broome of New York University.

FOREWORD

For Hansje and Willem:

WHEN I was twelve or thirteen years old, an uncle of mine who gave me my love for books and pictures promised to take me upon a memorable expedition. I was to go with him to the top of the tower of Old Saint Lawrence in Rotterdam.

And so, one fine day, a sexton with a key as large as that of Saint Peter opened a mysterious door. "Ring the bell," he said, "when you come back and want to get out," and with a great grinding of rusty old hinges he separated us from the noise of the busy street and locked us into a world of new and strange experiences.

For the first time in my life I was confronted by the phenomenon of audible silence. When we had climbed the first flight of stairs, I added another discovery to my limited knowledge of natural phenomena—that of tangible darkness. A match showed us where the upward road continued. We went to the next floor and then to the next and the next until I had lost count and then there came still another floor, and suddenly we had plenty of light. This floor was on an even height with the roof of the church, and it was used as a storeroom. Covered with many inches of dust, there lay the abandoned symbols of a venerable faith which had been discarded by the good people of the city many years ago. That which had meant life and death to our ancestors was here reduced to junk and rub-

bish. The industrious rat had built his nest among the carved
images and the ever watchful spider had opened up shop between the outspread arms of a kindly saint.

The next floor showed us from where we had derived our
light. Enormous open windows with heavy iron bars made
the high and barren room the roosting place of hundreds of
pigeons. The wind blew through the iron bars and the air was
filled with a weird and pleasing music. It was the noise of the
town below us, but a noise which had been purified and cleansed
by the distance. The rumbling of heavy carts and the clinking
of horses' hoofs, the winding of cranes and pulleys, the hissing
sound of the patient steam which had been set to do the work
of man in a thousand different ways—they had all been
blended into a softly rustling whisper which provided a beautiful background for the trembling cooing of the pigeons.

Here the stairs came to an end and the ladders began. And
after the first ladder (a slippery old thing which made one feel
his way with a cautious foot) there was a new and even greater
wonder, the town-clock. I saw the heart of time. I could hear
the heavy pulsebeats of the rapid seconds—one—two—three—
up to sixty. Then a sudden quivering noise when all the wheels
seemed to stop and another minute had been chopped off eternity. Without pause it began again—one—two—three—until
at last after a warning rumble and the scraping of many wheels
a thunderous voice, high above us, told the world that it was
the hour of noon.

On the next floor were the bells. The nice little bells and
their terrible sisters. In the centre the big bell, which made
me turn stiff with fright when I heard it in the middle of the
night telling a story of fire or flood. In solitary grandeur it
seemed to reflect upon those six hundred years during which
it had shared the joys and the sorrows of the good people of
Rotterdam. Around it, neatly arranged like the blue jars in
an old-fashioned apothecary shop, hung the little fellows, who
twice each week played a merry tune for the benefit of the
country-folk who had come to market to buy and sell and hear
what the big world had been doing. But in a corner—all alone

and shunned by the others—a big black bell, silent and stern, the bell of death.

Then darkness once more and other ladders, steeper and even more dangerous than those we had climbed before, and suddenly the fresh air of the wide heavens. We had reached the highest gallery. Above us the sky. Below us the city— a little toy-town, where busy ants were hastily crawling hither and thither, each one intent upon his or her particular business, and beyond the jumble of stones, the wide greenness of the open country.

It was my first glimpse of the big world.

Since then, whenever I have had the opportunity, I have gone to the top of the tower and enjoyed myself. It was hard work, but it repaid in full the mere physical exertion of climbing a few stairs.

Besides, I knew what my reward would be. I would see the land and the sky, and I would listen to the stories of my kind friend the watchman, who lived in a small shack, built in a sheltered corner of the gallery. He looked after the clock and was a father to the bells, and he warned of fires, but he enjoyed many free hours and then he smoked a pipe and thought his own peaceful thoughts. He had gone to school almost fifty years before and he had rarely read a book, but he had lived on the top of his tower for so many years that he had absorbed the wisdom of that wide world which surrounded him on all sides.

History he knew well, for it was a living thing with him. "There," he would say, pointing to a bend of the river, "there, my boy, do you see those trees? That is where the Prince of Orange cut the dikes to drown the land and save Leyden." Or he would tell me the tale of the old Meuse, until the broad river ceased to be a convenient harbour and became a wonderful highroad, carrying the ships of De Ruyter and Tromp upon that famous last voyage, when they gave their lives that the sea might be free to all.

Then there were the little villages, clustering around the protecting church which once, many years ago, had been the home of their Patron Saints. In the distance we could see the leaning tower of Delft. Within sight of its high arches, William the Silent had been murdered and there Grotius had learned to construe his first Latin sentences. And still further away, the long low body of the church of Gouda, the early home of the man whose wit had proved mightier than the armies of many an emperor, the charity-boy whom the world came to know as Erasmus.

Finally the silver line of the endless sea and as a contrast, immediately below us, the patchwork of roofs and chimneys and houses and gardens and hospitals and schools and railways, which we called our home. But the tower showed us the old home in a new light. The confused commotion of the streets and the market-place, of the factories and the workshop, became the well-ordered expression of human energy and purpose. Best of all, the wide view of the glorious past, which surrounded us on all sides, gave us new courage to face the problems of the future when we had gone back to our daily tasks.

History is the mighty Tower of Experience, which Time has built amidst the endless fields of bygone ages. It is no easy task to reach the top of this ancient structure and get the benefit of the full view. There is no elevator, but young feet are strong and it can be done.

Here I give you the key that will open the door.

When you return, you too will understand the reason for my enthusiasm.

HENDRIK WILLEM VAN LOON.

CONTENTS

CONTENTS xiii

xiv

CONTENTS

CONTENTS

LIST OF ILLUSTRATIONS

LIST OF PICTURES AND ANIMATED MAPS

THE STORY OF MANKIND

HIGH up in the North in the land called Svithjod, there stands a rock. It is a hundred miles high and a hundred miles wide. Once every thousand years a little bird comes to this rock to sharpen its beak.

When the rock has thus been worn away, then a single day of eternity will have gone by.

THE SETTING OF THE STAGE

WE live under the shadow of a gigantic question mark.
Who are we?
Where do we come from?
Whither are we bound?

Slowly, but with persistent courage, we have been pushing this question mark further and further towards that distant line, beyond the horizon, where we hope to find our answer.

We have not gone very far.

We still know very little but we have reached the point where (with a fair degree of accuracy) we can guess at many things.

In this chapter I shall tell you how (according to our best belief) the stage was set for the first appearance of man.

If we represent the time during which it has been possible for animal life to exist upon our planet by a line of this length,

then the tiny line just below indicates the age during which man (or a creature more or less resembling man) has lived upon this earth.

Man was the last to come but the first to use his brain for the purpose of conquering the forces of nature. That is the reason why we are going to study him, rather than cats or dogs or horses or any of the other animals, who, all in their own way, have a very interesting historical development behind them.

IT RAINED INCESSANTLY

In the beginning, the planet upon which we live was (as far as we now know) a large ball of flaming matter, a tiny cloud of smoke in the endless ocean of space. Gradually, in the course of millions of years, the surface burned itself out, and was covered with a thin layer of rocks. Upon these lifeless rocks the rain descended in endless torrents, wearing out the hard granite and carrying the dust to the valleys that lay hidden between the high cliffs of the steaming earth.

Finally the hour came when the sun broke through the clouds and saw how this little planet was covered with a few small puddles which were to develop into the mighty oceans of the eastern and western hemispheres.

Then one day the great wonder happened. What had been dead, gave birth to life.

The first living cell floated upon the waters of the sea.

For millions of years it drifted aimlessly with the currents. But during all that time it was developing certain habits that it might survive more easily upon the inhospitable earth. Some of these cells were happiest in the dark depths of the lakes and the pools. They took root in the slimy sediments which had been carried down from the tops of the hills and they became plants. Others preferred to move about and they grew strange jointed legs, like scorpions and began to crawl along the bottom of the sea amidst the plants and the pale green things that looked like jelly-fishes. Still others (covered with scales) depended upon a swimming motion to go from place to place in their search for food, and gradually they populated the ocean with myriads of fishes.

Meanwhile the plants had increased in number and they had to search for new dwelling places. There was no more room ror them at the bottom of the sea. Reluctantly they left the water and made a new home in the marshes and on the mud-banks that lay at the foot of the mountains. Twice a day the tides of the ocean covered them with their brine. For the rest of the time, the plants made the best of their uncomfortable situation and tried to survive in the thin air which surrounded the surface of the planet. After centuries of training, they learned how to live as comfortably in the air as they had done in the water. They increased in size and became shrubs and trees and at last they learned how to grow lovely flowers which attracted the attention of the busy big bumble-bees and the

THE ASCENT OF MAN

birds who carried the seeds far
and wide until the whole earth
had become covered with green
pastures, or lay dark under the
shadow of the big trees.

But some of the fishes too
had begun to leave the sea, and
they had learned how to breathe
with lungs as well as with gills.
We call such creatures amphibious, which means that they are
able to live with equal ease on
the land and in the water. The
first frog who crosses your path

THE PLANTS LEAVE THE SEA

can tell you all about the pleasures of the double existence of
the amphibian.

Once outside of the water, these animals gradually adapted
themselves more and more to life on land. Some became reptiles (creatures who crawl like lizards) and they shared the
silence of the forests with the insects. That they might move
faster through the soft soil, they improved upon their legs
and their size increased until the world was populated with
gigantic forms (which the hand-books of biology list under
the names of Ichthyosaurus and Megalosaurus and Bron-
tosaurus) who grew to be thirty to forty feet long and who
could have played with elephants as a full grown cat plays with
her kittens.

Some of the members of this reptilian family began to live in
the tops of the trees, which were then often more than a hundred
feet high. They no longer needed their legs for the purpose
of walking, but it was necessary for them to move quickly from
branch to branch. And so they changed a part of their skin
into a sort of parachute, which stretched between the sides of
their bodies and the small toes of their fore-feet, and gradually
they covered this skinny parachute with feathers and made
their tails into a steering gear and flew from tree to tree and
developed into true birds.

Then a strange thing happened. All the gigantic reptiles died within a short time. We do not know the reason. Perhaps it was due to a sudden change in climate. Perhaps they had grown so large that they could neither swim nor walk nor crawl, and they starved to death within sight but not within reach of the big ferns and trees. Whatever the cause, the million year old world-empire of the big reptiles was over.

The world now began to be occupied by very different creatures. They were the descendants of the reptiles but they were quite unlike these because they fed their young from the "mammæ" or the breasts of the mother. Wherefore modern science calls these animals "mammals." They had shed the scales of the fish. They did not adopt the feathers of the bird, but they covered their bodies with hair. The mammals however developed other habits which gave their race a great advantage over the other animals. The female of the species carried the eggs of the young inside her body until they were hatched and while all other living beings, up to that time, had left their children exposed to the dangers of cold and heat, and the attacks of wild beasts, the mammals kept their young with them for a long time and sheltered them while they were still too weak to fight their enemies. In this way the young mammals were given a much better chance to survive, because they learned many things from their mothers, as you will know if you have ever watched a cat teaching her kittens to take care of themselves and how to wash their faces and how to catch mice.

But of these mammals I need not tell you much for you know them well. They surround you on all sides. They are your daily companions in the streets and in your home, and you can see your less familiar cousins behind the bars of the zoological garden.

And now we come to the parting of the ways when man suddenly leaves the endless procession of dumbly living and dying creatures and begins to use his reason to shape the destiny of his race.

One mammal in particular seemed to surpass all others in

its ability to find food and shelter. It had learned to use its fore-feet for the purpose of holding its prey, and by dint of practice it had developed a hand-like claw. After innumerable attempts it had learned how to balance the whole of the body upon the hind legs. (This is a difficult act, which every child has to learn anew although the human race has been doing it for over a million years.)

This creature, half ape and half monkey but superior to both, became the most successful hunter and could make a living in every clime. For greater safety, it usually moved about in groups. It learned how to make strange grunts to warn its young of approaching danger and after many hundreds of thousands of years it began to use these throaty noises for the purpose of talking.

This creature, though you may hardly believe it, was your first "man-like" ancestor.

OUR EARLIEST ANCESTORS

WE know very little about the first "true" men. We have never seen their pictures. In the deepest layer of clay of an ancient soil we have sometimes found pieces of their bones. These lay buried amidst the broken skeletons of other animals that have long since disappeared from the face of the earth. Anthropologists (learned scientists who devote their lives to the study of man as a member of the animal kingdom) have taken these bones and they have been able to reconstruct our earliest ancestors with a fair degree of accuracy.

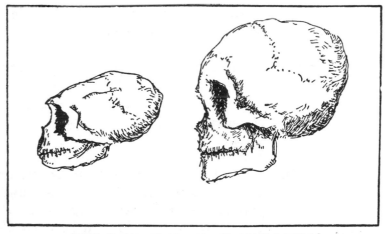

THE GROWTH OF THE HUMAN SKULL

The great-great-grandfather of the human race was a very ugly and unattractive mammal. He was quite small, much

9

smaller than the people of today. The heat of the sun and the biting wind of the cold winter had coloured his skin a dark brown. His head and most of his body, his arms and legs too, were covered with long, coarse hair. He had very thin but strong fingers which made his hands look like those of a monkey. His forehead was low and his jaw was like the jaw of a wild animal which uses its teeth both as fork and knife. He wore no clothes. He had seen no fire except the flames of the rumbling volcanoes which filled the earth with their smoke and their lava.

He lived in the damp blackness of vast forests, as the pygmies of Africa do to this very day. When he felt the pangs of hunger he ate raw leaves and the roots of plants or he took the eggs away from an angry bird and fed them to his own young. Once in a while, after a long and patient chase, he would catch a sparrow or a small wild dog or perhaps a rabbit. These he would eat raw for he had never discovered that food tasted better when it was cooked.

During the hours of day, this primitive human being prowled about looking for things to eat.

When night descended upon the earth, he hid his wife and his children in a hollow tree or behind some heavy boulders, for he was surrounded on all sides by ferocious animals and when it was dark these animals began to prowl about, looking for something to eat for their mates and their own young, and they liked the taste of human beings. It was a world where you must either eat or be eaten, and life was very unhappy because it was full of fear and misery.

In summer, man was exposed to the scorching rays of the sun, and during the winter his children would freeze to death in his arms. When such a creature hurt itself, (and hunting animals are forever breaking their bones or spraining their ankles) he had no one to take care of him and he must die a horrible death.

Like many of the animals who fill the Zoo with their strange noises, early man liked to jabber. That is to say, he endlessly repeated the same unintelligible gibberish because it

THE SHORT HEAVY LINE INDICATES THE DURATION OF HISTORIC TIMES

HISTORY

ABOUT 6000 YEARS AGO THE WRITTEN RECORD OF HISTORY BEGINS

AT LAST IT DEVELOPED INTO A TRUE MAN

IT SURVIVED HUNGER AND COLD AND DISEASE

THIS WILD CREATURE STRUGGLED UPWARDS FOR HUNDREDS OF THOUSANDS OF YEARS

THE ASCENT OF MAN WAS VERY SLOW

THE WORLD WAS MILLIONS OF YEARS OLD WHEN A CREATURE APPEARED WHICH WAS TO BE OUR ANGESTOR

THE ASCENT OF MAN.

THE ZIGZAG LINE INDICATES THE DURATION OF PREHISTORIC TIMES

PREHISTORY AND HISTORY

pleased him to hear the sound of his voice. In due time he learned that he could use this guttural noise to warn his fellow beings whenever danger threatened and he gave certain little shrieks which came to mean "there is a tiger!" or "here come five elephants." Then the others grunted something back at him and their growl meant, "I see them," or "let us run away and hide." And this was probably the origin of all language.

But, as I have said before, of these beginnings we know so very little. Early man had no tools and he built himself no houses. He lived and died and left no trace of his existence except a few collar-bones and a few pieces of his skull. These tell us that many thousands of years ago the world was inhabited by certain mammals who were quite different from all the other animals—who had probably developed from another unknown ape-like animal which had learned to walk on its hind-legs and use its fore-paws as hands—and who were most probably connected with the creatures who happen to be our own immediate ancestors.

It is little enough we know and the rest is darkness.

PREHISTORIC MAN

PREHISTORIC MAN BEGINS TO MAKE THINGS FOR HIMSELF

EARLY man did not know what time meant. He kept no records of birthdays or wedding anniversaries or the hour of death. He had no idea of days or weeks or even years. But in a general way he kept track of the seasons for he had noticed that the cold winter was invariably followed by the mild spring—that spring grew into the hot summer when fruits ripened and the wild ears of corn were ready to be eaten and that summer ended when sudden gusts of wind swept the leaves from the trees and a number of animals were getting ready for the long hibernal sleep.

But now, something unusual and rather frightening had happened. Something was the matter with the weather. The warm days of summer had come very late. The fruits had not ripened. The tops of the mountains which used to be covered with grass now lay deeply hidden underneath a heavy burden of snow.

Then, one morning, a number of wild people, different from the other creatures who lived in that neighbourhood, came wandering down from the region of the high peaks. They looked lean and appeared to be starving. They uttered sounds which no one could understand. They seemed to say that they were hungry. There was not food enough for both the old inhabitants and the newcomers. When they tried to stay

13

more than a few days there was a terrible battle with claw-like hands and feet and whole families were killed. The others fled back to their mountain slopes and died in the next blizzard.

But the people in the forest were greatly frightened. All the time the days grew shorter and the nights grew colder than they ought to have been.

Finally, in a gap between two high hills, there appeared a tiny speck of greenish ice. Rapidly it increased in size. A gigantic glacier came sliding downhill. Huge stones were being pushed into the valley. With the noise of a dozen thunderstorms torrents of ice and mud and blocks of granite suddenly tumbled among the people of the forest and killed them while they slept. Century old trees were crushed into kindling wood. And then it began to snow.

It snowed for months and months. All the plants died and the animals fled in search of the southern sun. Man hoisted his young upon his back and followed them. But he could not travel as fast as the wilder creatures and he was forced to choose between quick thinking or quick dying. He seems to have preferred the former for he has managed to survive the terrible glacial periods which upon four different occasions threatened to kill every human being on the face of the earth

In the first place it was necessary that man clothe himself lest he freeze to death. He learned how to dig holes and cover them with branches and leaves and in these traps he caught bears and hyenas, which he then killed with heavy stones and whose skins he used as coats for himself and his family.

Next came the housing problem. This was simple. Many animals were in the habit of sleeping in dark caves. Man now followed their example, drove the animals out of their warm homes and claimed them for his own.

Even so, the climate was too severe for most people and the old and the young died at a terrible rate. Then a genius bethought himself of the use of fire. Once, while out hunting, he had been caught in a forest-fire. He remembered that he had been almost roasted to death by the flames. Thus far fire had been an enemy. Now it became a friend. A dead tree

THE GLACIERS
ARE
RETREATING

ARCTIC
SEA

THE BALTIC

ATLANTIC
OCEAN

ELBE

MAN IS MOVING BACK
INTO THE DESERTED
PLAINS
OF
EUROPE

THAMES

RHINE

DANUBE

PYRENEES

THE ALPS
STILL COVERED WITH ICE

BLACK
SEA

THE FORESTS ARE ONCE MORE
MOVING NORTHWARD

THE BEGINNING
OF THE
MEDITERRANEAN
SEA

THIS IS AFRICA

was dragged into the cave and lighted by means of smouldering branches from a burning wood. This turned the cave into
a cozy little room.

And then one evening a dead chicken fell into the fire. It
was not rescued until it had been well roasted. Man discovered
that meat tasted better when cooked and he then and there
discarded one of the old habits which he had shared with the
other animals and began to prepare his food.

In this way thousands of years passed. Only the people
with the cleverest brains survived. They had to struggle day
and night against cold and hunger. They were forced to invent
tools. They learned how to sharpen stones into axes and how
to make hammers. They were obliged to put up large stores
of food for the endless days of the winter and they found that
clay could be made into bowls and jars and hardened in the
rays of the sun. And so the glacial period, which had threatened to destroy the human race, became its greatest teacher
because it forced man to use his brain.

HIEROGLYPHICS

THE EGYPTIANS INVENT THE ART OF WRITING AND THE RECORD OF HISTORY BEGINS

THESE earliest ancestors of ours who lived in the great European wilderness were rapidly learning many new things It is safe to say that in due course of time they would have given up the ways of savages and would have developed a civilisation of their own. But suddenly there came an end to their isolation. They were discovered.

A traveller from an unknown southland who had dared to cross the sea and the high mountain passes had found his way to the wild people of the European continent. He came from Africa. His home was in Egypt.

The valley of the Nile had developed a high stage of civilisation thousands of years before the people of the west had dreamed of the possibilities of a fork or a wheel or a house. And we shall therefore leave our great-great-grandfathers in their caves, while we visit the southern and eastern shores of the Mediterranean, where stood the earliest school of the human race.

The Egyptians have taught us many things. They were excellent farmers. They knew all about irrigation. They built temples which were afterwards copied by the Greeks and which served as the earliest models for the churches in which we worship nowadays. They had invented a calendar which proved such a useful instrument for the purpose of measuring time that it has survived with a few changes until today. But most important of all, the Egyptians had learned how to preserve speech for the benefit of future generations. They had invented the art of writing.

We are so accustomed to newspapers and books and magazines that we take it for granted that the world has always been able to read and write. As a matter of fact, writing, the most important of all inventions, is quite new. Without written documents we should be like cats and dogs, who can only teach their kittens and their puppies a few simple things and who, because they cannot write, possess no way in which they can make use of the experience of those generations of cats and dogs that have gone before.

In the first century before our era, when the Romans came to Egypt, they found the valley full of strange little pictures which seemed to have something to do with the history of the country. But the Romans were not interested in "anything foreign" and did not inquire into the origin of these queer figures which covered the walls of the temples and the walls of the palaces and endless reams of flat sheets made out of the papyrus reed. The last of the Egyptian priests who had understood the holy art of making such pictures had died several years before. Egypt deprived of its independence had become a store-house filled with important historical documents which no one could decipher and which were of no earthly use to either man or beast.

Seventeen centuries went by and Egypt remained a land of mystery. But in the year 1798 a French general by the name of Bonaparte happened to visit eastern Africa to prepare for an attack upon the British Indian Colonies. He did not get beyond the Nile, and his campaign was a failure. But, quite accidentally, the famous French expedition solved the problem of the ancient Egyptian picture-language.

One day a young French officer, much bored by the dreary life of his little fortress on the Rosetta river (a mouth of the Nile) decided to spend a few idle hours rummaging among

the ruins of the Nile Delta. And behold! he found a stone
which greatly puzzled him. Like everything else in Egypt
it was covered with little figures. But this particular slab of
black basalt was different from anything that had ever been
discovered. It carried three inscriptions. One of these was
in Greek. The Greek language was known. "All that is
necessary," so he reasoned, "is to compare the Greek text with
the Egyptian figures, and they will at once tell their secrets."

The plan sounded simple enough but it took more than
twenty years to solve the riddle. In the year 1802 a French
professor by the name of Champollion began to compare the
Greek and the Egyptian texts of the famous Rosetta stone. In
the year 1823 he announced that he had discovered the meaning of fourteen little figures. A short time later he died from
overwork, but the main principles of Egyptian writing had
become known. Today the story of the valley of the Nile is
better known to us than the story of the Mississippi River.
We possess a written record which covers four thousand years
of chronicled history.

As the ancient Egyptian hieroglyphics (the word means
"sacred writing") have played such a very great rôle in history, (a few of them in modified form have even found their
way into our own alphabet,) you ought to know something
about the ingenious system which was used fifty centuries ago
to preserve the spoken word for the benefit of the coming
generations.

Of course, you know what a sign language is. Every
Indian story of our western plains has a chapter devoted to
strange messages written in the form of little pictures which
tell how many buffaloes were killed and how many hunters
there were in a certain party. As a rule it is not difficult to
understand the meaning of such messages.

Ancient Egyptian, however, was not a sign language. The
clever people of the Nile had passed beyond that stage long
before. Their pictures meant a great deal more than the object
which they represented, as I shall try to explain to you now.

Suppose that you were Champollion, and that you were examining a stack of papyrus sheets, all covered with hieroglyphics. Suddenly you came across a picture of a man with a saw. "Very well," you would say, "that means of course that a farmer went out to cut down a tree." Then you take another papyrus. It tells the story of a queen who had died at the age of eighty-two. In the midst of a sentence appears the picture of the man with the saw. Queens of eighty-two do not handle saws. The picture therefore must mean something else. But what?

That is the riddle which the Frenchman finally solved. He discovered that the Egyptians were the first to use what we now call "phonetic writing"—a system of characters which reproduce the "sound" (or phone) of the spoken word and which make it possible for us to translate all our spoken words into a written form, with the help of only a few dots and dashes and pothooks.

Let us return for a moment to the little fellow with the saw. The word "saw" either means a certain tool which you will find in a carpenter's shop, or it means the past tense of the verb "to see."

This is what had happened to the word during the course of centuries. First of all it had meant only the particular tool which it represented. Then that meaning had been lost and it had become the past participle of a verb. After several hundred years, the Egyptians lost sight of both these meanings and

the picture came to stand for a single letter, the

letter S. A short sentence will show you what I mean. Here is a modern English sentence as it would have been written in

hieroglyphics.

The either means one of these two round objects

in your head, which allow you to see or it means "I," the person who is talking.

A is either an insect which gathers honey, or it

represents the verb "to be" which means to exist. Again, it may be the first part of a verb like "be-come" or "be-have."

In this particular instance it is followed by which

means a "leaf" or "leave" or "lieve" (the sound of all three words is the same).

The "eye" you know all about.

Finally you get the picture of a   It is a giraffe.

It is part of the old sign-language out of which the hieroglyphics developed.

You can now read that sentence without much difficulty. "I believe I saw a giraffe."

Having invented this system the Egyptians developed it during thousands of years until they could write anything they wanted, and they used these "canned words" to send messages to friends, to keep business accounts and to keep a record of the history of their country, that future generations might benefit by the mistakes of the past.

THE NILE VALLEY

THE BEGINNING OF CIVILISATION IN THE VALLEY OF THE NILE

THE history of man is the record of a hungry creature in search of food. Wherever food was plentiful, thither man has travelled to make his home.

The fame of the Valley of the Nile must have spread at an early date. From the interior of Africa and from the desert of Arabia and from the western part of Asia people had flocked to Egypt to claim their share of the rich farms. Together these invaders had formed a new race which called itself "Remi" or "the Men" just as we sometimes call America "God's own country." They had good reason to be grateful to a Fate which had carried them to this narrow strip of land. In the summer of each year the Nile turned the valley into a shallow lake and when the waters receded all the grainfields and the pastures were covered with several inches of the most fertile clay.

In Egypt a kindly river did the work of a million men and made it possible to feed the teeming population of the first large cities of which we have any record. It is true that all the arable land was not in the valley. But a complicated system of small canals and well-sweeps carried water from the river-level to the top of the highest banks and an even more intricate system of irrigation trenches spread it throughout the land.

THE VALLEY OF EGYPT

While man of the prehistoric age had been obliged to spend sixteen hours out of every twenty-four gathering food for himself and the members of his tribe, the Egyptian peasant or the inhabitant of the Egyptian city found himself possessed of a certain leisure. He used this spare time to make himself many things that were merely ornamental and not the least bit useful.

More than that. One day he discovered that his brain was capable of thinking all kinds of thoughts which had nothing to do with the problems of eating and sleeping and finding a home for the children. The Egyptian began to speculate upon many strange problems that confronted him. Where did the stars come from? Who made the noise of the thunder which frightened him so terribly? Who made the River Nile rise with such regularity that it was possible to base the calendar upon the appearance and the disappearance of the annual floods? Who was he, himself, a strange little creature surrounded on all sides by death and sickness and yet happy and full of laughter?

He asked these many questions and certain people obligingly stepped forward to answer these inquiries to the best of their ability. The Egyptians called them "priests" and they became the guardians of his thoughts and gained great respect in the community. They were highly learned men who were entrusted with the sacred task of keeping the written records. They understood that it is not good for man to think only of his immediate advantage in this world and they drew his attention to the days of the future when his soul would dwell beyond the mountains of the west and must give an account of his deeds to Osiris, the mighty God who was the Ruler of the Living and the Dead and who judged the acts of men according to their merits. Indeed, the priests made so much of that future day in the realm of Isis and Osiris that the Egyptians began to regard life merely as a short preparation for the Hereafter and turned the teeming valley of the Nile into a land devoted to the Dead.

In a strange way, the Egyptians had come to believe that no soul could enter the realm of Osiris without the possession of the body which had been its place of residence in this world. Therefore as soon as a man was dead his relatives took his corpse and had it embalmed. For weeks it was soaked in a solution of natron and then it was filled with pitch. The Persian word for pitch was "Mumiai" and the embalmed body was called a "Mummy." It was wrapped in yards and yards of specially prepared linen and it was placed in a specially prepared coffin ready to be removed to its final home. But an Egyptian grave was a real home where the body was surrounded by pieces of furniture and musical instruments (to while away the dreary hours of waiting) and by little statues of cooks and bakers and barbers (that the occupant of this

THE BUILDING OF THE PYRAMIDS

dark home might be decently provided with food and need not
go about unshaven).

Originally these graves had been dug into the rocks of the
western mountains but as the Egyptians moved northward
they were obliged to build their cemeteries in the desert. The
desert however is full of wild animals and equally wild robbers
and they broke into the graves and disturbed the mummy or
stole the jewelry that had been buried with the body. To prevent such unholy desecration the Egyptians used to build small
mounds of stones on top of the graves. These little mounds
gradually grew in size, because the rich people built higher
mounds than the poor and there was a good deal of competition to see who could make the highest hill of stones. The

record was made by King Khufu, whom the Greeks called Cheops and who lived thirty centuries before our era. His mound, which the Greeks called a pyramid (because the Egyptian word for high was pir-em-us) was over five hundred feet high.

It covered more than thirteen acres of desert which is three times as much space as that occupied by the church of St. Peter, the largest edifice of the Christian world.

During twenty years, over a hundred thousand men were busy carrying the necessary stones from the other side of the river—ferrying them across the Nile (how they ever managed to do this, we do not understand), dragging them in many instances a long distance across the desert and finally hoisting them into their correct position. But so well did the King's architects and engineers perform their task that the narrow passage-way which leads to the royal tomb in the heart of the stone monster has never yet been pushed out of shape by the weight of those thousands of tons of stone which press upon it from all sides.

THE STORY OF EGYPT

THE RISE AND FALL OF EGYPT

THE river Nile was a kind friend but occasionally it was a hard taskmaster. It taught the people who lived along its banks the noble art of "team-work." They depended upon each other to build their irrigation trenches and keep their dikes in repair. In this way they learned how to get along with their neighbours and their mutual-benefit-association quite easily developed into an organised state.

Then one man grew more powerful than most of his neighbours and he became the leader of the community and their commander-in-chief when the envious neighbours of western Asia invaded the prosperous valley. In due course of time he became their King and ruled all the land from the Mediterranean to the mountains of the west.

But these political adventures of the old Pharaohs (the word meant "the Man who lived in the Big House") rarely interested the patient and toiling peasant of the grain fields. Provided he was not obliged to pay more taxes to his King than he thought just, he accepted the rule of Pharaoh as he accepted the rule of Mighty Osiris.

It was different however when a foreign invader came and robbed him of his possessions. After twenty centuries of independent life, a savage Arab tribe of shepherds, called the Hyksos, attacked Egypt and for five hundred years they were the masters of the valley of the Nile. They were highly unpopular and great hate was also felt for the Hebrews who came to the land of Goshen to find a shelter after their long wandering through the desert and who helped the foreign usurper by acting as his tax-gatherers and his civil servants.

But shortly after the year 1700 B.C. the people of Thebes began a revolution and after a long struggle the Hyksos were driven out of the country and Egypt was free once more.

A thousand years later, when Assyria conquered all of western Asia, Egypt became part of the empire of Sardanapalus. In the seventh century B.C. it became once more an independent state which obeyed the rule of a king who lived in the city of Saïs in the Delta of the Nile. But in the year 525 B.C., Cambyses, the king of the Persians, took possession of Egypt and in the fourth century B.C., when Persia was conquered by Alexander the Great, Egypt too became a Macedonian province. It regained a semblance of independence when one of Alexander's generals set himself up as king of a new Egyptian state and founded the dynasty of the Ptolemies, who resided in the newly built city of Alexandria.

Finally, in the year 39 B.C., the Romans came. The last Egyptian queen, Cleopatra, tried her best to save the country. Her beauty and charm were more dangerous to the Roman generals than half a dozen Egyptian army corps. Twice she was successful in her attacks upon the hearts of her Roman conquerors. But in the year 30 B.C., Augustus, the nephew and heir of Cæsar, landed in Alexandria. He did not share his late uncle's admiration for the lovely princess. He destroyed her armies, but spared her life that he might make her march in his triumph as part of the spoils of war. When Cleopatra heard of this plan, she killed herself by taking poison. And Egypt became a Roman province.

MESOPOTAMIA

MESOPOTAMIA—THE SECOND CENTRE OF EASTERN CIVILISATION

I AM going to take you to the top of the highest pyramid and I am going to ask that you imagine yourself possessed of the eyes of a hawk. Way, way off, in the distance, far beyond the yellow sands of the desert, you will see something green and shimmering. It is a valley situated between two rivers. It is the Paradise of the Old Testament. It is the land of mystery and wonder which the Greeks called Mesopotamia—the "country between the rivers."

The names of the two rivers are the Euphrates (which the Babylonians called the Purattu) and the Tigris (which was known as the Diklat). They begin their course amidst the snows of the mountains of Armenia where Noah's Ark found a resting place and slowly they flow through the southern plain until they reach the muddy banks of the Persian gulf. They perform a very useful service. They turn the arid regions of western Asia into a fertile garden.

The valley of the Nile had attracted people because it had offered them food upon fairly easy terms. The "land between the rivers" was popular for the same reason. It was a country full of promise and both the inhabitants of the northern mountains and the tribes which roamed through the southern deserts tried to claim this territory as their own and most exclusive possession. The constant rivalry between the

mountaineers and the desert-nomads led to endless warfare.
Only the strongest and the bravest could hope to survive and
that will explain why Mesopotamia became the home of a very
strong race of men who were capable of creating a civilisation
which was in every respect as important as that of Egypt.

THE SUMERIANS

THE SUMERIAN NAIL WRITERS, WHOSE CLAY TABLETS TELL US THE STORY OF ASSYRIA AND BABYLONIA, THE GREAT SEMITIC MELTING-POT

THE fifteenth century was an age of great discoveries. Columbus tried to find a way to the island of Kathay and stumbled upon a new and unsuspected continent. An Austrian bishop equipped an expedition which was to travel eastward and find the home of the Grand Duke of Muscovy, a voyage which led to complete failure, for Moscow was not visited by western men until a generation later. Meanwhile a certain Venetian by the name of Barbero had explored the ruins of western Asia and had brought back reports of a most curious language which he had found carved in the rocks of the temples of Shiraz and engraved upon endless pieces of baked clay.

But Europe was busy with many other things and it was not until the end of the eighteenth century that the first "cuneiform inscriptions" (so-called because the letters were wedge-shaped and wedge is called "Cuneus" in Latin) were brought to Europe by a Danish surveyor, named Niebuhr. Then it took thirty years before a patient German schoolmaster by the name of Grotefend had deciphered the first four letters, the D, the A, the R and the SH, the name of the Persian King Darius. And another twenty years had to go by

until a British officer, Henry Rawlinson, who found the famous
inscription of Behistun, gave us a workable key to the nail-
writing of western Asia.

Compared to the problem of deciphering these nail-writ-
ings, the job of Champollion had been an easy one. The
Egyptians used pictures. But the Sumerians, the earliest
inhabitants of Mesopotamia, who had hit upon the idea of
scratching their words in tablets of clay, had discarded pictures
entirely and had evolved a system of V-shaped figures which
showed little connection with the pictures out of which they
had been developed. A few examples will show you what I
mean. In the beginning a star, when drawn with a nail into

a brick looked as follows: This sign however was too

cumbersome and after a short while when the meaning of
"heaven" was added to that of star the picture was simplified

in this way which made it even more of a puzzle.

In the same way an ox changed from into

and a fish changed from 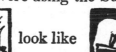 into The sun

was originally a plain circle and became

If we were using the Sumerian script today we would make an

look like . This system of writing down our

ideas looks rather complicated but for more than thirty centuries it was used by the Sumerians and the Babylonians and
the Assyrians and the Persians and all the different races
which forced their way into the fertile valley.

The story of Mesopotamia is one of endless warfare and
conquest.   First the Sumerians came from the North.   They
were a white people who had lived in the mountains.   They

A TOWER OF BABEL

had been accustomed to worship their Gods on the tops of
hills.   After they had entered the plain they constructed artificial little hills on top of which they built their altars.   They
did not know how to build stairs and they therefore surrounded their towers with sloping galleries.   Our engineers
have borrowed this idea, as you may see in our big railroad
stations where ascending galleries lead from one floor to another.   We may have borrowed other ideas from the Sumerians but we do not know it.   The Sumerians were entirely ab

sorbed by those races that entered the fertile valley at a later date. Their towers however still stand amidst the ruins of Mesopotamia. The Jews saw them when they went into exile in the land of Babylon and they called them towers of Bab-Illi, or towers of Babel.

In the fortieth century before our era, the Sumerians had entered Mesopotamia. They were soon afterwards over-

NINEVEH

powered by the Akkadians, one of the many tribes from the desert of Arabia who speak a common dialect and who are known as the "Semites," because in the olden days people believed them to be the direct descendants of Shem, one of the three sons of Noah. A thousand years later, the Akkadians were forced to submit to the rule of the Amorites, another Semitic desert tribe whose great King Hammurabi built himself a magnificent palace in the holy city of Babylon and who gave his people a set of laws which made the Babylonian state the best administered empire of the ancient world. **Next the Hittites**, whom you will also meet in the Old Testament, overran the Fertile Valley and destroyed whatever they could not carry away. They in turn were vanquished by the followers of the great desert God, Ashur, who called themselves Assyrians and who made the city of Nineveh the center of a vast and terrible empire which conquered all of western Asia and Egypt and gathered taxes from countless subject races until the end of the seventh century before the birth of Christ when

THE HOLY CITY OF BABYLON

the Chaldeans, also a Semitic tribe, re-established Babylon and made that city the most important capital of that day. Nebuchadnezzar, the best known of their Kings, encouraged the study of science, and our modern knowledge of astronomy and mathematics is all based upon certain first principles which were discovered by the Chaldeans. In the year 538 B.C. a crude tribe of Persian shepherds invaded this old land and overthrew the empire of the Chaldeans. Two hundred years later, they in turn were overthrown by Alexander the Great, who turned the Fertile Valley, the old melting-pot of so many Semitic races, into a Greek province. Next came the Romans and after the Romans, the Turks, and Mesopotamia, the second centre of the world's civilisation, became a vast wilderness where huge mounds of earth told a story of ancient glory.

```
┌─────────────────────────────────────────────┐
│                                               │
│                    MOSES                      │
│                                               │
└─────────────────────────────────────────────┘
```

THE STORY OF MOSES, THE LEADER OF THE JEWISH PEOPLE

SOME time during the twentieth century before our era, a small and unimportant tribe of Semitic shepherds had left its old home, which was situated in the land of Ur on the mouth of the Euphrates, and had tried to find new pastures within the domain of the Kings of Babylonia. They had been driven away by the royal soldiers and they had moved westward looking for a little piece of unoccupied territory where they might set up their tents.

This tribe of shepherds was known as the Hebrews or, as we call them, the Jews. They had wandered far and wide, and after many years of dreary peregrinations they had been given shelter in Egypt. For more than five centuries they had dwelt among the Egyptians and when their adopted country had been overrun by the Hyksos marauders (as I told you in the story of Egypt) they had managed to make themselves useful to the foreign invader and had been left in the undisturbed possession of their grazing fields. But after a long war of independence the Egyptians had driven the Hyksos out of the valley of the Nile and then the Jews had come upon evil times for they had been degraded to the rank of common slaves and they had been forced to work on the royal roads and on the Pyramids. And as the frontiers were

38

THE WANDERINGS OF THE JEWS

guarded by the Egyptian soldiers it had been impossible for the Jews to escape.

After many years of suffering they were saved from their miserable fate by a young Jew, called Moses, who for a long time had dwelt in the desert and there had learned to appreciate the simple virtues of his earliest ancestors, who had kept away from cities and city-life and had refused to let themselves be corrupted by the ease and the luxury of a foreign civilisation.

Moses decided to bring his people back to a love of the ways of the patriarchs. He succeeded in evading the Egyptian troops that were sent after him and led his fellow tribesmen into the heart of the plain at the foot of Mount Sinai. During his long and lonely life in the desert, he had learned to revere the strength of the great God of the Thunder and the Storm, who ruled the high heavens and upon whom the shepherds depended for life and light and breath. This God, one of the many divinities who were widely worshipped in western Asia, was called Jehovah, and through the teaching of Moses, he became the sole Master of the Hebrew race.

One day, Moses disappeared from the camp of the Jews. It was whispered that he had gone away carrying two tablets of rough-hewn stone. That afternoon, the top of the mountain was lost to sight. The darkness of a terrible storm hid it from the eye of man. But when Moses returned, behold! there stood engraved upon the tablets the words which Jehovah had spoken unto the people of Israel amidst the crash of his thunder and the blinding flashes of his lightning. And from that moment, Jehovah was recognised by all the Jews as the Highest Master of their Fate, the only True God, who had taught them how to live holy lives when he bade them to follow the wise lessons of his Ten Commandments.

They followed Moses when he bade them continue their journey through the desert. They obeyed him when he told them what to eat and drink and what to avoid that they might keep well in the hot climate. And finally after many years of wandering they came to a land which seemed pleasant and prosperous. It was called Palestine, which means the country of the "Pilistu" the Philistines, a small tribe of Cretans who had settled along the coast after they had been driven away from their own island. Unfortunately, the mainland, Palestine, was already inhabited by another Semitic race, called the Canaanites. But the Jews forced their way into the valleys and built themselves cities and constructed a mighty temple

MOSES SEES THE HOLY LAND

in a town which they named Jerusalem, the Home of Peace.
As for Moses, he was no longer the leader of his people. He had been allowed to see the mountain ridges of Palestine from afar. Then he had closed his tired eyes for all time. He had worked faithfully and hard to please Jehovah. Not only had he guided his brethren out of foreign slavery into the free and independent life of a new home but he had also made the Jews the first of all nations to worship a single God.

THE PHŒNICIANS

THE PHŒNICIANS WHO GAVE US OUR ALPHABET

THE Phœnicians, who were the neighbours of the Jews, were a Semitic tribe which at a very early age had settled along the shores of the Mediterranean. They had built themselves two well-fortified towns, Tyre and Sidon, and within a short time they had gained a monopoly of the trade of the western seas. Their ships went regularly to Greece and Italy and

THE PHŒNICIAN TRADER

Spain and they even ventured beyond the straits of Gibraltar
to visit the Scilly islands where they could buy tin. Wherever
they went, they built themselves small trading stations, which
they called colonies. Many of these were the origin of modern cities, such as Cadiz and Marseilles.

They bought and sold whatever promised to bring them a
good profit. They were not troubled by a conscience. If we
are to believe all their neighbours they did not know what the
words honesty or integrity meant. They regarded a well-filled
treasure chest the highest ideal of all good citizens. Indeed
they were very unpleasant people and did not have a single
friend. Nevertheless they have rendered all coming generations one service of the greatest possible value. They gave
us our alphabet.

The Phœnicians had been familiar with the art of writing.
invented by the Sumerians. But they regarded these pothooks
as a clumsy waste of time. They were practical business men
and could not spend hours engraving two or three letters.
They set to work and invented a new system of writing which
was greatly superior to the old one. They borrowed a few
pictures from the Egyptians and they simplified a number of
the wedge-shaped figures of the Sumerians. They sacrificed
the pretty looks of the older system for the advantage of speed
and they reduced the thousands of different images to a short
and handy alphabet of twenty-two letters.

In due course of time, this alphabet travelled across the
Ægean Sea and entered Greece. The Greeks added a few
letters of their own and carried the improved system to Italy.
The Romans modified the figures somewhat and in turn taught
them to the wild barbarians of western Europe. Those wild
barbarians were our own ancestors, and that is the reason why
this book is written in characters that are of Phœnician origin
and not in the hieroglyphics of the Egyptians or in the nail-
script of the Sumerians.

THE INDO-EUROPEANS

THE INDO-EUROPEAN PERSIANS CONQUER THE SEMITIC AND THE EGYPTIAN WORLD

THE world of Egypt and Babylon and Assyria and Phœ--nicia had existed almost thirty centuries and the venerable races of the Fertile Valley were getting old and tired. Their doom was sealed when a new and more energetic race appeared upon the horizon. We call this race the Indo-European race, because it conquered not only Europe but also made itself the ruling class in the country which is now known as British India.

These Indo-Europeans were white men like the Semites but they spoke a different language which is regarded as the common ancestor of all European tongues with the exception of Hungarian and Finnish and the Basque dialects of Northern Spain.

When we first hear of them, they had been living along the shores of the Caspian Sea for many centuries. But one day they had packed their tents and they had wandered forth in search of a new home. Some of them had moved into the mountains of Central Asia and for many centuries they had lived among the peaks which surround the plateau of Iran and that is why we call them Aryans. Others had followed the setting sun and they had taken possession of the plains of Europe as I shall tell you when I give you the story of Greece and Rome.

For the moment we must follow the Aryans. Under the leadership of Zarathustra (or Zoroaster) who was their great teacher many of them had left their mountain homes to follow the swiftly flowing Indus river on its way to the sea.

Others had preferred to stay among the hills of western Asia and there they had founded the half-independent communities of the Medes and the Persians, two peoples whose

THE STORY OF A WORD

names we have copied from the old Greek history-books. In the seventh century before the birth of Christ, the Medes had established a kingdom of their own called Media, but this perished when Cyrus, the chief of a clan known as the Anshan, made himself king of all the Persian tribes and started upon a career of conquest which soon made him and his children the undisputed masters of the whole of western Asia and of Egypt.

Indeed, with such energy did these Indo-European Persians push their triumphant campaigns in the west that they soon

THE INDO-EUROPEANS AND THEIR NEIGHBOURS

found themselves in serious difficulties with certain other Indo-European tribes which centuries before had moved into Europe and had taken possession of the Greek peninsula and the islands of the Ægean Sea.

These difficulties led to the three famous wars between Greece and Persia during which King Darius and King Xerxes of Persia invaded the northern part of the peninsula. They ravaged the lands of the Greeks and tried very hard to get a foothold upon the European continent.

But in this they did not succeed. The navy of Athens proved unconquerable. By cutting off the lines of supplies of the Persian armies, the Greek sailors invariably forced the Asiatic rulers to return to their base.

It was the first encounter between Asia, the ancient teacher, and Europe, the young and eager pupil. A great many of the other chapters of this book will tell you how the struggle between east and west has continued until this very day.

THE ÆGEAN SEA

THE PEOPLE OF THE ÆGEAN SEA CARRIED THE CIVILISATION OF OLD ASIA INTO THE WILDERNESS OF EUROPE

THE TROJAN HORSE

WHEN Heinrich Schliemann was a little boy his father told him the story of Troy. He liked that story better than anything else he had ever heard and he made up his mind, that as soon as he was big enough to leave home, he would travel to Greece and "find Troy." That he was the son of a poor country parson in a Mecklenburg village did not bother him. He knew that he would need money but he decided to gather a fortune first and do the digging afterwards. As a matter of fact, he managed to get a large fortune within a very short time, and as soon as he had enough money to equip an expedition, he went to the northwest corner of Asia Minor, where he supposed that Troy had been situated.

In that particular nook of old Asia Minor, stood a high mound covered with grainfields. According to tradition it had been the home of Priamus the king of Troy. Schliemann,

48

SCHLIEMANN DIGS FOR TROY

whose enthusiasm was somewhat greater than his knowledge, wasted no time in preliminary explorations. At once he began to dig. And he dug with such zeal and such speed that his trench went straight through the heart of the city for which he was looking and carried him to the ruins of another buried town which was at least a thousand years older than the Troy of which Homer had written. Then something very interesting occurred. If Schliemann had found a few polished stone hammers and perhaps a few pieces of crude pottery, no one would have been surprised. Instead of discovering such objects, which people had generally associated with the prehistoric men who had lived in these regions before the coming of the Greeks, Schliemann found beautiful statuettes and very costly jewelry and ornamented vases of a pattern that was unknown to the Greeks. He ventured the suggestion that

fully ten centuries before the great Trojan war, the coast of
the Ægean had been inhabited by a mysterious race of men
who in many ways had been the superiors of the wild Greek
tribes who had invaded their country and had destroyed their
civilisation or absorbed it until it had lost all trace of origi-
nality. And this proved to be the case. In the late seventies of

MYCENÆ IN ARGOLIS

the last century, Schliemann visited the ruins of Mycenæ, ruins
which were so old that Roman guide-books marvelled at their
antiquity. There again, beneath the flat slabs of stone of a
small round enclosure, Schliemann stumbled upon a wonderful
treasure-trove, which had been left behind by those mysterious
people who had covered the Greek coast with their cities and
who had built walls, so big and so heavy and so strong, that
the Greeks called them the work of the Titans, those god-like

giants who in very olden days had used to play ball with mountain peaks.

A very careful study of these many relics has done away with some of the romantic features of the story. The makers of these early works of art and the builders of these strong fortresses were no sorcerers, but simple sailors and traders. They had lived in Crete, and on the many small islands of the

THE ÆGEAN SEA

Ægean Sea. They had been hardy mariners and they had turned the Ægean into a center of commerce for the exchange of goods between the highly civilised east and the slowly developing wilderness of the European mainland.

For more than a thousand years they had maintained an island empire which had developed a very high form of art. Indeed their most important city, Cnossus, on the northern coast of Crete, had been entirely modern in its insistence upon hygiene and comfort. The palace had been properly drained and the houses had been provided with stoves and the Cnossians

LAND ROUTE FROM ASIA TO GREECE

MOUNT OLYMPUS

TROY

THE ISLANDS WHICH
WERE THE BRIDGES
OF
THE AEGEAN SEA

LESBOS

GREECE

ASIA
MINOR

SCOPELOS SCYROS PSYRA CHIOS

EUBOEA

RIDGE 1

ATHENS

ANDROS

SAMOS

TENOS MYCONOS ICARIA

MYCENAE
TIRYNS

CEOS

BRIDGE 2

PATMOS

CYTHNOS

SERIPHOS

DONUSSA

PAROS NAXOS

BRIDGE 3

RHODOS

CAPE MALEA

CARPATHOS

AEGILIA

CRETE

BRIDGE 4

CNOSSUS

TO
EGYPT

THE ISLAND-BRIDGES BETWEEN ASIA AND EUROPE

had been the first people to make a daily use of the hitherto unknown bathtub. The palace of their King had been famous for its winding staircases and its large banqueting hall. The cellars underneath this palace, where the wine and the grain and the olive-oil were stored, had been so vast and had so greatly impressed the first Greek visitors, that they had given rise to the story of the "labyrinth," the name which we give to a structure with so many complicated passages that it is almost impossible to find our way out, once the front door has closed upon our frightened selves.

But what finally became of this great Ægean Empire and what caused its sudden downfall, that I can not tell.

The Cretans were familiar with the art of writing, but no one has yet been able to decipher their inscriptions. Their history therefore is unknown to us. We have to reconstruct the record of their adventures from the ruins which the Ægeans have left behind. These ruins make it clear that the Ægean world was suddenly conquered by a less civilised race which had recently come from the plains of northern Europe. Unless we are very much mistaken, the savages who were responsible for the destruction of the Cretan and the Ægean civilisation were none other than certain tribes of wandering shepherds who had just taken possession of the rocky peninsula between the Adriatic and the Ægean seas and who are known to us as Greeks.

THE GREEKS

THE Pyramids were a thousand years old and were beginning to show the first signs of decay, and Hammurabi, the
wise king of Babylon, had been dead and buried several centuries, when a small tribe of shepherds left their homes along

AN ÆGEAN CITY ON THE GREEK MAINLAND

54

THE ACHÆANS TAKE AN ÆGEAN CITY

the banks of the River Danube and wandered southward in search of fresh pastures. They called themselves Hellenes, after Hellen, the son of Deucalion and Pyrrha. According to the old myths these were the only two human beings who had escaped the great flood, which countless years before had destroyed all the people of the world, when they had grown so wicked that they disgusted Zeus, the mighty God, who lived on Mount Olympus.

Of these early Hellenes we know nothing. Thucydides, the historian of the fall of Athens, describing his earliest ancestors, said that they "did not amount to very much," and this was probably true. They were very ill-mannered. They lived like pigs and threw the bodies of their enemies to the wild dogs who guarded their sheep. They had very little respect for other people's rights, and they killed the natives of the Greek peninsula (who were called the Pelasgians) and stole their farms and took their cattle and made their wives and daughters slaves and wrote endless songs praising the courage of the clan of the Achæans, who had led the Hellenic advance-guard into the mountains of Thessaly and the Peloponnesus.

But here and there, on the tops of high rocks, they saw the castles of the Ægeans and those they did not attack for they feared the metal swords and the spears of the Ægean soldiers and knew that they could not hope to defeat them with their clumsy stone axes.

For many centuries they continued to wander from valley to valley and from mountain side to mountain side. Then the whole of the land had been occupied and the migration had come to an end.

That moment was the beginning of Greek civilisation. The Greek farmer, living within sight of the Ægean colonies, was finally driven by curiosity to visit his haughty neighbours. He discovered that he could learn many useful things from the men who dwelt behind the high stone walls of Mycenæ and Tiryns.

He was a clever pupil. Within a short time he mastered the art of handling those strange iron weapons which the Ægeans had brought from Babylon and from Thebes. He came to understand the mysteries of navigation. He began to build little boats for his own use.

And when he had learned everything the Ægeans could

THE FALL OF CNOSSUS

THE GREEKS 57

teach him he turned upon his teachers and drove them back
to their islands. Soon afterwards he ventured forth upon the
sea and conquered all the cities of the Ægean. Finally in the
fifteenth century before our era he plundered and ravaged
Cnossus and ten centuries after their first appearance upon
the scene the Hellenes were the undisputed rulers of Greece,
of the Ægean and of the coastal regions of Asia Minor. Troy,
the last great commercial stronghold of the older civilisation,
was destroyed in the eleventh century B.C. European history
was to begin in all seriousness.

THE GREEK CITIES

THE GREEK CITIES THAT WERE REALLY STATES

WE modern people love the sound of the word "big." We pride ourselves upon the fact that we belong to the "biggest" country in the world and possess the "biggest" navy and grow the "biggest" oranges and potatoes, and we love to live in cities of "millions" of inhabitants and when we are dead we are buried in the "biggest cemetery of the whole state."

A citizen of ancient Greece, could he have heard us talk, would not have known what we meant. "Moderation in all things" was the ideal of his life and mere bulk did not impress him at all. And this love of moderation was not merely a hollow phrase used upon special occasions: it influenced the life of the Greeks from the day of their birth to the hour of their death. It was part of their literature and it made them build small but perfect temples. It found expression in the clothes which the men wore and in the rings and the bracelets of their wives. It followed the crowds that went to the theatre and made them hoot down any playwright who dared to sin against the iron law of good taste or good sense.

The Greeks even insisted upon this quality in their politicians and in their most popular athletes. When a powerful runner came to Sparta and boasted that he could stand longer on one foot than any other man in Hellas the people drove him from the city because he prided himself upon an accomplishment at which he could be beaten by any common goose.

"That is all very well," you will say, "and no doubt it is a great virtue to care so much for moderation and perfection, but why should the Greeks have been the only people to develop this quality in olden times?" For an answer I shall point to the way in which the Greeks lived.

The people of Egypt or Mesopotamia had been the "subjects" of a mysterious Supreme Ruler who lived miles and

MOUNT OLYMPUS WHERE THE GODS LIVED

miles away in a dark palace and who was rarely seen by the masses of the population. The Greeks on the other hand, were "free citizens" of a hundred independent little "cities" the largest of which counted fewer inhabitants than a large modern village. When a peasant who lived in Ur said that he was a Babylonian he meant that he was one of millions of other people who paid tribute to the king who at that particular moment happened to be master of western Asia. But when a Greek said proudly that he was an Athenian or a Theban he spoke of a small town, which was both his home and his country and which recognised no master but the will of the people in the market-place.

To the Greek, his fatherland was the place where he was born; where he had spent his earliest years playing hide and seek amidst the forbidden rocks of the Acropolis; where he had grown into manhood with a thousand other boys and girls, whose nicknames were as familiar to him as those of your own schoolmates. His Fatherland was the holy soil where his father and mother lay buried. It was the small house within the high city-walls where his wife and children lived in safety. It was a complete world which covered no more than four or five acres of rocky land. Don't you see how these surroundings must have influenced a man in everything he did and said and thought? The people of Babylon and Assyria and Egypt had been part of a vast mob. They had been lost in the multitude. The Greek on the other hand had never lost touch with his immediate surroundings. He never ceased to be part of a little town where everybody knew every one else. He felt that his intelligent neighbours were watching him. Whatever he did, whether he wrote plays or made statues out of marble or composed songs, he remembered that his efforts were going to be judged by all the free-born citizens of his home-town who knew about such things. This knowledge forced him to strive after perfection, and perfection, as he had been taught from childhood, was not possible without moderation.

In this hard school, the Greeks learned to excel in many things. They created new forms of government and new forms of literature and new ideals in art which we have never been able to surpass. They performed these miracles in little villages that covered less ground than four or five modern city blocks.

And look, what finally happened!

In the fourth century before our era, Alexander of Macedonia conquered the world. As soon as he had done with fighting, Alexander decided that he must bestow the benefits of the true Greek genius upon all mankind. He took it away from the little cities and the little villages and tried to make

it blossom and bear fruit amidst the vast royal residences of
his newly acquired Empire. But the Greeks, removed from
the familiar sight of their own temples, removed from the well-
known sounds and smells of their own crooked streets, at once
lost the cheerful joy and the marvellous sense of moderation
which had inspired the work of their hands and brains while
they laboured for the glory of their old city-states. They became cheap artisans, content with second-rate work. The day
the little city-states of old Hellas lost their independence and
were forced to become part of a big nation, the old Greek spirit
died. And it has been dead ever since.

GREEK SELF-GOVERNMENT

THE GREEKS WERE THE FIRST PEOPLE TO TRY THE DIFFICULT EXPERIMENT OF SELF-GOVERNMENT

In the beginning, all the Greeks had been equally rich and equally poor. Every man had owned a certain number of cows and sheep. His mud-hut had been his castle. He had been free to come and go as he wished. Whenever it was necessary to discuss matters of public importance, all the citizens had gathered in the market-place. One of the older men of the village was elected chairman and it was his duty to see that everybody had a chance to express his views. In case of war, a particularly energetic and self-confident villager was chosen commander-in-chief, but the same people who had voluntarily given this man the right to be their leader, claimed an equal right to deprive him of his job, once the danger had been averted.

But gradually the village had grown into a city. Some people had worked hard and others had been lazy. A few had been unlucky and still others had been just plain dishonest in dealing with their neighbours and had gathered wealth. As a result, the city no longer consisted of a number of men who were equally well-off. On the contrary it was inhabited by a small class of very rich people and a large class of very poor ones.

There had been another change. The old commander-in-

THE TEMPLE

chief who had been willingly recognised as "headman" or "King" because he knew how to lead his men to victory, had disappeared from the scene. His place had been taken by the nobles—a class of rich people who during the course of time had got hold of an undue share of the farms and estates.

These nobles enjoyed many advantages over the common crowd of freemen. They were able to buy the best weapons which were to be found on the market of the eastern Mediterranean. They had much spare time in which they could prac-

A GREEK CITY-STATE

tise the art of fighting. They lived in strongly built houses and they could hire soldiers to fight for them. They were constantly quarrelling among each other to decide who should rule the city. The victorious nobleman then assumed a sort of Kingship over all his neighbours and governed the town until he in turn was killed or driven away by still another ambitious nobleman.

Such a King, by the grace of his soldiers, was called a "Tyrant" and during the seventh and sixth centuries before our era every Greek city was for a time ruled by such Tyrants, many of whom, by the way, happened to be exceedingly capa-

ble men.   But in the long run, this state of affairs became unbearable.   Then attempts were made to bring about reforms
and out of these reforms grew the first democratic government
of which the world has a record.

It was early in the seventh century that the people of
Athens decided to do some housecleaning and give the large
number of freemen once more a voice in the government as
they were supposed to have had in the days of their Achæan
ancestors.   They asked a man by the name of Draco to provide them with a set of laws that would protect the poor against
the aggressions of the rich.   Draco set to work.   Unfortunately he was a professional lawyer and very much out of touch
with ordinary life.   In his eyes a crime was a crime and when
he had finished his code, the people of Athens discovered that
these Draconian laws were so severe that they could not possibly be put into effect.   There would not have been rope
enough to hang all the criminals under their new system of
jurisprudence which made the stealing of an apple a capital
offence.

The Athenians looked about for a more humane reformer.
At last they found some one who could do that sort of thing
better than anybody else.   His name was Solon.   He belonged
to a noble family and he had travelled all over the world and
had studied the forms of government of many other countries.
After a careful study of the subject, Solon gave Athens a set
of laws which bore testimony to that wonderful principle of
moderation which was part of the Greek character.   He tried
to improve the condition of the peasant without however destroying the prosperity of the nobles who were (or rather who
could be) of such great service to the state as soldiers.   To protect the poorer classes against abuse on the part of the judges
(who were always elected from the class of the nobles because
they received no salary) Solon made a provision whereby a
citizen with a grievance had the right to state his case before
a jury of thirty of his fellow Athenians.

Most important of all, Solon forced the average freeman
to take a direct and personal interest in the affairs of the city.

No longer could he stay at home and say "oh, I am too busy today" or "it is raining and I had better stay indoors." He was expected to do his share; to be at the meeting of the town council; and carry part of the responsibility for the safety and the prosperity of the state.

This government by the "demos," the people, was often far from successful. There was too much idle talk. There were too many hateful and spiteful scenes between rivals for official honor. But it taught the Greek people to be independent and to rely upon themselves for their salvation and that was a very good thing.

GREEK LIFE

HOW THE GREEKS LIVED

BUT how, you will ask, did the ancient Greeks have time to look after their families and their business if they were forever running to the market-place to discuss affairs of state? In this chapter I shall tell you.

In all matters of government, the Greek democracy recognised only one class of citizens—the freemen. Every Greek city was composed of a small number of free born citizens, a large number of slaves and a sprinkling of foreigners.

At rare intervals (usually during a war, when men were needed for the army) the Greeks showed themselves willing to confer the rights of citizenship upon the "barbarians" as they called the foreigners. But this was an exception. Citizenship was a matter of birth. You were an Athenian because your father and your grandfather had been Athenians before you. But however great your merits as a trader or a soldier, if you were born of non-Athenian parents, you remained a "foreigner" until the end of time.

The Greek city, therefore, whenever it was not ruled by a king or a tyrant, was run by and for the freemen, and this would not have been possible without a large army of slaves who outnumbered the free citizens at the rate of six or five to one and who performed those tasks to which we modern people must devote most of our time and energy if we wish to provide for our families and pay the rent of our apartments.

The slaves did all the cooking and baking and candlestick making of the entire city. They were the tailors and the carpenters and the jewelers and the school-teachers and the bookkeepers and they tended the store and looked after the factory while the master went to the public meeting to discuss questions of war and peace or visited the theatre to see the latest play of Æschylus or hear a discussion of the revolutionary ideas

GREEK SOCIETY

of Euripides, who had dared to express certain doubts upon the omnipotence of the great god Zeus.

Indeed, ancient Athens resembled a modern club. All the freeborn citizens were hereditary members and all the slaves were hereditary servants, and waited upon the needs of their masters, and it was very pleasant to be a member of the organisation.

But when we talk about slaves, we do not mean the sort of

people about whom you have read in the pages of "Uncle Tom's Cabin." It is true that the position of those slaves who tilled the fields was a very unpleasant one, but the average freeman who had come down in the world and who had been obliged to hire himself out as a farm hand led just as miserable a life. In the cities, furthermore, many of the slaves were more prosperous than the poorer classes of the freemen. For the Greeks, who loved moderation in all things, did not like to treat their slaves after the fashion which afterward was so common in Rome, where a slave had as few rights as an engine in a modern factory and could be thrown to the wild animals upon the smallest pretext.

The Greeks accepted slavery as a necessary institution, without which no city could possibly become the home of a truly civilised people.

The slaves also took care of those tasks which nowadays are performed by the business men and the professional men. As for those household duties which take up so much of the time of your mother and which worry your father when he comes home from his office, the Greeks, who understood the value of leisure, had reduced such duties to the smallest possible minimum by living amidst surroundings of extreme simplicity.

To begin with, their homes were very plain. Even the rich nobles spent their lives in a sort of adobe barn, which lacked all the comforts which a modern workman expects as his natural right. A Greek home consisted of four walls and a roof. There was a door which led into the street but there were no windows. The kitchen, the living rooms and the sleeping quarters were built around an open courtyard in which there was a small fountain, or a statue and a few plants to make it look bright. Within this courtyard the family lived when it did not rain or when it was not too cold. In one corner of the yard the cook (who was a slave) prepared the meal and in another corner, the teacher (who was also a slave) taught the children the alpha beta gamma and the tables of multiplication and in still another corner the lady of the house, who rarely left her domain (since it was not considered good form for a married woman to be seen on the street too often) was repairing her husband's coat with her seamstresses (who were slaves,) and in the little office, right off the door, the master was inspecting the accounts which the overseer of his farm (who was a slave) had just brought to him.

When dinner was ready the family came together but the meal was a very simple one and did not take much time. The Greeks seem to have regarded eating as an unavoidable evil and not a pastime, which kills many dreary hours and eventually kills many dreary people. They lived on bread and on wine, with a little meat and some green vegetables. They drank water only when nothing else was available because they did not think it very healthy. They loved to call on each other for dinner, but our idea of a festive meal, where everybody is supposed to eat much more than is good for him, would have disgusted them. They came together at the table for the purpose of a good talk and a good glass of wine and water, but as they were moderate people they despised those who drank too much.

The same simplicity which prevailed in the dining room also dominated their choice of clothes. They liked to be clean and well groomed, to have their hair and beards neatly cut, to feel their bodies strong with the exercise and the swimming of the gymnasium, but they never followed the Asiatic fashion which prescribed loud colours and strange patterns. They wore a long white coat and they managed to look as smart as a modern Italian officer in his long blue cape.

They loved to see their wives wear ornaments but they thought it very vulgar to display their wealth (or their wives) in public and whenever the women left their home they were as inconspicuous as possible.

In short, the story of Greek life is a story not only of moderation but also of simplicity. "Things," chairs and tables and books and houses and carriages, are apt to take up a great deal of their owner's time. In the end they invariably make him their slave and his hours are spent looking after their wants, keeping them polished and brushed and painted. The Greeks, before everything else, wanted to be "free," both in mind and in body. That they might maintain their liberty, and be truly free in spirit, they reduced their daily needs to the lowest possible point.

THE GREEK THEATRE

THE ORIGINS OF THE THEATRE, THE FIRST FORM OF PUBLIC AMUSEMENT

At a very early stage of their history the Greeks had begun to collect the poems, which had been written in honor of their brave ancestors who had driven the Pelasgians out of Hellas and had destroyed the power of Troy. These poems were recited in public and everybody came to listen to them. But the theatre, the form of entertainment which has become almost a necessary part of our own lives, did not grow out of these recited heroic tales. It had such a curious origin that I must tell you something about it in a separate chapter.

The Greeks had always been fond of parades. Every year they held solemn processions in honor of Dionysos the God of the wine. As everybody in Greece drank wine (the Greeks thought water only useful for the purpose of swimming and sailing) this particular Divinity was as popular as a God of the Soda-Fountain would be in our own land.

And because the Wine-God was supposed to live in the vineyards, amidst a merry mob of Satyrs (strange creatures who were half man and half goat), the crowd that joined the procession used to wear goat-skins and to hee-haw like real billy-goats. The Greek word for goat is "tragos" and the Greek word for singer is "oidos." The singer who meh-mehed like a goat therefore was called a "tragos-oidos" or goat singer, and it is this strange name which developed into the modern

71

word "Tragedy," which means in the theatrical sense a piece with an unhappy ending, just as Comedy (which really means the singing of something "comos" or gay) is the name given to a play which ends happily.

But how, you will ask, did this noisy chorus of masquer- aders, stamping around like wild goats, ever develop into the noble tragedies which have filled the theatres of the world for almost two thousand years?

The connecting link between the goat-singer and Hamlet is really very simple as I shall show you in a moment.

The singing chorus was very amusing in the beginning and attracted large crowds of spectators who stood along the side of the road and laughed. But soon this business of hee-hawing grew tiresome and the Greeks thought dullness an evil only comparable to ugliness or sickness. They asked for some- thing more entertaining. Then an inventive young poet from the village of Icaria in Attica hit upon a new idea which proved a tremendous success. He made one of the members of the goat-chorus step forward and engage in conversation with the leader of the musicians who marched at the head of the parade playing upon their pipes of Pan. This individual was al- lowed to step out of line. He waved his arms and gesticulated while he spoke (that is to say he "acted" while the others merely stood by and sang) and he asked a lot of questions, which the bandmaster answered according to the roll of papyrus upon which the poet had written down these answers before the show began.

This rough and ready conversation—the dialogue—which told the story of Dionysos or one of the other Gods, became at once popular with the crowd. Henceforth every Diony- sian procession had an "acted scene" and very soon the "acting" was considered more important than the procession and the meh-mehing.

Æschylus, the most successful of all "tragedians" who wrote no less than eighty plays during his long life (from 526 to 455) made a bold step forward when he introduced two "actors" instead of one. A generation later Sophocles increased the number of actors to three. When Euripides began to write his terrible tragedies in the middle of the fifth century, B.C., he was allowed as many actors as he liked and when Aristophanes wrote those famous comedies in which he poked fun at everybody and everything, including the Gods of Mount Olympus, the chorus had been reduced to the rôle of mere bystanders who were lined up behind the principal performers and who sang "this is a terrible world" while the hero in the foreground committed a crime against the will of the Gods.

This new form of dramatic entertainment demanded a proper setting, and soon every Greek city owned a theatre, cut out of the rock of a nearby hill. The spectators sat upon wooden benches and faced a wide circle (our present orchestra where you pay three dollars and thirty cents for a seat). Upon this half-circle, which was the stage, the actors and the chorus took their stand. Behind them there was a tent where they made up with large clay masks which hid their faces and which showed the spectators whether the actors were supposed to be happy and smiling or unhappy and weeping. The Greek word for tent is "skene" and that is the reason why we talk of the "scenery" of the stage.

When once the tragedy had become part of Greek life, the people took it very seriously and never went to the theatre to give their minds a vacation. A new play became as important an event as an election and a successful playwright was received with greater honors than those bestowed upon a general who had just returned from a famous victory.

THE PERSIAN WARS

HOW THE GREEKS DEFENDED EUROPE AGAINST ASIATIC INVASION AND DROVE THE PERSIANS BACK ACROSS THE ÆGEAN SEA

THE Greeks had learned the art of trading from the Ægeans who had been the pupils of the Phœnicians. They had founded colonies after the Phœnician pattern. They had even improved upon the Phœnician methods by a more general use of money in dealing with foreign customers. In the sixth century before our era they had established themselves firmly along the coast of Asia Minor and they were taking away trade from the Phœnicians at a fast rate. This the Phœnicians of course did not like but they were not strong enough to risk a war with their Greek competitors. They sat and waited nor did they wait in vain.

In a former chapter, I have told you how a humble tribe of Persian shepherds had suddenly gone upon the warpath and had conquered the greater part of western Asia. The Persians were too civilised to plunder their new subjects. They contented themselves with a yearly tribute. When they reached the coast of Asia Minor they insisted that the Greek colonies of Lydia recognize the Persian Kings as their over-Lords and pay them a stipulated tax. The Greek colonies objected. The Persians insisted. Then the Greek colonies appealed to the home-country and the stage was set for a quarrel.

For if the truth be told, the Persian Kings regarded the Greek city-states as very dangerous political institutions and bad examples for all other people who were supposed to be the patient slaves of the mighty Persian Kings.

Of course, the Greeks enjoyed a certain degree of safety because their country lay hidden beyond the deep waters of the

THE PERSIAN FLEET IS DESTROYED NEAR MOUNT ATHOS

Ægean. But here their old enemies, the Phœnicians, stepped forward with offers of help and advice to the Persians. If the Persian King would provide the soldiers, the Phœnicians would guarantee to deliver the necessary ships to carry them to Europe. It was the year 492 before the birth of Christ, and Asia made ready to destroy the rising power of Europe.

As a final warning the King of Persia sent messengers to the Greeks asking for "earth and water" as a token of their submission. The Greeks promptly threw the messengers into the nearest well where they would find both "earth and water" in large abundance and thereafter of course peace was impossible.

But the Gods of High Olympus watched over their children and when the Phœnician fleet carrying the Persian troops was near Mount Athos, the Storm-God blew his cheeks until he almost burst the veins of his brow, and the fleet was destroyed by a terrible hurricane and the Persians were all drowned.

Two years later more Persians came. This time they sailed across the Ægean Sea and landed near the village of

THE BATTLE OF MARATHON

Marathon. As soon as the Athenians heard this they sent their army of ten thousand men to guard the hills that surrounded the Marathonian plain. At the same time they despatched a fast runner to Sparta to ask for help. But Sparta was envious of the fame of Athens and refused to come to her assistance. The other Greek cities followed her example with the exception of tiny Plataea which sent a thousand men. On the twelfth of September of the year 490, Miltiades, the Athenian commander, threw this little army against the hordes of the

Persians. The Greeks broke through the Persian barrage of arrows and their spears caused terrible havoc among the disorganised Asiatic troops who had never been called upon to resist such an enemy.

That night the people of Athens watched the sky grow red with the flames of burning ships. Anxiously they waited for news. At last a little cloud of dust appeared upon the road that led to the North. It was Pheidippides, the runner. He stumbled and gasped for his end was near. Only a few days before had he returned from his errand to Sparta. He had hastened to join Miltiades. That morning he had taken part in the attack and later he had volunteered to carry the news of victory to his beloved city. The people saw him fall and they rushed forward to support him. "We have won," he whispered and then he died, a glorious death which made him envied of all men.

As for the Persians, they tried, after this defeat, to land near Athens but they found the coast guarded and disappeared, and once more the land of Hellas was at peace.

Eight years they waited and during this time the Greeks were not idle. They knew that a final attack was to be expected but they did not agree upon the best way to avert the danger. Some people wanted to increase the army. Others said that a strong fleet was necessary for success. The two parties led by Aristides (for the army) and Themistocles (the leader of the bigger-navy men) fought each other bitterly and nothing was done until Aristides was exiled. Then Themistocles had his chance and he built all the ships he could and turned the Piræus into a strong naval base.

In the year 481 B.C. a tremendous Persian army appeared in Thessaly, a province of northern Greece. In this hour of danger, Sparta, the great military city of Greece, was elected commander-in-chief. But the Spartans cared little what happened to northern Greece provided their own country was not invaded. They neglected to fortify the passes that led into Greece.

THERMOPYLAE

A small detachment of Spartans under Leonidas had been told to guard the narrow road between the high mountains and the sea which connected Thessaly with the southern provinces. Leonidas obeyed his orders. He fought and held the pass with unequalled bravery. But a traitor by the name of Ephialtes who knew the little byways of Malis guided a regiment of Persians through the hills and made it possible for them to attack Leonidas in the rear. Near the Warm Wells— the Thermopylae —a terrible battle was fought. When night came Leonidas and his faithful soldiers lay dead under the corpses of their enemies.

But the pass had been lost and the greater part of Greece fell into the hands of the Persians. They marched upon Athens, threw the garrison from the rocks of the Acropolis and

THE BATTLE OF THERMOPYLAE

GREECE

burned the city. The people fled to the Island of Salamis. All seemed lost. But on the 20th of September of the year 480 Themistocles forced the Persian fleet to give battle within the narrow straits which separated the Island of Salamis from the mainland and within a few hours he destroyed three quarters of the Persian ships.

In this way the victory of Thermopylae came to naught.

THE PERSIANS BURN ATHENS

Xerxes was forced to retire. The next year, so he decreed, would bring a final decision. He took his troops to Thessaly and there he waited for spring.

But this time the Spartans understood the seriousness of the hour. They left the safe shelter of the wall which they had built across the isthmus of Corinth and under the leadership of Pausanias they marched against Mardonius the Persian general. The united Greeks (some one hundred thousand men from a dozen different cities) attacked the three hundred thousand men of the enemy near Plataea. Once more the heavy Greek infantry broke through the Persian barrage of arrows. The Persians were defeated, as they had been at Marathon, and this time they left for good. By a strange coincidence, the same day that the Greek armies won their victory near Plataea, the Athenian ships destroyed the enemy's fleet near Cape Mycale in Asia Minor.

Thus did the first encounter between Asia and Europe end. Athens had covered herself with glory and Sparta had fought bravely and well. If these two cities had been able to come to an agreement, if they had been willing to forget their little jealousies, they might have become the leaders of a strong and united Hellas.

But alas, they allowed the hour of victory and enthusiasm to slip by, and the same opportunity never returned.

ATHENS vs. SPARTA

HOW ATHENS AND SPARTA FOUGHT A LONG AND DISASTROUS WAR FOR THE LEADERSHIP OF GREECE

ATHENS and Sparta were both Greek cities and their people spoke a common language. In every other respect they were different. Athens rose high from the plain. It was a city exposed to the fresh breezes from the sea, willing to look at the world with the eyes of a happy child. Sparta, on the other hand, was built at the bottom of a deep valley, and used the surrounding mountains as a barrier against foreign thought. Athens was a city of busy trade. Sparta was an armed camp where people were soldiers for the sake of being soldiers. The people of Athens loved to sit in the sun and discuss poetry or listen to the wise words of a philosopher. The Spartans, on the other hand, never wrote a single line that was considered literature, but they knew how to fight, they liked to fight, and they sacrificed all human emotions to their ideal of military preparedness.

No wonder that these sombre Spartans viewed the success of Athens with malicious hate. The energy which the defence of the common home had developed in Athens was now used for purposes of a more peaceful nature. The Acropolis was rebuilt and was made into a marble shrine to the Goddess Athena. Pericles, the leader of the Athenian democracy, sent far and wide to find famous sculptors and painters and scientists to make the city more beautiful and the young Athenians more worthy of their home. At the same time he kept a watchful eye on Sparta and built high walls which connected Athens with the sea and made her the strongest fortress of that day.

An insignificant quarrel between two little Greek cities led to the final conflict. For thirty years the war between Athens and Sparta continued. It ended in a terrible disaster for Athens.

During the third year of the war the plague had entered the city. More than half of the people and Pericles, the great leader, had been killed. The plague was followed by a period of bad and untrustworthy leadership. A brilliant young fel⸗ low by the name of Alcibiades had gained the favor of the popular assembly. He suggested a raid upon the Spartan colony of Syracuse in Sicily. An expedition was equipped and everything was ready. But Alcibiades got mixed up in a street brawl and was forced to flee. The general who succeeded him was a bungler. First he lost his ships and then he lost his army, and the few surviving Athenians were thrown into the stone-quarries of Syracuse, where they died from hunger and thirst.

The expedition had killed all the young men of Athens. The city was doomed. After a long siege the town surrendered in April of the year 404. The high walls were demolished. The navy was taken away by the Spartans. Athens ceased to exist as the center of the great colonial empire which it had conquered during the days of its prosperity. But that won derful desire to learn and to know and to investigate which had distinguished her free citizens during the days of great ness and prosperity did not perish with the walls and the ships. It continued to live. It became even more brilliant.

Athens no longer shaped the destinies of the land of Greece. But now, as the home of the first great university the city be gan to influence the minds of intelligent people far beyond the narrow frontiers of Hellas.

ALEXANDER THE GREAT

ALEXANDER THE MACEDONIAN ESTAB-LISHES A GREEK WORLD-EMPIRE, AND WHAT BECAME OF THIS HIGH AMBITION

W HEN the Achæans had left their homes along the banks of the Danube to look for pastures new, they had spent some time among the mountains of Macedonia. Ever since, the Greeks had maintained certain more or less formal relations with the people of this northern country. The Macedonians from their side had kept themselves well informed about conditions in Greece.

Now it happened, just when Sparta and Athens had finished their disastrous war for the leadership of Hellas, that Macedonia was ruled by an extraordinarily clever man by the name of Philip. He admired the Greek spirit in letters and art but he despised the Greek lack of self-control in political affairs. It irritated him to see a perfectly good people waste its men and money upon fruitless quarrels. So he settled the difficulty by making himself the master of all Greece and then he asked his new subjects to join him on a voyage which he meant to pay to Persia in return for the visit which Xerxes had paid the Greeks one hundred and fifty years before.

Unfortunately Philip was murdered before he could start upon this well-prepared expedition. The task of avenging the destruction of Athens was left to Philip's son Alexander, the beloved pupil of Aristotle, wisest of all Greek teachers.

Alexander bade farewell to Europe in the spring of the year 334 B.C. Seven years later he reached India. In the meantime he had destroyed Phœnicia, the old rival of the Greek merchants. He had conquered Egypt and had been worshipped by the people of the Nile valley as the son and heir of the Pharaohs. He had defeated the last Persian king—he had overthrown the Persian empire—he had given orders to rebuild Babylon—he had led his troops into the heart of the Himalayan mountains and had made the entire world a Macedonian province and dependency. Then he stopped and announced even more ambitious plans.

The newly formed Empire must be brought under the influence of the Greek mind. The people must be taught the Greek language—they must live in cities built after a Greek model. The Alexandrian soldier now turned school-master. The military camps of yesterday became the peaceful centres of the newly imported Greek civilisation. Higher and higher did the flood of Greek manners and Greek customs rise, when suddenly Alexander was stricken with a fever and died in the old palace of King Hammurabi of Babylon in the year 323.

Then the waters receded. But they left behind the fertile clay of a higher civilisation and Alexander, with all his childish ambitions and his silly vanities, had performed a most valuable service. His Empire did not long survive him. A number of ambitious generals divided the territory among themselves. But they too remained faithful to the dream of a great world brotherhood of Greek and Asiatic ideas and knowledge.

They maintained their independence until the Romans added western Asia and Egypt to their other domains. The strange inheritance of this Hellenistic civilisation (part Greek, part Persian, part Egyptian and Babylonian) fell to the Roman conquerors. During the following centuries, it got such a firm hold upon the Roman world, that we feel its influence in our own lives this very day.

A SUMMARY

A SHORT SUMMARY OF CHAPTERS 1 to 20

THUS far, from the top of our high tower we have been looking eastward. But from this time on, the history of Egypt and Mesopotamia is going to grow less interesting and I must take you to study the western landscape.

Before we do this, let us stop a moment and make clear to ourselves what we have seen.

First of all I showed you prehistoric man—a creature very simple in his habits and very unattractive in his manners. I told you how he was the most defenceless of the many animals that roamed through the early wilderness of the five continents, but being possessed of a larger and better brain, he managed to hold his own.

Then came the glaciers and the many centuries of cold weather, and life on this planet became so difficult that man was obliged to think three times as hard as ever before if he wished to survive. Since, however, that "wish to survive" was (and is) the mainspring which keeps every living being going full tilt to the last gasp of its breath, the brain of glacial man was set to work in all earnestness. Not only did these hardy people manage to exist through the long cold spells which killed many ferocious animals, but when the earth became warm and comfortable once more, prehistoric man had learned a number of things which gave him such great advantages over his less intelligent neighbors that the danger of extinction (a very serious one during the first half million years of man's residence upon this planet) became a very remote one.

I told you how these earliest ancestors of ours were slowly plodding along when suddenly (and for reasons that are not well understood) the people who lived in the valley of the Nile rushed ahead and almost over night, created the first centre of civilisation.

Then I showed you Mesopotamia, "the land between the rivers," which was the second great school of the human race. And I made you a map of the little island bridges of the Ægean Sea, which carried the knowledge and the science of the old east to the young west, where lived the Greeks.

Next I told you of an Indo-European tribe, called the Hellenes, who thousands of years before had left the heart of Asia and who had in the eleventh century before our era pushed their way into the rocky peninsula of Greece and who, since then, have been known to us as the Greeks. And I told you the story of the little Greek cities that were really states, where the civilisation of old Egypt and Asia was transfigured (that is a big word, but you can "figure out" what it means) into something quite new, something that was much nobler and finer than anything that had gone before.

When you look at the map you will see how by this time civilisation has described a semi-circle. It begins in Egypt, and by way of Mesopotamia and the Ægean Islands it moves westward until it reaches the European continent. The first four thousand years, Egyptians and Babylonians and Phœnicians and a large number of Semitic tribes (please remember that the Jews were but one of a large number of Semitic peoples) have carried the torch that was to illuminate the world. They now hand it over to the Indo-European Greeks, who become the teachers of another Indo-European tribe, called the Romans. But meanwhile the Semites have pushed westward along the northern coast of Africa and have made themselves the rulers of the western half of the Mediterranean just when the eastern half has become a Greek (or Indo-European) possession.

This, as you shall see in a moment, leads to a terrible con-flict between the two rival races, and out of their struggle arises the victorious Roman Empire, which is to take this Egyptian-Mesopotamian-Greek civilisation to the furthermost corners of the European continent, where it serves as the foundation upon which our modern society is based.

I know all this sounds very complicated, but if you get hold of these few principles, the rest of our history will become a great deal simpler. The maps will make clear what the words fail to tell. And after this short intermission, we go back to our story and give you an account of the famous war between Carthage and Rome.

ROME AND CARTHAGE

THE SEMITIC COLONY OF CARTHAGE ON THE
NORTHERN COAST OF AFRICA AND THE
INDO-EUROPEAN CITY OF ROME ON THE
WEST COAST OF ITALY FOUGHT EACH
OTHER FOR THE POSSESSION OF THE
WESTERN MEDITERRANEAN AND CARTH-
AGE WAS DESTROYED

THE little Phœnician trading post of Kart-hadshat stood
on a low hill which overlooked the African Sea, a stretch of
water ninety miles wide which separates Africa from Europe.
It was an ideal spot for a commercial centre. Almost too ideal.
It grew too fast and became too rich. When in the sixth century before our era, Nebuchadnezzar of Babylon destroyed
Tyre, Carthage broke off all further relations with the Mother
Country and became an independent state—the great western
advance-post of the Semitic races.

Unfortunately the city had inherited many of the traits
which for a thousand years had been characteristic of the
Phœnicians. It was a vast business-house, protected by a
strong navy, indifferent to most of the finer aspects of life.
The city and the surrounding country and the distant colonies
were all ruled by a small but exceedingly powerful group of
rich men. The Greek word for rich is "ploutos" and the Greeks
88

called such a government by "rich men" a "Plutocracy." Carthage was a plutocracy and the real power of the state lay in the hands of a dozen big ship-owners and mine-owners and merchants who met in the back room of an office and regarded their common Fatherland as a business enterprise which ought

CARTHAGE

to yield them a decent profit. They were however wide awake and full of energy and worked very hard.

As the years went by the influence of Carthage upon her neighbours increased until the greater part of the African coast, Spain and certain regions of France were Carthaginian possessions, and paid tribute, taxes and dividends to the mighty city on the African Sea.

Of course, such a "plutocracy" was forever at the mercy of

the crowd. As long as there was plenty of work and wages were high, the majority of the citizens were quite contented, allowed their "betters" to rule them and asked no embarrassing questions. But when no ships left the harbor, when no ore was brought to the smelting-ovens, when dockworkers and

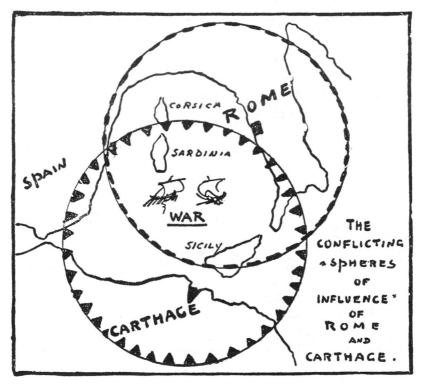

SPHERES OF INFLUENCE

stevedores were thrown out of employment, then there were grumblings and there was a demand that the popular assembly be called together as in the olden days when Carthage had been a self-governing republic.

To prevent such an occurrence the plutocracy was obliged to keep the business of the town going at full speed. They had managed to do this very successfully for almost five hundred years when they were greatly disturbed by certain rumors which reached them from the western coast of Italy. It was said that a little village on the banks of the Tiber had suddenly risen to great power and was making itself the acknowledged leader of all the Latin tribes who inhabited central Italy. It was also said that this village, which by the way was called Rome, intended to build ships and go after the commerce of Sicily and the southern coast of France.

Carthage could not possibly tolerate such competition. The young rival must be destroyed lest the Carthaginian rulers lose their prestige as the absolute rulers of the western Mediterranean. The rumors were duly investigated and in a general way these were the facts that came to light.

The west coast of Italy had long been neglected by civilisation. Whereas in Greece all the good harbours faced eastward and enjoyed a full view of the busy islands of the Ægean, the west coast of Italy contemplated nothing more exciting than the desolate waves of the Mediterranean. The country was poor. It was therefore rarely visited by foreign merchants and the natives were allowed to live in undisturbed possession of their hills and their marshy plains.

The first serious invasion of this land came from the north. At an unknown date certain Indo-European tribes had managed to find their way through the passes of the Alps and had pushed southward until they had filled the heel and the toe of the famous Italian boot with their villages and their flocks. Of these early conquerors we know nothing. No Homer sang their glory. Their own accounts of the foundation of Rome (written eight hundred years later when the little city had become the centre of an Empire) are fairy stories and do not belong in a history. Romulus and Remus jumping across each other's walls (I always forget who jumped across whose wall) make entertaining reading, but the foundation of the City of Rome was a much more prosaic affair. Rome began as a thousand American cities have done, by being a convenient place for barter and horse-trading. It lay in the heart of the plains

HOW THE CITY OF ROME HAPPENED

of central Italy. The Tiber provided direct access to the sea. The land-road from north to south found here a convenient ford which could be used all the year around. And seven little hills along the banks of the river offered the inhabitants a safe shelter against their enemies who lived in the mountains and those who lived beyond the horizon of the nearby sea.

The mountaineers were called the Sabines. They were a rough crowd with an unholy desire for easy plunder. But they were very backward. They used stone axes and wooden shields and were no match for the Romans with their steel swords. The sea-people on the other hand were dangerous foes. They were called the Etruscans and they were (and still are) one of the great mysteries of history. Nobody knew (or knows) whence they came; who they were; what had driven them away from their original homes. We have found the remains of their cities and their cemeteries and their waterworks all along the Italian coast. We are familiar with their inscriptions. But as no one has ever been able to decipher the Etruscan alphabet, these written messages are, so far, merely annoying and not at all useful.

Our best guess is that the Etruscans came originally from Asia Minor and that a great war or a pestilence in that country had forced them to go away and seek a new home elsewhere. Whatever the reason for their coming, the Etruscans played a great rôle in history. They carried the pollen of the ancient civilisation from the east to the west and they taught the Romans who, as we know, came from the north, the first principles of architecture and street-building and fighting and art and cookery and medicine and astronomy.

But just as the Greeks had not loved their Ægean teachers, in this same way did the Romans hate their Etruscan masters. They got rid of them as soon as they could and the opportunity offered itself when Greek merchants discovered the commercial possibilities of Italy and when the first Greek vessels reached Rome. The Greeks came to trade, but they stayed to instruct. They found the tribes who inhabited the

Roman country-side (and who were called the Latins) quite willing to learn such things as might be of practical use. At once they understood the great benefit that could be derived from a written alphabet and they copied that of the Greeks. They also understood the commercial advantages of a well-regulated system of coins and measures and weights. Eventually the Romans swallowed Greek civilisation hook, line and sinker.

They even welcomed the Gods of the Greeks to their country. Zeus was taken to Rome where he became known as Jupiter and the other divinities followed him. The Roman Gods however never were quite like their cheerful cousins who had accompanied the Greeks on their road through life and through history. The Roman Gods were State Functionaries. Each one managed his own department with great prudence and a deep sense of justice, but in turn he was exact in demanding the obedience of his worshippers. This obedience the Romans rendered with scrupulous care. But they never established the cordial personal relations and that charming friendship which had existed between the old Hellenes and the mighty residents of the high Olympian peak.

The Romans did not imitate the Greek form of government, but being of the same Indo-European stock as the people of Hellas, the early history of Rome resembles that of Athens and the other Greek cities. They did not find it difficult to get rid of their kings, the descendants of the ancient tribal chieftains. But once the kings had been driven from the city, the Romans were forced to bridle the power of the nobles, and it took many centuries before they managed to establish a system which gave every free citizen of Rome a chance to take a personal interest in the affairs of his town.

Thereafter the Romans enjoyed one great advantage over the Greeks. They managed the affairs of their country without making too many speeches. They were less imaginative than the Greeks and they preferred an ounce of action to a pound of words. They understood the tendency of the multitude (the "plebs," as the assemblage of free citizens was called) only too well to waste valuable time upon mere talk. They therefore placed the actual business of running the city into the hands of two "consuls" who were assisted by a council of Elders, called the Senate (because the word "senex" means an old man). As a matter of custom and practical advantage the senators were elected from the nobility. But their power had been strictly defined.

Rome at one time had passed through the same sort of struggle between the poor and the rich which had forced Athens to adopt the laws of Draco and Solon. In Rome this conflict had occurred in the fifth century B. C. As a result the freemen had obtained a written code of laws which protected them against the despotism of the aristocratic judges by the institution of the "Tribune." These Tribunes were city-magistrates, elected by the freemen. They had the right to protect any citizen against those actions of the government officials which were thought to be unjust. A consul had the right to condemn a man to death, but if the case had not been absolutely proved the Tribune could interfere and save the poor fellow's life.

But when I use the word Rome, I seem to refer to a little city of a few thousand inhabitants. And the real strength of Rome lay in the country districts outside her walls. And it was in the government of these outlying provinces that Rome at an early age showed her wonderful gift as a colonising power.

In very early times Rome had been the only strongly fortified city in central Italy, but it had always offered a hospitable refuge to other Latin tribes who happened to be in danger of attack. The Latin neighbours had recognised the advantages of a close union with such a powerful friend and they had tried to find a basis for some sort of defensive and offensive alliance. Other nations, Egyptians, Babylonians, Phœnicians, even Greeks, would have insisted upon a treaty of submission on the part of the "barbarians." The Romans did nothing of

the sort. They gave the "outsider" a chance to become partners in a common "res publica"—or common-wealth.

"You want to join us," they said. "Very well, go ahead
and join. We shall treat you as if you were full-fledged citizens of Rome. In return for this privilege we expect you to
fight for our city, the mother of us all, whenever it shall be necessary."

The "outsider" appreciated this generosity and he showed
his gratitude by his unswerving loyalty.

Whenever a Greek city had been attacked, the foreign residents had moved out as quickly as they could. Why defend
something which meant nothing to them but a temporary
boarding house in which they were tolerated as long as they
paid their bills? But when the enemy was before the gates
of Rome, all the Latins rushed to her defence. It was their
Mother who was in danger. It was their true "home" even if
they lived a hundred miles away and had never seen the walls
of the sacred Hills.

No defeat and no disaster could change this sentiment. In
the beginning of the fourth century B.C. the wild Gauls forced
their way into Italy. They had defeated the Roman army near
the River Allia and had marched upon the city. They had
taken Rome and then they expected that the people would
come and sue for peace. They waited, but nothing happened.
After a short time the Gauls found themselves surrounded by
a hostile population which made it impossible for them to obtain
supplies. After seven months, hunger forced them to withdraw. The policy of Rome to treat the "foreigner" on equal
terms had proved a great success and Rome stood stronger than
ever before.

This short account of the early history of Rome shows you
the enormous difference between the Roman ideal of a healthy
state, and that of the ancient world which was embodied in the
town of Carthage. The Romans counted upon the cheerful
and hearty co-operation between a number of "equal citizens." The Carthaginians, following the example of Egypt

and western Asia, insisted upon the unreasoning (and therefore unwilling) obedience of "Subjects" and when these failed
they hired professional soldiers to do their fighting for them.

You will now understand why Carthage was bound to fear
such a clever and powerful enemy and why the plutocracy of
Carthage was only too willing to pick a quarrel that they might
destroy the dangerous rival before it was too late.

But the Carthaginians, being good business men, knew that

A FAST ROMAN WARSHIP

it never pays to rush matters. They proposed to the Romans
that their respective cities draw two circles on the map and
that each town claim one of these circles as her own "sphere
of influence" and promise to keep out of the other fellow's circle. The agreement was promptly made and was broken just
as promptly when both sides thought it wise to send their
armies to Sicily where a rich soil and a bad government invited foreign interference.

The war which followed (the so-called first Punic War)
lasted twenty-four years. It was fought out on the high seas
and in the beginning it seemed that the experienced Car-

thaginian navy would defeat the newly created Roman fleet. Following their ancient tactics, the Carthaginian ships would either ram the enemy vessels or by a bold attack from the side they would break their oars and would then kill the sailors of the helpless vessel with their arrows and with fire balls. But Roman engineers invented a new craft which carried a boarding bridge across which the Roman infantrymen stormed the hostile ship. Then there was a sudden end to Carthaginian victories. At the battle of Mylae their fleet was badly defeated. Carthage was obliged to sue for peace, and Sicily became part of the Roman domains.

Twenty-three years later new trouble arose. Rome (in quest of copper) had taken the island of Sardinia. Carthage (in quest of silver) thereupon occupied all of southern Spain. This made Carthage a direct neighbour of the Romans. The latter did not like this at all and they ordered their troops to cross the Pyrenees and watch the Carthaginian army of occupation.

The stage was set for the second outbreak between the two rivals. Once more a Greek colony was the pretext for a war. The Carthaginians were besieging Saguntum on the east coast of Spain. The Saguntians appealed to Rome and Rome, as usual, was willing to help. The Senate promised the help of the Latin armies, but the preparation for this expedition took some time, and meanwhile Saguntum had been taken and had been destroyed. This had been done in direct opposition to the will of Rome. The Senate decided upon war. One Roman army was to cross the African sea and make a landing on Carthaginian soil. A second division was to keep the Carthaginian armies occupied in Spain to prevent them from rushing to the aid of the home town. It was an excellent plan and everybody expected a great victory. But the Gods had decided otherwise.

It was the fall of the year 218 before the birth of Christ and the Roman army which was to attack the Carthaginians in Spain had left Italy. People were eagerly waiting for news of

HANNIBAL CROSSES THE ALPS

an easy and complete victory when a terrible rumour began to spread through the plain of the Po. Wild mountaineers, their lips trembling with fear, told of hundreds of thousands of brown men accompanied by strange beasts "each one as big as a house," who had suddenly emerged from the clouds of snow which surrounded the old Graian pass through which Hercules, thousands of years before, had driven the oxen of Geryon on his way from Spain to Greece. Soon an endless stream of bedraggled refugees appeared before the gates of Rome, with more complete details. Hannibal, the son of Hamilcar, with fifty thousand soldiers, nine thousand horsemen and thirty-seven fighting elephants, had crossed the Pyrenees. He had defeated the Roman army of Scipio on the banks of the Rhone and he had guided his army safely across the mountain passes of the Alps although it was October and the roads were thickly covered with snow and ice. Then he had joined forces with the Gauls and together they had defeated a second Roman army just before they crossed the Trebia and laid siege to Placentia, the northern terminus of the road which connected Rome with the province of the Alpine districts.

The Senate, surprised but calm and energetic as usual, hushed up the news of these many defeats and sent two fresh armies to stop the invader. Hannibal managed to surprise these troops on a narrow road along the shores of the Trasimene Lake and there he killed all the Roman officers and most of their men. This time there was a panic among the people of Rome, but the Senate kept its nerve. A third army was organised and the command was given to Quintus Fabius Maximus with full power to act "as was necessary to save the state."

Fabius knew that he must be very careful lest all be lost. His raw and untrained men, the last available soldiers, were no match for Hannibal's veterans. He refused to accept battle but forever he followed Hannibal, destroyed everything eatable, destroyed the roads, attacked small detachments and generally weakened the morale of the Carthaginian troops by a most distressing and annoying form of guerilla warfare.

UNKNOWN LAND

UNKNOWN LAND

CROSSES THE ALPS LATE IN THE FALL OF 218

CROSSES THE RHONE 218

HANNIBAL LEAVES SPAIN IN THE SUMMER OF 218

SAGUNTUM

HANNIBAL GOES TO SPAIN AS A BOY

HANNIBAL

ZAMA 202

CARTHAGE

LAKE TRASIMENE 217

ROME

CAPUA

CANNAE

216

216

216

203

SICILY

BACK TO CARTHAGE 203

GOES EAST FOR HELP 207

HANNIBAL AND THE C. R. E.

Such methods however did not satisfy the fearsome crowds who had found safety behind the walls of Rome. They wanted "action." Something must be done and must be done quickly. A popular hero by the name of Varro, the sort of man who went about the city telling everybody how much better he could do things than slow old Fabius, the "Delayer," was made commander-in-chief by popular acclamation. At the battle of Cannae (216) he suffered the most terrible defeat of Roman history. More than seventy thousand men were killed. Hannibal was master of all Italy.

He marched from one end of the peninsula to the other, proclaiming himself the "deliverer from the yoke of Rome" and asking the different provinces to join him in warfare upon the mother city. Then once more the wisdom of Rome bore noble fruit. With the exceptions of Capua and Syracuse, all Roman cities remained loyal. Hannibal, the deliverer, found himself opposed by the people whose friend he pretended to be. He was far away from home and did not like the situation. He sent messengers to Carthage to ask for fresh supplies and new men. Alas, Carthage could not send him either.

The Romans with their boarding-bridges, were the masters of the sea. Hannibal must help himself as best he could. He continued to defeat the Roman armies that were sent out against him, but his own numbers were decreasing rapidly and the Italian peasants held aloof from this self-appointed "deliverer."

After many years of uninterrupted victories, Hannibal found himself besieged in the country which he had just conquered. For a moment, the luck seemed to turn. Hasdrubal, his brother, had defeated the Roman armies in Spain. He had crossed the Alps to come to Hannibal's assistance. He sent messengers to the south to tell of his arrival and ask the other army to meet him in the plain of the Tiber. Unfortunately the messengers fell into the hands of the Romans and Hannibal waited in vain for further news until his brother's head, neatly packed in a basket, came rolling into his camp and told him of the fate of the last of the Carthaginian troops.

With Hasdrubal out of the way, young Publius Scipio easily reconquered Spain and four years later the Romans were ready for a final attack upon Carthage. Hannibal was called back. He crossed the African Sea and tried to organise the defences of his home-city. In the year 202 at the battle of Zama, the Carthaginians were defeated. Hannibal fled to Tyre. From there he went to Asia Minor to stir up the Syrians and the Macedonians against Rome. He accomplished very little but his activities among these Asiatic powers gave the Romans an excuse to carry their warfare into the territory of the east and annex the greater part of the Ægean world.

Driven from one city to another, a fugitive without a home, Hannibal at last knew that the end of his ambitious dream had come. His beloved city of Carthage had been ruined by the war. She had been forced to sign a terrible peace. Her navy had been sunk. She had been forbidden to make war without Roman permission. She had been condemned to pay the Romans millions of dollars for endless years to come. Life offered no hope of a better future. In the year 190 B.C. Hannibal took poison and killed himself.

THE DEATH OF HANNIBAL

Forty years later, the Romans forced their last war upon Carthage. Three long years the inhabitants of the old Phœnician colony held out against the power of the new republic. Hunger forced them to surrender. The few men and women who had survived the siege were sold as slaves. The city was set on fire. For two whole weeks the store-houses and the palaces and the great arsenal burned.   Then a terrible curse was pronounced upon the blackened ruins and the Roman legions returned to Italy to enjoy their victory.

For the next thousand years, the Mediterranean remained a European sea.   But as soon as the Roman Empire had been destroyed, Asia made another attempt to dominate this great inland sea, as you will learn when I tell you about Mohammed,

THE RISE OF ROME

HOW ROME HAPPENED

THE Roman Empire was an accident. No one planned it. It "happened." No famous general or statesman or cut-throat ever got up and said "Friends, Romans, Citizens, we must found an Empire. Follow me and together we shall conquer all the land from the Gates of Hercules to Mount Taurus."

Rome produced famous generals and equally distinguished statesmen and cut-throats, and Roman armies fought all over the world. But the Roman empire-making was done without

HOW ROME HAPPENED
105

a preconceived plan. The average Roman was a very matter-of-fact citizen. He disliked theories about government. When someone began to recite "eastward the course of Roman Empire, etc., etc.," he hastily left the forum. He just continued to take more and more land because circumstances forced him to do so. He was not driven by ambition or by greed. Both by nature and inclination he was a farmer and wanted to stay at home. But when he was attacked he was obliged to defend himself and when the enemy happened to cross the sea to ask for aid in a distant country then the patient Roman marched many dreary miles to defeat this dangerous foe and when this had been accomplished, he stayed behind to adminster his newly conquered provinces lest they fall into the hands of wandering Barbarians and become themselves a menace to Roman safety. It sounds rather complicated and yet to the contemporaries it was so very simple, as you shall see in a moment.

In the year 203 B.C. Scipio had crossed the African Sea and had carried the war into Africa. Carthage had called Hannibal back. Badly supported by his mercenaries, Hannibal had been defeated near Zama. The Romans had asked for his surrender and Hannibal had fled to get aid from the kings of Macedonia and Syria, as I told you in my last chapter.

The rulers of these two countries (remnants of the Empire of Alexander the Great) just then were contemplating an expedition against Egypt. They hoped to divide the rich Nile valley between themselves. The king of Egypt had heard of this and he had asked Rome to come to his support. The stage was set for a number of highly interesting plots and counter-plots. But the Romans, with their lack of imagination, rang the curtain down before the play had been fairly started. Their legions completely defeated the heavy Greek phalanx which was still used by the Macedonians as their battle formation. That happened in the year 197 B.C. at the battle in the plains of Cynoscephalæ or "Dogs' Heads," in central Thessaly.

The Romans then marched southward to Attica and informed the Greeks that they had come to "deliver the Hellenes

from the Macedonian yoke." The Greeks, having learned
nothing in their years of semi-slavery, used their new freedom
in a most unfortunate way. All the little city-states once more
began to quarrel with each other as they had done in the good
old days. The Romans, who had little understanding and less
love for these silly bickerings of a race which they rather despised, showed great forbearance. But tiring of these endless

CIVILIZATION GOES WESTWARD

dissensions they lost patience, invaded Greece, burned down
Corinth (to "encourage the other Greeks") and sent a Roman
governor to Athens to rule this turbulent province. In this
way, Macedonia and Greece became buffer states which protected Rome's eastern frontier.

Meanwhile right across the Hellespont lay the Kingdom of
Syria, and Antiochus III, who ruled that vast land, had shown
great eagerness when his distinguished guest, General Han-

nibal, explained to him how easy it would be to invade Italy and sack the city of Rome.

Lucius Scipio, a brother of Scipio the African fighter who had defeated Hannibal and his Carthaginians at Zama, was sent to Asia Minor. He destroyed the armies of the Syrian king near Magnesia (in the year 190 B.C.) Shortly afterwards, Antiochus was lynched by his own people. Asia Minor became a Roman protectorate and the small City-Republic of Rome was mistress of most of the lands which bordered upon the Mediterranean.

THE ROMAN EMPIRE

HOW THE REPUBLIC OF ROME AFTER CENTURIES OF UNREST AND REVOLUTION BECAME AN EMPIRE

WHEN the Roman armies returned from these many victorious campaigns, they were received with great jubilation. Alas and alack! this sudden glory did not make the country any happier. On the contrary. The endless campaigns had ruined the farmers who had been obliged to do the hard work of Empire making. It had placed too much power in the hands of the successful generals (and their private friends) who had used the war as an excuse for wholesale robbery.

The old Roman Republic had been proud of the simplicity which had characterised the lives of her famous men. The new Republic felt ashamed of the shabby coats and the high principles which had been fashionable in the days of its grandfathers. It became a land of rich people ruled by rich people for the benefit of rich people. As such it was doomed to disastrous failure, as I shall now tell you.

Within less than a century and a half, Rome had become the mistress of practically all the land around the Mediterranean. In those early days of history a prisoner of war lost his freedom and became a slave. The Roman regarded war as a very serious business and he showed no mercy to a conquered foe. After the fall of Carthage, the Carthaginian women and children were sold into bondage together with their own slaves.

And a like fate awaited the obstinate inhabitants of Greece and
Macedonia and Spain and Syria when they dared to revolt
against the Roman power.

Two thousand years ago a slave was merely a piece of
machinery. Nowadays a rich man invests his money in factories. The rich people of Rome (senators, generals and war-
profiteers) invested theirs in land and in slaves. The land
they bought or took in the newly-acquired provinces. The
slaves they bought in open market wherever they happened to
be cheapest. During most of the third and second centuries
before Christ there was a plentiful supply, and as a result the
landowners worked their slaves until they dropped dead in their
tracks, when they bought new ones at the nearest bargain-coun-
ter of Corinthian or Carthaginian captives.

And now behold the fate of the freeborn farmer!

He had done his duty toward Rome and he had fought her
battles without complaint. But when he came home after ten,
fifteen or twenty years, his lands were covered with weeds and
his family had been ruined. But he was a strong man and
willing to begin life anew. He sowed and planted and waited
for the harvest. He carried his grain to the market together
with his cattle and his poultry, to find that the large landowners
who worked their estates with slaves could underbid him all
along the line. For a couple of years he tried to hold his own.
Then he gave up in despair. He left the country and he went
to the nearest city. In the city he was as hungry as he had been
before on the land. But he shared his misery with thousands
of other disinherited beings. They crouched together in filthy
hovels in the suburbs of the large cities. They were apt
to get sick and die from terrible epidemics. They were all profoundly discontented. They had fought for their country and
this was their reward. They were always willing to listen to
those plausible spell-binders who gather around a public grievance like so many hungry vultures, and soon they became a
grave menace to the safety of the state.

But the class of the newly-rich shrugged its shoulders.
"We have our army and our policemen," they argued, "they

ROME

will keep the mob in order." And they hid themselves behind the high walls of their pleasant villas and cultivated their gardens and read the poems of a certain Homer which a Greek slave had just translated into very pleasing Latin hexameters.

In a few families however the old tradition of unselfish service to the Commonwealth continued. Cornelia, the daughter of Scipio Africanus, had been married to a Roman by the name of Gracchus. She had two sons, Tiberius and Gaius. When the boys grew up they entered politics and tried to bring about certain much-needed reforms. A census had shown that most of the land of the Italian peninsula was owned by two thousand noble families. Tiberius Gracchus, having been elected a Tribune, tried to help the freemen. He revived two ancient laws which restricted the number of acres which a single owner might possess. In this way he hoped to revive the valuable old class of small and independent freeholders. The newly-rich called him a robber and an enemy of the state. There were street riots. A party of thugs was hired to kill the popular Tribune. Tiberius Gracchus was attacked when he entered the assembly and was beaten to death. Ten years later his brother Gaius tried the experiment of reforming a nation against the expressed wishes of a strong privileged class. He passed a "poor law" which was meant to help the destitute farmers. Eventually it made the greater part of the Roman citizens into professional beggars.

He established colonies of destitute people in distant parts of the empire, but these settlements failed to attract the right sort of people. Before Gaius Gracchus could do more harm he too was murdered and his followers were either killed or exiled. The first two reformers had been gentlemen. The two who came after were of a very different stamp. They were professional soldiers. One was called Marius. The name of the other was Sulla. Both enjoyed a large personal following.

Sulla was the leader of the landowners. Marius, the victor in a great battle at the foot of the Alps when the Teutons and the Cimbri had been annihilated, was the popular hero of the disinherited freemen.

Now it happened in the year 88 B.C. that the Senate of Rome was greatly disturbed by rumours that came from Asia. Mithridates, king of a country along the shores of the Black Sea, and a Greek on his mother's side, had seen the possibility of establishing a second Alexandrian Empire. He began his campaign for world-domination with the murder of all Roman citizens who happened to be in Asia Minor, men, women and children. Such an act, of course, meant war. The Senate equipped an army to march against the King of Pontus and punish him for his crime. But who was to be commander-in-chief? "Sulla," said the Senate, "because he is Consul." "Marius," said the mob, "because he has been Consul five times and because he is the champion of our rights."

Possession is nine points of the law. Sulla happened to be in actual command of the army. He went east to defeat Mithridates and Marius fled to Africa. There he waited until he heard that Sulla had crossed into Asia. He then returned to Italy, gathered a motley crew of malcontents, marched on Rome and entered the city with his professional highwaymen, spent five days and five nights, slaughtering his enemies in the Senatorial party, got himself elected Consul and promptly died from the excitement of the last fortnight.

There followed four years of disorder. Then Sulla, having defeated Mithridates, announced that he was ready to return to Rome and settle a few old scores of his own. He was as good as his word. For weeks his soldiers were busy executing those of their fellow citizens who were suspected of democratic sympathies. One day they got hold of a young fellow who had been often seen in the company of Marius. They were going to hang him when some one interfered. "The boy is too young," he said, and they let him go. His name was Julius Cæsar. You shall meet him again on the next page.

As for Sulla, he became "Dictator," which meant sole and supreme ruler of all the Roman possessions. He ruled Rome for four years, and he died quietly in his bed, having spent the last year of his life tenderly raising his cabbages, as was the custom of so many Romans who had spent a lifetime killing their fellow-men.

But conditions did not grow better. On the contrary, they grew worse. Another general, Gnæus Pompeius, or Pompey, a close friend of Sulla, went east to renew the war against the ever troublesome Mithridates. He drove that energetic potentate into the mountains where Mithridates took poison and killed himself, well knowing what fate awaited him as a Roman captive. Next he re-established the authority of Rome over Syria, destroyed Jerusalem, roamed through western Asia, trying to revive the myth of Alexander the Great, and at last (in the year 62) returned to Rome with a dozen ship-loads of defeated Kings and Princes and Generals, all of whom were forced to march in the triumphal procession of this enormously popular Roman who presented his city with the sum of forty million dollars in plunder.

It was necessary that the government of Rome be placed in the hands of a strong man. Only a few months before, the town had almost fallen into the hands of a good-for-nothing young aristocrat by the name of Catiline, who had gambled away his money and hoped to reimburse himself for his losses by a little plundering. Cicero, a public-spirited lawyer, had discovered the plot, had warned the Senate, and had forced Catiline to flee. But there were other young men with similar ambitions and it was no time for idle talk.

Pompey organised a triumvirate which was to take charge of affairs. He became the leader of this Vigilante Committee. Gaius Julius Cæsar, who had made a reputation for himself as governor of Spain, was the second in command. The third was an indifferent sort of person by the name of Crassus. He had been elected because he was incredibly rich, having been a successful contractor of war supplies. He soon went upon an expedition against the Parthians and was killed.

As for Cæsar, who was by far the ablest of the three, he decided that he needed a little more military glory to become a popular hero. He crossed the Alps and conquered that part of the world which is now called France. Then he hammered a solid wooden bridge across the Rhine and invaded the land of the wild Teutons. Finally he took ship and visited England. Heaven knows where he might have ended if he had not been forced to return to Italy. Pompey, so he was informed, had been appointed dictator for life. This of course meant that Cæsar was to be placed on the list of the "retired officers," and the idea did not appeal to him. He remembered that he had begun life as a follower of Marius. He decided to teach the

CÆSAR GOES WEST

Senators and their "dictator" another lesson. He crossed the Rubicon River which separated the province of Cis-alpine Gaul from Italy. Everywhere he was received as the "friend of the people." Without difficulty Cæsar entered Rome and Pompey fled to Greece. Cæsar followed him and defeated his followers near Pharsalus. Pompey sailed across the Mediterranean and escaped to Egypt. When he landed he was murdered by order of young king Ptolemy. A few days later Cæsar arrived. He found himself caught in a trap. Both the Egyptians and the Roman garrison which had remained faithful to Pompey, attacked his camp.

Fortune was with Cæsar. He succeeded in setting fire to the Egyptian fleet. Incidentally the sparks of the burning vessels fell on the roof of the famous library of Alexandria (which was just off the water front,) and destroyed it. Next he attacked the Egyptian army, drove the soldiers into the Nile, drowned Ptolemy, and established a new government under Cleopatra, the sister of the late king. Just then word reached him that Pharnaces, the son and heir of Mithridates, had gone on the war-path. Cæsar marched northward, defeated Pharnaces in a war which lasted five days, sent word of his victory to Rome in the famous sentence "veni, vidi, vici," which is Latin for "I came, I saw, I conquered," and returned to Egypt where he fell desperately in love with Cleopatra, who followed him to Rome when he returned to take charge of the government, in the year 46. He marched at the head of not less than four different victory-parades, having won four different campaigns.

Then Cæsar appeared in the Senate to report upon his adventures, and the grateful Senate made him "dictator" for ten years. It was a fatal step.

The new dictator made serious attempts to reform the Roman state. He made it possible for freemen to become members of the Senate. He conferred the rights of citizenship upon distant communities as had been done in the early days of Roman history. He permitted "foreigners" to exercise influence upon the government. He reformed the administration of the distant provinces which certain aristocratic families had come to regard as their private possessions. In short he did many things for the good of the majority of the people but which made him thoroughly unpopular with the most powerful men in the state. Half a hundred young aristocrats formed a plot "to save the Republic." On the Ides of March (the fifteenth of March according to that new calendar which Cæsar had brought with him from Egypt) Cæsar was murdered when he entered the Senate. Once more Rome was without a master

ULTIMA THULE
OR
THE END OF
THE WORLD

WILDERNESS

DESERT

THE ROMAN
EMPIRE

THE GREAT ROMAN EMPIRE

There were two men who tried to continue the tradition of Cæsar's glory. One was Antony, his former secretary. The other was Octavian, Cæsar's grand-nephew and heir to his estate. Octavian remained in Rome, but Antony went to Egypt to be near Cleopatra with whom he too had fallen in love, as seems to have been the habit of Roman generals.

A war broke out between the two. In the battle of Actium, Octavian defeated Antony. Antony killed himself and Cleopatra was left alone to face the enemy. She tried very hard to make Octavian her third Roman conquest. When she saw that she could make no impression upon this very proud aristocrat, she killed herself, and Egypt became a Roman province.

As for Octavian, he was a very wise young man and he did not repeat the mistake of his famous uncle. He knew how people will shy at words. He was very modest in his demands when he returned to Rome. He did not want to be a "dictator." He would be entirely satisfied with the title of "the Honourable." But when the Senate, a few years later, addressed him as Augustus—the Illustrious—he did not object and a few years later the man in the street called him Cæsar, or Kaiser, while the soldiers, accustomed to regard Octavian as their Commander-in-chief referred to him as the Chief, the Imperator or Emperor. The Republic had become an Empire, but the average Roman was hardly aware of the fact.

In 14 A.D. his position as the Absolute Ruler of the Roman people had become so well established that he was made an object of that divine worship which hitherto had been reserved for the Gods. And his successors were true "Emperors"—the absolute rulers of the greatest empire the world had ever seen.

If the truth be told, the average citizen was sick and tired of anarchy and disorder. He did not care who ruled him provided the new master gave him a chance to live quietly and without the noise of eternal street riots. Octavian assured his subjects forty years of peace. He had no desire to extend the frontiers of his domains. In the year 9 A.D. he had contemplated an invasion of the northwestern wilderness which was inhabited by the Teutons. But Varus, his general, had been killed with all his men in the Teutoburg Woods, and after that the Romans made no further attempts to civilise these wild people.

They concentrated their efforts upon the gigantic problem of internal reform. But it was too late to do much good. Two centuries of revolution and foreign war had repeatedly killed the best men among the younger generations. It had ruined the class of the free farmers. It had introduced slave labor, against which no freeman could hope to compete. It had turned the cities into beehives inhabited by pauperized and unhealthy mobs of runaway peasants. It had created a large bureaucracy—petty officials who were underpaid and who were forced to take graft in order to buy bread and clothing for their families. Worst of all, it had accustomed people to violence, to blood shed, to a barbarous pleasure in the pain and suffering of others.

Outwardly, the Roman state during the first century of our era was a magnificent political structure, so large that Alexander's empire became one of its minor provinces. Underneath this glory there lived millions upon millions of poor and tired human beings, toiling like ants who have built a nest underneath a heavy stone. They worked for the benefit of some one else. They shared their food with the animals of the fields. They lived in stables. They died without hope.

It was the seven hundred and fifty-third year since the founding of Rome. Gaius Julius Cæsar Octavianus Augustus was living in the palace of the Palatine Hill, busily engaged upon the task of ruling his empire.

In a little village of distant Syria, Mary, the wife of Joseph the Carpenter, was tending her little boy, born in a stable of Bethlehem.

This is a strange world.

Before long, the palace and the stable were to meet in open combat.

And the stable was to emerge victorious.

JOSHUA OF NAZARETH

THE STORY OF JOSHUA OF NAZARETH, WHOM THE GREEKS CALLED JESUS

In the autumn of the year of the city 815 (which would be 62 A.D., in our way of counting time) Æsculapius Cultellus, a Roman physician, wrote to his nephew who was with the army in Syria as follows:

My dear Nephew,

A few days ago I was called in to prescribe for a sick man named Paul. He appeared to be a Roman citizen of Jewish parentage, well educated and of agreeable manners. I had been told that he was here in connection with a law-suit, an appeal from one of our provincial courts, Cæsarea or some such place in the eastern Mediterranean. He had been described to me as a "wild and violent" fellow who had been making speeches against the People and against the Law. I found him very intelligent and of great honesty.

A friend of mine who used to be with the army in Asia Minor tells me that he heard something about him in Ephesus where he was preaching sermons about a strange new God. I asked my patient if this were true and whether he had told the people to rebel against the will of our beloved Emperor. Paul answered me that the Kingdom of which he had spoken was not of this world and he added many strange utterances which I did not understand, but which were probably due to his fever.

His personality made a great impression upon me and I was sorry to hear that he was killed on the Ostian Road a few days ago. Therefore I am writing this letter to you. When next you visit Jerusalem, I want you to find out something about my friend Paul and the strange Jewish prophet, who seems to have been his teacher. Our slaves are getting much excited about this so-called Messiah, and a few of them, who openly talked of the new kingdom (whatever that means) have been crucified. I would like to know the truth about all these rumours and I am

Your devoted Uncle,
ÆSCULAPIUS CULTELLUS.

Six weeks later, Gladius Ensa, the nephew, a captain of the VII Gallic Infantry, answered as follows:

My dear Uncle,
I received your letter and I have obeyed your instructions.
Two weeks ago our brigade was sent to Jerusalem. There have been several revolutions during the last century and there is not much left of the old city. We have been here now for a month and to-morrow we shall continue our march to Petra, where there has been trouble with some of the Arab tribes. I shall use this evening to answer your questions, but pray do not expect a detailed report.
I have talked with most of the older men in this city but few have been able to give me any definite information. A few days ago a pedler came to the camp. I bought some of his olives and I asked him whether he had ever heard of the famous Messiah who was killed when he was young. He said that he remembered it very clearly, because his father had taken him to Golgotha (a hill just outside the city) to see the execution, and to show him what became of the enemies of the laws of the people of Judæa. He gave me the address of one Joseph, who had been a personal friend of the Messiah and told me that I had better go and see him if I wanted to know more.

This morning I went to call on Joseph. He was quite an old man. He had been a fisherman on one of the fresh-water lakes. His memory was clear, and from him at last I got a fairly definite account of what had happened during the troublesome days before I was born.

Tiberius, our great and glorious emperor, was on the throne, and an officer of the name of Pontius Pilatus was governor of

THE HOLY LAND

Judæa and Samaria. Joseph knew little about this Pilatus. He seemed to have been an honest enough official who left a decent reputation as procurator of the province. In the year 783 or 784 (Joseph had forgotten when) Pilatus was called to Jerusalem on account of a riot. A certain young man (the son of a carpenter of Nazareth) was said to be planning a revolution against the Roman government. Strangely enough our own intelligence officers, who are usually well informed, appear to have heard nothing about it, and when they investigated the matter they reported that the carpenter was an excellent citizen and that there was no reason to proceed against him. But the old-fashioned leaders of the Jewish faith, according to Joseph, were much upset. They greatly disliked his popularity with the masses of the poorer Hebrews. The "Nazarene" (so they told Pilatus) had publicly claimed that a Greek or a Roman or even a Philistine, who tried to live a decent and honourable life, was quite as good as a Jew who spent his days studying the ancient laws of Moses. Pilatus does not seem to have been impressed by this argument, but when the crowds around the temple threatened to lynch Jesus, and kill all his followers, he decided to take the carpenter into custody to save his life.

He does not appear to have understood the real nature of the quarrel. Whenever he asked the Jewish priests to explain their grievances, they shouted "heresy" and "treason" and got terribly excited. Finally, so Joseph told me, Pilatus sent for Joshua (that was the name of the Nazarene, but the Greeks who live in this part of the world always refer to him as Jesus) to examine him personally. He talked to him for several hours. He asked him about the "dangerous doctrines" which he was said to have preached on the shores of the sea of Galilee. But Jesus answered that he never referred to politics. He was not so much interested in the bodies of men as in Man's soul. He wanted all people to regard their neighbours as their brothers and to love one single God, who was the father of all living beings.

Pilatus, who seems to have been well versed in the doctrines of the Stoics and the other Greek philosophers, does not appear to have discovered anything seditious in the talk of Jesus. According to my informant he made another attempt to save the life of the kindly prophet. He kept putting the execution off. Meanwhile the Jewish people, lashed into fury by their priests, got frantic with rage. There had been many riots in Jerusalem before this and there were only a few Roman soldiers within calling distance. Reports were being sent to the

Roman authorities in Cæsarea that Pilatus had "fallen a victim to the teachings of the Nazarene." Petitions were being circulated all through the city to have Pilatus recalled, because he was an enemy of the Emperor. You know that our governors have strict instructions to avoid an open break with their foreign subjects. To save the country from civil war, Pilatus finally sacrificed his prisoner, Joshua, who behaved with great dignity and who forgave all those who hated him. He was crucified amidst the howls and the laughter of the Jerusalem mob.

That is what Joseph told me, with tears running down his old cheeks. I gave him a gold piece when I left him, but he refused it and asked me to hand it to one poorer than himself. I also asked him a few questions about your friend Paul. He had known him slightly. He seems to have been a tent maker who gave up his profession that he might preach the words of a loving and forgiving God, who was so very different from that Jehovah of whom the Jewish priests are telling us all the time. Afterwards, Paul appears to have travelled much in Asia Minor and in Greece, telling the slaves that they were all children of one loving Father and that happiness awaits all, both rich and poor, who have tried to live honest lives and have done good to those who were suffering and miserable.

I hope that I have answered your questions to your satisfaction. The whole story seems very harmless to me as far as the safety of the state is concerned. But then, we Romans never have been able to understand the people of this province. I am sorry that they have killed your friend Paul. I wish that I were at home again, and I am, as ever,

Your dutiful nephew,
GLADIUS ENSA.

THE FALL OF ROME

THE TWILIGHT OF ROME

THE text-books of ancient History give the date 476 as the year in which Rome fell, because in that year the last emperor was driven off his throne. But Rome, which was not built in a day, took a long time falling. The process was so slow and so gradual that most Romans did not realise how their old world was coming to an end. They complained about the unrest of the times—they grumbled about the high prices of food and about the low wages of the workmen—they cursed the profiteers who had a monopoly of the grain and the wool and the gold coin. Occasionally they rebelled against an unusually rapacious governor. But the majority of the people during the first four centuries of our era ate and drank (whatever their purse allowed them to buy) and hated or loved (according to their nature) and went to the theatre (whenever there was a free show of fighting gladiators) or starved in the slums of the big cities, utterly ignorant of the fact that their empire had outlived its usefulness and was doomed to perish.

How could they realise the threatened danger? Rome made a fine showing of outward glory. Well-paved roads connected the different provinces, the imperial police were active and showed little tenderness for highwaymen. The frontier was closely guarded against the savage tribes who seemed to be occupying the waste lands of northern Europe. The whole world was paying tribute to the mighty city of Rome, and a

124

score of able men were working day and night to undo the mistakes of the past and bring about a return to the happier conditions of the early Republic.

But the underlying causes of the decay of the State, of which I have told you in a former chapter, had not been removed and reform therefore was impossible.

Rome was, first and last and all the time, a city-state as Athens and Corinth had been city-states in ancient Hellas. It had been able to dominate the Italian peninsula. But Rome as the ruler of the entire civilised world was a political impossibility and could not endure. Her young men were killed in her endless wars. Her farmers were ruined by long military service and by taxation. They either became professional beggars or hired themselves out to rich landowners who gave them board and lodging in exchange for their services and made them "serfs," those unfortunate human beings who are neither slaves nor freemen, but who have become part of the soil upon which they work, like so many cows, and the trees.

The Empire, the State, had become everything. The common citizen had dwindled down to less than nothing. As for the slaves, they had heard the words that were spoken by Paul. They had accepted the message of the humble carpenter of Nazareth. They did not rebel against their masters. On the contrary, they had been taught to be meek and they obeyed their superiors. But they had lost all interest in the affairs of this world which had proved such a miserable place of abode. They were willing to fight the good fight that they might enter into the Kingdom of Heaven. But they were not willing to engage in warfare for the benefit of an ambitious emperor who aspired to glory by way of a foreign campaign in the land of the Parthians or the Numidians or the Scots.

And so conditions grew worse as the centuries went by. The first Emperors had continued the tradition of "leadership" which had given the old tribal chieftains such a hold upon their subjects. But the Emperors of the second and third centuries were Barrack-Emperors, professional soldiers, who existed by the grace of their body-guards, the so-called Prætorians. They succeeded each other with terrifying rapidity, murdering their way into the palace and being murdered out of it as soon as their successors had become rich enough to bribe the guards into a new rebellion.

Meanwhile the barbarians were hammering at the gates of the northern frontier. As there were no longer any native Roman armies to stop their progress, foreign mercenaries had to be hired to fight the invader. As the foreign soldier happened to be of the same blood as his supposed enemy, he was

WHEN THE BARBARIANS GOT THROUGH WITH A ROMAN CITY

apt to be quite lenient when he engaged in battle. Finally, by way of experiment, a few tribes were allowed to settle within the confines of the Empire. Others followed. Soon these tribes complained bitterly of the greedy Roman tax-gatherers, who took away their last penny. When they got no redress they marched to Rome and loudly demanded that they be heard.

This made Rome very uncomfortable as an Imperial residence. Constantine (who ruled from 323 to 337) looked for a new capital. He chose Byzantium, the gate-way for the commerce between Europe and Asia. The city was renamed

Constantinople, and the court moved eastward. When Constantine died, his two sons, for the sake of a more efficient administration, divided the Empire between them. The elder lived in Rome and ruled in the west. The younger stayed in Constantinople and was master of the east.

Then came the fourth century and the terrible visitation of the Huns, those mysterious Asiatic horsemen who for more than two centuries maintained themselves in Northern Europe and continued their career of bloodshed until they were defeated near Chalons-sur-Marne in France in the year 451. As soon as the Huns had reached the Danube they had begun to press hard upon the Goths. The Goths, in order to save themselves, were thereupon obliged to invade Rome. The Emperor Valens tried to stop them, but was killed near Adrianople in the year 378. Twenty-two years later, under their king, Alaric, these same West Goths marched westward and attacked Rome. They did not plunder, and destroyed only a few palaces. Next came the Vandals, and showed less respect for the venerable traditions of the city. Then the Burgundians. Then the East Goths. Then the Alemanni. Then the Franks. There was no end to the invasions. Rome at last was at the mercy of every ambitious highway robber who could gather a few followers.

In the year 402 the Emperor fled to Ravenna, which was a sea-port and strongly fortified, and there, in the year 475, Odoacer, commander of a regiment of the German mercenaries, who wanted the farms of Italy to be divided among themselves, gently but effectively pushed Romulus Augustulus, the last of the emperors who ruled the western division, from his throne, and proclaimed himself Patrician or ruler of Rome. The eastern Emperor, who was very busy with his own affairs, recognised him, and for ten years Odoacer ruled what was left of the western provinces.

A few years later, Theodoric, King of the East Goths, invaded the newly formed Patriciate, took Ravenna, murdered Odoacer at his own dinner table, and established a Gothic

THE INVASIONS OF THE BARBARIANS

Kingdom amidst the ruins of the western part of the Empire. This Patriciate state did not last long. In the sixth century a motley crowd of Longobards and Saxons and Slavs and Avars invaded Italy, destroyed the Gothic kingdom, and established a new state of which Pavia became the capital.

Then at last the imperial city sank into a state of utter neglect and despair. The ancient palaces had been plundered time and again. The schools had been burned down. The teachers had been starved to death. The rich people had been thrown out of their villas which were now inhabited by evil-smelling and hairy barbarians. The roads had fallen into decay. The old bridges were gone and commerce had come to a standstill. Civilisation—the product of thousands of years of patient labor on the part of Egyptians and Babylonians and Greeks and Romans, which had lifted man high above the most daring dreams of his earliest ancestors, threatened to perish from the western continent.

It is true that in the far east, Constantinople continued to be the centre of an Empire for another thousand years. But it hardly counted as a part of the European continent. Its interests lay in the east. It began to forget its western origin. Gradually the Roman language was given up for the Greek. The Roman alphabet was discarded and Roman law was written in Greek characters and explained by Greek judges. The Emperor became an Asiatic despot, worshipped as the god-like kings of Thebes had been worshipped in the valley of the Nile, three thousand years before. When missionaries of the Byzantine church looked for fresh fields of activity, they went eastward and carried the civilisation of Byzantium into the vast wilderness of Russia.

As for the west, it was left to the mercies of the Barbarians. For twelve generations, murder, war, arson, plundering were the order of the day. One thing—and one thing alone—saved Europe from complete destruction, from a return to the days of cave-men and the hyena.

This was the church—the flock of humble men and women

who for many centuries had confessed themselves the followers of Jesus, the carpenter of Nazareth, who had been killed that the mighty Roman Empire might be saved the trouble of a street-riot in a little city somewhere along the Syrian frontier.

RISE OF THE CHURCH

HOW ROME BECAME THE CENTRE OF THE CHRISTIAN WORLD

THE average intelligent Roman who lived under the Empire had taken very little interest in the gods of his fathers. A few times a year he went to the temple, but merely as a matter of custom. He looked on patiently when the people celebrated a religious festival with a solemn procession. But he regarded the worship of Jupiter and Minerva and Neptune as something rather childish, a survival from the crude days of the early republic and not a fit subject of study for a man who had mastered the works of the Stoics and the Epicureans and the other great philosophers of Athens.

This attitude made the Roman a very tolerant man. The government insisted that all people, Romans, foreigners, Greeks, Babylonians, Jews, should pay a certain outward respect to the image of the Emperor which was supposed to stand in every temple, just as a picture of the President of the United States is apt to hang in an American Post Office. But this was a formality without any deeper meaning. Generally speaking everybody could honour, revere and adore whatever gods he pleased, and as a result, Rome was filled with all sorts of queer little temples and synagogues, dedicated to the worship of Egyptian and African and Asiatic divinities.

When the first disciples of Jesus reached Rome and began to preach their new doctrine of a universal brotherhood of man, nobody objected. The man in the street stopped and listened. Rome, the capital of the world, had always been full of wandering preachers, each proclaiming his own "mystery." Most of the self-appointed priests appealed to the senses—promised golden rewards and endless pleasure to the followers of their own particular god. Soon the crowd in the street noticed that the so-called Christians (the followers of the Christ or "anointed") spoke a very different language. They did not appear to be impressed by great riches or a noble position. They extolled the beauties of poverty and humility and meekness. These were not exactly the virtues which had made Rome the mistress of the world. It was rather interesting to listen to a "mystery" which told people in the hey-day of their glory that their worldly success could not possibly bring them lasting happiness.

Besides, the preachers of the Christian mystery told dreadful stories of the fate that awaited those who refused to listen to the words of the true God. It was never wise to take chances. Of course the old Roman gods still existed, but were they strong enough to protect their friends against the powers of this new deity who had been brought to Europe from distant Asia? People began to have doubts. They returned to listen to further explanations of the new creed. After a while they began to meet the men and women who preached the words of Jesus. They found them very different from the average Roman priests. They were all dreadfully poor. They were kind to slaves and to animals. They did not try to gain riches, but gave away whatever they had. The example of their unselfish lives forced many Romans to forsake the old religion. They joined the small communities of Christians who met in the back rooms of private houses or somewhere in an open field, and the temples were deserted.

This went on year after year and the number of Christians continued to increase. Presbyters or priests (the original Greek meant "elder") were elected to guard the interests of the small churches. A bishop was made the head of all the communities within a single province. Peter, who had followed **Paul** to **Rome**, was the first Bishop of **Rome**. In due time his successors (who were addressed as Father or Papa) came to be known as Popes.

The church became a powerful institution within the Empire. The Christian doctrines appealed to those who despaired of this world. They also attracted many strong men who found it impossible to make a career under the Imperial gov-

A CLOISTER

ernment, but who could exercise their gifts of leadership among the humble followers of the Nazarene teacher. At last the state was obliged to take notice. The Roman Empire (I have said this before) was tolerant through indifference. It allowed everybody to seek salvation after his or her own fashion. But it insisted that the different sects keep the peace among themselves and obey the wise rule of "live and let live."

The Christian communities however, refused to practise any

sort of tolerance. They publicly declared that their God, and
their God alone, was the true ruler of Heaven and Earth,
and that all other gods were impostors. This seemed unfair
to the other sects and the police discouraged such utterances.
The Christians persisted.

Soon there were further difficulties. The Christians refused
to go through the formalities of paying homage to the emperor. They refused to appear when they were called upon
to join the army. The Roman magistrates threatened to

THE GOTHS ARE COMING

punish them. The Christians answered that this miserable
world was only the ante-room to a very pleasant Heaven and
that they were more than willing to suffer death for their
principles. The Romans, puzzled by such conduct, sometimes
killed the offenders, but more often they did not. There was
a certain amount of lynching during the earliest years of the
church, but this was the work of that part of the mob which
accused their meek Christian neighbours of every conceivable
crime, (such as slaughtering and eating babies, bringing about
sickness and pestilence, betraying the country in times of danger) because it was a harmless sport and devoid of danger, as
the Christians refused to fight back.

Meanwhile, Rome continued to be invaded by the Barbarians and when her armies failed, Christian missionaries went forth to preach their gospel of peace to the wild Teutons. They were strong men without fear of death. They spoke a language which left no doubt as to the future of unrepentant sinners. The Teutons were deeply impressed. They still had a deep respect for the wisdom of the ancient city of Rome. Those men were Romans. They probably spoke the truth. Soon the Christian missionary became a power in the savage regions of the Teutons and the Franks. Half a dozen missionaries were as valuable as a whole regiment of soldiers. The Emperors began to understand that the Christian might be of great use to them. In some of the provinces they were given equal rights with those who remained faithful to the old gods. The great change however came during the last half of the fourth century.

Constantine, sometimes (Heaven knows why) called Constantine the Great, was emperor. He was a terrible ruffian, but people of tender qualities could hardly hope to survive in that hard-fighting age. During a long and checkered career, Constantine had experienced many ups and downs. Once, when almost defeated by his enemies, he thought that he would try the power of this new Asiatic deity of whom everybody was talking. He promised that he too would become a Christian if he were successful in the coming battle. He won the victory and thereafter he was convinced of the power of the Christian God and allowed himself to be baptised.

From that moment on, the Christian church was officially recognised and this greatly strengthened the position of the new faith.

But the Christians still formed a very small minority of all the people, (not more than five or six percent,) and in order to win, they were forced to refuse all compromise. The old gods must be destroyed. For a short spell the emperor Julian, a lover of Greek wisdom, managed to save the pagan Gods from further destruction. But Julian died of his wounds during a campaign in Persia and his successor Jovian re-established the church in all its glory. One after the other the doors of the ancient temples were then closed. Then came the emperor Justinian (who built the church of Saint Sophia in Constantinople), who discontinued the school of philosophy at Athens which had been founded by Plato.

That was the end of the old Greek world, in which man had been allowed to think his own thoughts and dream his own dreams according to his desires. The somewhat vague rules of conduct of the philosophers had proved a poor compass by which to steer the ship of life after a deluge of savagery and ignorance had swept away the established order of things There was need of something more positive and more definite. This the Church provided.

During an age when nothing was certain, the church stood like a rock and never receded from those principles which it held to be true and sacred. This steadfast courage gained the admiration of the multitudes and carried the church of Rome safely through the difficulties which destroyed the Roman state.

There was however, a certain element of luck in the final success of the Christian faith. After the disappearance of Theodoric's Roman-Gothic kingdom, in the fifth century, Italy was comparatively free from foreign invasion. The Lombards and Saxons and Slavs who succeeded the Goths were weak and backward tribes. Under those circumstances it was possible for the bishops of Rome to maintain the independence of their city. Soon the remnants of the empire, scattered throughout the peninsula, recognised the Dukes of Rome (or bishops) as their political and spiritual rulers.

The stage was set for the appearance of a strong man. He came in the year 590 and his name was Gregory. He belonged to the ruling classes of ancient Rome, and he had been "prefect" or mayor of the city. Then he had become a monk and a bishop and finally, and much against his will, (for he wanted to be a missionary and preach Christianity to the heathen of England,) he had been dragged to the Church of Saint Peter to be made Pope. He ruled only fourteen years but when he died the Christian world of western Europe had officially recognised the bishops of Rome, the Popes, as the head of the entire church.

This power, however, did not extend to the east. In Constantinople the Emperors continued the old custom which had recognised the successors of Augustus and Tiberius both as head of the government and as High Priest of the Established Religion. In the year 1453 the eastern Roman Empire was conquered by the Turks. Constantinople was taken, and Constantine Paleologue, the last Roman Emperor, was killed on the steps of the Church of the Holy Sophia.

A few years before, Zoë, the daughter of his brother Thomas, had married Ivan III of Russia. In this way did the grand-dukes of Moscow fall heir to the traditions of Constantinople. The double-eagle of old Byzantium (reminiscent of the days when Rome had been divided into an eastern and a western part) became the coat of arms of modern Russia The Tsar who had been merely the first of the Russian nobles, assumed the aloofness and the dignity of a Roman emperor before whom all subjects, both high and low, were inconsiderable slaves.

The court was refashioned after the oriental pattern which the eastern Emperors had imported from Asia and from Egypt and which (so they flattered themselves) resembled the court of Alexander the Great. This strange inheritance which the dying Byzantine Empire bequeathed to an unsuspecting world continued to live with great vigour for six more centuries. amidst the vast plains of Russia. The last man to wear the crown with the double eagle of Constantinople, Tsar Nicholas, was murdered only the other day, so to speak. His body was thrown into a well. His son and his daughters were all killed. All his ancient rights and prerogatives were abolished, and the church was reduced to the position which it had held in Rome before the days of Constantine.

The western church however fared very differently, as we shall see in the next chapter when the whole Christian world is going to be threatened with destruction by the rival creed of an Arab camel-driver.

MOHAMMED

AHMED, THE CAMEL-DRIVER, WHO BECAME
THE PROPHET OF THE ARABIAN DESERT,
AND WHOSE FOLLOWERS ALMOST CON-
QUERED THE ENTIRE KNOWN WORLD
FOR THE GREATER GLORY OF ALLAH, THE
ONLY TRUE GOD

SINCE the days of Carthage and Hannibal we have said nothing of the Semitic people. You will remember how they filled all the chapters devoted to the story of the Ancient World. The Babylonians, the Assyrians, the Phœnicians, the Jews, the Arameans, the Chaldeans, all of them Semites, had been the rulers of western Asia for thirty or forty centuries. They had been conquered by the Indo-European Persians who had come from the east and by the Indo-European Greeks who had come from the west. A hundred years after the death of Alexander the Great, Carthage, a colony of Semitic Phœnicians, had fought the Indo-European Romans for the mastery of the Mediterranean. Carthage had been defeated and de-stroyed and for eight hundred years the Romans had been mas-ters of the world. In the seventh century, however, another Semitic tribe appeared upon the scene and challenged the power of the west. They were the Arabs, peaceful shepherds who had roamed through the desert since the beginning of time without showing any signs of imperial ambitions.

Then they listened to Mohammed, mounted their horses and

in less than a century they had pushed to the heart of Europe and proclaimed the glories of Allah, "the only God," and Mohammed, "the prophet of the only God," to the frightened peasants of France.

The story of Ahmed, the son of Abdallah and Aminah, (usually known as Mohammed, or "he who will be praised,") reads like a chapter in the "Thousand and One Nights." He was a camel-driver, born in Mecca. He seems to have been an epileptic and he suffered from spells of unconsciousness when he dreamed strange dreams and heard the voice of the angel Gabriel, whose words were afterwards written down in a book called the Koran. His work as a caravan leader carried him all over Arabia and he was constantly falling in with Jewish merchants and with Christian traders, and he came to see that the worship of a single God was a very excellent thing. His own people, the Arabs, still revered queer stones and trunks of trees as their ancestors had done, tens of thousands of years before. In Mecca, their holy city, stood a little square building, the Kaaba, full of idols and strange odds and ends of Hoo-doo worship.

Mohammed decided to be the Moses of the Arab people. He could not well be a prophet and a camel-driver at the same time. So he made himself independent by marrying his employer, the rich widow Chadija. Then he told his neighbours in Mecca that he was the long-expected prophet sent by Allah to save the world. The neighbours laughed most heartily and when Mohammed continued to annoy them with his speeches they decided to kill him. They regarded him as

THE FLIGHT OF MOHAMMED

a lunatic and a public bore who deserved no mercy. Mohammed heard of the plot and in the dark of night he fled to Medina together with Abu Bekr, his trusted pupil. This happened in the year 622. It is the most important date in Mohammedan history and is known as the Hegira—the year of the Great Flight.

In Medina, Mohammed, who was a stranger, found it easier to proclaim himself a prophet than in his home city, where every one had known him as a simple camel-driver. Soon he was surrounded by an increasing number of followers, or Moslems, who accepted the Islam, "the submission to the will of God," which Mohammed praised as the highest of all virtues. For seven years he preached to the people of Medina. Then he believed himself strong enough to begin a campaign against his former neighbours who had dared to sneer at him and his Holy Mission in his old camel-driving days. At the head of an army of Medinese he marched across the desert. His followers took Mecca without great difficulty, and having slaughtered a number of the inhabitants, they found it quite easy to convince the others that Mohammed was really a great prophet.

From that time on until the year of his death, Mohammed was fortunate in everything he undertook.

There are two reasons for the success of Islam. In the first place, the creed which Mohammed taught to his followers was very simple. The disciples were told that they must love Allah, the Ruler of the World, the Merciful and Compassionate. They must honour and obey their parents. They were warned against dishonesty in dealing with their neighbours and were admonished to be humble and charitable, to the poor and to the sick. Finally they were ordered to abstain from strong drink and to be very frugal in what they ate. That was all. There were no priests, who acted as shepherds of their flocks and asked that they be supported at the common expense. The Mohammedan churches or mosques were merely large stone halls without benches or pictures, where the faithful could gather (if they felt so inclined) to read and discuss chapters from the Koran, the Holy Book. But the average Mohammedan carried his religion with him and never felt himself hemmed in by the restrictions and regulations of an established church. Five times a day he turned his face toward Mecca, the Holy City, and said a simple prayer. For the rest of the time he let Allah rule the world as he saw fit and accepted whatever fate brought him with patient resignation.

Of course such an attitude towards life did not encourage the Faithful to go forth and invent electrical machinery or bother about railroads and steamship lines. But it gave every Mohammedan a certain amount of contentment. It bade him be at peace with himself and with the world in which he lived and that was a very good thing.

The second reason which explains the success of the Moslems in their warfare upon the Christians, had to do with the conduct of those Mohammedan soldiers who went forth to do battle for the true faith. The Prophet promised that those who fell, facing the enemy, would go directly to Heaven. This made sudden death in the field preferable to a long but dreary existence upon this earth. It gave the Mohammedans an enormous advantage over the Crusaders who were in constant dread of a dark hereafter, and who stuck to the good things of this world as long as they possibly could. Incidentally it explains why even to-day Moslem soldiers will charge into the fire of European machine guns quite indifferent to the fate that awaits them and why they are such dangerous and persistent enemies.

Having put his religious house in order, Mohammed now began to enjoy his power as the undisputed ruler of a large number of Arab tribes. But success has been the undoing of a large number of men who were great in the days of adversity. He tried to gain the good will of the rich people by a number of regulations which could appeal to those of wealth. He allowed the Faithful to have four wives. As one wife was a costly investment in those olden days when brides were bought directly from the parents, four wives became a positive luxury except to those who possessed camels and dromedaries and date orchards beyond the dreams of avarice. A religion which at first had been meant for the hardy hunters of the high-skied desert was gradually transformed to suit the needs of the smug merchants who lived in the bazaars of the cities. It was a regrettable change from the original program and it did very little good to the cause of Mohammedanism. As for the prophet himself, he went on preaching the truth of Allah and proclaiming new rules of conduct until he died, quite suddenly, of a fever on June the seventh of the year 632.

His successor as Caliph (or leader) of the Moslems was his father-in-law, Abu-Bekr, who had shared the early dangers of the prophet's life. Two years later, Abu-Bekr died and Omar ibn Al-Khattab followed him. In less than ten years he conquered Egypt, Persia, Phœnicia, Syria and Palestine and made Damascus the capital of the first Mohammedan world empire.

Omar was succeeded by Ali, the husband of Mohammed's daughter, Fatima, but a quarrel broke out upon a point of Moslem doctrine and Ali was murdered. After his death, the caliphate was made hereditary and the leaders of the faithful who had begun their career as the spiritual head of a religious sect became the rulers of a vast empire. They built a new city on the shores of the Euphrates, near the ruins of Babylon and called it Bagdad, and organising the Arab horsemen into regiments of cavalry, they set forth to bring the happiness of their Moslem faith to all unbelievers. In the year 700 A.D. a Mohammedan general by the name of Tarik crossed the old Gates of Hercules and reached the high rock on the European side which he called the Gibel-al-tarik, the Hill of Tarik or Gibraltar.

Eleven years later in the battle of Xeres de la Frontera, he defeated the king of the Visigoths and then the Moslem army moved northward and following the route of Hannibal, they crossed the passes of the Pyrenees. They defeated the Duke of Aquitania, who tried to halt them near Bordeaux, and marched upon Paris. But in the year 732 (one hundred years after the death of the prophet,) they were beaten in a battle between Tours and Poitiers. On that day, Charles Martel (Charles the Hammer), the Frankish chieftain, saved Europe from a Mohammedan conquest. He drove the Moslems out of France, but they maintained themselves in Spain where Abd-ar-Rahman founded the Caliphate of Cordova, which became the greatest centre of science and art of mediæval Europe.

This Moorish kingdom, so-called because the people came from Mauretania in Morocco, lasted seven centuries. It was only after the capture of Granada, the last Moslem stronghold,

THE STRUGGLE BETWEEN THE CROSS AND THE CRESCENT

in the year 1492, that Columbus received the royal grant which allowed him to go upon a voyage of discovery. The Mohammedans soon regained their strength in the new conquests which they made in Asia and Africa and to-day there are as many followers of Mohammed as there are of Christ.

CHARLEMAGNE

HOW CHARLEMAGNE, THE KING OF THE FRANKS, CAME TO BEAR THE TITLE OF EMPEROR AND TRIED TO REVIVE THE OLD IDEAL OF WORLD-EMPIRE

THE battle of Poitiers had saved Europe from the Mohammedans. But the enemy within—the hopeless disorder which had followed the disappearance of the Roman police officer—that enemy remained. It is true that the new converts of the Christian faith in Northern Europe felt a deep respect for the mighty Bishop of Rome. But that poor bishop did not feel any too safe when he looked toward the distant mountains. Heaven knew what fresh hordes of barbarians were ready to cross the Alps and begin a new attack on Rome. It was necessary—very necessary—for the spiritual head of the world to find an ally with a strong sword and a powerful fist who was willing to defend His Holiness in case of danger.

And so the Popes, who were not only very holy but also very practical, cast about for a friend, and presently they made overtures to the most promising of the Germanic tribes who had occupied north-western Europe after the fall of Rome. They were called the Franks. One of their earliest kings, called Merovech, had helped the Romans in the battle of the Catalaunian fields in the year 451 when they defeated the Huns. His descendants, the Merovingians, had continued to take little bits of imperial territory until the year 486 when king Clovis (the old French word for "Louis") felt himself strong enough to beat the Romans in the open. But his descendants were weak men who left the affairs of state to their Prime minister, the "Major Domus" or Master of the Palace.

Pepin the Short, the son of the famous Charles Martel, who succeeded his father as Master of the Palace, hardly knew how to handle the situation. His royal master was a devout theologian, without any interest in politics. Pepin asked the Pope for advice. The Pope who was a practical person answered that the "power in the state belonged to him who was actually possessed of it." Pepin took the hint. He persuaded Childeric, the last of the Merovingians to become a monk and then made himself king with the approval of the other Germanic chieftains. But this did not satisfy the shrewd Pepin. He wanted to be something more than a barbarian chieftain. He staged an elaborate ceremony at which Boniface, the great missionary of the European northwest, anointed him and made him a "King by the grace of God." It was easy to slip those words, "Dei gratia," into the coronation service. It took almost fifteen hundred years to get them out again.

Pepin was sincerely grateful for this kindness on the part of the church. He made two expeditions to Italy to defend the Pope against his enemies. He took Ravenna and several other cities away from the Longobards and presented them to His Holiness, who incorporated these new domains into the so-called Papal State, which remained an independent country until half a century ago.

After Pepin's death, the relations between Rome and Aix-la-Chapelle or Nymwegen or Ingelheim, (the Frankish Kings did not have one official residence, but travelled from place to place with all their ministers and court officers,) became more and more cordial. Finally the Pope and the King took a step which was to influence the history of Europe in a most profound way.

Charles, commonly known as Carolus Magnus or Char-

lemagne, succeeded Pepin in the year 768. He had conquered
the land of the Saxons in eastern Germany and had
built towns and monasteries all over the greater part of northern Europe. At the request of certain enemies of Abd-ar-
Rahman, he had invaded Spain to fight the Moors. But in
the Pyrenees he had been attacked by the wild Basques and
had been forced to retire. It was upon this occasion that Roland, the great Margrave of Brittany, showed what a Frankish
chieftain of those early days meant when he promised to be
faithful to his King, and gave his life and that of his trusted
followers to safeguard the retreat of the royal army.

During the last ten years of the eighth century, however.
Charles was obliged to devote himself exclusively to affairs of
the South. The Pope, Leo III, had been attacked by a band
of Roman rowdies and had been left for dead in the street.
Some kind people had bandaged his wounds and had helped
him to escape to the camp of Charles, where he asked for
help. An army of Franks soon restored quiet and carried Leo
back to the Lateran Palace which ever since the days of Constantine, had been the home of the Pope. That was in December of the year 799. On Christmas day of the next year,
Charlemagne, who was staying in Rome, attended the service
in the ancient church of St. Peter. When he arose from prayer,
the Pope placed a crown upon his head, called him Emperor of
the Romans and hailed him once more with the title of "Augustus" which had not been heard for hundreds of years.

Once more Northern Europe was part of a Roman Empire.
but the dignity was held by a German chieftain who could
read just a little and never learned to write. But he could
fight and for a short while there was order and even the rival
emperor in Constantinople sent a letter of approval to his
"dear Brother."

Unfortunately this splendid old man died in the year 814.
His sons and his grandsons at once began to fight for the
largest share of the imperial inheritance. Twice the Carolingian lands were divided, by the treaties of Verdun in the
year 843 and by the treaty of Mersen-on-the-Meuse in the

THE HOLY ROMAN EMPIRE OF GERMAN NATIONALITY

year 870. The latter treaty divided the entire Frankish Kingdom into two parts. Charles the Bold received the western
half. It contained the old Roman province called Gaul where
the language of the people had become thoroughly romanized.
The Franks soon learned to speak this language and this
accounts for the strange fact that a purely Germanic land
like France should speak a Latin tongue.

The other grandson got the eastern part, the land which
the Romans had called Germania. Those inhospitable regions had never been part of the old Empire. Augustus had
tried to conquer this "far east," but his legions had been annihilated in the Teutoburg Wood in the year 9 and the people had
never been influenced by the higher Roman civilisation. They
spoke the popular Germanic tongue. The Teuton word for
"people" was "thiot." The Christian missionaries therefore
called the German language the "lingua theotisca" or the
"lingua teutisca," the "popular dialect" and this word "teutisca" was changed into "Deutsch" which accounts for the name
"Deutschland."

As for the famous Imperial Crown, it very soon slipped
off the heads of the Carolingian successors and rolled back onto
the Italian plain, where it became a sort of plaything of a
number of little potentates who stole the crown from each other
amidst much bloodshed and wore it (with or without the permission of the Pope) until it was the turn of some more ambitious neighbour. The Pope, once more sorely beset by his
enemies, sent north for help. He did not appeal to the ruler
of the west-Frankish kingdom, this time. His messengers
crossed the Alps and addressed themselves to Otto, a Saxon
Prince who was recognised as the greatest chieftain of the
different Germanic tribes.

Otto, who shared his people's affection for the blue skies
and the gay and beautiful people of the Italian peninsula,
hastened to the rescue. In return for his services, the Pope,
Leo VIII, made Otto "Emperor," and the eastern half of
Charles' old kingdom was henceforth known as the "Holy
Roman Empire of the German Nation."

THE MOUNTAIN PASS

This strange political creation managed to live to the ripe old age of eight hundred and thirty-nine years. In the year 1801, (during the presidency of Thomas Jefferson,) it was most unceremoniously relegated to the historical scrapheap. The brutal fellow who destroyed the old Germanic Empire was the son of a Corsican notary-public who had made a brilliant career in the service of the French Republic. He was ruler of Europe by the grace of his famous Guard Regiments, but he desired to be something more. He sent to Rome for the Pope and the Pope came and stood by while General Napoleon placed the imperial crown upon his own head and proclaimed himself heir to the tradition of Charlemagne. For history is like life. The more things change, the more they remain the same.

THE NORSEMEN

WHY THE PEOPLE OF THE TENTH CENTURY PRAYED THE LORD TO PROTECT THEM FROM THE FURY OF THE NORSEMEN

IN the third and fourth centuries, the Germanic tribes of central Europe had broken through the defences of the Empire that they might plunder Rome and live on the fat of the land. In the eighth century it became the turn of the Germans to be the "plundered-ones." They did not like this at all, even if their enemies were their first cousins, the Norsemen, who lived in Denmark and Sweden and Norway.

What forced these hardy sailors to turn pirate we do not know, but once they had discovered the advantages and pleasures of a buccaneering career there was no one who could stop them. They would suddenly descend upon a peaceful Frankish or Frisian village, situated on the mouth of a river. They would kill all the men and steal all the women. Then they would sail away in their fast-sailing ships and when the soldiers of the king or emperor arrived upon the scene, the robbers were gone and nothing remained but a few smouldering ruins.

During the days of disorder which followed the death of Charlemagne, the Northmen developed great activity. Their fleets made raids upon every country and their sailors established small independent kingdoms along the coast of Holland and France and England and Germany, and they even found

THE NORSEMEN ARE COMING

their way into Italy.   The Northmen were very intelligent.
They soon learned to speak the language of their subjects and
gave up the uncivilised ways of the early Vikings (or Sea-
Kings) who had been very picturesque but also very unwashed
and terribly cruel.

THE HOME OF THE NORSEMEN

Early in the tenth century a Viking by the name of Rollo
had repeatedly attacked the coast of France.   The king of
France, too weak to resist these northern robbers, tried to
bribe them into "being good."   He offered them the province
of Normandy, if they would promise to stop bothering the rest
of his domains.   Rollo accepted this bargain and became "Duke
of Normandy."

THE NORSEMEN GO TO RUSSIA

But the passion of conquest was strong in the blood of his children. Across the channel, only a few hours away from the European mainland, they could see the white cliffs and the green fields of England. Poor England had passed through difficult days. For two hundred years it had been a Roman colony. After the Romans left, it had been conquered by the

THE NORMANS LOOK ACROSS THE CHANNEL

THE WORLD OF THE NORSEMEN

Angles and the Saxons, two German tribes from Schleswig. Next the Danes had taken the greater part of the country and had established the kingdom of Cnut. The Danes had been driven away and now (it was early in the eleventh century) another Saxon king, Edward the Confessor, was on the throne. But Edward was not expected to live long and he had no children. The circumstances favoured the ambitious dukes of Normandy.

In 1066 Edward died. Immediately William of Normandy crossed the channel, defeated and killed Harold of Wessex (who had taken the crown) at the battle of Hastings, and proclaimed himself king of England.

In another chapter I have told you how in the year 800 a German chieftain had become a Roman Emperor. Now in the year 1066 the grandson of a Norse pirate was recognised as King of England.

Why should we ever read fairy stories, when the truth of history is so much more interesting and entertaining?

FEUDALISM

HOW CENTRAL EUROPE, ATTACKED FROM
THREE SIDES, BECAME AN ARMED CAMP
AND WHY EUROPE WOULD HAVE PER-
ISHED WITHOUT THOSE PROFESSIONAL
SOLDIERS AND ADMINISTRATORS WHO
WERE PART OF THE FEUDAL SYSTEM

THE following, then, is the state of Europe in the year one
thousand, when most people were so unhappy that they welcomed the prophecy foretelling the approaching end of the
world and rushed to the monasteries, that the Day of Judgement might find them engaged upon devout duties.

At an unknown date, the Germanic tribes had left their old
home in Asia and had moved westward into Europe. By
sheer pressure of numbers they had forced their way into the
Roman Empire. They had destroyed the great western empire, but the eastern part, being off the main route of the
great migrations, had managed to survive and feebly continued
the traditions of Rome's ancient glory.

During the days of disorder which had followed, (the true
"dark ages" of history, the sixth and seventh centuries of our
era,) the German tribes had been persuaded to accept the
Christian religion and had recognised the Bishop of Rome
as the Pope or spiritual head of the world. In the ninth century, the organising genius of Charlemagne had revived the
Roman Empire and had united the greater part of western

155

Europe into a single state. During the tenth century this empire had gone to pieces. The western part had become a separate kingdom, France. The eastern half was known as the Holy Roman Empire of the German nation, and the rulers of this federation of states then pretended that they were the direct heirs of Cæsar and Augustus.

Unfortunately the power of the kings of France did not stretch beyond the moat of their royal residence, while the Holy Roman Emperor was openly defied by his powerful subjects whenever it suited their fancy or their profit.

To increase the misery of the masses of the people, the triangle of western Europe (look at page 128, please) was for ever exposed to attacks from three sides. On the south lived the ever dangerous Mohammedans. The western coast was ravaged by the Northmen. The eastern frontier (defenceless except for the short stretch of the Carpathian mountains) was at the mercy of hordes of Huns, Hungarians, Slavs and Tartars.

The peace of Rome was a thing of the remote past, a dream of the "Good Old Days" that were gone for ever. It was a question of "fight or die," and quite naturally people preferred to fight. Forced by circumstances, Europe became an armed camp and there was a demand for strong leadership. Both King and Emperor were far away. The frontiersmen (and most of Europe in the year 1000 was "frontier") must help themselves. They willingly submitted to the representatives of the king who were sent to administer the outlying districts, *provided they could protect them against their enemies.*

Soon central Europe was dotted with small principalities, each one ruled by a duke or a count or a baron or a bishop, as the case might be, and organised as a fighting unit. These dukes and counts and barons had sworn to be faithful to the king who had given them their "feudum" (hence our word "feudal,") in return for their loyal services and a certain amount of taxes. But travel in those days was slow and the means of communication were exceedingly poor. The royal or imperial administrators therefore enjoyed great independence, and within the boundaries of their own province they assumed most of the rights which in truth belonged to the king.

But you would make a mistake if you supposed that the people of the eleventh century objected to this form of government. They supported Feudalism because it was a very practical and necessary institution. Their Lord and Master usually lived in a big stone house erected on the top of a steep rock or built between deep moats, but within sight of his subjects. In case of danger the subjects found shelter behind the walls of the baronial stronghold. That is why they tried to live as near the castle as possible and it accounts for the many European cities which began their career around a feudal fortress.

But the knight of the early middle ages was much more than a professional soldier. He was the civil servant of that day. He was the judge of his community and he was the chief of police. He caught the highwaymen and protected the wandering pedlars who were the merchants of the eleventh century. He looked after the dikes so that the countryside should not be flooded (just as the first noblemen had done in the valley of the Nile four thousand years before). He encouraged the Troubadours who wandered from place to place telling the stories of the ancient heroes who had fought in the great wars of the migrations. Besides, he protected the churches and the monasteries within his territory, and although he could neither read nor write, (it was considered unmanly to know such things,) he employed a number of priests who kept his accounts and who registered the marriages and the births and the deaths which occurred within the baronial or ducal domains.

In the fifteenth century the kings once more became strong enough to exercise those powers which belonged to them because they were "anointed of God." Then the feudal knights lost their former independence. Reduced to the rank of country squires, they no longer filled a need and soon they became a nuisance. But Europe would have perished without the "feudal system" of the dark ages. There were many bad knights as there are many bad people to-day. But generally speaking, the rough-fisted barons of the twelfth and thirteenth century were hard-working administrators who rendered a most useful service to the cause of progress. During that era the noble torch of learning and art which had illuminated the world of the Egyptians and the Greeks and the Romans was burning very low. Without the knights and their good friends, the monks, civilisation would have been extinguished entirely, and the human race would have been forced to begin once more where the cave-man had left off.

CHIVALRY

CHIVALRY

CHIVALRY

IT was quite natural that the professional fighting-men of the Middle Ages should try to establish some sort of organisation for their mutual benefit and protection. Out of this need for close organisation, Knighthood or Chivalry was born.

We know very little about the origins of Knighthood. But as the system developed, it gave the world something which it needed very badly—a definite rule of conduct which softened the barbarous customs of that day and made life more livable than it had been during the five hundred years of the Dark Ages. It was not an easy task to civilise the rough frontiersmen who had spent most of their time fighting Mohammedans and Huns and Norsemen. Often they were guilty of back-sliding, and having vowed all sorts of oaths about mercy and charity in the morning, they would murder all their prisoners before evening. But progress is ever the result of slow and ceaseless labour, and finally the most unscrupulous of knights was forced to obey the rules of his "class" or suffer the consequences.

These rules were different in the various parts of Europe, but they all made much of "service" and "loyalty to duty." The Middle Ages regarded service as something very noble and beautiful. It was no disgrace to be a servant, provided you were a good servant and did not slacken on the job. As for loyalty, at a time when life depended upon the faithful per-

159

formance of many unpleasant duties, it was the chief virtue of the fighting man.

A young knight therefore was asked to swear that he would be faithful as a servant to God and as a servant to his King. Furthermore, he promised to be generous to those whose need was greater than his own. He pledged his word that he would be humble in his personal behaviour and would never boast of his own accomplishments and that he would be a friend of all those who suffered, (with the exception of the Mohammedans, whom he was expected to kill on sight).

Around these vows, which were merely the Ten Commandments expressed in terms which the people of the Middle Ages could understand, there developed a complicated system of manners and outward behaviour. The knights tried to model their own lives after the example of those heroes of Arthur's Round Table and Charlemagne's court of whom the Troubadours had told them and of whom you may read in many delightful books which are enumerated at the end of this volume. They hoped that they might prove as brave as Lancelot and as faithful as Roland. They carried themselves with dignity and they spoke careful and gracious words that they might be known as True Knights, however humble the cut of their coat or the size of their purse.

In this way the order of Knighthood became a school of those good manners which are the oil of the social machinery. Chivalry came to mean courtesy and the feudal castle showed the rest of the world what clothes to wear, how to eat, how to ask a lady for a dance and the thousand and one little things of every-day behaviour which help to make life interesting and agreeable.

Like all human institutions, Knighthood was doomed to perish as soon as it had outlived its usefulness.

The crusades, about which one of the next chapters tells, were followed by a great revival of trade. Cities grew overnight. The townspeople became rich, hired good school teachers and soon were the equals of the knights. The invention of gun-powder deprived the heavily armed "Chevalier" of his former advantage and the use of mercenaries made it impossible to conduct a battle with the delicate niceties of a chess tournament. The knight became superfluous. Soon he became a ridiculous figure, with his devotion to ideals that had no longer any practical value. It was said that the noble Don Quixote de la Mancha had been the last of the true knights. After his death, his trusted sword and his armour were sold to pay his debts.

But somehow or other that sword seems to have fallen into the hands of a number of men. Washington carried it during the hopeless days of Valley Forge. It was the only defence of Gordon, when he had refused to desert the people who had been entrusted to his care, and stayed to meet his death in the besieged fortress of Khartoum.

And I am not quite sure but that it proved of invaluable strength in winning the Great War.

POPE vs. EMPEROR

THE STRANGE DOUBLE LOYALTY OF THE PEOPLE OF THE MIDDLE AGES AND HOW IT LED TO ENDLESS QUARRELS BETWEEN THE POPES AND THE HOLY ROMAN EMPERORS

IT is very difficult to understand the people of by-gone ages. Your own grandfather, whom you see every day, is a mysterious being who lives in a different world of ideas and clothes and manners. I am now telling you the story of some of your grandfathers who are twenty-five generations removed, and I do not expect you to catch the meaning of what I write without re-reading this chapter a number of times.

The average man of the Middle Ages lived a very simple and uneventful life. Even if he was a free citizen, able to come and go at will, he rarely left his own neighbourhood. There were no printed books and only a few manuscripts. Here and there, a small band of industrious monks taught reading and writing and some arithmetic. But science and history and geography lay buried beneath the ruins of Greece and Rome.

Whatever people knew about the past they had learned by listening to stories and legends. Such information, which goes from father to son, is often slightly incorrect in details, but it will preserve the main facts of history with astonishing accuracy. After more than two thousand years, the mothers of India still frighten their naughty children by telling them that

162

"Iskander will get them," and Iskander is none other than
Alexander the Great, who visited India in the year 330 before
the birth of Christ, but whose story has lived through all these
ages.

The people of the early Middle Ages never saw a text-
book of Roman history. They were ignorant of many things
which every school-boy to-day knows before he has entered
the third grade. But the Roman Empire, which is merely a
name to you, was to them something very much alive. They
felt it. They willingly recognised the Pope as their spiritual
leader because he lived in Rome and represented the idea of
the Roman super-power. And they were profoundly grateful when Charlemagne, and afterwards Otto the Great, revived the idea of a world-empire and created the Holy Roman
Empire, that the world might again be as it always had been.

But the fact that there were two different heirs to the
Roman tradition placed the faithful burghers of the Middle
Ages in a difficult position. The theory behind the mediæval
political system was both sound and simple. While the worldly
master (the emperor) looked after the physical well-being of
his subjects, the spiritual master (the Pope) guarded their
souls.

In practice, however, the system worked very badly. The
Emperor invariably tried to interfere with the affairs of the
church and the Pope retaliated and told the Emperor how
he should rule his domains. Then they told each other to mind
their own business in very unceremonious language and the
inevitable end was war.

Under those circumstances, what were the people to do?
A good Christian obeyed both the Pope and his King. But
the Pope and the Emperor were enemies. Which side should
a dutiful subject and an equally dutiful Christian take?

It was never easy to give the correct answer. When the
Emperor happened to be a man of energy and was sufficiently
well provided with money to organise an army, he was very
apt to cross the Alps and march on Rome, besiege the Pope

in his own palace if need be, and force His Holiness to obey the imperial instructions or suffer the consequences.

But more frequently the Pope was the stronger. Then the Emperor or the King together with all his subjects was excommunicated. This meant that all churches were closed, that no one could be baptised, that no dying man could be given absolution—in short, that half of the functions of mediæval government came to an end.

More than that, the people were absolved from their oath of loyalty to their sovereign and were urged to rebel against their master. But if they followed this advice of the distant Pope and were caught, they were hanged by their near-by Liege Lord and that too was very unpleasant.

Indeed, the poor fellows were in a difficult position and none fared worse than those who lived during the latter half of the eleventh century, when the Emperor Henry IV of Germany and Pope Gregory VII fought a two-round battle which decided nothing and upset the peace of Europe for almost fifty years.

In the middle of the eleventh century there had been a strong movement for reform in the church. The election of the Popes, thus far, had been a most irregular affair. It was to the advantage of the Holy Roman Emperors to have a well-disposed priest elected to the Holy See. They frequently came to Rome at the time of election and used their influence for the benefit of one of their friends.

In the year 1059 this had been changed. By a decree of Pope Nicholas II the principal priests and deacons of the churches in and around Rome were organised into the so-called College of Cardinals, and this gathering of prominent churchmen (the word "Cardinal" meant principal) was given the exclusive power of electing the future Popes.

In the year 1073 the College of Cardinals elected a priest by the name of Hildebrand, the son of very simple parents in Tuscany, as Pope, and he took the name of Gregory VII. His energy was unbounded. His belief in the supreme powers of his holy office was built upon a granite rock of conviction and courage. In the mind of Gregory, the Pope was not only the absolute head of the Christian church, but also the highest Court of Appeal in all worldly matters. The Pope who had elevated simple German princes to the dignity of Emperor could depose them at will. He could veto any law passed by duke or king or emperor, but whosoever should question a papal decree, let him beware, for the punishment would be swift and merciless.

Gregory sent ambassadors to all the European courts to inform the potentates of Europe of his new laws and asked them to take due notice of their contents. William the Conqueror promised to be good, but Henry IV, who since the age of six had been fighting with his subjects, had no intention of submitting to the Papal will. He called together a college of German bishops, accused Gregory of every crime under the sun and then had him deposed by the council of Worms.

The Pope answered with excommunication and a demand that the German princes rid themselves of their unworthy ruler. The German princes, only too happy to be rid of Henry, asked the Pope to come to Augsburg and help them elect a new Emperor.

HENRY IV AT CANOSSA

Gregory left Rome and travelled northward. Henry, who was no fool, appreciated the danger of his position. At all costs he must make peace with the Pope, and he must do it at once. In the midst of winter he crossed the Alps and hastened to Canossa where the Pope had stopped for a short rest. Three long days, from the 25th to the 28th of January of the year 1077, Henry, dressed as a penitent pilgrim (but with a warm sweater underneath his monkish garb), waited outside the gates of the castle of Canossa. Then he was allowed to enter and was pardoned for his sins. But the repentance did not last long. As soon as Henry had returned to Germany, he behaved exactly as before. Again he was excommunicated. For the second time a council of German bishops deposed Gregory, but this time, when Henry crossed the Alps he was at the head of a large army, besieged Rome and forced Gregory to retire to Salerno, where he died in exile. This first violent outbreak decided nothing. As soon as Henry was back in Germany, the struggle between Pope and Emperor was continued.

The Hohenstaufen family which got hold of the Imperial German Throne shortly afterwards, were even more independent than their predecessors. Gregory had claimed that the Popes were superior to all kings because they (the Popes) at the Day of Judgement would be responsible for the behaviour of all the sheep of their flock, and in the eyes of God, a king was one of that faithful herd.

Frederick of Hohenstaufen, commonly known as Barbarossa or Red Beard, set up the counter-claim that the Empire had been bestowed upon his predecessor "by God himself" and as the Empire included Italy and Rome, he began a campaign which was to add these "lost provinces" to the northern country. Barbarossa was accidentally drowned in Asia Minor during the second Crusade, but his son Frederick II, a brilliant young man who in his youth had been exposed to the civilisation of the Mohammedans of Sicily, continued the war. The Popes accused him of heresy. It is true that Frederick seems to have felt a deep and serious contempt for the rough Christian world of the North, for the boorish German Knights and the intriguing Italian priests. But he held his tongue, went on a Crusade and took Jerusalem from the infidel and was duly crowned as King of the Holy City. Even this act did not placate the Popes. They deposed Frederick and gave his Italian possessions to Charles of Anjou, the brother of that King Louis of France who became famous as Saint Louis.

THE CASTLE

This led to more warfare. Conrad V, the son of Conrad IV, and the last of the Hohenstaufens, tried to regain the kingdom, and was defeated and decapitated at Naples. But twenty years later, the French who had made themselves thoroughly unpopular in Sicily were all murdered during the so-called Sicilian Vespers, and so it went.

The quarrel between the Popes and the Emperors was never settled, but after a while the two enemies learned to leave each other alone.

In the year 1273, Rudolph of Hapsburg was elected Emperor. He did not take the trouble to go to Rome to be crowned. The Popes did not object and in turn they kept away from Germany. This meant peace but two entire centuries which might have been used for the purpose of internal organisation had been wasted in useless warfare.

It is an ill wind however that bloweth no good to some one. The little cities of Italy, by a process of careful balancing, had managed to increase their power and their independence at the expense of both Emperors and Popes. When the rush for the Holy Land began, they were able to handle the transportation problem of the thousands of eager pilgrims who were clamoring for passage, and at the end of the Crusades they had built themselves such strong defences of brick and of gold that they could defy Pope and Emperor with equal indifference.

Church and State fought each other and a third party—the mediæval city—ran away with the spoils.

THE CRUSADES

BUT ALL THESE DIFFERENT QUARRELS WERE FORGOTTEN WHEN THE TURKS TOOK THE HOLY LAND, DESECRATED THE HOLY PLACES AND INTERFERED SERIOUSLY WITH THE TRADE FROM EAST TO WEST. EUROPE WENT CRUSADING

DURING three centuries there had been peace between Christians and Moslems except in Spain and in the eastern Roman Empire, the two states defending the gateways of Europe. The Mohammedans having conquered Syria in the seventh century were in possession of the Holy Land. But they regarded Jesus as a great prophet (though not quite as great as Mohammed), and they did not interfere with the pilgrims who wished to pray in the church which Saint Helena, the mother of the Emperor Constantine, had built on the spot of the Holy Grave. But early in the eleventh century, a Tartar tribe from the wilds of Asia, called the Seljuks or Turks, became masters of the Mohammedan state in western Asia and then the period of tolerance came to an end. The Turks took all of Asia Minor away from the eastern Roman Emperors and they made an end to the trade between east and west.

Alexis, the Emperor, who rarely saw anything of his Christian neighbours of the west, appealed for help and pointed to the danger which threatened Europe should the Turks take Constantinople.

The Italian cities which had established colonies along the coast of Asia Minor and Palestine, in fear for their posses- sions, reported terrible stories of Turkish atrocities and Chris tian suffering. All Europe got excited.

Pope Urban II, a Frenchman from Reims, who had been educated at the same famous cloister of Cluny which had trained Gregory VII, thought that the time had come for action. The general state of Europe was far from satisfactory. The primitive agricultural methods of that day (unchanged since Roman times) caused a constant scarcity of food. There was unemployment and hunger and these are apt to lead to discontent and riots. Western Asia in older days had fed mil- lions. It was an excellent field for the purpose of immigration.

Therefore at the council of Clermont in France in the year 1095 the Pope arose, described the terrible horrors which the infidels had inflicted upon the Holy Land, gave a glowing de- scription of this country which ever since the days of Moses had been overflowing with milk and honey, and exhorted the knights of France and the people of Europe in general to leave wife and child and deliver Palestine from the Turks.

A wave of religious hysteria swept across the continent. All reason stopped. Men would drop their hammer and saw, walk out of their shop and take the nearest road to the east to go and kill Turks. Children would leave their homes to "go to Palestine" and bring the terrible Turks to their knees by the mere appeal of their youthful zeal and Christian piety. Fully ninety percent of those enthusiasts never got within sight of the Holy Land. They had no money. They were forced to beg or steal to keep alive. They became a danger to the safety of the highroads and they were killed by the angry country people.

The first Crusade, a wild mob of honest Christians, default- ing bankrupts, penniless noblemen and fugitives from justice, following the lead of half-crazy Peter the Hermit and Walter- without-a-Cent, began their campaign against the Infidels by murdering all the Jews whom they met by the way. They got as far as Hungary and then they were all killed.

This experience taught the Church a lesson. Enthusiasm alone would not set the Holy Land free. Organisation was as necessary as good-will and courage. A year was spent in training and equipping an army of 200,000 men. They were placed under command of Godfrey of Bouillon, Robert, duke of Normandy, Robert, count of Flanders, and a number of other noblemen, all experienced in the art of war.

In the year 1096 this second crusade started upon its long voyage. At Constantinople the knights did homage to the

THE FIRST CRUSADE

Emperor. (For as I have told you, traditions die hard, and a Roman Emperor, however poor and powerless, was still held in great respect). Then they crossed into Asia, killed all the Moslems who fell into their hands, stormed Jerusalem, massacred the Mohammedan population, and marched to the Holy Sepulchre to give praise and thanks amidst tears of piety and gratitude. But soon the Turks were strengthened by the arrival of fresh troops. Then they retook Jerusalem and in turn killed the faithful followers of the Cross.

THE WORLD OF THE CRUSADERS

During the next two centuries, seven other crusades took place. Gradually the Crusaders learned the technique of the trip. The land voyage was too tedious and too dangerous. They preferred to cross the Alps and go to Genoa or Venice where they took ship for the east. The Genoese and the Venetians made this trans-Mediterranean passenger service a very profitable business. They charged exorbitant rates, and when the Crusaders (most of whom had very little money) could not pay the price, these Italian "profiteers" kindly allowed them to "work their way across." In return for a fare from Venice to Acre, the Crusader undertook to do a stated amount of fighting for the owners of his vessel. In this way Venice greatly increased her territory along the coast of the Adriatic and in Greece, where Athens became a Venetian colony, and in the islands of Cyprus and Crete and Rhodes.

All this, however, helped little in settling the question of the Holy Land. After the first enthusiasm had worn off, a short crusading trip became part of the liberal education of every well-bred young man, and there never was any lack of candidates for service in Palestine. But the old zeal was gone. The Crusaders, who had begun their warfare with deep hatred for the Mohammedans and great love for the Christian people of the eastern Roman Empire and Armenia, suffered a complete change of heart.

THE CRUSADERS TAKE JERUSALEM

They came to despise the Greeks of Byzantium, who cheated them and frequently betrayed the cause of the Cross, and the Armenians and all the other Levantine races, and they began to appreciate the virtues of their enemies who proved to be generous and fair opponents.

Of course, it would never do to say this openly. But when the Crusader returned home, he was likely to imitate the manners which he had learned from his heathenish foe, compared to whom the average western knight was still a good deal of a country bumpkin. He also brought with him several new food-stuffs, such as peaches and spinach which he planted in his garden and grew for his own benefit. He gave up the barbarous custom of wearing a load of heavy armour and appeared in the flowing robes of silk or cotton which were the traditional habit of the followers of the Prophet and were originally worn by the Turks. Indeed the Crusades, which had begun as a punitive expedition against the Heathen, became a course of general instruction in civilisation for millions of young Europeans.

From a military and political point of view the Crusades were a failure. Jerusalem and a number of cities were taken and lost. A dozen little kingdoms were established in Syria and Palestine and Asia Minor, but they were re-conquered by the Turks and after the year 1244 (when Jerusalem became definitely Turkish) the status of the Holy Land was the same as it had been before 1095.

THE CRUSADER'S GRAVE

But Europe had undergone a great change. The people of the west had been allowed a glimpse of the light and the sunshine and the beauty of the east. Their dreary castles no longer satisfied them. They wanted a broader life. Neither Church nor State could give this to them.

They found it in the cities.

THE MEDIÆVAL CITY

WHY THE PEOPLE OF THE MIDDLE AGES SAID THAT "CITY AIR IS FREE AIR"

THE early part of the Middle Ages had been an era of pioneering and of settlement. A new people, who thus far had lived outside the wild range of forest, mountains and marshes which protected the north-eastern frontier of the Roman Empire, had forced its way into the plains of western Europe and had taken possession of most of the land. They were restless, as all pioneers have been since the beginning of time. They liked to be "on the go." They cut down the forests and they cut each other's throats with equal energy. Few of them wanted to live in cities. They insisted upon being "free," they loved to feel the fresh air of the hillsides fill their lungs while they drove their herds across the wind-swept pastures. When they no longer liked their old homes, they pulled up stakes and went away in search of fresh adventures.

The weaker ones died. The hardy fighters and the cou rageous women who had followed their men into the wilderness survived. In this way they developed a strong race of men. They cared little for the graces of life. They were too busy to play the fiddle or write pieces of poetry. They had little love for discussions. The priest, "the learned man" of the village (and before the middle of the thirteenth century, a layman who could read and write was regarded as a "sissy") was supposed to settle all questions which had no direct practical value. Meanwhile the German chieftain, the Frankish Baron, the Northman Duke (or whatever their names and titles) occupied their share of the territory which once had been part of the great Roman Empire and among the ruins of past glory, they built a world of their own which pleased them mightily and which they considered quite perfect.

They managed the affairs of their castle and the surrounding country to the best of their ability. They were as faithful to the commandments of the Church as any weak mortal could hope to be. They were sufficiently loyal to their king or emperor to keep on good terms with those distant but always dangerous potentates. In short, they tried to do right and to be fair to their neighbours without being exactly unfair to their own interests·

It was not an ideal world in which they found themselves. The greater part of the people were serfs or "villeins," farmhands who were as much a part of the soil upon which they lived as the cows and sheep whose stables they shared. Their fate was not particularly happy nor was it particularly unhappy. But what was one to do? The good Lord who ruled the world of the Middle Ages had undoubtedly ordered everything for the best. If He, in his wisdom, had decided that there must be both knights and serfs, it was not the duty of these faithful sons of the church to question the arrangement. The serfs therefore did not complain but when they were too hard driven, they would die off like cattle which are not fed and stabled in the right way, and then something would be hastily done to better their condition. But if the progress of the world had been left to the serf and his feudal master, we would still be living after the fashion of the twelfth century, saying "abracadabra" when we tried to stop a tooth-ache, and feeling a deep contempt and hatred for the dentist who offered to help us with his "science," which most likely was of Mohammedan or heathenish origin and therefore both wicked and useless.

When you grow up you will discover that many people do not believe in "progress" and they will prove to you by the terrible deeds of some of our own contemporaries that "the world does not change." But I hope that you will not pay much attention to such talk. You see, it took our ancestors almost a million years to learn how to walk on their hind legs. Other centuries had to go by before their animal-like grunts developed into an understandable language. Writing—the art of preserving our ideas for the benefit of future generations, without which no progress is possible—was invented only four thousand years ago. The idea of turning the forces of nature into the obedient servants of man was quite new in the days of your own grandfather. It seems to me, therefore, that we are making progress at an unheard-of rate of speed. Perhaps we have paid a little too much attention to the mere physical comforts of life. That will change in due course of time and we shall then attack the problems which are not related to health and to wages and plumbing and machinery in general.

But please do not be too sentimental about the "good old days." Many people who only see the beautiful churches and the great works of art which the Middle Ages have left behind grow quite eloquent when they compare our own ugly civilisation with its hurry and its noise and the evil smells of back-firing motor trucks with the cities of a thousand years ago. But these mediæval churches were invariably surrounded by miserable hovels compared to which a modern tenement house stands forth as a luxurious palace. It is true that the noble Lancelot and the equally noble Parsifal, the pure young hero who went in search of the Holy Grail, were not bothered by the odor of gasoline. But there were other smells of the barn-yard variety—odors of decaying refuse which had been thrown into the street—of pig-sties surrounding the Bishop's palace— of unwashed people who had inherited their coats and hats from their grandfathers and who had never learned the bless-ing of soap. I do not want to paint too unpleasant a picture. But when you read in the ancient chronicles that the King of France, looking out of the windows of his palace, fainted at the stench caused by the pigs rooting in the streets of Paris, when an ancient manuscript recounts a few details of an epi-demic of the plague or of small-pox, then you begin to understand that "progress" is something more than a catchword used by modern advertising men.

No, the progress of the last six hundred years would not have been possible without the existence of cities. I shall, therefore, have to make this chapter a little longer than many of the others. It is too important to be reduced to three or four pages, devoted to mere political events.

The ancient world of Egypt and Babylonia and Assyria had been a world of cities. Greece had been a country of City-States. The history of Phœnicia was the history of two cities called Sidon and Tyre. The Roman Empire was the "hinterland" of a single town. Writing, art, science, astronomy, architecture, literature, the theatre—the list is endless—have all been products of the city.

For almost four thousand years the wooden bee-hive which we call a town had been the workshop of the world. Then came the great migrations. The Roman Empire was destroyed. The cities were burned down and Europe once more became a land of pastures and little agricultural villages. During the Dark Ages the fields of civilisation had lain fallow.

The Crusades had prepared the soil for a new crop. It was time for the harvest, but the fruit was plucked by the burghers of the free cities.

I have told you the story of the castles and the monasteries, with their heavy stone enclosures—the homes of the knights and the monks, who guarded men's bodies and their souls. You have seen how a few artisans (butchers and bakers and an occasional candle stick maker) came to live near the castle to tend to the wants of their masters and to find protection in case of danger. Sometimes the feudal lord allowed these people to surround their houses with a stockade. But they were dependent for their living upon the good-will of the mighty Seigneur of the castle. When he went about they knelt before him and kissed his hand.

Then came the Crusades and many things changed. The migrations had driven people from the north-east to the west. The Crusades made millions of people travel from the west to the highly civilised regions of the south-east. They discovered that the world was not bounded by the four walls of their little settlement. They came to appreciate better clothes, more comfortable houses, new dishes, products of the mysterious Orient. After their return to their old homes, they insisted that they be supplied with those articles. The peddler with his pack upon his back—the only merchant of the Dark Ages—added these goods to his old merchandise, bought a cart, hired a few ex-crusaders to protect him against the crime wave which followed this great international war, and went forth to do business upon a more modern and larger scale. His career was not an easy one. Every time he entered the domains of another Lord he had to pay tolls and taxes. But the business was profitable all the same and the peddler continued to make his rounds.

Soon certain energetic merchants discovered that the goods which they had always imported from afar could be made at home. They turned part of their homes into a work shop. They ceased to be merchants and became manufacturers. They sold their products not only to the lord of the castle and to the abbot in his monastery, but they exported them to nearby towns. The lord and the abbot paid them with products of their farms, eggs and wines, and with honey, which in those early days was used as sugar. But the citizens of distant towns were obliged to pay in cash and the manufacturer and the merchant began to own little pieces of gold, which entirely changed their position in the society of the early Middle Ages.

It is difficult for you to imagine a world without money. In a modern city one cannot possibly live without money. All day long you carry a pocket full of small discs of metal to "pay your way." You need a nickel for the street-car, a dollar for a dinner, three cents for an evening paper. But many people of the early Middle Ages never saw a piece of coined money from the time they were born to the day of their death. The gold and silver of Greece and Rome lay buried beneath the ruins of their cities. The world of the migrations, which had succeeded the Empire, was an agricultural world. Every farmer raised enough grain and enough sheep and enough cows for his own use.

The mediæval knight was a country squire and was rarely forced to pay for materials in money. His estates produced

THE CASTLE AND THE CITY

everything that he and his family ate and drank and wore on their backs. The bricks for his house were made along the banks of the nearest river. Wood for the rafters of the hall was cut from the baronial forest. The few articles that had to come from abroad were paid for in goods—in honey—in eggs —in fagots.

But the Crusades upset the routine of the old agricultural
life in a very drastic fashion. Suppose that the Duke of Hil-
desheim was going to the Holy Land. He must travel thousands of miles and he must pay his passage and his hotel-bills.
At home he could pay with products of his farm. But he
could not well take a hundred dozen eggs and a cart-load of
hams with him to satisfy the greed of the shipping agent of
Venice or the inn-keeper of the Brenner Pass. These gentlemen insisted upon cash. His Lordship therefore was obliged
to take a small quantity of gold with him upon his voyage.
Where could he find this gold? He could borrow it from the
Lombards, the descendants of the old Longobards, who had
turned professional money-lenders, who seated behind their
exchange-table (commonly known as "banco" or bank) were
glad to let his Grace have a few hundred gold pieces in exchange for a mortgage upon his estates, that they might be repaid in case His Lordship should die at the hands of the Turks.

That was dangerous business for the borrower. In the end,
the Lombards invariably owned the estates and the Knight
became a bankrupt, who hired himself out as a fighting man to
a more powerful and more careful neighbour.

His Grace could also go to that part of the town where the
Jews were forced to live. There he could borrow money at a
rate of fifty or sixty percent. interest. That, too, was bad
business. But was there a way out? Some of the people of the
little city which surrounded the castle were said to have money.
They had known the young lord all his life. His father and
their fathers had been good friends. They would not be unreasonable in their demands. Very well. His Lordship's
clerk, a monk who could write and keep accounts, sent a note
to the best known merchants and asked for a small loan. The
townspeople met in the work-room of the jeweller who made
chalices for the nearby churches and discussed this demand.
They could not well refuse. It would serve no purpose to
ask for "interest." In the first place, it was against the religious principles of most people to take interest and in the

second place, it would never be paid except in agricultural products and of these the people had enough and to spare.

"But," suggested the tailor who spent his days quietly sitting upon his table and who was somewhat of a philosopher, "suppose that we ask some favour in return for our money. We are all fond of fishing. But his Lordship won't let us fish in his brook. Suppose that we let him have a hundred ducats and that he give us in return a written guarantee allowing us to fish all we want in all of his rivers. Then he gets the hundred which he needs, but we get the fish and it will be good business all around."

The day his Lordship accepted this proposition (it seemed such an easy way of getting a hundred gold pieces) he signed the death-warrant of his own power. His clerk drew up the agreement. His Lordship made his mark (for he could not sign his name) and departed for the East. Two years later he came back, dead broke. The townspeople were fishing in the castle pond. The sight of this silent row of anglers annoyed his Lordship. He told his equerry to go and chase the crowd away. They went, but that night a delegation of merchants visited the castle. They were very polite. They congratulated his Lordship upon his safe return. They were sorry his Lordship had been annoyed by the fishermen, but as his Lordship might perhaps remember he had given them permission to do so himself, and the tailor produced the Charter which had been kept in the safe of the jeweller ever since the master had gone to the Holy Land.

His Lordship was much annoyed. But once more he was in dire need of some money. In Italy he had signed his name to certain documents which were now in the possession of Salvestro dei Medici, the well-known banker. These documents were "promissory notes" and they were due two months from date. Their total amount came to three hundred and forty pounds, Flemish gold. Under these circumstances, the noble knight could not well show the rage which filled his heart and his proud soul. Instead, he suggested another little loan. The merchants retired to discuss the matter.

After three days they came back and said "yes." They were only too happy to be able to help their master in his difficulties, but in return for the 345 golden pounds would he give them another written promise (another charter) that they, the townspeople, might establish a council of their own to be elected by all the merchants and free citizens of the city, said council to manage civic affairs without interference from the side of the castle?

His Lordship was confoundedly angry. But again, he needed the money. He said yes, and signed the charter. Next week, he repented. He called his soldiers and went to the house of the jeweller and asked for the documents which his crafty subjects had cajoled out of him under the pressure of circumstances. He took them away and burned them. The townspeople stood by and said nothing. But when next his Lordship needed money to pay for the dowry of his daughter, he was unable to get a single penny. After that little affair at the jeweller's his credit was not considered good.

THE BELFRY

He was forced to eat humble-pie and offer to make certain reparations. Before his Lordship got the first installment of the stipulated sum, the townspeople were once more in possession of all their old charters and a brand new one which permitted them to build a "city-hall" and a strong tower where all the charters might be kept protected against fire and theft, which really meant protected against future violence on the part of the Lord and his armed followers.

This, in a very general way, is what happened during the centuries which followed the Crusades. It was a slow process,

THE MEDIÆVAL TOWN

this gradual shifting of power from the castle to the city. There was some fighting. A few tailors and jewellers were killed and a few castles went up in smoke. But such occurrences were not common. Almost imperceptibly the towns grew richer and the feudal lords grew poorer. To maintain themselves they were for ever forced to exchange charters of civic liberty in return for ready cash. The cities grew. They offered an asylum to run away serfs who gained their liberty after they had lived a number of years behind the city walls. They came to be the home of the more energetic elements of the surrounding country districts. They were proud of their new importance and expressed their power in the churches and public buildings which they erected around the old market place, where centuries before the barter of eggs and sheep and honey and salt had taken place. They wanted their children to have a better chance in life than they had enjoyed themselves. They hired

GUNPOWDER

monks to come to their city and be school teachers. When they heard of a man who could paint pictures upon boards of wood, they offered him a pension if he would come and cover the walls of their chapels and their town hall with scenes from the Holy Scriptures.

Meanwhile his Lordship, in the dreary and drafty halls of his castle, saw all this up-start splendour and regretted the day when first he had signed away a single one of his sovereign rights and prerogatives. But he was helpless. The towns-people with their well-filled strong-boxes snapped their fingers at him. They were free men, fully prepared to hold what they had gained by the sweat of their brow and after a struggle which had lasted for more than ten generations.

MEDIÆVAL SELF-GOVERNMENT

HOW THE PEOPLE OF THE CITIES ASSERTED THEIR RIGHT TO BE HEARD IN THE ROYAL COUNCILS OF THEIR COUNTRY

As long as people were "nomads," wandering tribes of shepherds, all men had been equal and had been responsible for the welfare and safety of the entire community.

But after they had settled down and some had become rich and others had grown poor, the government was apt to fall into the hands of those who were not obliged to work for their living and who could devote themselves to politics.

I have told you how this had happened in Egypt and in Mesopotamia and in Greece and in Rome. It occurred among the Germanic population of western Europe as soon as order had been restored. The western European world was ruled in the first place by an emperor who was elected by the seven or eight most important kings of the vast Roman Empire of the German nation and who enjoyed a great deal of imaginary and very little actual power. It was ruled by a number of kings who sat upon shaky thrones. The every-day government was in the hands of thousands of feudal princelets. Their subjects were peasants or serfs. There were few cities. There was hardly any middle class. But during the thirteenth century (after an absence of almost a thousand years) the middle class—the merchant class—once more appeared upon the his-

ICELAND

THE ICELANDERS ESTABLISHED A FORM OF SELF GOVERNMENT IN THE NINTH CENTURY.

HOLLAND

BY THE ACT OF ABJURATION OF 1581 THE ESTATES GENERAL DECLARE THAT KING PHILIP HAD FORFEITED HIS SOVEREIGNTY OVER THEM.

SWITZERLAND

BETWEEN 1290 AND 1309 THREE SWISS CANTONS GAINED THEIR INDEPENDENCE FROM THE HABSBURGS.

THE ATLANTIC OCEAN

ENGLAND

FRANCE

THE UNITED STATES

ON JULY 4. OF THE YEAR 1776 THE THIRTEEN COLONIES OF THE NORTH AMERICAN CONTINENT DECLARED THEMSELVES INDEPENDENT FROM ENGLAND.

ON JANUARY 30. 1649 THE ENGLISH PEOPLE DECAPITATED KING CHARLES I

DECEMBER 22. 1688 KING JAMES II AFTER A QUARREL WITH HIS SUBJECTS FLEES TO FRANCE

ON JANUARY 21. 1793 THE FRENCH PEOPLE DECAPITATED KING LOUIS XVI

THE DEVELOPMENT OF THE IDEA OF POPULAR SOVEREIGNTY

THE SPREADING OF THE IDEA OF POPULAR SOVEREIGNTY

torical stage and its rise in power, as we saw in the last chapter, had meant a decrease in the influence of the castle folk.

Thus far, the king, in ruling his domains, had only paid attention to the wishes of his noblemen and his bishops. But the new world of trade and commerce which grew out of the Crusades forced him to recognise the middle class or suffer from an ever-increasing emptiness of his exchequer. Their majesties (if they had followed their hidden wishes) would have as lief consulted their cows and their pigs as the good burghers of their cities. But they could not help themselves. They swallowed the bitter pill because it was gilded, but not without a struggle.

In England, during the absence of Richard the Lion Hearted (who had gone to the Holy Land, but who was spending the greater part of his crusading voyage in an Austrian jail) the government of the country had been placed in the hands of John, a brother of Richard, who was his inferior in the art of war, but his equal as a bad administrator. John had begun his career as a regent by losing Normandy and the greater part of the French possessions. Next, he had managed to get into a quarrel with Pope Innocent III, the famous enemy of the Hohenstaufens. The Pope had excommunicated John (as Gregory VII had excommunicated the Emperor Henry IV two centuries before). In the year 1213 John had been obliged to make an ignominious peace just as Henry IV had been obliged to do in the year 1077.

Undismayed by his lack of success, John continued to abuse his royal power until his disgruntled vassals made a prisoner of their anointed ruler and forced him to promise that he would be good and would never again interfere with the ancient rights of his subjects. All this happened on a little island in the Thames, near the village of Runnymede, on the 15th of June of the year 1215. The document to which John signed his name was called the Big Charter—the Magna Carta. It contained very little that was new. It re-stated in short and direct sentences the ancient duties of the king and enumerated the privileges of his vassals. It paid little attention to the rights (if any) of the vast majority of the people, the peasants, but it offered certain securities to the rising class of the merchants. It was a charter of great importance because it defined the powers of the king with more precision than had ever been done before. But it was still a purely mediæval document. It did not refer to common human beings, unless they happened to be the property of the vassal, which must be safe-guarded against royal tyranny just as the Baronial woods and cows were protected against an excess of zeal on the part of the royal foresters.

A few years later, however, we begin to hear a very different note in the councils of His Majesty.

John, who was bad, both by birth and inclination, solemnly had promised to obey the great charter and then had broken every one of its many stipulations. Fortunately, he soon died and was succeeded by his son Henry III, who was forced to recognise the charter anew. Meanwhile, Uncle Richard, the Crusader, had cost the country a great deal of money and the king was obliged to ask for a few loans that he might pay his obligations to the Jewish money-lenders. The large land-owners and the bishops who acted as councillors to the king could not provide him with the necessary gold and silver. The king then gave orders that a few representatives of the cities be called upon to attend the sessions of his Great Council. They made their first appearance in the year 1265. They were supposed to act only as financial experts who were not supposed to take a part in the general discussion of matters of state, but to give advice exclusively upon the question of taxation.

Gradually, however, these representatives of the "commons" were consulted upon many of the problems and the meeting of noblemen, bishops and city delegates developed into a regular Parliament, a place "où l'on parlait," which means in English where people talked, before important affairs of state were decided upon.

But the institution of such a general advisory board with certain executive powers was not an English invention, as seems to be the general belief, and government by a "king and his parliament" was by no means restricted to the British Isles. You will find it in every part of Europe. In some countries, like France, the rapid increase of the Royal power after the Middle Ages reduced the influence of the "parliament" to nothing. In the year 1302 representatives of the cities had been admitted to the meeting of the French Parliament, but five centuries had to pass before this "Parliament" was strong enough to assert the rights of the middle class, the so-called

THE HOME OF SWISS LIBERTY

Third Estate, and break the power of the king. Then they made up for lost time and during the French Revolution, abolished the king, the clergy and the nobles and made the representatives of the common people the rulers of the land. In Spain the "cortes" (the king's council) had been opened to the commoners as early as the first half of the twelfth century. In the German Empire, a number of important cities had obtained the rank of "imperial cities" whose representatives must be heard in the imperial diet.

In Sweden, representatives of the people attended the sessions of the Riksdag at the first meeting of the year 1359. In

Denmark the Daneholf, the ancient national assembly, was re-
established in 1314, and, although the nobles often regained control of the country at the expense of the king and the people,
the representatives of the cities were never completely deprived
of their power.

In the Scandinavian country, the story of representative
government is particularly interesting. In Iceland, the "Al-
thing," the assembly of all free landowners, who managed the
affairs of the island, began to hold regular meetings in the ninth

THE ABJURATION OF PHILIP II

century and continued to do so for more than a thousand
years.

In Switzerland, the freemen of the different cantons defended their assemblies against the attempts of a number of
feudal neighbours with great success.

Finally, in the Low Countries, in Holland, the councils of
the different duchies and counties were attended by representatives of the third estate as early as the thirteenth century.

In the sixteenth century a number of these small provinces
rebelled against their king, abjured his majesty in a solemn
meeting of the "Estates General," removed the clergy from

the discussions, broke the power of the nobles and assumed full executive authority over the newly-established Republic of the United Seven Netherlands. For two centuries, the representatives of the town-councils ruled the country without a king, without bishops and without noblemen. The city had become supreme and the good burghers had become the rulers of the land.

THE MEDIÆVAL WORLD

THE MEDIÆVAL WORLD

WHAT THE PEOPLE OF THE MIDDLE AGES THOUGHT OF THE WORLD IN WHICH THEY HAPPENED TO LIVE

DATES are a very useful invention. We could not do without them but unless we are very careful, they will play tricks with us. They are apt to make history too precise. For example, when I talk of the point-of-view of mediæval man, I do not mean that on the 31st of December of the year 476, suddenly all the people of Europe said, "Ah, now the Roman Empire has come to an end and we are living in the Middle Ages. How interesting!"

You could have found men at the Frankish court of Charlemagne who were Romans in their habits, in their manners, in their out-look upon life. On the other hand, when you grow up you will discover that some of the people in this world have never passed beyond the stage of the cave-man. All times and all ages overlap, and the ideas of succeeding generations play tag with each other. But it is possible to study the minds of a good many true representatives of the Middle Ages and then give you an idea of the average man's attitude toward life and the many difficult problems of living.

First of all, remember that the people of the Middle Ages never thought of themselves as free-born citizens, who could come and go at will and shape their fate according to their ability or energy or luck. On the contrary, they all considered themselves part of the general scheme of things, which included emperors and serfs, popes and heretics, heroes and swashbucklers, rich men, poor men, beggar men and thieves. They accepted this divine ordinance and asked no questions. In this, of course, they differed radically from modern people who accept nothing and who are forever trying to improve their own financial and political situation.

To the man and woman of the thirteenth century, the world hereafter—a Heaven of wonderful delights and a Hell of brimstone and suffering—meant something more than empty words or vague theological phrases. It was an actual fact and the mediæval burghers and knights spent the greater part of their time preparing for it. We modern people regard a noble death after a well-spent life with the quiet calm of the ancient Greeks and Romans. After three score years of work and effort, we go to sleep with the feeling that all will be well.

But during the Middle Ages, the King of Terrors with his grinning skull and his rattling bones was man's steady companion. He woke his victims up with terrible tunes on his scratchy fiddle—he sat down with them at dinner—he smiled at them from behind trees and shrubs when they took a girl out for a walk. If you had heard nothing but hair-raising yarns about cemeteries and coffins and fearful diseases when you were very young, instead of listening to the fairy stories of Andersen and Grimm, you, too, would have lived all your days in a dread of the final hour and the gruesome day of Judgment. That is exactly what happened to the children of the Middle Ages. They moved in a world of devils and spooks and only a few occasional angels. Sometimes, their fear of the future filled their souls with humility and piety, but often it influenced them the other way and made them cruel and sentimental. They would first of all murder all the women and children of a captured city and then they would devoutly march to a holy spot and with their hands gory with the blood of innocent victims, they would pray that a merciful heaven forgive them their sins. Yea, they would do more than pray, they would weep bitter tears and would confess themselves the most wicked of sinners. But the next day, they would once more butcher a camp of Saracen enemies without a spark of mercy in their hearts.

Of course, the Crusaders were Knights and obeyed a somewhat different code of manners from the common men. But in such respects the common man was just the same as his master. He, too, resembled a shy horse, easily frightened by a shadow or a silly piece of paper, capable of excellent and faithful service but liable to run away and do terrible damage when his feverish imagination saw a ghost.

In judging these good people, however, it is wise to remember the terrible disadvantages under which they lived. They were really barbarians who posed as civilised people. Charlemagne and Otto the Great were called "Roman Emperors," but they had as little resemblance to a real Roman Emperor (say Augustus or Marcus Aurelius) as "King" Wumba Wumba of the Upper Congo has to the highly educated rulers of Sweden or Denmark. They were savages who lived amidst glorious ruins but who did not share the benefits of the civilisation which their fathers and grandfathers had destroyed. They knew nothing. They were ignorant of almost every fact which a boy of twelve knows to-day. They were obliged to go to one single book for all their information. That was the Bible. But those parts of the Bible which have influenced the history of the human race for the better are those chapters of the New Testament which teach us the great moral lessons of love, charity and forgiveness. As a handbook of astronomy, zoölogy, botany, geometry and all the other sciences, the venerable book is not entirely reliable. In the twelfth century, a second book was added to the mediæval library, the great encyclopædia of useful knowledge, compiled by Aristotle, the Greek philosopher of the fourth century before Christ. Why the Christian church should have been willing to accord such high honors to the teacher of Alexander the Great, whereas they condemned all other Greek philosophers on account of their heathenish doctrines, I really do not know. But next to the Bible, Aristotle was recognized as the only reliable teacher

whose works could be safely placed into the hands of true
Christians.

His works had reached Europe in a somewhat roundabout
way. They had gone from Greece to Alexandria. They had
then been translated from the Greek into the Arabic language
by the Mohammedans who conquered Egypt in the seventh
century. They had followed the Moslem armies into Spain and
the philosophy of the great Stagirite (Aristotle was a native of
Stagira in Macedonia) was taught in the Moorish universities
of Cordova. The Arabic text was then translated into Latin
by the Christian students who had crossed the Pyrenees to get
a liberal education and this much travelled version of the famous books was at last taught at the different schools of north-
western Europe. It was not very clear, but that made it all
the more interesting.

With the help of the Bible and Aristotle, the most brilliant
men of the Middle Ages now set to work to explain all things
between Heaven and Earth in their relation to the expressed
will of God. These brilliant men, the so-called Scholiasts or
Schoolmen, were really very intelligent, but they had obtained
their information exclusively from books, and never from actual observation. If they wanted to lecture on the sturgeon
or on caterpillars, they read the Old and New Testaments and
Aristotle, and told their students everything these good books
had to say upon the subject of caterpillars and sturgeons.
They did not go out to the nearest river to catch a sturgeon.
They did not leave their libraries and repair to the backyard
to catch a few caterpillars and look at these animals and study
them in their native haunts. Even such famous scholars as
Albertus Magnus and Thomas Aquinas did not inquire whether
the sturgeons in the land of Palestine and the caterpillars of
Macedonia might not have been different from the sturgeons
and the caterpillars of western Europe.

When occasionally an exceptionally curious person like
Roger Bacon appeared in the council of the learned and began
to experiment with magnifying glasses and funny little tele-
scopes and actually dragged the sturgeon and the caterpillar

into the lecturing room and proved that they were different from the creatures described by the Old Testament and by Aristotle, the Schoolmen shook their dignified heads. Bacon was going too far. When he dared to suggest that an hour of actual observation was worth more than ten years with Aristotle and that the works of that famous Greek might as well have remained untranslated for all the good they had ever done, the scholiasts went to the police and said, "This man is a danger to the safety of the state. He wants us to study Greek that we may read Aristotle in the original. Why should he not be contented with our Latin-Arabic translation which has satisfied our faithful people for so many hundred years? Why is he so curious about the insides of fishes and the insides of insects? He is probably a wicked magician trying to upset the established order of things by his Black Magic." And so well did they plead their cause that the frightened guardians of the peace forbade Bacon to write a single word for more than ten years. When he resumed his studies he had learned a lesson. He wrote his books in a queer cipher which made it impossible for his contemporaries to read them, a trick which became common as the Church became more desperate in its attempts to prevent people from asking questions which would lead to doubts and infidelity.

This, however, was not done out of any wicked desire to keep people ignorant. The feeling which prompted the heretic hunters of that day was really a very kindly one. They firmly believed—nay, they knew—that this life was but the preparation for our real existence in the next world. They felt convinced that too much knowledge made people uncomfortable, filled their minds with dangerous opinions and led to doubt and hence to perdition. A mediæval Schoolman who saw one of his pupils stray away from the revealed authority of the Bible and Aristotle, that he might study things for himself, felt as uncomfortable as a loving mother who sees her young child approach a hot stove. She knows that he will burn his little fingers if he is allowed to touch it and she tries to keep him back, if necessary she will use force. But she really loves the child and if he will only obey her, she will be as good to him as she possibly can be. In the same way the mediæval guardians of people's souls, while they were strict in all matters pertaining to the Faith, slaved day and night to render the greatest possible service to the members of their flock. They held out a helping hand whenever they could and the society of that day shows the influence of thousands of good men and pious women who tried to make the fate of the average mortal as bearable as possible.

A serf was a serf and his position would never change. But the Good Lord of the Middle Ages who allowed the serf to remain a slave all his life had bestowed an immortal soul upon this humble creature and therefore he must be protected in his rights, that he might live and die as a good Christian. When he grew too old or too weak to work he must be taken care of by the feudal master for whom he had worked. The serf, therefore, who led a monotonous and dreary life, was never haunted by fear of to-morrow. He knew that he was "safe"— that he could not be thrown out of employment, that he would always have a roof over his head (a leaky roof, perhaps, but a roof all the same), and that he would always have something to eat.

This feeling of "stability" and of "safety" was found in all classes of society. In the towns the merchants and the artisans established guilds which assured every member of a steady income. It did not encourage the ambitious to do better than their neighbours. Too often the guilds gave protection to the "slacker" who managed to "get by." But they established a general feeling of content and assurance among the labouring classes which no longer exists in our day of general competition. The Middle Ages were familiar with the dangers of what we modern people call "corners," when a single rich man gets hold of all the available grain or soap or pickled herring, and then forces the world to buy from him at his own price. The authorities, therefore, discouraged wholesale trading and regulated the price at which merchants were allowed to sell their goods.

The Middle Ages disliked competition. Why compete and fill the world with hurry and rivalry and a multitude of pushing men, when the Day of Judgement was near at hand, when riches would count for nothing and when the good serf would enter the golden gates of Heaven while the bad knight was sent to do penance in the deepest pit of Inferno?

In short, the people of the Middle Ages were asked to surrender part of their liberty of thought and action, that they might enjoy greater safety from poverty of the body and poverty of the soul.

And with a very few exceptions, they did not object. They firmly believed that they were mere visitors upon this planet— that they were here to be prepared for a greater and more important life. Deliberately they turned their backs upon a world which was filled with suffering and wickedness and injustice. They pulled down the blinds that the rays of the sun might not distract their attention from that chapter in the Apocalypse which told them of that heavenly light which was to illumine their happiness in all eternity. They tried to close their eyes to most of the joys of the world in which they lived that they might enjoy those which awaited them in the near future. They accepted life as a necessary evil and welcomed death as the beginning of a glorious day.

The Greeks and the Romans had never bothered about the future but had tried to establish their Paradise right here upon this earth. They had succeeded in making life extremely pleasant for those of their fellow men who did not happen to be slaves. Then came the other extreme of the Middle Ages, when man built himself a Paradise beyond the highest clouds and turned this world into a vale of tears for high and low, for rich and poor, for the intelligent and the dumb. It was time for the pendulum to swing back in the other direction, as I shall tell you in my next chapter.

MEDIÆVAL TRADE

HOW THE CRUSADES ONCE MORE MADE THE MEDITERRANEAN A BUSY CENTRE OF TRADE AND HOW THE CITIES OF THE ITALIAN PENINSULA BECAME THE GREAT DISTRIBUTING CENTRE FOR THE COMMERCE WITH ASIA AND AFRICA

THERE were three good reasons why the Italian cities should have been the first to regain a position of great importance during the late Middle Ages. The Italian peninsula had been settled by Rome at a very early date. There had been more roads and more towns and more schools than anywhere else in Europe.

The barbarians had burned as lustily in Italy as elsewhere, but there had been so much to destroy that more had been able to survive. In the second place, the Pope lived in Italy and as the head of a vast political machine, which owned land and serfs and buildings and forests and rivers and conducted courts of law, he was in constant receipt of a great deal of money. The Papal authorities had to be paid in gold and silver as did the merchants and ship-owners of Venice and Genoa. The cows and the eggs and the horses and all the other agricultural products of the north and the west must be changed into actual cash before the debt could be paid in the distant city of Rome.

THE MEDITERRANEAN WAS THE COMMERCIAL DISTRIBUTING CENTER OF THE MIDDLE AGES

MEDIÆVAL TRADE

This made Italy the one country where there was a comparative abundance of gold and silver. Finally, during the Crusades, the Italian cities had become the point of embarkation for the Crusaders and had profiteered to an almost unbelievable extent.

And after the Crusades had come to an end, these same Italian cities remained the distributing centres for those Oriental goods upon which the people of Europe had come to depend during the time they had spent in the near east.

Of these towns, few were as famous as Venice. Venice was a republic built upon a mud bank. Thither people from the mainland had fled during the invasions of the barbarians in the fourth century. Surrounded on all sides by the sea they had engaged in the business of salt-making. Salt had been very scarce during the Middle Ages, and the price had been high. For hundreds of years Venice had enjoyed a monopoly of this indispensable table commodity (I say indispensable, because people, like sheep, fall ill unless they get a certain amount of salt in their food). The people had used this monopoly to increase the power of their city. At times they had even dared to defy the power of the Popes. The town had grown rich and had begun to build ships, which engaged in trade with the Orient. During the Crusades, these ships were used to carry passengers to the Holy Land, and when the passengers could not pay for their tickets in cash, they were obliged to help the Venetians who were for ever increasing their colonies in the Ægean Sea, in Asia Minor and in Egypt.

By the end of the fourteenth century, the population had grown to two hundred thousand, which made Venice the biggest city of the Middle Ages. The people were without influence upon the government which was the private affair of a small number of rich merchant families. They elected a senate and a Doge (or Duke), but the actual rulers of the city were the members of the famous Council of Ten,—who maintained themselves with the help of a highly organised system of secret-service men and professional murderers, who kept watch upon all citizens and quietly removed those who might be dangerous to the safety of their high-handed and unscrupulous Committee of Public Safety.

The other extreme of government, a democracy of very turbulent habits, was to be found in Florence. This city controlled the main road from northern Europe to Rome and used the money which it had derived from this fortunate economic position to engage in manufacturing. The Florentines tried to follow the example of Athens. Noblemen, priests and members of the guilds all took part in the discussions of civic affairs. This led to great civic upheaval. People were forever being divided into political parties and these parties fought each other with intense bitterness and exiled their enemies and confiscated their possessions as soon as they had gained a victory in the council. After several centuries of this rule by organised mobs, the inevitable happened. A powerful family made itself master of the city and governed the town and the surrounding country after the fashion of the old Greek "tyrants." They were called the Medici. The earliest Medici had been physicians (medicus is Latin for physician, hence their name), but later they had turned banker. Their banks and their pawnshops were to be found in all the more important centres of trade. Even to-day our American pawn-shops display the three golden balls which were part of the coat of arms of the mighty house of the Medici, who became rulers of Florence and married their daughters to the kings of France and were buried in graves worthy of a Roman Cæsar.

Then there was Genoa, the great rival of Venice, where the merchants specialised in trade with Tunis in Africa and the grain depots of the Black Sea. Then there were more than two hundred other cities, some large and some small, each a perfect commercial unit, all of them fighting their neighbours and rivals with the undying hatred of neighbours who are depriving each other of their profits.

Once the products of the Orient and Africa had been brought to these distributing centres, they must be prepared for the voyage to the west and the north.

Genoa carried her goods by water to Marseilles, from where

they were reshipped to the cities along the Rhone, which in turn served as the market places of northern and western France.

Venice used the land route to northern Europe. This ancient road led across the Brenner pass, the old gateway for the barbarians who had invaded Italy. Past Innsbrück, the merchandise was carried to Basel. From there it drifted down the Rhine to the North Sea and England, or it was taken to

GREAT NOVGOROD

Augsburg where the Fugger family (who were both bankers and manufacturers and who prospered greatly by "shaving" the coins with which they paid their workmen), looked after the further distribution to Nuremberg and Leipzig and the cities of the Baltic and to Wisby (on the Island of Gotland) which looked after the needs of the Northern Baltic and dealt directly with the Republic of Novgorod, the old commercial centre of Russia which was destroyed by Ivan the Terrible in the middle of the sixteenth century.

The little cities on the coast of north-western Europe had an interesting story of their own. The mediæval world ate a great deal of fish. There were many fast days and then people were not permitted to eat meat. For those who lived away from the coast and from the rivers, this meant a diet of eggs or nothing at all. But early in the thirteenth century a Dutch fisherman had discovered a way of curing herring, so that it could be transported to distant points. The herring fisheries of the North Sea then became of great importance. But some time during the thirteenth century, this useful little fish (for reasons of its own) moved from the North Sea to the Baltic and the cities of that inland sea began to make money. All the world now sailed to the Baltic to catch herring and as that fish could only be caught during a few months each year (the rest of the time it spends in deep water, raising large families of little herrings) the ships would have been idle during the rest of the time unless they had found another occupation. They were then used to carry the wheat of northern and central Russia to southern and western Europe. On the return voyage they brought spices and silks and carpets and Oriental rugs from Venice and Genoa to Bruges and Hamburg and Bremen.

Out of such simple beginnings there developed an important system of international trade which reached from the manufacturing cities of Bruges and Ghent (where the almighty guilds fought pitched battles with the kings of France and England and established a labour tyranny which completely ruined both the employers and the workmen) to the Republic of Novgorod in northern Russia, which was a mighty city until Tsar Ivan, who distrusted all merchants, took the town and killed sixty thousand people in less than a month's time and reduced the survivors to beggary.

That they might protect themselves against pirates and excessive tolls and annoying legislation, the merchants of the north founded a protective league which was called the "Hansa." The Hansa, which had its headquarters in Lübeck, was a voluntary association of more than one hundred cities. The association maintained a navy of its own which patrolled the seas and fought and defeated the Kings of England and Denmark when they dared to interfere with the rights and the privileges of the mighty Hanseatic merchants.

I wish that I had more space to tell you some of the won‑ derful stories of this strange commerce which was carried on across the high mountains and across the deep seas amidst such dangers that every voyage became a glorious adventure. But it would take several volumes and it cannot be done here.

THE HANSA SHIP

The Middle Ages, as I have tried to show you, had been a period of very slow progress. The people who were in power believed that "progress" was a very undesirable invention of the Evil One and ought to be discouraged, and as they hap‑ pened to occupy the seats of the mighty, it was easy to enforce their will upon the patient serfs and the illiterate knights. Here and there a few brave souls sometimes ventured forth into the forbidden region of science, but they fared badly and were considered lucky when they escaped with their lives and a jail sentence of twenty years.

In the twelfth and thirteenth centuries the flood of international commerce swept over western Europe as the Nile had swept across the valley of ancient Egypt. It left behind a fertile sediment of prosperity. Prosperity meant leisure hours and these leisure hours gave both men and women a chance to buy manuscripts and take an interest in literature and art and music.

Then once more was the world filled with that divine curiosity which has elevated man from the ranks of those other mammals who are his distant cousins but who have remained dumb, and the cities, of whose growth and development I have told you in my last chapter, offered a safe shelter to these brave pioneers who dared to leave the very narrow domain of the established order of things.

They set to work. They opened the windows of their cloistered and studious cells. A flood of sunlight entered the dusty rooms and showed them the cobwebs which had gathered during the long period of semi-darkness.

They began to clean house. Next they cleaned their gardens.

Then they went out into the open fields, outside the crumbling town walls, and said, "This is a good world. We are glad that we live in it."

At that moment, the Middle Ages came to an end and a new world began.

THE RENAISSANCE

PEOPLE ONCE MORE DARED TO BE HAPPY
JUST BECAUSE THEY WERE ALIVE. THEY
TRIED TO SAVE THE REMAINS OF THE
OLDER AND MORE AGREEABLE CIVILISA-
TION OF ROME AND GREECE AND THEY
WERE SO PROUD OF THEIR ACHIEVE-
MENTS THAT THEY SPOKE OF A RENAIS-
SANCE OR RE-BIRTH OF CIVILISATION

THE Renaissance was not a political or religious movement. It was a state of mind.

The men of the Renaissance continued to be the obedient
sons of the mother church. They were subjects of kings and
emperors and dukes and murmured not.

But their outlook upon life was changed. They began to
wear different clothes—to speak a different language—to live
different lives in different houses.

They no longer concentrated all their thoughts and their
efforts upon the blessed existence that awaited them in Heaven.
They tried to establish their Paradise upon this planet, and,
truth to tell, they succeeded in a remarkable degree.

I have quite often warned you against the danger that
lies in historical dates. People take them too literally. They
think of the Middle Ages as a period of darkness and ignor-

ance. "Click," says the clock, and the Renaissance begins and cities and palaces are flooded with the bright sunlight of an eager intellectual curiosity.

As a matter of fact, it is quite impossible to draw such sharp lines. The thirteenth century belonged most decidedly to the Middle Ages. All historians agree upon that. But was it a time of darkness and stagnation merely? By no means. People were tremendously alive. Great states were being founded. Large centres of commerce were being developed. High above the turretted towers of the castle and the peaked roof of the town-hall, rose the slender spire of the newly built Gothic cathedral. Everywhere the world was in motion. The high and mighty gentlemen of the city-hall, who had just become conscious of their own strength (by way of their recently acquired riches) were struggling for more power with their feudal masters. The members of the guilds who had just become aware of the important fact that "numbers count" were fighting the high and mighty gentlemen of the city-hall. The king and his shrewd advisers went fishing in these troubled waters and caught many a shining bass of profit which they proceeded to cook and eat before the noses of the surprised and disappointed councillors and guild brethren.

To enliven the scenery during the long hours of evening when the badly lighted streets did not invite further political and economic dispute, the Troubadours and Minnesingers told their stories and sang their songs of romance and adventure and heroism and loyalty to all fair women. Meanwhile youth, impatient of the slowness of progress, flocked to the universities, and thereby hangs a story.

The Middle Ages were "internationally minded." That sounds difficult, but wait until I explain it to you. We modern people are "nationally minded." We are Americans or Englishmen or Frenchmen or Italians and speak English or French or Italian and go to English and French and Italian universities, unless we want to specialise in some particular branch of learning which is only taught elsewhere, and then we learn another language and go to Munich or Madrid or Moscow. But the people of the thirteenth or fourteenth century rarely talked of themselves as Englishmen or Frenchmen or Italians. They said, "I am a citizen of Sheffield or Bordeaux or Genoa." Because they all belonged to one and the same church they felt a certain bond of brotherhood. And as all educated men could speak Latin, they possessed an international language which removed the stupid language barriers which have grown up in modern Europe and which place the small nations at such an enormous disadvantage. Just as an example, take the case of Erasmus, the great preacher of tolerance and laughter, who wrote his books in the sixteenth century. He was the native of a small Dutch village. He wrote in Latin and all the world was his audience. If he were alive to-day, he would write in Dutch. Then only five or six million people would be able to read him. To be understood by the rest of Europe and America, his publishers would be obliged to translate his books into twenty different languages. That would cost a lot of money and most likely the publishers would never take the trouble or the risk.

Six hundred years ago that could not happen. The greater part of the people were still very ignorant and could not read or write at all. But those who had mastered the difficult art of handling the goose quill belonged to an international republic of letters which spread across the entire continent and which knew of no boundaries and respected no limitations of language or nationality. The universities were the strongholds of this republic. Unlike modern fortifications, they did not follow the frontier. They were to be found wherever a teacher and a few pupils happened to find themselves together. There again the Middle Ages and the Renaissance differed from our own time. Nowadays, when a new university is built, the process (almost invariably) is as follows: Some rich man wants to do something for the community in which he lives or a particular religious sect wants to build a school to keep its faithful children under decent supervision, or a state needs doc-

tors and lawyers and teachers. The university begins as a
large sum of money which is deposited in a bank. This money
is then used to construct buildings and laboratories and dormi-
tories. Finally professional teachers are hired, entrance exami-
nations are held and the university is on the way.

But in the Middle
Ages things were done
differently. A wise man
said to himself, "I have
discovered a great truth.
I must impart my knowl-
edge to others." And he
began to preach his wis-
dom wherever and when-
ever he could get a few
people to listen to him,
like a modern soap-box
orator. If he was an in-
teresting speaker, the
crowd came and stayed.
If he was dull, they
shrugged their shoulders
and continued their way.

THE MEDIÆVAL LABORATORY

By and by certain young men began to come regularly to hear
the words of wisdom of this great teacher. They brought copy-
books with them and a little bottle of ink and a goose quill and
wrote down what seemed to be important. One day it rained.
The teacher and his pupils retired to an empty basement or
the room of the "Professor." The learned man sat in his chair
and the boys sat on the floor. That was the beginning of the
University, the "universitas," a corporation of professors and
students during the Middle Ages, when the "teacher" counted
for everything and the building in which he taught counted for
very little.

As an example, let me tell you of something that happened
in the ninth century. In the town of Salerno near Naples there
were a number of excellent physicians. They attracted people

desirous of learning the medical profession and for almost a thousand years (until 1817) there was a university of Salerno which taught the wisdom of Hippocrates, the great Greek doctor who had practised his art in ancient Hellas in the fifth century before the birth of Christ.

Then there was Abelard, the young priest from Brittany, who early in the twelfth century began to lecture on theology and logic in Paris. Thousands of eager young men flocked to the French city to hear him. Other priests who disagreed with him stepped forward to explain their point of view. Paris was soon filled with a clamouring multitude of Englishmen and Germans and Italians and students from Sweden and Hungary and around the old cathedral which stood on a little island in the Seine there grew the famous University of Paris.

In Bologna in Italy, a monk by the name of Gratian had compiled a text-book for those whose business it was to know the laws of the church. Young priests and many laymen then came from all over Europe to hear Gratian explain his ideas. To protect themselves against the landlords and the innkeepers and the boarding-house ladies of the city, they formed a corporation (or University) and behold the beginning of the university of Bologna.

Next there was a quarrel in the University of Paris. We do not know what caused it, but a number of disgruntled teachers together with their pupils crossed the channel and found a hospitable home in a little village on the Thames called Oxford, and in this way the famous University of Oxford came into being. In the same way, in the year 1222, there had been a split in the University of Bologna. The discontented teachers (again followed by their pupils) had

THE RENAISSANCE

moved to Padua and their proud city thenceforward boasted of a university of its own. And so it went from Valladolid in Spain to Cracow in distant Poland and from Poitiers in France to Rostock in Germany.

It is quite true that much of the teaching done by these early professors would sound absurd to our ears, trained to listen to logarithms and geometrical theorems. The point, however, which I want to make is this—the Middle Ages and especially the thirteenth century were not a time when the world stood entirely still. Among the younger generation, there was life, there was enthusiasm, and there was a restless if somewhat bashful asking of questions. And out of this turmoil grew the Renaissance.

But just before the curtain went down upon the last scene of the Mediæval world, a solitary figure crossed the stage, of whom you ought to know more than his mere name. This man was called Dante. He was the son of a Florentine lawyer who belonged to the Alighieri family and he saw the light of day in the year 1265. He grew up in the city of his ancestors while Giotto was painting his stories of the life of St. Francis of Assisi upon the walls of the Church of the Holy Cross, but often when he went to school, his frightened eyes would see the puddles of blood which told of the terrible and endless warfare that raged forever between the Guelphs and the Ghibellines, the followers of the Pope and the adherents of the Emperors.

When he grew up, he became a Guelph, because his father had been one before him, just as an American boy might become a Democrat or a Republican, simply because his father had happened to be a Democrat or a Republican. But after a few years, Dante saw that Italy, unless united under a single head, threatened to perish as a victim of the disordered jealousies of a thousand little cities. Then he became a Ghibelline.

He looked for help beyond the Alps. He hoped that a mighty emperor might come and re-establish unity and order. Alas! he hoped in vain. The Ghibellines were driven out of Florence in the year 1302. From that time on until the day of his death amidst the dreary ruins of Ravenna, in the year 1321, Dante was a homeless wanderer, eating the bread of charity at the table of rich patrons whose names would have sunk into the deepest pit of oblivion but for this single fact, that they had been kind to a poet in his misery. During the many years of exile, Dante felt compelled to justify himself and his actions when he had been a political leader in his home-town, and when he had spent his days walking along the banks of the Arno that he might catch a glimpse of the lovely Beatrice Portinari, who died the wife of another man, a dozen years before the Ghibelline disaster.

DANTE

He had failed in the ambitions of his career. He had faithfully served the town of his birth and before a corrupt court he had been accused of stealing the public funds and had been condemned to be burned alive should he venture back within the realm of the city of Florence. To clear himself before his own conscience and before his contemporaries, Dante then created an Imaginary World and with great detail he described the circumstances which had led to his defeat and depicted the hopeless condition of greed and lust and hatred which had turned his fair and beloved Italy into a battlefield for the pitiless mercenaries of wicked and selfish tyrants.

He tells us how on the Thursday before Easter of the year 1300 he had lost his way in a dense forest and how he found his path barred by a leopard and a lion and a wolf. He gave himself up for lost when a white figure appeared amidst the trees. It was Virgil, the Roman poet and philosopher, sent upon his errand of mercy by the Blessed Virgin and by Beatrice, who from high Heaven watched over the fate of her true lover. Virgil then takes Dante through Purgatory and through Hell. Deeper and deeper the path leads them until they reach the lowest pit where Lucifer himself stands frozen into the eternal ice surrounded by the most terrible of sinners, traitors and liars and those who have achieved fame and success by lies and by deceit. But before the two wanderers have reached this terrible spot, Dante has met all those who in some way or other have played a rôle in the history of his beloved city. Emperors and Popes, dashing knights and whining usurers, they are all there, doomed to eternal punishment or awaiting the day of deliverance, when they shall leave Purgatory for Heaven.

It is a curious story. It is a handbook of everything the people of the thirteenth century did and felt and feared and prayed for. Through it all moves the figure of the lonely Florentine exile, forever followed by the shadow of his own despair.

And behold! when the gates of death were closing upon the sad poet of the Middle Ages, the portals of life swung open to the child who was to be the first of the men of the Renaissance. That was Francesco Petrarca, the son of the notary public of the little town of Arezzo.

Francesco's father had belonged to the same political party as Dante. He too had been exiled and thus it happened that Petrarca (or Petrarch, as we call him) was born away from Florence. At the age of fifteen he was sent to Montpellier in France that he might become a lawyer like his father. But the boy did not want to be a jurist. He hated the law. He wanted to be a scholar and a poet—and because he wanted to be a scholar and a poet beyond everything else, he became one. as people of a strong will are apt to do. He made long voyages, copying manuscripts in Flanders and in the cloisters along the Rhine and in Paris and Liège and finally in Rome. Then he went to live in a lonely valley of the wild mountains

of Vaucluse, and there he studied and wrote and soon he had
become so famous for his verse and for his learning that both
the University of Paris and the king of Naples invited him
to come and teach their students and subjects. On the way
to his new job, he was obliged to pass through Rome. The
people had heard of his fame as an editor of half-forgotten
Roman authors. They decided to honour him and in the
ancient forum of the Imperial City, Petrarch was crowned with
the laurel wreath of the Poet.

From that moment on, his life was an endless career of
honour and appreciation. He wrote the things which people
wanted most to hear. They were tired of theological dispu-
tations. Poor Dante could wander through hell as much as
he wanted. But Petrarch wrote of love and of nature and the
sun and never mentioned those gloomy things which seemed
to have been the stock in trade of the last generation. And
when Petrarch came to a city, all the people flocked out to
meet him and he was received like a conquering hero. If he
happened to bring his young friend Boccaccio, the story teller,
with him, so much the better. They were both men of their
time, full of curiosity, willing to read everything once, digging
in forgotten and musty libraries that they might find still another manuscript of Virgil or Ovid or Lucretius or any of the
other old Latin poets. They were good Christians. Of course
they were! Everyone was. But no need of going around with
a long face and wearing a dirty coat just because some day
or other you were going to die. Life was good. People were
meant to be happy. You desired proof of this? Very well.
Take a spade and dig into the soil. What did you find?
Beautiful old statues. Beautiful old vases. Ruins of ancient
buildings. All these things were made by the people of the
greatest empire that ever existed. They ruled all the world
for a thousand years. They were strong and rich and handsome (just look at that bust of the Emperor Augustus!). Of
course, they were not Christians and they would never be
able to enter Heaven. At best they would spend their days
in purgatory, where Dante had just paid them a visit.

But who cared? To have lived in a world like that of
ancient Rome was heaven enough for any mortal being. And
anyway, we live but once. Let us be happy and cheerful for
the mere joy of existence.

Such, in short, was the spirit that had begun to fill the
narrow and crooked streets of the many little Italian cities.

You know what we mean by the "bicycle craze" or the
"automobile craze." Some one invents a bicycle. People who
for hundreds of thousands of years have moved slowly and
painfully from one place to another go "crazy" over the pros-
pect of rolling rapidly and easily over hill and dale. Then
a clever mechanic makes the first automobile. No longer is it
necessary to pedal and pedal and pedal. You just sit and
let little drops of gasoline do the work for you. Then everybody wants an automobile. Everybody talks about Rolls-
Royces and Flivvers and carburetors and mileage and oil. Explorers penetrate into the hearts of unknown countries that
they may find new supplies of gas. Forests arise in Sumatra
and in the Congo to supply us with rubber. Rubber and oil
become so valuable that people fight wars for their possession.
The whole world is "automobile mad" and little children can
say "car" before they learn to whisper "papa" and "mamma."

In the fourteenth century, the Italian people went crazy
about the newly discovered beauties of the buried world of
Rome. Soon their enthusiasm was shared by all the people of
western Europe. The finding of an unknown manuscript became the excuse for a civic holiday. The man who wrote a
grammar became as popular as the fellow who nowadays invents
a new spark-plug. The humanist, the scholar who devoted his
time and his energies to a study of "homo" or mankind (instead
of wasting his hours upon fruitless theological investigations),
that man was regarded with greater honour and a deeper respect than was ever bestowed upon a hero who had just conquered all the Cannibal Islands.

In the midst of this intellectual upheaval, an event occurred
which greatly favoured the study of the ancient philosophers
and authors. The Turks were renewing their attacks upon

Europe. Constantinople, capital of the last remnant of the original Roman Empire, was hard pressed. In the year 1393 the Emperor, Manuel Paleologue, sent Emmanuel Chrysoloras to western Europe to explain the desperate state of old Byzantium and to ask for aid. This aid never came. The Roman Catholic world was more than willing to see the Greek Catholic world go to the punishment that awaited such wicked heretics. But however indifferent western Europe might be to the fate of the Byzantines, they were greatly interested in the ancient Greeks whose colonists had founded the city on the Bosphorus five centuries after the Trojan war. They wanted to learn Greek that they might read Aristotle and Homer and Plato. They wanted to learn it very badly, but they had no books and no grammars and no teachers. The magistrates of Florence heard of the visit of Chrysoloras. The people of their city were "crazy to learn Greek." Would he please come and teach them? He would, and behold! the first professor of Greek teaching alpha, beta, gamma to hundreds of eager young men, begging their way to the city of the Arno, living in stables and in dingy attics that they might learn how to decline the verb παιδευω παιδευεις παιδευει and enter into the companionship of Sophocles and Homer.

Meanwhile in the universities, the old schoolmen, teaching their ancient theology and their antiquated logic; explaining the hidden mysteries of the old Testament and discussing the strange science of their Greek-Arabic-Spanish-Latin edition of Aristotle, looked on in dismay and horror. Next, they turned angry. This thing was going too far. The young men were deserting the lecture halls of the established universities to go and listen to some wild-eyed "humanist" with his new-fangled notions about a "reborn civilization."

They went to the authorities. They complained. But one cannot force an unwilling horse to drink and one cannot make unwilling ears listen to something which does not really interest them. The schoolmen were losing ground rapidly. Here and there they scored a short victory. They combined forces with those fanatics who hated to see other people enjoy a happiness which was foreign to their own souls. In Florence, the centre of the Great Rebirth, a terrible fight was fought between the old order and the new. A Dominican monk, sour of face and bitter in his hatred of beauty, was the leader of the mediæval rear-guard. He fought a valiant battle. Day after day he thundered his warnings of God's holy wrath through the wide halls of Santa Maria del Fiore. "Repent," he cried, "repent of your godlessness, of your joy in things that are not holy!" He began to hear voices and to see flaming swords that flashed through the sky. He preached to the little children that they might not fall into the errors of these ways which were leading their fathers to perdition. He organised companies of boy-scouts, devoted to the service of the great God whose prophet he claimed to be. In a sudden moment of frenzy, the frightened people promised to do penance for their wicked love of beauty and pleasure. They carried their books and their statues and their paintings to the market place and celebrated a wild "carnival of the vanities" with holy singing and most unholy dancing, while Savonarola applied his torch to the accumulated treasures.

But when the ashes cooled down, the people began to realise what they had lost. This terrible fanatic had made them destroy that which they had come to love above all things. They turned against him, Savonarola was thrown into jail. He was tortured. But he refused to repent for anything he had done. He was an honest man. He had tried to live a holy life. He had willingly destroyed those who deliberately refused to share his own point of view. It had been his duty to eradicate evil wherever he found it. A love of heathenish books and heathenish beauty in the eyes of this faithful son of the Church, had been an evil. But he stood alone. He had fought the battle of a time that was dead and gone. The Pope in Rome never moved a finger to save him. On the contrary, he approved of his "faithful Florentines" when they dragged Savonarola to the gallows, hanged him and burned his body amidst the cheerful howling and yelling of the mob.

It was a sad ending, but quite inevitable. Savonarola

would have been a great man in the eleventh century. In the fifteenth century he was merely the leader of a lost cause. For better or worse, the Middle Ages had come to an end when the Pope had turned humanist and when the Vatican became the most important museum of Roman and Greek antiquities.

THE AGE OF EXPRESSION

THE PEOPLE BEGAN TO FEEL THE NEED OF
GIVING EXPRESSION TO THEIR NEWLY
DISCOVERED JOY OF LIVING. THEY EX-
PRESSED THEIR HAPPINESS IN POETRY
AND IN SCULPTURE AND IN ARCHITEC-
TURE AND IN PAINTING AND IN THE
BOOKS THEY PRINTED

IN the year 1471 there died a pious old man who had spent
seventy-two of his ninety-one years behind the sheltering walls
of the cloister of Mount St. Agnes near the good town of
Zwolle, the old Dutch Hanseatic city on the river Ysel. He
was known as Brother Thomas and because he had been born
in the village of Kempen, he was called Thomas à Kempis.
At the age of twelve he had been sent to Deventer, where
Gerhard Groot, a brilliant graduate of the universities of
Paris, Cologne and Prague, and famous as a wandering
preacher, had founded the Society of the Brothers of the
Common Life. The good brothers were humble laymen who
tried to live the simple life of the early Apostles of Christ
while working at their regular jobs as carpenters and house-
painters and stone masons. They maintained an excellent
school, that deserving boys of poor parents might be taught
the wisdom of the Fathers of the church. At this school,
little Thomas had learned how to conjugate Latin verbs and
how to copy manuscripts. Then he had taken his vows, had

put his little bundle of books upon his back, had wandered to Zwolle and with a sigh of relief he had closed the door upon a turbulent world which did not attract him.

Thomas lived in an age of turmoil, pestilence and sudden death. In central Europe, in Bohemia, the devoted disciples of Johannes Huss, the friend and follower of John Wycliffe, the English reformer, were avenging with a terrible warfare the death of their beloved leader who had been burned at the stake by order of that same Council of Constance, which had promised him a safe-conduct if he would come to Switzerland and explain his doctrines to the Pope, the Emperor, twenty-three cardinals, thirty-three archbishops and bishops, one hundred and fifty abbots and more than a hundred princes and dukes who had gathered together to reform their church.

In the west, France had been fighting for a hundred years that she might drive the English from her territories and just then was saved from utter defeat by the fortunate appearance of Joan of Arc. And no sooner had this struggle come to an end than France and Burgundy were at each other's throats, engaged upon a struggle of life and death for the supremacy of western Europe.

JOHN HUSS

In the south, a Pope at Rome was calling the curses of Heaven down upon a second Pope who resided at Avignon, in southern France, and who retaliated in kind. In the far east the Turks were destroying the last remnants of the Roman Empire and the Russians had started upon a final crusade to crush the power of their Tartar masters.

But of all this, Brother Thomas in his quiet cell never heard. He had his manuscripts and his own thoughts and he was contented. He poured his love of God into a little volume. He called it the Imitation of Christ. It has since been translated into more languages than any other book save the Bible. It has been read by quite as many people as ever studied the Holy Scriptures. It has influenced the lives of countless millions. And it was the work of a man whose highest ideal of existence was expressed in the simple wish that "he might quietly spend his days sitting in a little corner with a little book."

Good Brother Thomas represented the purest ideals of the Middle Ages. Surrounded on all sides by the forces of the victorious Renaissance, with the humanists loudly proclaiming the coming of modern times, the Middle Ages gathered strength for a last sally. Monasteries were reformed. Monks gave up the habits of riches and vice. Simple, straightforward and honest men, by the example of their blameless and devout lives, tried to bring the people back to the ways of righteousness and humble resignation to the will of God. But all to no avail. The new world rushed past these good people. The days of quiet meditation were gone. The great era of "expression" had begun.

Here and now let me say that I am sorry that I must use so many "big words." I wish that I could write this history in words of one syllable. But it cannot be done. You cannot write a text-book of geometry without reference to a hypotenuse and triangles and a rectangular parallelopiped. You simply have to learn what those words mean or do without mathematics. In history (and in all life) you will eventually be obliged to learn the meaning of many strange words of Latin and Greek origin. Why not do it now?

When I say that the Renaissance was an era of expression, I mean this: People were no longer contented to be the audience and sit still while the emperor and the pope told them what to do and what to think. They wanted to be actors

upon the stage of life. They insisted upon giving "expression"
to their own individual ideas. If a man happened to be interested in statesmanship like the Florentine historian, Niccolò
Macchiavelli, then he "expressed" himself in his books which
revealed his own idea of a successful state and an efficient
ruler. If on the other hand he had a liking for painting, he

A.D. 1400
ONE MAN COPIES A BOOK
IN A HUNDRED DAYS

A.D. 1500
A HUNDRED
BOOKS
ARE PRINTED
IN A DAY.

THE MANUSCRIPT AND THE PRINTED BOOK

"expressed" his love for beautiful lines and lovely colours in
the pictures which have made the names of Giotto, Fra An-
gelico, Rafael and a thousand others household words wherever people have learned to care for those things which express
a true and lasting beauty.

If this love for colour and line happened to be combined with
an interest in mechanics and hydraulics, the result was a Leo-
nardo da Vinci, who painted his pictures, experimented with
his balloons and flying machines, drained the marshes of the
Lombardian plains and "expressed" his joy and interest in all

THE CATHEDRAL

things between Heaven and Earth in prose, in painting, in
sculpture and in curiously conceived engines. When a man of
gigantic strength, like Michael Angelo, found the brush and
the palette too soft for his strong hands, he turned to sculpture
and to architecture, and hacked the most terrific creatures out
of heavy blocks of marble and drew the plans for the church
of St. Peter, the most concrete "expression" of the glories
of the triumphant church. And so it went.

All Italy (and very soon all of Europe) was filled with
men and women who lived that they might add their mite to
the sum total of our accumulated treasures of knowledge and
beauty and wisdom. In Germany, in the city of Mainz, Johann
zum Gänsefleisch, commonly known as Johann Gutenberg, had
just invented a new method of copying books. He had studied
the old woodcuts and had perfected a system by which individual letters of soft lead could be placed in such a way that
they formed words and whole pages. It is true, he soon lost
all his money in a law-suit which had to do with the original
invention of the press. He died in poverty, but the "expression" of his particular inventive genius lived after him.

Soon Aldus in Venice and Etienne in Paris and Plantin in
Antwerp and Froben in Basel were flooding the world with
carefully edited editions of the classics printed in the Gothic
letters of the Gutenberg Bible, or printed in the Italian type
which we use in this book, or printed in Greek letters, or in
Hebrew.

Then the whole world became the eager audience of those
who had something to say. The day when learning had been
a monopoly of a privileged few came to an end. And the
last excuse for ignorance was removed from this world, when
Elzevier of Haarlem began to print his cheap and popular
editions. Then Aristotle and Plato, Virgil and Horace and
Pliny, all the goodly company of the ancient authors and
philosophers and scientists, offered to become man's faithful
friend in exchange for a few paltry pennies. Humanism had
made all men free and equal before the printed word.

THE GREAT DISCOVERIES

BUT NOW THAT PEOPLE HAD BROKEN THROUGH THE BONDS OF THEIR NARROW MEDIÆVAL LIMITATIONS, THEY HAD TO HAVE MORE ROOM FOR THEIR WANDERINGS. THE EUROPEAN WORLD HAD GROWN TOO SMALL FOR THEIR AMBITIONS. IT WAS THE TIME OF THE GREAT VOYAGES OF DISCOVERY

THE Crusades had been a lesson in the liberal art of travelling. But very few people had ever ventured beyond the well-known beaten track which led from Venice to Jaffe. In the thirteenth century the Polo brothers, merchants of Venice, had wandered across the great Mongolian desert and after climbing mountains as high as the moon, they had found their way to the court of the great Khan of Cathay, the mighty emperor of China. The son of one of the Polos, by the name of Marco, had written a book about their adventures, which covered a period of more than twenty years. The astonished world had gaped at his descriptions of the golden towers of the strange island of Zipangu, which was his Italian way of spelling Japan. Many people had wanted to go east, that they might find this gold-land and grow rich. But the trip was too far and too dangerous and so they stayed at home.

Of course, there was always the possibility of making the

voyage by sea. But the sea was very unpopular in the Middle Ages and for many very good reasons. In the first place, ships were very small. The vessels on which Magellan made his famous trip around the world, which lasted many years, were not as large as a modern ferryboat. They carried from twenty to fifty men, who lived in dingy quarters (too low to allow any of them to stand up straight) and the sailors were obliged to

MARCO POLO

eat poorly cooked food as the kitchen arrangements were very bad and no fire could be made whenever the weather was the least bit rough. The mediæval world knew how to pickle herring and how to dry fish. But there were no canned goods and fresh vegetables were never seen on the bill of fare as soon as the coast had been left behind. Water was carried in small barrels. It soon became stale and then tasted of rotten wood and iron rust and was full of slimy growing things. As the people of the Middle Ages knew nothing about microbes

(Roger Bacon, the learned monk of the thirteenth century seems to have suspected their existence, but he wisely kept his discovery to himself) they often drank unclean water and sometimes the whole crew died of typhoid fever. Indeed the mortality on board the ships of the earliest navigators was terrible. Of the two hundred sailors who in the year 1519 left Seville to accompany Magellan on his famous voyage around the world, only eighteen returned. As late as the seventeenth century when there was a brisk trade between western Europe and the Indies, a mortality of 40 percent was nothing unusual for a trip from Amsterdam to Batavia and back. The greater part of these victims died of scurvy, a disease which is caused by lack of fresh vegetables and which affects the gums and poisons the blood until the patient dies of sheer exhaustion.

Under those circumstances you will understand that the sea did not attract the best elements of the population. Famous discoverers like Magellan and Columbus and Vasco da Gama travelled at the head of crews that were almost entirely composed of ex-jailbirds, future murderers and pickpockets out of a job.

These navigators certainly deserve our admiration for the courage and the pluck with which they accomplished their hopeless tasks in the face of difficulties of which the people of our own comfortable world can have no conception. Their ships were leaky. The rigging was clumsy. Since the middle of the thirteenth century they had possessed some sort of a compass (which had come to Europe from China by way of Arabia and the Crusades) but they had very bad and incorrect maps. They set their course by God and by guess. If luck was with them they returned after one or two or three years. In the other case, their bleached bones remained behind on some lonely beach. But they were true pioneers. They gambled with luck. Life to them was a glorious adventure. And all the suffering, the thirst and the hunger and the pain were forgotten when their eyes beheld the dim outlines of a new coast or the placid waters of an ocean that had lain forgotten since the beginning of time.

HOW THE WORLD GREW LARGER

Again I wish that I could make this book a thousand pages long. The subject of the early discoveries is so fascinating. But history, to give you a true idea of past times, should be like those etchings which Rembrandt used to make. It should cast a vivid light on certain important causes, on those which are best and greatest. All the rest should be left in the shadow or should be indicated by a few lines. And in this chapter I can only give you a short list of the most important discoveries.

Keep in mind that all during the fourteenth and fifteenth centuries the navigators were trying to accomplish just *one thing*—they wanted to find a comfortable and safe road to the empire of Cathay (China), to the island of Zipangu (Japan) and to those mysterious islands, where grew the spices which the mediæval world had come to like since the days of the Crusades, and which people needed in those days before the introduction of cold storage, when meat and fish spoiled very quickly and could only be eaten after a liberal sprinkling of pepper or nutmeg.

The Venetians and the Genoese had been the great navigators of the Mediterranean, but the honour for exploring the coast of the Atlantic goes to the Portuguese. Spain and Portugal were full of that patriotic energy which their age-old struggle against the Moorish invaders had developed. Such energy, once it exists, can easily be forced into new channels. In the thirteenth century, King Alphonso III had conquered the kingdom of Algarve in the southwestern corner of the Spanish peninsula and had added it to his dominions. In the next century, the Portuguese had turned the tables on the Mohammedans, had crossed the straits of Gibraltar and had taken possession of Ceuta, opposite the Arabic city of Ta'Rifa (a word which in Arabic means "inventory" and which by way of the Spanish language has come down to us as "tariff,") and Tangiers, which became the capital of an African addition to Algarve.

They were ready to begin their career as explorers.

In the year 1415, Prince Henry, known as Henry the

Navigator, the son of John I of Portugal and Philippa, the daughter of John of Gaunt (about whom you can read in Richard II, a play by William Shakespeare) began to make preparations for the systematic exploration of northwestern Africa. Before this, that hot and sandy coast had been visited by the Phœnicians and by the Norsemen, who remembered it as the home of the hairy "wild man" whom we have come to know as the gorilla. One after another, Prince Henry and his captains discovered the Canary Islands—re-discovered the island of Madeira which a century before had been visited by a Genoese ship, carefully charted the Azores which had been vaguely known to both the Portuguese and the Spaniards, and caught a glimpse of the mouth of the Senegal River on the west coast of Africa, which they supposed to be the western mouth of the Nile. At last, by the middle of the Fifteenth Century, they saw Cape Verde, or the Green Cape, and the Cape Verde Islands, which lie almost halfway between the coast of Africa and Brazil.

But Henry did not restrict himself in his investigations to the waters of the Ocean. He was Grand Master of the Order of Christ. This was a Portuguese continuation of the crusading order of the Templars which had been abolished by Pope Clement V in the year 1312 at the request of King Philip the Fair of France, who had improved the occasion by burning his own Templars at the stake and stealing all their possessions. Prince Henry used the revenues of the domains of his religious order to equip several expeditions which explored the hinterland of the Sahara and of the coast of Guinea.

But he was still very much a son of the Middle Ages and spent a great deal of time and wasted a lot of money upon a search for the mysterious "Prester John," the mythical Christian Priest who was said to be the Emperor of a vast empire "situated somewhere in the east." The story of this strange potentate had first been told in Europe in the middle of the twelfth century. For three hundred years people had tried to find "Prester John" and his descendants. Henry took part in the search.   Thirty years after his death, the riddle was solved.

In the year 1486 Bartholomew Diaz, trying to find the land

THE WORLD OF COLUMBUS

of Prester John by sea, had reached the southernmost point of Africa.   At first he called it the Storm Cape, on account of the strong winds which had prevented him from continuing his voyage toward the east, but the Lisbon pilots who understood the importance of this discovery in their quest for the India water route, changed the name into that of the Cape of Good Hope.

One year later, Pedro de Covilham, provided with letters of credit on the house of Medici, started upon a similar mission by land. He crossed the Mediterranean and after leaving Egypt, he travelled southward. He reached Aden, and from there, travelling through the waters of the Persian Gulf which few white men had seen since the days of Alexander the Great, eighteen centuries before, he visited Goa and Calicut on the coast of India where he got a great deal of news about the island of the Moon (Madagascar) which was supposed to lie halfway between Africa and India. Then he returned, paid a secret visit to Mecca and to Medina, crossed the Red Sea once more and in the year 1490 he discovered the realm of Prester John, who was no one less than the Black Negus (or King) of Abyssinia, whose ancestors had adopted Christianity in the fourth century, seven hundred years before the Christian missionaries had found their way to Scandinavia.

These many voyages had convinced the Portuguese geographers and cartographers that while the voyage to the Indies by an eastern sea-route was possible, it was by no means easy. Then there arose a great debate. Some people wanted to continue the explorations east of the Cape of Good Hope. Others said, "No, we must sail west across the Atlantic and then we shall reach Cathay."

Let us state right here that most intelligent people of that day were firmly convinced that the earth was not as flat as a pancake but was round. The Ptolemean system of the universe, invented and duly described by Claudius Ptolemy, the great Egyptian geographer, who had lived in the second century of our era, which had served the simple needs of the men of the Middle Ages, had long been discarded by the scientists of the Renaissance. They had accepted the doctrine of the Polish mathematician, Nicolaus Copernicus, whose studies had convinced him that the earth was one of a number of round planets which turned around the sun, a discovery which he did not venture to publish for thirty-six years (it was printed in 1543, the year of his death) from fear of the Holy Inquisition, a Papal court which had been established in the thirteenth century when the heresies of the Albigenses and the Waldenses in France and in Italy (very mild heresies of devoutly pious people who did not believe in private property and preferred to live in Christ-like poverty) had for a moment threatened the absolute power of the bishops of Rome. But the belief in the roundness of the earth was common among the nautical experts and, as I said, they were now debating the respective advantages of the eastern and the western routes.

Among the advocates of the western route was a Genoese mariner by the name of Cristoforo Colombo. He was the son of a wool merchant. He seems to have been a student at the University of Pavia where he specialised in mathematics and geometry. Then he took up his father's trade but soon we find him in Chios in the eastern Mediterranean travelling on business. Thereafter we hear of voyages to England but whether he went north in search of wool or as the captain of a ship we do not know. In February of the year 1477, Colombo (if we are to believe his own words) visited Iceland, but very likely he only got as far as the Faröe Islands which are cold enough in February to be mistaken for Iceland by any one. Here Colombo met the descendants of those brave Norsemen who in the tenth century had settled in Greenland and who had visited America in the eleventh century, when Leif's vessel had been blown to the coast of Vineland, or Labrador.

What had become of those far western colonies no one knew. The American colony of Thorfinn Karlsefne, the husband of the widow of Leif's brother Thorstein, founded in the year 1003, had been discontinued three years later on account of the hostility of the Esquimaux. As for Greenland, not a word had been heard from the settlers since the year 1440. Very likely the Greenlanders had all died of the Black Death, which had just killed half the people of Norway. However that might be, the tradition of a "vast land in the distant west" still survived among the people of the Faröe and Iceland, and

THE GREAT DISCOVERIES, WESTERN HEMISPHERE

Colombo must have heard of it. He gathered further information among the fishermen of the northern Scottish islands and then went to Portugal where he married the daughter of one of the captains who had served under Prince Henry the Navigator.

From that moment on (the year 1478) he devoted himself

THE GREAT DISCOVERIES, EASTERN HEMISPHERE

to the quest of the western route to the Indies. He sent his plans for such a voyage to the courts of Portugal and Spain. The Portuguese, who felt certain that they possessed a monopoly of the eastern route, would not listen to his plans. In Spain, Ferdinand of Aragon and Isabella of Castile, whose marriage in 1469 had made Spain into a single kingdom, were busy driving the Moors from their last stronghold, Granada. They had no money for risky expeditions. They needed every peseta for their soldiers.

Few people were ever forced to fight as desperately for their ideas as this brave Italian. But the story of Colombo (or Colon or Columbus, as we call him,) is too well known to bear repeating. The Moors surrendered Granada on the second of January of the year 1492. In the month of April of the same year, Columbus signed a contract with the King and Queen of Spain. On Friday, the 3rd of August, he left Palos with three little ships and a crew of 88 men, many of whom were criminals who had been offered indemnity of punishment if they joined the expedition. At two o'clock in the morning of Friday, the 12th of October, Columbus discovered land. On the fourth of January of the year 1493, Columbus waved farewell to the 44 men of the little fortress of La Navidad (none of whom was ever again seen alive) and returned homeward. By the middle of February he reached the Azores where the Portuguese threatened to throw him into gaol. On the fifteenth of March, 1493, the admiral reached Palos and together with his Indians (for he was convinced that he had discovered some outlying islands of the Indies and called the natives red Indians) he hastened to Barcelona to tell his faithful patrons that he had been successful and that the road to the gold and the silver of Cathay and Zipangu was at the disposal of their most Catholic Majesties.

Alas, Columbus never knew the truth. Towards the end of his life, on his fourth voyage, when he had touched the mainland of South America, he may have suspected that all was not well with his discovery. But he died in the firm belief that there was no solid continent between Europe and Asia and that he had found the direct route to China.

Meanwhile, the Portuguese, sticking to their eastern route,

had been more fortunate. In the year 1498, Vasco da Gama had been able to reach the coast of Malabar and return safely to Lisbon with a cargo of spice. In the year 1502 he had repeated the visit. But along the western route, the work of exploration had been most disappointing. In 1497 and 1498 John and Sebastian Cabot had tried to find a passage to Japan but they had seen nothing but the snowbound coasts and the rocks of Newfoundland, which had first been sighted by the Northmen, five centuries before. Amerigo Vespucci, a Florentine who became the Pilot Major of Spain, and who gave his name to our continent, had explored the coast of Brazil, but had found not a trace of the Indies.

In the year 1513, seven years after the death of Columbus, the truth at last began to dawn upon the geographers of Europe. Vasco Nuñez de Balboa had crossed the Isthmus of Panama, had climbed the famous peak in Darien, and had looked down upon a vast expanse of water which seemed to suggest the existence of another ocean.

Finally in the year 1519 a fleet of five small Spanish ships under command of the Portuguese navigator, Ferdinand de Magellan, sailed westward (and not eastward since that route, was absolutely in the hands of the Portuguese who allowed no competition) in search of the Spice Islands. Magellan crossed the Atlantic between Africa and Brazil and sailed southward. He reached a narrow channel between the southernmost point of Patagonia, the "land of the people with the big feet," and the Fire Island (so named on account of a fire, the only sign of the existence of natives, which the sailors watched one night). For almost five weeks the ships of Magellan were at the mercy of the terrible storms and blizzards which swept through the straits. A mutiny broke out among the sailors. Magellan suppressed it with terrible severity and sent two of his men on shore where they were left to repent of their sins at leisure. At last the storms quieted down, the channel broadened, and Magellan entered a new ocean. Its waves were quiet and placid. He called it the Peaceful Sea, the Mare Pacifico,

Then he continued in a western direction. He sailed for ninety-eight days without seeing land. His people almost perished from hunger and thirst and ate the rats that infested the ships, and when these were all gone they chewed pieces of sail to still their gnawing hunger.

In March of the year 1521 they saw land. Magellan called

MAGELLAN

it the land of the Ladrones (which means robbers) because the natives stole everything they could lay hands on. Then further westward to the Spice Islands!

Again land was sighted. A group of lonely islands. Magellan called them the Philippines, after Philip, the son of his master Charles V, the Philip II of unpleasant historical memory. At first Magellan was well received, but when he used the guns of his ships to make Christian converts he was killed by the aborigines, together with a number of his captains and sailors. The survivors burned one of the three remaining ships and continued their voyage. They found the Moluccas, the famous Spice Islands; they sighted Borneo and reached Tidoɪ. There, one of the two ships, too leaky to be of further use, remained behind with her crew. The "Vittoria," under Sebastian del Cano, crossed the Indian Ocean, missed seeing the northern coast of Australia (which was not discovered until the first half of the seventeenth century when ships of the Dutch East India Company explored this flat and inhospitable land), and after great hardships reached Spain.

This was the most notable of all voyages. It had taken three years. It had been accomplished at a great cost both of men and money. But it had established the fact that the earth was round and that the new lands discovered by Columbus were not a part of the Indies but a separate continent. From that time on, Spain and Portugal devoted all their energies to the development of their Indian and American trade. To prevent an armed conflict between the rivals, Pope Alexander VI (the only avowed heathen who was ever elected to this most holy office) had obligingly divided the world into two equal parts by a line of demarcation which followed the 50th degree of longitude west of Greenwich, the so-called division of Tordesillas of 1494. The Portuguese were to establish their colonies to the east of this line, the Spaniards were to have theirs to the west. This accounts for the fact that the entire American continent with the exception of Brazil became Spanish and that all of the Indies and most of Africa became Portuguese until the English and the Dutch colonists (who had no respect for Papal decisions) took these possessions away in the seventeenth and eighteenth centuries.

When news of the discovery of Columbus reached the Rialto of Venice, the Wall street of the Middle Ages, there was a terrible panic. Stocks and bonds went down 40 and 50 percent. After a short while, when it appeared that Columbus had failed to find the road to Cathay, the Venetian merchants

A NEW WORLD

recovered from their fright. But the voyages of da Gama and Magellan proved the practical possibilities of an eastern water-route to the Indies. Then the rulers of Genoa and Venice, the two great commercial centres of the Middle Ages and the Renaissance, began to be sorry that they had refused to listen to Columbus. But it was too late. Their Mediterranean became an inland sea. The overland trade to the Indies and China dwindled to insignificant proportions. The old days of Italian glory were gone. The Atlantic became the new centre of commerce and therefore the centre of civilisation. It has remained so ever since.

See how strangely civilisation has progressed since those carly days, fifty centuries before, when the inhabitants of the Valley of the Nile began to keep a written record of history, From the river Nile, it went to Mesopotamia, the land be· tween the rivers. Then came the turn of Crete and Greece and Rome. An inland sca became the centre of trade and thc cities along the Mediterranean were the home of art and science and philosophy and learning. In the sixteenth century it moved westward once more and made the countrics that border upon the Atlantic become the masters of thc earth.

There are those who say that the world war and the suicide of the great European nations has greatly diminished the importance of the Atlantic Ocean. They expect to see civilisation cross the American continent and find a new home in the Pacific. But I doubt this.

The westward trip was accompanied by a steady increase in the size of ships and a broadening of the knowledge of the navigators. The flat-bottomed vessels of the Nile and the Euphrates were replaced by the sailing vessels of the Phœnicians, the Ægeans, the Greeks, the Carthaginians and the Romans. These in turn were discarded for the square rigged vessels of the Portuguese and the Spaniards. And the latter were driven from the ocean by the full-rigged craft of the English and the Dutch.

At present, however, civilisation no longer depends upon

ships.   Aircraft has taken and will continue to take the place of the sailing vessel and the steamer.   The next centre of civilisation will depend upon the development of aircraft and water power.   And the sea once more shall be the undisturbed home of the little fishes, who once upon a time shared their deep residence with the earliest ancestors of the human race.

BUDDHA AND CONFUCIUS

CONCERNING BUDDHA AND CONFUCIUS

THE discoveries of the Portuguese and the Spaniards had brought the Christians of western Europe into close contact with the people of India and of China. They knew of course that Christianity was not the only religion on this earth. There were the Mohammedans and the heathenish tribes of northern Africa who worshipped sticks and stones and dead trees. But in India and in China the Christian conquerors found new millions who had never heard of Christ and who did not want to hear of Him, because they thought their own religion, which was thousands of years old, much better than that of the West As this is a story of mankind and not an exclusive history of the people of Europe and our western hemisphere, you ought to know something of two men whose teaching and whose example continue to influence the actions and the thoughts of the majority of our fellow-travellers on this earth.

In India, Buddha was recognised as the great religious teacher. His history is an interesting one. He was born in the Sixth Century before the birth of Christ, within sight of the mighty Himalaya Mountains, where four hundred years before Zarathustra (or Zoroaster), the first of the great leaders of the Aryan race (the name which the Eastern branch of the Indo-European race had given to itself), had taught his people to regard life as a continuous struggle between Ahriman, and Ormuzd, the Gods of Evil and Good. Buddha's father was Suddhodana, a mighty chief among the tribe of the Sakiyas. His mother, Maha Maya, was the daughter of a neighbouring king. She had been married when she was a very young girl. But many moons had passed beyond the distant ridge of hills and still her husband was without an heir who should rule his lands after him. At last, when she was fifty years old, her day came and she went forth that she might be among her own people when her baby should come into this world.

It was a long trip to the land of the Koliyans, where Maha Maya had spent her earliest years. One night she was resting among the cool trees of the garden of Lumbini. There her son was born. He was given the name of Siddhartha, but we know him as Buddha, which means the Enlightened One.

In due time, Siddhartha grew up to be a handsome young prince and when he was nineteen years old, he was married to his cousin Yasodhara. During the next ten years he lived far away from all pain and all suffering, behind the protecting walls of the royal palace, awaiting the day when he should succeed his father as King of the Sakiyas.

But it happened that when he was thirty years old, he drove outside of the palace gates and saw a man who was old and worn out with labour and whose weak limbs could hardly carry the burden of life. Siddhartha pointed him out to his coachman, Channa, but Channa answered that there were lots of poor people in this world and that one more or less did not matter. The young prince was very sad but he did not say anything and went back to live with his wife and his father and his mother and tried to be happy. A little while later he left the palace a second time. His carriage met a man who suffered from a terrible disease. Siddhartha asked Channa what had been the cause of this man's suffering, but the coachman answered that there were many sick people in this world and that such things could not be helped and did not matter very much. The young prince was very sad when he heard this but again he returned to his people.

A few weeks passed. One evening Siddhartha ordered his

THE THREE GREAT RELIGION

HERE VERY FEW PEOPLE LIVE. HEATHEN

SIBERIA

HEATHEN

SIBERIA

HEATHEN

HEATHEN

HIMALAYA MTS.

VINDHYA MTS. HERE

HERE CONFUCIUS WAS BORN

CHINA

BUDDHISTS

BUDDHA WAS BORN

BRAHMANS

INDIA

Japan

Philippines

MOHAMMEDANS SINCE THE 15TH CENTURY

BUDDHIST

CHRISTIANS

HERE CHRIST WAS BORN

MOHAMMEDANS

MECCA

ARABIA

HEATHEN

THE RELIGIONS OF THE OLD WORLD

carriage in order to go to the river and bathe. Suddenly his horses were frightened by the sight of a dead man whose rotting body lay sprawling in the ditch beside the road. The young prince, who had never been allowed to see such things, was frightened, but Channa told him not to mind such trifles. The world was full of dead people. It was the rule of life that all things must come to an end. Nothing was eternal. The grave awaited us all and there was no escape.

That evening, when Siddhartha returned to his home, he was received with music. While he was away his wife had given birth to a son. The people were delighted because now they knew that there was an heir to the throne and they celebrated the event by the beating of many drums. Siddhartha, however, did not share their joy. The curtain of life had been lifted and he had learned the horror of man's existence. The sight of death and suffering followed him like a terrible dream.

That night the moon was shining brightly. Siddhartha woke up and began to think of many things. Never again could he be happy until he should have found a solution to the riddle of existence. He decided to find it far away from all those whom he loved. Softly he went into the room where Yasodhara was sleeping with her baby. Then he called for his faithful Channa and told him to follow.

Together the two men went into the darkness of the night, one to find rest for his soul, the other to be a faithful servant unto a beloved master.

The people of India among whom Siddhartha wandered for many years were just then in a state of change. Their ancestors, the native Indians, had been conquered without great difficulty by the war-like Aryans (our distant cousins) and thereafter the Aryans had been the rulers and masters of tens of millions of docile little brown men. To maintain themselves in the seat of the mighty, they had divided the population into different classes and gradually a system of "caste" of the most rigid sort had been enforced upon the natives. The descendants of the Indo-European conquerors belonged to the highest "caste," the class of warriors and nobles. Next came the caste of the priests. Below these followed the peasants and the business men. The ancient natives, however, who were called Pariahs, formed a class of despised and miserable slaves and never could hope to be anything else.

Even the religion of the people was a matter of caste. The old Indo-Europeans, during their thousands of years of wandering, had met with many strange adventures. These had been collected in a book called the Veda. The language of this book was called Sanskrit, and it was closely related to the different languages of the European continent, to Greek and Latin and Russian and German and two-score others. The three highest castes were allowed to read these holy scriptures. The Pariah, however, the despised member of the lowest caste, was not permitted to know its contents. Woe to the man of noble or priestly caste who should teach a Pariah to study the sacred volume!

The majority of the Indian people, therefore, lived in misery. Since this planet offered them very little joy, salvation from suffering must be found elsewhere. They tried to derive a little consolation from meditation upon the bliss of their future existence.

Brahma, the all-creator who was regarded by the Indian people as the supreme ruler of life and death, was worshipped as the highest ideal of perfection. To become like Brahma, to lose all desires for riches and power, was recognised as the most exalted purpose of existence. Holy thoughts were regarded as more important than holy deeds, and many people went into the desert and lived upon the leaves of trees and starved their bodies that they might feed their souls with the glorious contemplation of the splendours of Brahma, the Wise, the Good and the Merciful.

Siddhartha, who had often observed these solitary wanderers who were seeking the truth far away from the turmoil of the cities and the villages, decided to follow their example. He cut his hair. He took his pearls and his rubies and sent them back to his family with a message of farewell, which the ever faithful Channa carried. Without a single follower, the young prince then moved into the wilderness.

Soon the fame of his holy conduct spread among the mountains. Five young men came to him and asked that they might be allowed to listen to his words of wisdom. He agreed to be their master if they would follow him. They consented, and he took them into the hills and for six years he taught them all he knew amidst the lonely peaks of the Vindhya Mountains. But at the end of this period of study, he felt that he was still far from perfection. The world that he had left continued to tempt him. He now asked that his pupils leave him and then he fasted for forty-nine days and nights, sitting upon the roots of an old tree. At last he received his reward. In the dusk of the fiftieth evening, Brahma revealed himself to his faithful servant. From that moment on, Siddhartha was called Buddha and he was revered as the Enlightened One who had come to save men from their unhappy mortal fate.

The last forty-five years of his life, Buddha spent within the valley of the Ganges River, teaching his simple lesson of submission and meekness unto all men. In the year 488 before our era, he died, full of years and beloved by millions of people. He had not preached his doctrines for the benefit of a single class. Even the lowest Pariah might call himself his disciple.

This, however, did not please the nobles and the priests and the merchants who did their best to destroy a creed which recognised the equality of all living creatures and offered men the hope of a second life (a reincarnation) under happier circumstances. As soon as they could, they encouraged the people of India to return to the ancient doctrines of the Brahmin creed with its fasting and its tortures of the sinful body. But Buddhism could not be destroyed. Slowly the disciples of the Enlightened One wandered across the valleys of the Himalayas, and moved into China. They crossed the Yellow Sea and preached the wisdom of their master unto the people of Japan, and they faithfully obeyed the will of their great master, who had forbidden them to use force. To-day more people recognise Buddha as their teacher than ever before and their

BUDDHA GOES INTO THE MOUNTAINS

number surpasses that of the combined followers of Christ and Mohammed.

As for Confucius, the wise old man of the Chinese, his story is a simple one. He was born in the year 550 B.C. He led a quiet, dignified and uneventful life at a time when China was without a strong central government and when the Chinese people were at the mercy of bandits and robber-barons who went from city to city, pillaging and stealing and murdering and turning the busy plains of northern and central China into a wilderness of starving people.

Confucius, who loved his people, tried to save them. He did not have much faith in the use of violence. He was a very peaceful person. He did not think that he could make people over by giving them a lot of new laws. He knew that the only possible salvation would come from a change of heart, and he set out upon the seemingly hopeless task of changing the character of his millions of fellow men who inhabited the wide plains of eastern Asia. The Chinese had never been much interested in religion as we understand that word. They believed in devils and spooks as most primitive people do. But they had no prophets and recognised no "revealed truth." Confucius is almost the only one among the great moral leaders who did not see visions, who did not proclaim himself as the messenger of a divine power; who did not, at some time or another, claim that he was inspired by voices from above.

He was just a very sensible and kindly man, rather given to lonely wanderings and melancholy tunes upon his faithful flute. He asked for no recognition. He did not demand that any one should follow him or worship him. He reminds us of the ancient Greek philosophers, especially those of the Stoic School, men who believed in right living and righteous thinking without the hope of a reward but simply for the peace of the soul that comes with a good conscience.

Confucius was a very tolerant man. He went out of his way to visit Lao-Tse, the other great Chinese leader and the founder of a philosophic system called "Taoism," which was merely an early Chinese version of the Golden Rule.

Confucius bore no hatred to any one. He taught the virtue of supreme self-possession. A person of real worth, according to the teaching of Confucius, did not allow himself to be ruffled by anger and suffered whatever fate brought him with the resignation of those sages who understand that everything which happens, in one way or another, is meant for the best.

At first he had only a few students. Gradually the number increased. Before his death, in the year 478 B.C., several of the kings and the princes of China confessed themselves his disciples. When Christ was born in Bethlehem, the philosophy of Confucius had already become a part of the mental make-up of most Chinamen. It has continued to influence their lives ever since. Not however in its pure, original form. Most religions change as time goes on. Christ preached humility and meekness and absence from worldly ambitions, but fifteen centuries after Golgotha, the head of the Christian church was spending millions upon the erection of a building that bore little relation to the lonely stable of Bethlehem.

Lao-Tse taught the Golden Rule, and in less than three centuries the ignorant masses had made him into a real and very cruel God and had buried his wise commandments under a rubbish-heap of superstition which made the lives of the average Chinese one long series of frights and fears and horrors.

Confucius had shown his students the beauties of honouring their Father and their Mother. They soon began to be more interested in the memory of their departed parents than in the happiness of their children and their grandchildren. Deliberately they turned their backs upon the future and tried to peer into the vast darkness of the past. The worship of the ancestors became a positive religious system. Rather than disturb a cemetary situated upon the sunny and fertile side of a mountain, they would plant their rice and wheat upon the barren rocks of the other slope where nothing could possibly grow. And they preferred hunger and famine to the desecration of the ancestral grave.

At the same time the wise words of Confucius never quite lost their hold upon the increasing millions of eastern Asia.

1300 B C
MOSES
THE LEADER OF
THE JEWS

1000 B C
ZARATHUSTRA
THE LEADER OF
THE ARYAN PEOPLES

600 B.C
BUDDHA
THE ENLIGHTENED ONE
OF THE INDIAN PEOPLE

500 B.C
CONFUCIUS
THE WISE OLD MAN
OF THE CHINESE

400 B.C
THE GREAT GREEK
PHILOSOPHERS

A D 30
JESUS CHRIST

A D 622
MOHAMMED
THE PROPHET OF THE
ARABIAN DESERT

THE GREAT MORAL LEADERS

Confucianism, with its profound sayings and shrewd observations, added a touch of common-sense philosophy to the soul of every Chinaman and influenced his entire life, whether he was a simple laundryman in a steaming basement or the ruler of vast provinces who dwelt behind the high walls of a secluded palace.

In the sixteenth century the enthusiastic but rather uncivilised Christians of the western world came face to face with the older creeds of the East. The early Spaniards and Portuguese looked upon the peaceful statues of Buddha and contemplated the venerable pictures of Confucius and did not in the least know what to make of those worthy prophets with their far-away smile. They came to the easy conclusion that these strange divinities were just plain devils who represented something idolatrous and heretical and did not deserve the respect of the true sons of the Church. Whenever the spirit of Buddha or Confucius seemed to interfere with the trade in spices and silks, the Europeans attacked the "evil influence" with bullets and grapeshot. That system had certain very definite disadvantages. It has left us an unpleasant heritage of ill-will which promises little good for the immediate future.

THE REFORMATION

THE PROGRESS OF THE HUMAN RACE IS BEST
COMPARED TO A GIGANTIC PENDULUM
WHICH FOREVER SWINGS FORWARD AND
BACKWARD. THE RELIGIOUS INDIFFER-
ENCE AND THE ARTISTIC AND LITERARY
ENTHUSIASM OF THE RENAISSANCE
WERE FOLLOWED BY THE ARTISTIC AND
LITERARY INDIFFERENCE AND THE RE-
LIGIOUS ENTHUSIASM OF THE REFORMA-
TION

OF course you have heard of the Reformation. You think
of a small but courageous group of pilgrims who crossed the
ocean to have "freedom of religious worship." Vaguely in the
course of time (and more especially in our Protestant countries) the Reformation has come to stand for the idea of
"liberty of thought." Martin Luther is represented as the
leader of the vanguard of progress. But when history is
something more than a series of flattering speeches addressed
to our own glorious ancestors, when to use the words of the
German historian Ranke, we try to discover what "actually
happened," then much of the past is seen in a very different
light.

Few things in human life are either entirely good or entirely
bad. Few things are either black or white. It is the duty of

the honest chronicler to give a true account of all the good and bad sides of every historical event. It is very difficult to do this because we all have our personal likes and dislikes. But we ought to try and be as fair as we can be, and must not allow our prejudices to influence us too much.

Take my own case as an example. I grew up in the very Protestant centre of a very Protestant country. I never saw any Catholics until I was about twelve years old. Then I felt very uncomfortable when I met them. I was a little bit afraid. I knew the story of the many thousand people who had been burned and hanged and quartered by the Spanish Inquisition when the Duke of Alba tried to cure the Dutch people of their Lutheran and Calvinistic heresies. All that was very real to me. It seemed to have happened only the day before. It might occur again. There might be another Saint Bartholomew's night, and poor little me would be slaughtered in my nightie and my body would be thrown out of the window, as had happened to the noble Admiral de Coligny.

Much later I went to live for a number of years in a Catholic country. I found the people much pleasanter and much more tolerant and quite as intelligent as my former countrymen. To my great surprise, I began to discover that there was a Catholic side to the Reformation, quite as much as a Protestant.

Of course the good people of the sixteenth and seventeenth centuries, who actually lived through the Reformation, did not see things that way. They were always right and their enemy was always wrong. It was a question of hang or be hanged, and both sides preferred to do the hanging. Which was no more than human and for which they deserve no blame.

When we look at the world as it appeared in the year 1500, an easy date to remember, and the year in which the Emperor Charles V was born, this is what we see. The feudal disorder of the Middle Ages has given way before the order of a number of highly centralised kingdoms. The most powerful of all sovereigns is the great Charles, then a baby in a cradle. He is the grandson of Ferdinand and Isabella and of Maximilian of Habsburg, the last of the mediæval knights, and of his wife Mary, the daughter of Charles the Bold, the ambitious Burgundian duke who had made successful war upon France, but had been killed by the independent Swiss peasants. The child Charles, therefore, has fallen heir to the greater part of the map, to all the lands of his parents, grandparents, uncles, cousins and aunts in Germany, in Austria, in Holland, in Belgium, in Italy, and in Spain, together with all their colonies in Asia, Africa and America. By a strange irony of fate, he has been born in Ghent, in that same castle of the counts of Flanders, which the Germans used as a prison during their recent occupation of Belgium, and although a Spanish king and a German emperor, he receives the training of a Fleming.

As his father is dead (poisoned, so people say, but this is never proved), and his mother has lost her mind (she is travelling through her domains with the coffin containing the body of her departed husband), the child is left to the strict discipline of his Aunt Margaret. Forced to rule Germans and Italians and Spaniards and a hundred strange races, Charles grows up a Fleming, a faithful son of the Catholic Church, but quite averse to religious intolerance. He is rather lazy, both as a boy and as a man. But fate condemns him to rule the world when the world is in a turmoil of religious fervour. Forever he is speeding from Madrid to Innsbrück and from Bruges to Vienna. He loves peace and quiet and he is always at war. At the age of fifty-five, we see him turn his back upon the human race in utter disgust at so much hate and so much stupidity. Three years later he dies, a very tired and disappointed man.

So much for Charles the Emperor. How about the Church, the second great power in the world? The Church has changed greatly since the early days of the Middle Ages, when it started out to conquer the heathen and show them the advantages of a pious and righteous life. In the first place, the Church has grown too rich. The Pope is no longer the shepherd of a flock of humble Christians. He lives in a vast palace and surrounds himself with artists and musicians and famous literary men.

His churches and chapels are covered with new pictures in which the saints look more like Greek Gods than is strictly necessary. He divides his time unevenly between affairs of state and art. The affairs of state take ten percent of his time. The other ninety percent goes to an active interest in Roman statues, recently discovered Greek vases, plans for a new summer home, the rehearsal of a new play. The Archbishops and the Cardinals follow the example of their Pope. The Bishops try to imitate the Archbishops. The village priests, however, have remained faithful to their duties. They keep themselves aloof from the wicked world and the heathenish love of beauty and pleasure. They stay away from the monasteries where the monks seem to have forgotten their ancient vows of simplicity and poverty and live as happily as they dare without causing too much of a public scandal.

Finally, there are the common people. They are much better off than they have ever been before. They are more prosperous, they live in better houses, their children go to better schools, their cities are more beautiful than before, their firearms have made them the equal of their old enemies, the robber-barons, who for centuries have levied such heavy taxes upon their trade. So much for the chief actors in the Reformation.

Now let us see what the Renaissance has done to Europe, and then you will understand how the revival of learning and art was bound to be followed by a revival of religious interests. The Renaissance began in Italy. From there it spread to France. It was not quite successful in Spain, where five hundred years of warfare with the Moors had made the people very narrow minded and very fanatical in all religious matters. The circle had grown wider and wider, but once the Alps had been crossed, the Renaissance had suffered a change.

The people of northern Europe, living in a very different climate, had an outlook upon life which contrasted strangely with that of their southern neighbours. The Italians lived out in the open, under a sunny sky. It was easy for them to laugh and to sing and to be happy. The Germans. the Dutch, the

English, the Swedes, spent most of their time indoors, listening to the rain beating on the closed windows of their comfortable little houses. They did not laugh quite so much. They took everything more seriously. They were forever conscious of their immortal souls and they did not like to be funny about matters which they considered holy and sacred. The "humanistic" part of the Renaissance, the books, the studies of ancient authors, the grammar and the text-books, interested them greatly. But the general return to the old pagan civilisation of Greece and Rome, which was one of the chief results of the Renaissance in Italy, filled their hearts with horror.

But the Papacy and the College of Cardinals was almost entirely composed of Italians and they had turned the Church into a pleasant club where people discussed art and music and the theatre, but rarely mentioned religion. Hence the split between the serious north and the more civilised but easy-going and indifferent south was growing wider and wider all the time and nobody seemed to be aware of the danger that threatened the Church.

There were a few minor reasons which will explain why the Reformation took place in Germany rather than in Sweden or England. The Germans bore an ancient grudge against Rome. The endless quarrels between Emperor and Pope had caused much mutual bitterness. In the other European countries where the government rested in the hands of a strong king, the ruler had often been able to protect his subjects against the greed of the priests. In Germany, where a shadowy emperor ruled a turbulent crowd of little princelings, the good burghers were more directly at the mercy of their bishops and prelates. These dignitaries were trying to collect large sums of money for the benefit of those enormous churches which were a hobby of the Popes of the Renaissance. The Germans felt that they were being mulcted and quite naturally they did not like it.

And then there is the rarely mentioned fact that Germany was the home of the printing press. In northern Europe books were cheap and the Bible was no longer a mysterious manuscript owned and explained by the priest. It was a household book of many families where Latin was understood by the father and by the children. Whole families began to read it, which was against the law of the Church. They discovered that the priests were telling them many things which, according to the original text of the Holy Scriptures, were somewhat different. This caused doubt. People began to ask questions. And questions, when they cannot be answered, often cause a great deal of trouble.

The attack began when the humanists of the North opened fire upon the monks. In their heart of hearts they still had too much respect and reverence for the Pope to direct their sallies against his Most Holy Person. But the lazy, ignorant monks, living behind the sheltering walls of their rich monasteries, offered rare sport.

The leader in this warfare, curiously enough, was a very faithful son of the church. Gerard Gerardzoon, or Desiderius Erasmus, as he is usually called, was a poor boy, born in Rotterdam in Holland, and educated at the same Latin school of Deventer from which Thomas à Kempis had graduated. He had become a priest and for a time he had lived in a monastery. He had travelled a great deal and knew whereof he wrote. When he began his career as a public pamphleteer (he would have been called an editorial writer in our day) the world was greatly amused at an anonymous series of letters which had just appeared under the title of "Letters of Obscure Men." In these letters, the general stupidity and arrogance of the monks of the late Middle Ages was exposed in a strange German-Latin doggerel which reminds one of our modern limericks. Erasmus himself was a very learned and serious scholar, who knew both Latin and Greek and gave us the first reliable version of the New Testament, which he translated into Latin together with a corrected edition of the original Greek text. But he believed with Horace, the Roman poet, that nothing prevents us from "stating the truth with a smile upon our lips."

In the year 1500, while visiting Sir Thomas More in England, he took a few weeks off and wrote a funny little book, called the "Praise of Folly," in which he attacked the monks and their credulous followers with that most dangerous of all weapons, humor. The booklet was the best seller of the sixteenth century. It was translated into almost every language and it made people pay attention to those other books of Erasmus in which he advocated reform of the many abuses of the church and appealed to his fellow humanists to help him in his task of bringing about a great rebirth of the Christian faith.

But nothing came of these excellent plans. Erasmus was too reasonable and too tolerant to please most of the enemies of the church. They were waiting for a leader of a more robust nature.

LUTHER TRANSLATES
THE BIBLE

He came, and his name was Martin Luther.

Luther was a North-German peasant with a first-class brain and possessed of great personal courage. He was ordained an Augustinian friar and was an important figure in the Saxon province of the Order of Saint Augustine. Then he became a college professor at the theological school of Wittenberg and began to explain the scriptures to the indifferent ploughboys of his Saxon home. He had a lot of spare time and this he used to study the original texts of the Old and New Testaments. Soon he began to see the great difference which existed between the words of Christ and those that were preached by the Popes and the Bishops.

In the year 1511, he visited Rome on official business. Alexander VI, of the family of Borgia, who had enriched himself for the benefit of his son and daughter, was dead. But his

successor, Julius II, a man of irreproachable personal character, was spending most of his time fighting and building and
did not impress this serious minded German theologian with
his piety. Luther returned to Wittenberg a much disappointed
man. But worse was to follow.

The gigantic church of St. Peter which Pope Julius had
wished upon his innocent successors, although only half begun,
was already in need of repair. Alexander VI had spent every
penny of the Papal treasury. Leo X, who succeeded Julius
in the year 1513, was on the verge of bankruptcy. He reverted
to an old method of raising ready cash. He began to sell
"indulgences." An indulgence was a piece of parchment which
in return for a certain sum of money, promised a sinner a decrease of the time which he would have to spend in purgatory.
It was a perfectly correct thing according to the creed of the
late Middle Ages. Since the church had the power to forgive
the sins of those who truly repented before they died, the
church also had the right to shorten, through its intercession
with the Saints, the time during which the soul must be purified in the shadowy realms of Purgatory.

It was unfortunate that these Indulgences must be sold for
money. But they offered an easy form of revenue and besides,
those who were too poor to pay, received theirs for nothing.

Now it happened in the year 1517 that the exclusive territory for the sale of indulgences in Saxony was given to a
Dominican monk by the name of Johan Tetzel. Brother
Johan was a hustling salesman. To tell the truth he was a
little too eager. His business methods outraged the pious
people of the little duchy. And Luther, who was an honest
fellow, got so angry that he did a rash thing. On the 31st of
October of the year 1517, he went to the court church and upon
the doors thereof he posted a sheet of paper with ninety-five
statements (or theses), attacking the sale of indulgences.
These statements had been written in Latin. Luther had no
intention of starting a riot. He was not a revolutionist. He
objected to the institution of the Indulgences and he wanted his
fellow professors to know what he thought about them. But

this was still a private affair of the clerical and professorial world and there was no appeal to the prejudices of the community of laymen.

Unfortunately, at that moment when the whole world had begun to take an interest in the religious affairs of the day, it was utterly impossible to discuss anything, without at once creating a serious mental disturbance. In less than two months, all Europe was discussing the ninety-five theses of the Saxon monk. Every one must take sides. Every obscure little theologian must print his own opinion. The papal authorities began to be alarmed. They ordered the Wittenberg professor to proceed to Rome and give an account of his action. Luther wisely remembered what had happened to Huss. He stayed in Germany and he was punished with excommunication. Luther burned the papal bull in the presence of an admiring multitude and from that moment, peace between himself and the Pope was no longer possible.

Without any desire on his part, Luther had become the leader of a vast army of discontented Christians. German patriots like Ulrich von Hutten, rushed to his defence. The students of Wittenberg and Erfurt and Leipzig offered to defend him should the authorities try to imprison him. The Elector of Saxony reassured the eager young men. No harm would befall Luther as long as he stayed on Saxon ground.

All this happened in the year 1520. Charles V was twenty years old and as the ruler of half the world, was forced to remain on pleasant terms with the Pope. He sent out calls for a Diet or general assembly in the good city of Worms on the Rhine and commanded Luther to be present and give an account of his extraordinary behaviour. Luther, who now was the national hero of the Germans, went. He refused to take back a single word of what he had ever written or said. His conscience was controlled only by the word of God. He would live and die for his conscience.

The Diet of Worms, after due deliberation, declared Luther an outlaw before God and man, and forbade all Germans to give him shelter or food or drink, or to read a single word of the books which the dastardly heretic had written. But the great reformer was in no danger. By the majority of the Germans of the north the edict was denounced as a most unjust and outrageous document. For greater safety, Luther was hidden in the Wartburg, a castle belonging to the Elector of Saxony, and there he defied all papal authority by translating the entire Bible into the German language, that all the people might read and know the word of God for themselves.

By this time, the Reformation was no longer a spiritual and religious affair. Those who hated the beauty of the modern church building used this period of unrest to attack and destroy what they did not like because they did not understand it. Impoverished knights tried to make up for past losses by grabbing the territory which belonged to the monasteries. Discontented princes made use of the absence of the Emperor to increase their own power. The starving peasants, following the leadership of half-crazy agitators, made the best of the opportunity and attacked the castles of their masters and plundered and murdered and burned with the zeal of the old Crusaders.

A veritable reign of disorder broke loose throughout the Empire. Some princes became Protestants (as the "protesting" adherents of Luther were called) and persecuted their Catholic subjects. Others remained Catholic and hanged their Protestant subjects. The Diet of Speyer of the year 1526 tried to settle this difficult question of allegiance by ordering that "the subjects should all be of the same religious denomination as their princes." This turned Germany into a checkerboard of a thousand hostile little duchies and principalities and created a situation which prevented the normal political growth for hundreds of years.

In February of the year 1546 Luther died and was put to rest in the same church where twenty-nine years before he had proclaimed his famous objections to the sale of Indulgences. In less than thirty years, the indifferent, joking and laughing world of the Renaissance had been transformed into the arguing, quarrelling, back-biting, debating-society of the

Reformation. The universal spiritual empire of the Popes came to a sudden end and the whole of western Europe was turned into a battle-field, where Protestants and Catholics killed each other for the greater glory of certain theological doctrines which are as incomprehensible to the present generation as the mysterious inscriptions of the ancient Etruscans.

RELIGIOUS WARFARE

THE AGE OF THE GREAT RELIGIOUS
CONTROVERSIES

THE sixteenth and seventeenth centuries were the age of religious controversy.

If you will notice you will find that almost everybody around you is forever "talking economics" and discussing wages and hours of labor and strikes in their relation to the life of the community, for that is the main topic of interest of our own time.

The poor little children of the year 1600 or 1650 fared worse. They never heard anything but "religion." Their heads were filled with "predestination," "transubstantiation," "free will," and a hundred other queer words, expressing obscure points of "the true faith," whether Catholic or Protestant. According to the desire of their parents they were baptised Catholics or Lutherans or Calvinists or Zwinglians or Anabaptists. They learned their theology from the Augsburg catechism, composed by Luther, or from the "institutes of Christianity," written by Calvin, or they mumbled the Thirty-Nine Articles of Faith which were printed in the English Book of Common Prayer, and they were told that these alone represented the "True Faith."

They heard of the wholesale theft of church property perpetrated by King Henry VIII, the much-married monarch of England, who made himself the supreme head of the English

262

church, and assumed the old papal rights of appointing bishops and priests. They had a nightmare whenever some one mentioned the Holy Inquisition, with its dungeons and its many torture chambers, and they were treated to equally horrible stories of how a mob of outraged Dutch Protestants had got hold of a dozen defenceless old priests and hanged them for the sheer pleasure of killing those who professed a different faith. It was unfortunate that the two contending parties were so equally matched. Otherwise the struggle would have come to a quick solution. Now it dragged on for eight generations, and it grew so complicated that I can only tell you the most i m p o r t a n t details, and must ask you to get the rest from one of the many histories of the Reformation.

THE INQUISITION

The great reform movement of the Protestants had been followed by a thoroughgoing r e f o r m within the bosom of the Church. Those popes who had been merely amateur humanists and dealers in Roman and Greek antiquities, disappeared from the scene and their place was taken by serious men who spent twenty hours a day administering those holy duties which had been placed in their hands.

The long and rather disgraceful happiness of the monasteries came to an end. Monks and nuns were forced to be up at sunrise, to study the Church Fathers, to tend the sick and console the dying. The Holy Inquisition watched day and night that no dangerous doctrines should be spread by way of the printing press. Here it is customary to mention poor Galileo, who was locked up because he had been a little too indiscreet in explaining the heavens with his funny little telescope and had muttered certain opinions about the behaviour of the planets which were entirely opposed to the official views of the church. But in all fairness to the Pope, the clergy and the Inquisition, it ought to be stated that the Protestants were quite as much the enemies of science and medicine as the Catholics and with equal manifestations of ignorance and intolerance regarded the men who investigated things for themselves as the most dangerous enemies of mankind.

And Calvin, the great French reformer and the tyrant (both political and spiritual) of Geneva, not only assisted the French authorities when they tried to hang Michael Servetus (the Spanish theologian and physician who had become famous as the assistant of Vesalius, the first great anatomist), but when Servetus had managed to escape from his French jail and had fled to Geneva, Calvin threw this brilliant man into prison and after a prolonged trial, allowed him to be burned at the stake on account of his heresies, totally indifferent to his fame as a scientist.

And so it went. We have few reliable statistics upon the subject, but on the whole, the Protestants tired of this game long before the Catholics, and the greater part of honest men and women who were burned and hanged and decapitated on account of their religious beliefs fell as victims of the very energetic but also very drastic church of Rome.

For tolerance (and please remember this when you grow older), is of very recent origin and even the people of our own so-called "modern world" are apt to be tolerant only upon such matters as do not interest them very much. They are tolerant towards a native of Africa, and do not care whether he becomes a Buddhist or a Mohammedan, because neither Buddhism nor Mohammedanism means anything to them. But when they hear that their neighbour who was a Republican and believed in a high protective tariff, has joined the Socialist party and now wants to repeal all tariff laws, their tolerance ceases and they use almost the same words as those employed by a kindly Catholic (or Protestant) of the seventeenth century, who was informed that his best friend whom he had always respected and loved had fallen a victim to the terrible heresies of the Protestant (or Catholic) church.

"Heresy" until a very short time ago was regarded as a disease. Nowadays when we see a man neglecting the personal cleanliness of his body and his home and exposing himself and his children to the dangers of typhoid fever or another preventable disease, we send for the board-of-health and the health officer calls upon the police to aid him in removing this person who is a danger to the safety of the entire community. In the sixteenth and seventeenth centuries, a heretic, a man or a woman who openly doubted the fundamental principles upon which his Protestant or Catholic religion had been founded, was considered a more terrible menace than a typhoid carrier. Typhoid fever might (very likely would) destroy the body. But heresy, according to them, would positively destroy the immortal soul. It was therefore the duty of all good and logical citizens to warn the police against the enemies of the established order of things and those who failed to do so were as culpable as a modern man who does not telephone to the nearest doctor when he discovers that his fellow-tenants are suffering from cholera or small-pox.

In the years to come you will hear a great deal about preventive medicine. Preventive medicine simply means that our doctors do not wait until their patients are sick, then step forward and cure them. On the contrary, they study the patient and the conditions under which he lives when he (the patient) is perfectly well and they remove every possible cause of illness by cleaning up rubbish, by teaching him what to eat and what to avoid, and by giving him a few simple ideas of personal hygiene. They go even further than that, and these good doctors enter the schools and teach the children how to use tooth-brushes and how to avoid catching colds.

The sixteenth century which regarded (as I have tried to show you) bodily illness as much less important than sickness which threatened the soul, organised a system of spiritual preventive medicine. As soon as a child was old enough to spell his first words, he was educated in the true (and the"only true") principles of the Faith. Indirectly this proved to be a good thing for the general progress of the people of Europe. The Protestant lands were soon dotted with schools. They used a great deal of very valuable time to explain the Catechism, but they gave instruction in other things besides theology. They encouraged reading and they were responsible for the great prosperity of the printing trade.

But the Catholics did not lag behind. They too devoted much time and thought to education. The Church, in this matter, found an invaluable friend and ally in the newly-founded order of the Society of Jesus. The founder of this remarkable organisation was a Spanish soldier who after a life of unholy adventures had been converted and thereupon felt himself bound to serve the church just as many former sinners, who have been shown the errors of their way by the Salvation Army, devote the remaining years of their lives to the task of aiding and consoling those who are less fortunate.

The name of this Spaniard was Ignatius de Loyola. He was born in the year before the discovery of America. He had been wounded and lamed for life and while he was in the hospital he had seen a vision of the Holy Virgin and her Son, who bade him give up the wickedness of his former life. He decided to go to the Holy Land and finish the task of the Crusades. But a visit to Jerusalem had shown him the impossibility of the task and he returned west to help in the warfare upon the heresies of the Lutherans.

In the year 1534 he was studying in Paris at the Sorbonne. Together with seven other students he founded a fraternity. The eight men promised each other that they would lead holy lives, that they would not strive after riches but after righteousness, and would devote themselves, body and soul, to the service of the Church. A few years later this small fraternity had grown into a regular organisation and was recognised by Pope Paul III as the Society of Jesus.

Loyola had been a military man. He believed in discipline, and absolute obedience to the orders of the superior dignitaries became one of the main causes for the enormous success of the Jesuits. They specialised in education. They gave their teachers a most thorough-going education before they allowed them to talk to a single pupil. They lived with their students and they entered into their games. They watched them with tender care. And as a result they raised a new generation of faithful Catholics who took their religious duties as seriously as the people of the early Middle Ages.

The shrewd Jesuits, however, did not waste all their efforts upon the education of the poor. They entered the palaces of the mighty and became the private tutors of future emperors and kings. And what this meant you will see for yourself when I tell you about the Thirty Years War. But before this terrible and final outbreak of religious fanaticism, a great many other things had happened.

Charles V was dead. Germany and Austria had been left to his brother Ferdinand. All his other possessions, Spain and the Netherlands and the Indies and America had gone to his son Philip. Philip was the son of Charles and a Portuguese princess who had been first cousin to her own husband. The children that are born of such a union are apt to be rather queer. The son of Philip, the unfortunate Don Carlos, (murdered afterwards with his own father's consent,) was crazy. Philip was not quite crazy, but his zeal for the Church bordered closely upon religious insanity. He believed that Heaven had appointed him as one of the saviours of mankind. Therefore, whosoever was obstinate and refused to share his Majesty's views, proclaimed himself an enemy of the human race and must be exterminated lest his example corrupt the souls of his pious neighbours.

Spain, of course, was a very rich country. All the gold and silver of the new world flowed into the Castilian and Aragonian treasuries. But Spain suffered from a curious economic disease. Her peasants were hard working men and even harder working women. But the better classes maintained a supreme contempt for any form of labour, outside of employment in the army or navy or the civil service. As for the Moors, who had been very industrious artisans, they had been driven out of the country long before. As a result, Spain, the treasure chest of the world, remained a poor country because all her money had to be sent abroad in exchange for the wheat and the other necessities of life which the Spaniards neglected to raise for themselves.

THE NIGHT OF
ST. BARTHOLOMEW

Philip, ruler of the most powerful nation of the sixteenth century, depended for his revenue upon the taxes which were gathered in the busy commercial bee-hive of the Netherlands. But these Flemings and Dutchmen were devoted followers of the doctrines of Luther and Calvin and they had cleansed their churches of all images and holy paintings and they had informed the Pope that they no longer regarded him as their shepherd but intended to follow the dictates of their consciences and the commands of their newly translated Bible.

This placed the king in a very difficult position. He could not possibly tolerate the heresies of his Dutch subjects, but he needed their money. If he allowed them to be Protestants and took no measures to save their souls he was deficient in his duty toward God. If he sent the Inquisition to the Netherlands and burned his subjects at the stake, he would lose the greater part of his income.

Being a man of uncertain will-power he hesitated a long time. He tried kindness and sternness and promises and threats. The Hollanders remained obstinate, and continued to sing psalms and listen to the sermons of their Lutheran and Calvinist preachers. Philip in his despair sent his "man of iron," the Duke of Alba, to bring these hardened sinners to terms. Alba began by decapitating those leaders who had not wisely left the country before his arrival. In the year 1572 (the same year that the French Protestant leaders were all killed during the terrible night of Saint Bartholomew), he

LEYDEN DELIVERED BY THE CUTTING OF THE DYKES

attacked a number of Dutch cities and massacred the inhabitants as an example for the others. The next year he laid siege to the town of Leyden, the manufacturing center of Holland.

Meanwhile, the seven small provinces of the northern Netherlands had formed a defensive union, the so-called union of Utrecht, and had recognised William of Orange, a German prince who had been the private secretary of the Emperor Charles V, as the leader of their army and as commander of their freebooting sailors, who were known as the Beggars of the Sea. William, to save Leyden, cut the dykes, created a shallow inland sea, and delivered the town with the help of a strangely equipped navy consisting of scows and flat-bottomed barges which were rowed and pushed and pulled through the mud until they reached the city walls.

It was the first time that an army of the invincible Spanish king had suffered such a humiliating defeat. It surprised the world just as the Japanese victory of Mukden, in the Russian-Japanese war, surprised our own generation. The Protestant powers took fresh courage and Philip devised new means for the purpose of conquering his rebellious subjects. He hired a poor half-witted fanatic to go and murder William of Orange. But the sight of their dead leader did not bring the Seven Provinces to their knees. On the contrary it made them furiously angry. In the year 1581, the Estates General (the meeting of the representatives of the Seven Provinces) came together at the Hague and most solemnly abjured their "wicked king Philip" and themselves assumed the burden of sovereignty which thus far had been invested in their "King by the Grace of God."

THE MURDER OF WILLIAM
THE SILENT

This is a very important event in the history of the great struggle for political liberty. It was a step which reached much further than the uprising of the nobles which ended with the signing of the Magna Carta. These good burghers said "Between a king and his subjects there is a silent understanding that both sides shall perform certain services and shall recognize certain definite duties. If either party fails to live up to this contract, the other has the right to consider it terminated." The American subjects of King George III in the year 1776 came to a similar conclusion. But they had three thousand miles of ocean between themselves and their ruler and the Estates General took their decision (which meant a slow death in case of defeat) within hearing of the Spanish guns and although in constant fear of an avenging Spanish fleet.

The stories about a mysterious Spanish fleet that was to conquer both Holland and England, when Protestant Queen Elizabeth had succeeded Catholic "Bloody Mary" was an old one. For years the sailors of the waterfront had talked about it. In the eighties of the sixteenth century, the rumour took a definite shape. According to pilots who had been in Lisbon, all the Spanish and Portuguese wharves were building ships. And in the southern Netherlands (in Belgium) the Duke of Parma was collecting a large expeditionary force to be carried from Ostend to London and Amsterdam as soon as the fleet should arrive.

THE ARMADA IS COMING

In the year 1586 the Great Armada set sail for the north. But the harbours of the Flemish coast were blockaded by a Dutch fleet and the Channel was guarded by the English, and the Spaniards, accustomed to the quieter seas of the south, did not know how to navigate in this squally and bleak northern climate. What happened to the Armada once it was attacked by ships and by storms I need not tell you. A few ships, by sailing around Ireland, escaped to tell the terrible story of defeat. The others perished and lie at the bottom of the North Sea.

Turn about is fair play. The British and the Dutch Protestants now carried the war into the territory of the enemy. Before the end of the century, Houtman, with the help of a booklet written by Linschoten (a Hollander who had been in the Portuguese service), had at last discovered the route to the Indies. As a result the great Dutch East India Company was founded and a systematic war upon the Portuguese and Spanish colonies in Asia and Africa was begun in all seriousness.

It was during this early era of colonial conquest that a curious lawsuit was fought out in the Dutch courts. Early in the seventeenth century a Dutch Captain by the name of van Heemskerk, a man who had made himself famous as the head of an expedition which had tried to discover the North Eastern Passage to the Indies and who had spent a winter on the frozen shores of the island of Nova Zembla, had captured a Portuguese ship in the straits of Malacca. You will remember that the Pope had divided the world into two equal shares, one of which had been given to the Spaniards and the other to the Portuguese. The Portuguese quite naturally regarded the water which surrounded their Indian islands as part of their own property and since, for the moment, they were not at war with the United Seven Netherlands, they claimed that the captain of a private Dutch trading company had no right to enter their private domain and steal their ships. And they brought suit. The directors of the Dutch East India Company hired a bright young lawyer, by the name of De Groot or Grotius, to defend their case. He made the astonishing plea that the ocean is free to all comers. Once outside the distance which a cannon ball fired from the land can reach, the sea is or (according to Grotius) ought to be, a free and open highway to all the ships of all nations. It was the first time that this startling doctrine had been publicly pronounced in a court of law. It was opposed by all the other seafaring people. To counteract the effect of Grotius' famous plea for the "Mare Liberum," or "Open Sea," John Selden, the Englishman, wrote his famous treatise upon the "Mare Clausum" or "Closed Sea" which treated of the natural right of a sovereign to regard the seas which surrounded his country as belonging to his territory. I mention this here because the question had not yet been decided and during the last war caused all sorts of difficulties and complicatiⱼns.

To return to the warfare between Spaniard and Hollander and Englishman, before twenty years were over the most valuable colonies of the Indies and the Cape of Good Hope and Ceylon and those along the coast of China and even Japan were in Protestant hands. In 1621 a West Indian Company was founded which conquered Brazil and in North America built

THE DEATH OF HUDSON

a fortress called Nieuw Amsterdam at the mouth of the river which Henry Hudson had discovered in the year 1609.

These new colonies enriched both England and the Dutch Republic to such an extent that they could hire foreign soldiers to do their fighting on land while they devoted themselves to commerce and trade. To them the Protestant revolt meant independence and prosperity. But in many other parts of Europe it meant a succession of horrors compared to which the last war was a mild excursion of kindly Sunday-school boys.

The Thirty Years War which broke out in the year 1618 and which ended with the famous treaty of Westphalia in 1648 was the perfectly natural result of a century of ever increasing religious hatred. It was, as I have said, a terrible war. Every-body fought everybody else and the struggle ended only when all parties had been thoroughly exhausted and could fight no longer.

In less than a generation it turned many parts of central Europe into a wilderness, where the hungry peasants fought for the carcass of a dead horse with the even hungrier wolf. Five-sixths of all the German towns and villages were de-stroyed. The Palatinate, in western Germany, was plundered twenty-eight times. And a population of eighteen million people was reduced to four million.

The hostilities began almost as soon as Ferdinand II of the House of Habsburg had been elected Emperor. He was the product of a most careful Jesuit training and was a most obedient and devout son of the Church. The vow which he had made as a young man, that he would eradicate all sects and all heresies from his domains, Ferdinand kept to the best of his ability. Two days before his election, his chief opponent, Frederick, the Protestant Elector of the Palatinate and a son-in-law of James I of England, had been made King of Bohemia, in direct violation of Ferdinand's wishes.

At once the Habsburg armies marched into Bohemia. The young king looked in vain for assistance against this formid‑able enemy. The Dutch Republic was willing to help, but, engaged in a desperate war of its own with the Spanish branch of the Habsburgs, it could do little. The Stuarts in England were more interested in strengthening their own absolute power at home than spending money and men upon a forlorn adven‑ture in far away Bohemia. After a struggle of a few months, the Elector of the Palatinate was driven away and his domains were given to the Catholic house of Bavaria. This was the be-ginning of the great war.

Then the Habsburg armies, under Tilly and Wallenstein, fought their way through the Protestant part of Germany until they had reached the shores of the Baltic. A Catholic neighbour meant serious danger to the Protestant king of Denmark. Christian IV tried to defend himself by attacking

THE THIRTY YEARS WAR

his enemies before they had become too strong for him. The Danish armies marched into Germany but were defeated. Wallenstein followed up his victory with such energy and violence that Denmark was forced to sue for peace. Only one town of the Baltic then remained in the hands of the Protestants. That was Stralsund.

There, in the early summer of the year 1630, landed King Gustavus Adolphus of the house of Vasa, king of Sweden, and famous as the man who had defended his country against the Russians. A Protestant prince of unlimited ambition, desirous of making Sweden the centre of a great Northern Empire, Gustavus Adolphus was welcomed by the Protestant princes of Europe as the saviour of the Lutheran cause. He defeated Tilly, who had just successfully butchered the Protestant inhabitants of Magdeburg. Then his troops began their great march through the heart of Germany in an attempt to reach the Habsburg possessions in Italy. Threatened in the rear by the Catholics, Gustavus suddenly veered around and defeated the main Habsburg army in the battle of Lützen. Unfortunately the Swedish king was killed when he strayed away from his troops. But the Habsburg power had been broken.

Ferdinand, who was a suspicious sort of person, at once began to distrust his own servants. Wallenstein, his commander-in-chief, was murdered at his instigation. When the Catholic Bourbons, who ruled France and hated their Habsburg rivals, heard of this, they joined the Protestant Swedes. The armies of Louis XIII invaded the eastern part of Germany, and Turenne and Condé added their fame to that of Baner and Weimar, the Swedish generals, by murdering, pillaging and burning Habsburg property. This brought great fame and riches to the Swedes and caused the Danes to become envious. The Protestant Danes thereupon declared war upon the Protestant Swedes who were the allies of the Catholic French, whose political leader, the Cardinal de Richelieu, had just deprived the Huguenots (or French Protestants) of those

rights of public worship which the Edict of Nantes of the year
1598 had guaranteed them.

The war, after the habit of such encounters, did not decide
anything, when it came to an end with the treaty of Westphalia in 1648. The Catholic powers remained Catholic and
the Protestant powers stayed faithful to the doctrines of
Luther and Calvin and Zwingli. The Swiss and Dutch Protestants were recognised as independent republics. France
kept the cities of Metz and Toul and Verdun and a part of
Alsace. The Holy Roman Empire continued to exist as a sort
of scare-crow state, without men, without money, without hope
and without courage.

AMSTERDAM IN 1648

The only good the Thirty Years War accomplished was a
negative one. It discouraged both Catholics and Protestants
from ever trying it again. Henceforth they left each other in
peace. This however did not mean that religious feeling and
theological hatred had been removed from this earth. On the
contrary. The quarrels between Catholic and Protestant
came to an end, but the disputes between the different Protestant sects continued as bitterly as ever before. In Holland
a difference of opinion as to the true nature of predestination
(a very obscure point of theology, but exceedingly important
in the eyes of your great-grandfather) caused a quarrel which

ended with the decapitation of John of Oldenbarneveldt, the Dutch statesman, who had been responsible for the success of the Republic during the first twenty years of its independence, and who was the great organising genius of her Indian trading company. In England, the feud led to civil war.

But before I tell you of this outbreak which led to the first execution by process-of-law of a European king, I ought to say something about the previous history of England. In this book I am trying to give you only those events of the past which can throw a light upon the conditions of the present world. If I do not mention certain countries, the cause is not to be found in any secret dislike on my part. I wish that I could tell you what happened to Norway and Switzerland and Serbia and China. But these lands exercised no great influ‚ ence upon the development of Europe in the sixteenth and seventeenth centuries. I therefore pass them by with a polite and very respectful bow. England however is in a different position. What the people of that small island have done during the last five hundred years has shaped the course of history in every corner of the world. Without a proper knowledge of the background of English history, you cannot understand what you read in the newspapers. And it is therefore necessary that you know how England happened to develop a parliamentary form of government while the rest of the European continent was still ruled by absolute monarchs.

THE ENGLISH REVOLUTION

HOW THE STRUGGLE BETWEEN THE "DIVINE RIGHT" OF KINGS AND THE LESS DIVINE BUT MORE REASONABLE "RIGHT OF PARLIAMENT" ENDED DISASTROUSLY FOR KING CHARLES I

CÆSAR, the earliest explorer of north-western Europe, had crossed the Channel in the year 55 B.C. and had conquered England. During four centuries the country then remained a Roman province. But when the Barbarians began to threaten Rome, the garrisons were called back from the frontier that they might defend the home country and Britannia was left without a government and without protection.

As soon as this became known among the hungry Saxon tribes of northern Germany, they sailed across the North Sea and made themselves at home in the prosperous island. They founded a number of independent Anglo-Saxon kingdoms (so called after the original invaders, the Angles or English and the Saxons) but these small states were for ever quarrelling with each other and no King was strong enough to establish himself as the head of a united country. For more than five hundred years, Mercia and Northumbria and Wessex and Sussex and Kent and East Anglia, or whatever their names, were exposed to attacks from various Scandinavian pirates. Finally in the eleventh century, England, together with Norway and northern Germany became part of the large Danish Empire

279

of Canute the Great and the last vestiges of independence
disappeared.

The Danes, in the course of time, were driven away but no
sooner was England free, than it was conquered for the fourth
time. The new enemies were the descendants of another tribe
of Norsemen who early in the tenth century had invaded
France and had founded the Duchy of Normandy. William,

THE ENGLISH NATION

Duke of Normandy, who for a long time had looked across the
water with an envious eye, crossed the Channel in October
of the year 1066. At the battle of Hastings, on October the
fourteenth of that year, he destroyed the weak forces of Harold
of Wessex, the last of the Anglo-Saxon Kings and established
himself as King of England. But neither William nor his
successors of the House of Anjou and Plantagenet regarded
England as their true home. To them the island was merely a

part of their great inheritance on the continent—a sort of colony inhabited by rather backward people upon whom they forced their own language and civilisation. Gradually however the "colony" of England gained upon the "Mother country" of Normandy. At the same time the Kings of

THE HUNDRED YEARS WAR

France were trying desperately to get rid of the powerful Norman-English neighbours who were in truth no more than disobedient servants of the French crown. After a century of warfare the French people, under the leadership of a young girl by the name of Joan of Arc, drove the "foreigners" from their soil. Joan herself, taken a prisoner at the battle of Compiègne in the year 1430 and sold by her Burgundian captors to the English soldiers, was burned as a witch. But the English never gained foothold upon the continent and their Kings were at last able to devote all their time to their British possessions. As the feudal nobility of the island had been engaged in one of those strange feuds which were as common in the middle ages as measles and small-pox, and as the greater part of the old landed proprietors had been killed during these so-called Wars of the Roses, it was quite easy for the Kings to increase their royal power. And by the end of the fifteenth century, England was a strongly centralised country, ruled by Henry VII of the House of Tudor, whose famous Court of Justice, the "Star Chamber" of terrible memory, suppressed all attempts on the part of the surviving nobles to regain their old influence upon the government of the country with the utmost severity.

In the year 1509 Henry VII was succeeded by his son Henry VIII, and from that moment on the history of England gained a new importance for the country ceased to be a mediæval island and became a modern state.

Henry had no deep interest in religion. He gladly used a private disagreement with the Pope about one of his many divorces to declare himself independent of Rome and make the church of England the first of those "nationalistic churches" in which the worldly ruler also acts as the spiritual head of his subjects. This peaceful reformation of 1534 not only gave the house of Tudor the support of the English clergy, who for a long time had been exposed to the violent attacks of many Lutheran propagandists, but it also increased the Royal power through the confiscation of the former possessions of the monasteries. At the same time it made Henry popular with the merchants and tradespeople, who as the proud and prosperous inhabitants of an island which was separated from the rest of Europe by a wide and deep channel, had a great dislike for everything "foreign" and did not want an Italian bishop to rule their honest British souls.

In 1547 Henry died. He left the throne to his small son, aged ten. The guardians of the child, favoring the modern

Lutheran doctrines, did their best to help the cause of Protestantism. But the boy died before he was sixteen, and was succeeded by his sister Mary, the wife of Philip II of Spain, who burned the bishops of the new "national church" and in other ways followed the example of her royal Spanish husband.

Fortunately she died, in the year 1558, and was succeeded by Elizabeth, the daughter of Henry VIII and Anne Boleyn, the second of his six wives, whom he had decapitated when she no longer pleased him. Elizabeth, who had spent some time in prison, and who had been released only at the request of the Holy Roman Emperor, was a most cordial enemy of everything Catholic and Spanish. She shared her father's indifference in the matter of religion but she inherited his ability as a very shrewd judge of character, and spent the forty-five years of her reign in strengthening the power of the dynasty and in increasing the revenue and possessions of her merry islands. In this she was most ably assisted by a number of men who gathered around her throne and made the Elizabethan age a period of such importance that you ought to study it in detail in one of the special books of which I shall tell you in the bibliography at the end of this volume.

Elizabeth, however, did not feel entirely safe upon her throne. She had a rival and a very dangerous one. Mary, of the house of Stuart, daughter of a French duchess and a Scottish father, widow of king Francis II of France and daughter-in-law of Catherine of Medici (who had organised the murders of Saint Bartholomew's night), was the mother of a little boy who was afterwards to become the first Stuart king of England. She was an ardent Catholic and a willing friend to those who were the enemies of Elizabeth. Her own lack of political ability and the violent methods which she employed to punish her Calvinistic subjects, caused a revolution in Scotland and forced Mary to take refuge on English territory. For eighteen years she remained in England, plotting forever and a day against the woman who had given her shelter and who was at last obliged to follow the advice of her trusted councilors "to cutte off the Scottish Queen's heade."

The head was duly "cutte off" in the year 1587 and caused a war with Spain. But the combined navies of England and Holland defeated Philip's Invincible Armada, as we have already seen, and the blow which had been meant to destroy the power of the two great anti-Catholic leaders was turned into a profitable business adventure.

For now at last, after many years of hesitation, the English as well as the Dutch thought it their good right to invade the Indies and America and avenge the ills which their Protes-

JOHN AND SEBASTIAN CABOT SEE THE COAST OF NEWFOUNDLAND

tant brethren had suffered at the hands of the Spaniards. The English had been among the earliest successors of Columbus. British ships, commanded by the Venetian pilot Giovanni Caboto (or Cabot), had been the first to discover and explore the northern American continent in 1496. Labrador and Newfoundland were of little importance as a possible colony. But the banks of Newfoundland offered a rich reward to the English fishing fleet. A year later, in 1497, the same Cabot had explored the coast of Florida.

Then had come the busy years of Henry VII and Henry VIII when there had been no money for foreign explorations.

But under Elizabeth, with the country at peace and Mary Stuart in prison, the sailors could leave their harbour without fear for the fate of those whom they left behind. While Elizabeth was still a child, Willoughby had ventured to sail past the North Cape and one of his captains, Richard Chancellor, pushing further eastward in his quest of a possible road to the Indies, had reached Archangel, Russia, where he had established diplomatic and commercial relations with the mysterious rulers of this distant Muscovite Empire. During the first years of

THE ELIZABETHAN STAGE

Elizabeth's rule this voyage had been followed up by many others. Merchant adventurers, working for the benefit of a "joint stock Company" had laid the foundations of trading companies which in later centuries were to become colonies. Half pirate, half diplomat, willing to stake everything on a single lucky voyage, smugglers of everything that could be loaded into the hold of a vessel, dealers in men and merchandise with equal indifference to everything except their profit, the sailors of Elizabeth had carried the English flag and the fame of their Virgin Queen to the four corners of the Seven Seas. Meanwhile William Shakespeare kept her Majesty amused at home, and the best brains and the best wit of England co-operated with the queen in her attempt to change the feudal inheritance of Henry VIII into a modern national state.

In the year 1603 the old lady died at the age of seventy. Her cousin, the great-grandson of her own grandfather Henry VII and son of Mary Stuart, her rival and enemy, succeeded her as James I. By the Grace of God, he found himself the ruler of a country which had escaped the fate of its continental rivals. While the European Protestants and Catholics were killing each other in a hopeless attempt to break the power of their adversaries and establish the exclusive rule of their own particular creed, England was at peace and "reformed" at leisure without going to the extremes of either Luther or Loyola. It gave the island kingdom an enormous advantage in the coming struggle for colonial possessions. It assured England a leadership in international affairs which that country has maintained until the present day. Not even the disastrous adventure with the Stuarts was able to stop this normal development.

The Stuarts, who succeeded the Tudors, were "foreigners" in England. They do not seem to have appreciated or understood this fact. The native house of Tudor could steal a horse, but the "foreign" Stuarts were not allowed to look at the bridle without causing great popular disapproval. Old Queen Bess had ruled her domains very much as she pleased. In general however, she had always followed a policy which meant money in the pocket of the honest (and otherwise) British merchants. Hence the Queen had been always assured of the wholehearted support of her grateful people. And small liberties taken with some of the rights and prerogatives of Parliament were gladly overlooked for the ulterior benefits which were derived from her Majesty's strong and successful foreign policies.

Outwardly King James continued the same policy. But he lacked that personal enthusiasm which had been so very typical of his great predecessor. Foreign commerce continued to be encouraged. The Catholics were not granted any liberties. But when Spain smiled pleasantly upon England in an effort to establish peaceful relations, James was seen to smile back. The majority of the English people did not like this, but James was their King and they kept quiet.

Soon there were other causes of friction. King James and his son, Charles I, who succeeded him in the year 1625 both firmly believed in the principle of their "divine right" to administer their realm as they thought fit without consulting the wishes of their subjects. The idea was not new. The Popes, who in more than one way had been the successors of the Roman Emperors (or rather of the Roman Imperial ideal of a single and undivided state covering the entire known world), had always regarded themselves and had been publicly recognised as the "Vice-Regents of Christ upon Earth." No one questioned the right of God to rule the world as He saw fit. As a natural result, few ventured to doubt the right of the divine "Vice-Regent" to do the same thing and to demand the obedience of the masses because he was the direct representative of the Absolute Ruler of the Universe and responsible only to Almighty God.

When the Lutheran Reformation proved successful, those rights which formerly had been vested in the Papacy were taken over by the many European sovereigns who became Protestants. As head of their own national or dynastic churches they insisted upon being "Christ's Vice-Regents" within the limit of their own territory. The people did not question the right of their rulers to take such a step. They accepted it, just as we in our own day accept the idea of a representative system which to us seems the only reasonable and just form of government. It is unfair therefore to state that either Lutheranism or Calvinism caused the particular feeling of irritation which greeted King James's oft and loudly repeated assertion of his "Divine Right." There must have been other grounds for the genuine English disbelief in the Divine Right of Kings.

The first positive denial of the "Divine Right" of sovereigns had been heard in the Netherlands when the Estates General abjured their lawful sovereign King Philip II of Spain, in the year 1581. "The King," so they said, "has broken his contract and the King therefore is dismissed like any other unfaithful servant." Since then, this particular idea of a king's responsibilities towards his subjects had spread among many of the nations who inhabited the shores of the North Sea. They were in a very favourable position. They were rich. The poor people in the heart of central Europe, at the mercy of their Ruler's body-guard, could not afford to discuss a problem which would at once land them in the deepest dungeon of the nearest castle. But the merchants of Holland and England who possessed the capital necessary for the maintenance of great armies and navies, who knew how to handle the almighty weapon called "credit," had no such fear. They were willing to pit the "Divine Right" of their own good money against the "Divine Right" of any Habsburg or Bourbon or Stuart. They knew that their guilders and shillings could beat the clumsy feudal armies which were the only weapons of the King. They dared to act, where others were condemned to suffer in silence or run the risk of the scaffold.

When the Stuarts began to annoy the people of England with their claim that they had a right to do what they pleased and never mind the responsibility, the English middle classes used the House of Commons as their first line of defence against this abuse of the Royal Power. The Crown refused to give in and the King sent Parliament about its own business. Eleven long years, Charles I ruled alone. He levied taxes which most people regarded as illegal and he managed his British kingdom as if it had been his own country estate. He had capable assistants and we must say that he had the courage of his convictions.

Unfortunately, instead of assuring himself of the support of his faithful Scottish subjects, Charles became involved in a quarrel with the Scotch Presbyterians. Much against his will, but forced by his need for ready cash, Charles was at last obliged to call Parliament together once more. It met in April of 1640 and showed an ugly temper. It was dissolved a few weeks later. A new Parliament convened in November. This one was even less pliable than the first one. The members understood that the question of "Government by Divine Right" or "Government by Parliament" must be fought out for good and all. They attacked the King in his chief councillors and executed half a dozen of them. They announced that they would not allow themselves to be dissolved without their own approval. Finally on December 1, 1641, they presented to the King a "Grand Remonstrance" which gave a detailed account of the many grievances of the people against their Ruler.

Charles, hoping to derive some support for his own policy in the country districts, left London in January of 1642. Each side organised an army and prepared for open warfare between the absolute power of the crown and the absolute power of Parliament. During this struggle, the most powerful religious element of England, called the Puritans, (they were Anglicans who had tried to purify their doctrines to the most absolute limits), came quickly to the front. The regiments of "Godly men," commanded by Oliver Cromwell, with their iron discipline and their profound confidence in the holiness of their aims, soon became the model for the entire army of the opposition. Twice Charles was defeated. After the battle of Naseby, in 1645, he fled to Scotland. The Scotch sold him to the English.

There followed a period of intrigue and an uprising of the Scotch Presbyterians against the English Puritan. In August of the year 1648 after the three-days' battle of Preston Pans, Cromwell made an end to this second civil war, and took Edinburgh. Meanwhile his soldiers, tired of further talk and wasted hours of religious debate, had decided to act on their own initiative. They removed from Parliament all those who did not agree with their own Puritan views. Thereupon the "Rump," which was what was left of the old Parliament, accused the King of high treason. The House of Lords refused to sit as a tribunal. A special tribunal was appointed and it condemned the King to death. On the 30th of January of the year 1649, King Charles walked quietly out of a window of White Hall onto the scaffold. That day, the Sovereign People, acting through their chosen representatives, for the first time executed a ruler who had failed to understand his own position in the modern state.

The period which followed the death of Charles is usually called after Oliver Cromwell. At first the unofficial Dictator of England, he was officially made Lord Protector in the year 1653. He ruled five years. He used this period to continue the policies of Elizabeth. Spain once more became the arch enemy of England and war upon the Spaniard was made a national and sacred issue.

The commerce of England and the interests of the traders were placed before everything else, and the Protestant creed of the strictest nature was rigourously maintained. In maintaining England's position abroad, Cromwell was successful. As a social reformer, however, he failed very badly. The world is made up of a number of people and they rarely think alike. In the long run, this seems a very wise provision. A government of and by and for one single part of the entire community cannot possibly survive. The Puritans had been a great force for good when they tried to correct the abuse of the royal power. As the absolute Rulers of England they became intolerable.

When Cromwell died in 1658, it was an easy matter for the Stuarts to return to their old kingdom. Indeed, they were welcomed as "deliverers" by the people who had found the yoke of the meek Puritans quite as hard to bear as that of autocratic King Charles. Provided the Stuarts were willing to forget about the Divine Right of their late and lamented father and were willing to recognise the superiority of Parliament, the people promised that they would be loyal and faithful subjects.

Two generations tried to make a success of this new arrangement. But the Stuarts apparently had not learned their lesson and were unable to drop their bad habits. Charles II, who came back in the year 1660, was an amiable but worthless person. His indolence and his constitutional insistence upon following the easiest course, together with his conspicuous success as a liar, prevented an open outbreak between himself and his people. By the act of Uniformity in 1662 he broke the power of the Puritan clergy by banishing all dissenting clergymen from their parishes. By the so-called Conventicle Act of 1664 he tried to prevent the Dissenters from attending religious meetings by a threat of deportation to the West Indies. This looked too much like the good old days of Divine Right. People began to show the old and well-known signs of impatience, and Parliament suddenly experienced difficulty in providing the King with funds.

Since he could not get money from an unwilling Parliament, Charles borrowed it secretly from his neighbour and cousin, King Louis of France. He betrayed his Protestant allies in return for 200,000 pounds per year, and laughed at the poor simpletons of Parliament.

Economic independence suddenly gave the King great faith in his own strength. He had spent many years of exile among his Catholic relations and he had a secret liking for their religion. Perhaps he could bring England back to Rome! He passed a Declaration of Indulgence which suspended the old laws against the Catholics and Dissenters. This happened just when Charles' younger brother James was said to have become a Catholic. All this looked suspicious to the man in the street. People began to fear some terrible Popish plot. A new spirit of unrest entered the land. Most of the people wanted to prevent another outbreak of civil war. To them Royal Oppression and a Catholic King—yea, even Divine Right,—were preferable to a new struggle between members of the same race. Others however were less lenient. They were the much-feared Dissenters, who invariably had the courage of their convictions. They were led by several great noblemen who did not want to see a return of the old days of absolute royal power.

For almost ten years, these two great parties, the Whigs (the middle class element, called by this derisive name because in the year 1640 a lot of Scottish Whiggamores or horse-drovers headed by the Presbyterian clergy, had marched to Edinburgh to oppose the King) and the Tories (an epithet originally used against the Royalist Irish adherents but now applied to the supporters of the King) opposed each other, but neither wished to bring about a crisis. They allowed Charles to die peacefully in his bed and permitted the Catholic James II to succeed his brother in 1685. But when James, after threatening the country with the terrible foreign invention of a "standing army" (which was to be commanded by Catholic Frenchmen), issued a second Declaration of Indulgence in 1688, and ordered it to be read in all Anglican churches, he went just a trifle beyond that line of sensible demarcation which can only be transgressed by the most popular of rulers under very exceptional circumstances. Seven bishops refused to comply with the Royal Command. They were accused of "seditious libel." They were brought before a court. The jury which pronounced the verdict of "not guilty" reaped a rich harvest of popular approval.

At this unfortunate moment, James (who in a second marriage had taken to wife Maria of the Catholic house of Modena-Este) became the father of a son. This meant that the throne was to go to a Catholic boy rather than to his older sisters, Mary and Anne, who were Protestants. The man in the street again grew suspicious. Maria of Modena was too old to have children! It was all part of a plot! A strange baby had been brought into the palace by some Jesuit priest that England might have a Catholic monarch. And so on. It looked as if another civil war would break out. Then seven well-known men, Whigs and Tories, wrote a letter asking the husband of James's oldest daughter Mary, William III the Stadtholder or head of the Dutch Republic, to come to England and deliver the country from its lawful but entirely undesirable sovereign.

On the fifth of November of the year 1688, William landed at Torbay. As he did not wish to make a martyr out of his father-in-law, he helped him to escape safely to France. On the 22nd of January of 1689 he summoned Parliament. On the 13th of February of the same year he and his wife Mary were proclaimed joint sovereigns of England and the country was saved for the Protestant cause.

Parliament, having undertaken to be something more than a mere advisory body to the King, made the best of its opportunities. The old Petition of Rights of the year 1628 was fished out of a forgotten nook of the archives. A second and more drastic Bill of Rights demanded that the sovereign of England should belong to the Anglican church. Furthermore it stated that the king had no right to suspend the laws or permit certain privileged citizens to disobey certain laws. It stipulated that "without consent of Parliament no taxes could be levied and no army could be maintained." Thus in the year 1689 did England acquire an amount of liberty unknown in any other country of Europe.

But it is not only on account of this great liberal measure that the rule of William in England is still remembered. During his lifetime, government by a "responsible" ministry first developed No king of course can rule alone. He needs a few trusted advisors. The Tudors had their Great Council which was composed of Nobles and Clergy. This body grew too large. It was restricted to the small "Privy Council." In the course of time it became the custom of these councillors to meet the king in a cabinet in the palace. Hence they were called the "Cabinet Council." After a short while they were known as the "Cabinet."

William, like most English sovereigns before him, had chosen his advisors from among all parties. But with the increased strength of Parliament, he had found it impossible to direct the politics of the country with the help of the Tories while the Whigs had a majority in the house of Commons. Therefore the Tories had been dismissed and the Cabinet Council had been composed entirely of Whigs. A few years later when the Whigs lost their power in the House of Commons, the

king, for the sake of convenience, was obliged to look for his
support among the leading Tories. Until his death in 1702,
William was too busy fighting Louis of France to bother much
about the government of England. Practically all important
affairs had been left to his Cabinet Council. When William's
sister-in-law, Anne, succeeded him in 1702 this condition of
affairs continued. When she died in 1714 (and unfortunately
not a single one of her seventeen children survived her) the
throne went to George I of the House of Hanover, the son of
Sophie, grand-daughter of James I.

This somewhat rustic monarch, who never learned a word
of English, was entirely lost in the complicated mazes of England's political arrangements. He left everything to his Cabinet Council and kept away from their meetings, which bored
him as he did not understand a single sentence. In this way
the Cabinet got into the habit of ruling England and Scotland (whose Parliament had been joined to that of England
in 1707) without bothering the King, who was apt to spend
a great deal of his time on the continent.

During the reign of George I and George II, a succession of
great Whigs (of whom one, Sir Robert Walpole, held office for
twenty-one years) formed the Cabinet Council of the King.
Their leader was finally recognised as the official leader not
only of the actual Cabinet but also of the majority party in
power in Parliament. The attempts of George III to take
matters into his own hands and not to leave the actual business of government to his Cabinet were so disastrous that
they were never repeated. And from the earliest years of the
eighteenth century on, England enjoyed representative government, with a responsible ministry which conducted the affairs
of the land.

To be quite true, this government did not represent all
classes of society. Less than one man in a dozen had the right
to vote. But it was the foundation for the modern representative form of government. In a quiet and orderly fashion it
took the power away from the King and placed it in the hands

of an ever increasing number of popular representatives. It did not bring the millenium to England, but it saved that country from most of the revolutionary outbreaks which proved so disastrous to the European continent in the eighteenth and nineteenth centuries.

THE BALANCE OF POWER

IN FRANCE ON THE OTHER HAND THE "DIVINE RIGHT OF KINGS" CONTINUED WITH GREATER POMP AND SPLENDOUR THAN EVER BEFORE AND THE AMBITION OF THE RULER WAS ONLY TEMPERED BY THE NEWLY INVENTED LAW OF THE "BALANCE OF POWER"

As a contrast to the previous chapter, let me tell you what happened in France during the years when the English people were fighting for their liberty. The happy combination of the right man in the right country at the right moment is very rare in History. Louis XIV was a realisation of this ideal, as far as France was concerned, but the rest of Europe would have been happier without him.

The country over which the young king was called to rule was the most populous and the most brilliant nation of that day. Louis came to the throne when Mazarin and Richelieu, the two great Cardinals, had just hammered the ancient French Kingdom into the most strongly centralised state of the seventeenth century. He was himself a man of extraordinary ability. We, the people of the twentieth century, are still surrounded by the memories of the glorious age of the Sun King. Our social life is based upon the perfection of manners and the elegance of expression attained at the court of Louis. In international and diplomatic relations, French is still the official language of diplomacy and international gatherings because two centuries ago it reached a polished elegance and a purity of expression which no other tongue had as yet been able to equal. The theatre of King Louis still teaches us lessons which we are only too slow in learning. During his reign the French Academy (an invention of Richelieu) came to occupy a position in the world of letters which other countries have flattered by their imitation. We might continue this list for many pages. It is no matter of mere chance that our modern bill-of-fare is printed in French. The very difficult art of decent cooking, one of the highest expressions of civilisation, was first practised for the benefit of the great Monarch. The age of Louis XIV was a time of splendour and grace which can still teach us a lot.

Unfortunately this brilliant picture has another side which was far less encouraging. Glory abroad too often means misery at home, and France was no exception to this rule. Louis XIV succeeded his father in the year 1643. He died in the year 1715. That means that the government of France was in the hands of one single man for seventy-two years, almost two whole generations.

It will be well to get a firm grasp of this idea, "one single man." Louis was the first of a long list of monarchs who in many countries established that particular form of highly efficient autocracy which we call "enlightened despotism." He did not like kings who merely played at being rulers and turned official affairs into a pleasant picnic. The Kings of that enlightened age worked harder than any of their subjects. They got up earlier and went to bed later than anybody else, and felt their "divine responsibility" quite as strongly as their "divine right" which allowed them to rule without consulting their subjects.

Of course, the king could not attend to everything in person. He was obliged to surround himself with a few helpers and councillors. One or two generals, some experts upon foreign politics, a few clever financiers and economists would do for this purpose. But these dignitaries could act only through their Sovereign. They had no individual existence. To the mass of the people, the Sovereign actually represented in his own sacred person the government of their country. The glory of the common fatherland became the glory of a single dynasty. It meant the exact opposite of our own American ideal. France was ruled of and by and for the House of Bourbon.

The disadvantages of such a system are clear. The King grew to be everything. Everybody else grew to be nothing at all. The old and useful nobility was gradually forced to give up its former shares in the government of the provinces. A little Royal bureaucrat, his fingers splashed with ink, sitting behind the greenish windows of a government building in faraway Paris, now performed the task which a hundred years before had been the duty of the feudal Lord. The feudal Lord, deprived of all work, moved to Paris to amuse himself as best he could at the court. Soon his estates began to suffer from that very dangerous economic sickness, known as "Absentee Landlordism." Within a single generation, the industrious and useful feudal administrators had become the well-mannered but quite useless loafers of the court of Versailles.

Louis was ten years old when the peace of Westphalia was concluded and the House of Habsburg, as a result of the Thirty Years War, lost its predominant position in Europe. It was inevitable that a man with his ambition should use so favourable a moment to gain for his own dynasty the honours which had formerly been held by the Habsburgs. In the year 1660 Louis had married Maria Theresa, daughter of the King of Spain. Soon afterward, his father-in-law, Philip IV, one of the half-witted Spanish Habsburgs, died. At once Louis claimed the Spanish Netherlands (Belgium) as part of his wife's dowry. Such an acquisition would have been disastrous to the peace of Europe, and would have threatened the safety of the Protestant states. Under the leadership of Jan de Witt, Raadpensionaris or Foreign Minister of the United Seven Netherlands, the first great international alliance, the Triple Alliance of Sweden, England and Holland, of the year 1664, was concluded. It did not last long. With money and fair promises Louis bought up both King Charles and the Swedish Estates. Holland was betrayed by her allies and was left to her own fate. In the year 1672 the French invaded the low countries. They marched to the heart of the country. For a second time the dikes were opened and the Royal Sun of France set amidst the mud of the Dutch marshes. The peace

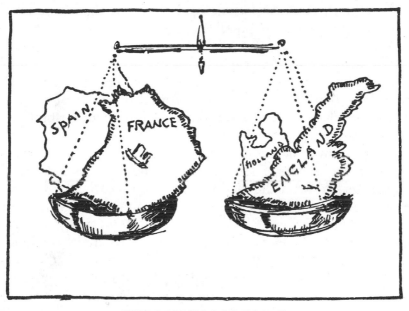

THE BALANCE OF POWER

of Nimwegen which was concluded in 1678 settled nothing but merely anticipated another war.

A second war of aggression from 1689 to 1697, ending with the Peace of Ryswick, also failed to give Louis that position in the affairs of Europe to which he aspired. His old enemy, Jan de Witt, had been murdered by the Dutch rabble, but his successor, William III (whom you met in the last chapter), had checkmated all efforts of Louis to make France the ruler of Europe.

The great war for the Spanish succession, begun in the

year 1701, immediately after the death of Charles II, the la
of the Spanish Habsburgs, and ended in 1713 by the Pea
of Utrecht, remained equally undecided, but it had ruined tl
treasury of Louis. On land the French king had been victo
ious, but the navies of England and Holland had spoiled a
hope for an ultimate French victory; besides the long strugg
had given birth to a new and fundamental principle of inte
national politics, which thereafter made it impossible for oi
single nation to rule the whole of Europe or the whole of tl
world for any length of time.

That was the so-called "balance of power." It was not
written law but for three centuries it has been obeyed as close
as are the laws of nature. The people who originated the ide
maintained that Europe, in its nationalistic stage of develo]
ment, could only survive when there should be an absolute ba
ance of the many conflicting interests of the entire continer
No single power or single dynasty must ever be allowed
dominate the others. During the Thirty Years War, tl
Habsburgs had been the victims of the application of this la\
They, however, had been unconscious victims. The issues du
ing that struggle were so clouded in a haze of religious stri
that we do not get a very clear view of the main tendenci
of that great conflict. But from that time on, we begin to s
how cold, economic considerations and calculations prevail
all matters of international importance. We discover the d
velopment of a new type of statesman, the statesman with tl
personal feelings of the slide-rule and the cash-register. Ja
de Witt was the first successful exponent of this new scho
of politics. William III was the first great pupil. And Lou
XIV with all his fame and glory, was the first conscious victin
There have been many others since.

THE RISE OF RUSSIA

IN the year 1492, as you know, Columbus discovered Amer·
a. Early in the year, a Tyrolese by the name of Schnups,
avelling as the head of a scientific expedition for the
rchbishop of Tyrol, and provided with the best letters
introduction and excellent credit tried to reach the mythical
wn of Moscow. He did not succeed. When he reached the
ontiers of this vast Moscovite state which was vaguely sup-
)sed to exist in the extreme Eastern part of Europe, he was
mly turned back. No foreigners were wanted. And
:hnups went to visit the heathen Turk in Constantinople, in
der that he might have something to report to his clerical
aster when he came back from his explorations.

Sixty-one years later, Richard Chancellor, trying to dis-
ver the North-eastern passage to the Indies, and blown by
ill wind into the White Sea, reached the mouth of the Dwina
id found the Moscovite village of Kholmogory, a few hours
om the spot where in 1584 the town of Archangel was found-
l. This time the foreign visitors were requested to come
Moscow and show themselves to the Grand Duke. They
ent and returned to England with the first commercial treaty
rer concluded between Russia and the western world. Other

301

nations soon followed and something became known of this mysterious land.

Geographically, Russia is a vast plain. The Ural mountains are low and form no barrier against invaders. The rivers are broad but often shallow. It was an ideal territory for nomads.

While the Roman Empire was founded, grew in power and disappeared again, Slavic tribes, who had long since left their homes in Central Asia, wandered aimlessly through the forests and plains of the region between the Dniester and Dnieper rivers. The Greeks had sometimes met these Slavs and a few travellers of the third and fourth centuries mention them. Otherwise they were as little known as were the Nevada Indians in the year 1800.

Unfortunately for the peace of these primitive peoples, a very convenient trade-route ran through their country. This was the main road from northern Europe to Constantinople. It followed the coast of the Baltic until the Neva was reached. Then it crossed Lake Ladoga and went southward along the Volkhov river. Then through Lake Ilmen and up the small Lovat river. Then there was a short portage until the Dnieper was reached. Then down the Dnieper into the Black Sea.

The Norsemen knew of this road at a very early date. In the ninth century they began to settle in northern Russia, just as other Norsemen were laying the foundation for independent states in Germany and France. But in the year 862, three Norsemen, brothers, crossed the Baltic and founded three small dynasties. Of the three brothers, only one, Rurik, lived for a number of years. He took possession of the territory of his brothers, and twenty years after the arrival of this first Norseman, a Slavic state had been established with Kiev as its capital.

From Kiev to the Black Sea is a short distance. Soon the existence of an organised Slavic State became known in Constantinople. This meant a new field for the zealous missionaries of the Christian faith. Byzantine monks followed the Dnieper on their way northward and soon reached the heart of

THE ORIGIN OF RUSSIA

Russia. They found the people worshipping strange gods who were supposed to dwell in woods and rivers and in mountain caves. They taught them the story of Jesus. There was no competition from the side of Roman missionaries. These good men were too busy educating the heathen Teutons to bother about the distant Slavs. Hence Russia received its religion and its alphabet and its first ideas of art and architecture from the Byzantine monks and as the Byzantine empire (a relic of the eastern Roman empire) had become very oriental and had lost many of its European traits, the Russians suffered in consequence.

Politically speaking these new states of the great Russian plains did not fare well. It was the Norse habit to divide every inheritance equally among all the sons. No sooner had a small state been founded but it was broken up among eight or nine heirs who in turn left their territory to an ever increasing number of descendants. It was inevitable that these small competing states should quarrel among themselves. Anarchy was the order of the day. And when the red glow of the eastern horizon told the people of the threatened invasion of a savage Asiatic tribe, the little states were too weak and too divided to render any sort of defence against this terrible enemy.

It was in the year 1224 that the first great Tartar invasion took place and that the hordes of Jenghiz Khan, the conqueror of China, Bokhara, Tashkent and Turkestan made their first appearance in the west. The Slavic armies were beaten near the Kalka river and Russia was at the mercy of the Mongolians. Just as suddenly as they had come they disappeared. Thirteen years later, in 1237, however, they returned. In less than five years they conquered every part of the vast Russian plains. Until the year 1380 when Dmitry Donskoi, Grand Duke of Moscow, beat them on the plains of Kulikovo, the Tartars were the masters of the Russian people.

All in all, it took the Russians two centuries to deliver themselves from this yoke. For a yoke it was and a most offensive and objectionable one. It turned the Slavic peasants into miserable slaves. No Russian could hope to survive unless he was willing to creep before a dirty little yellow man who sat in a tent somewhere in the heart of the steppes of southern Russia and spat at him. It deprived the mass of the people of all feeling of honour and independence. It made hunger and misery and maltreatment and personal abuse the normal state of human existence. Until at last the average Russian, were he peasant or nobleman, went about his business like a neglected dog who has been beaten so often that his spirit has been broken and he dare not wag his tail without permission.

There was no escape. The horsemen of the Tartar Khan were fast and merciless. The endless prairie did not give a man a chance to cross into the safe territory of his neighbour. He must keep quiet and bear what his yellow master decided to inflict upon him or run the risk of death. Of course, Europe might have interfered. But Europe was engaged upon business of its own, fighting the quarrels between the Pope and the emperor or suppressing this or that or the other heresy. And so Europe left the Slav to his fate, and forced him to work out his own salvation.

The final saviour of Russia was one of the many small states, founded by the early Norse rulers. It was situated in the heart of the Russian plain. Its capital, Moscow, was upon a steep hill on the banks of the Moskwa river. This little principality, by dint of pleasing the Tartar (when it was necessary to please), and opposing him (when it was safe to do so), had, during the middle of the fourteenth century made itself the leader of a new national life. It must be remembered that the Tartars were wholly deficient in constructive political ability. They could only destroy. Their chief aim in conquering new territories was to obtain revenue. To get this revenue in the form of taxes, it was necessary to allow certain remnants of the old political organization to continue. Hence there were many little towns, surviving by the grace of the Great Khan, that they might act as tax-gatherers and rob their neighbours for the benefit of the Tartar treasury.

The state of Moscow, growing fat at the expense of the surrounding territory, finally became strong enough to risk

open rebellion against its masters, the Tartars. It was successful and its fame as the leader in the cause of Russian independence made Moscow the natural centre for all those who
still believed in a better future for the Slavic race. In the year
1453, Constantinople was taken by the Turks. Ten years
later, under the rule of Ivan III, Moscow informed the
western world that the Slavic state laid claim to the worldly
and spiritual inheritance of the lost Byzantine Empire, and
such traditions of the Roman empire as had survived in Constantinople. A generation afterwards, under Ivan the Terrible,
the grand dukes of Moscow were strong enough to adopt the
title of Cæsar, or Tsar, and to demand recognition by the western powers of Europe.

In the year 1598, with Feodor the First, the old Muscovite
dynasty, descendants of the original Norseman Rurik, came to
an end. For the next seven years, a Tartar half-breed, by the
name of Boris Godunow, reigned as Tsar. It was during
this period that the future destiny of the large masses of the
Russian people was decided. This Empire was rich in land
but very poor in money. There was no trade and there were
no factories. Its few cities were dirty villages. It was composed of a strong central government and a vast number of
illiterate peasants. This government, a mixture of Slavic,
Norse, Byzantine and Tartar influences, recognised nothing beyond the interest of the state. To defend this state, it
needed an army. To gather the taxes, which were necessary
to pay the soldiers, it needed civil servants. To pay these many
officials it needed land. In the vast wilderness on the east
and west there was a sufficient supply of this commodity. But
land without a few labourers to till the fields and tend the
cattle, has no value. Therefore the old nomadic peasants
were robbed of one privilege after the other, until finally, during the first year of the seventeenth century, they were formally
made a part of the soil upon which they lived. The Russian
peasants ceased to be free men. They became serfs or slaves
and they remained serfs until the year 1861, when their fate
had become so terrible that they were beginning to die out.

In the seventeenth century, this new state with its growing territory which was spreading quickly into Siberia, had become a force with which the rest of Europe was obliged to reckon. In 1613, after the death of Boris Godunow, the Russian nobles had elected one of their own number to be Tsar. He was Michael, the son of Feodor, of the Moscow family of Romanow who lived in a little house just outside the Kremlin.

In the year 1672 his great-grandson, Peter, the son of another Feodor, was born. When the child was ten years old, his step-sister Sophia took possession of the Russian throne. The little boy was allowed to spend his days in the suburbs of the national capital, where the foreigners lived. Surrounded by Scotch barkeepers, Dutch traders, Swiss apothecaries, Italian barbers, French dancing teachers and German school-masters, the young prince obtained a first but rather extraordinary impression of that far-away and mysterious Europe where things were done differently.

When he was seventeen years old, he suddenly pushed Sister Sophia from the throne. Peter himself became the ruler of Russia. He was not contented with being the Tsar of a semi-barbarous and half-Asiatic people. He must be the sovereign head of a civilised nation. To change Russia overnight from a Byzantine-Tartar state into a European empire was no small undertaking. It needed strong hands and a capable head. Peter possessed both. In the year 1698, the great operation of grafting Modern Europe upon Ancient Russia was performed. The patient did not die. But he never got over the shock, as the events of the last five years have shown very plainly.

RUSSIA vs. SWEDEN

RUSSIA AND SWEDEN FIGHT MANY WARS TO DECIDE WHO SHALL BE THE LEADING POWER OF NORTH-EASTERN EUROPE

In the year 1698, Tsar Peter set forth upon his first voyage to western Europe. He travelled by way of Berlin and went to Holland and to England. As a child he had almost been drowned sailing a home-made boat in the duck pond of his father's country home. This passion for water remained with him to the end of his life. In a practical way it showed itself in his wish to give his land-locked domains access to the open sea.

PETER THE GREAT IN THE DUTCH SHIPYARD

While the unpopular and harsh young ruler was away from home, the friends of the old Russian ways in Moscow set to work to undo all his reforms. A sudden rebellion among his life-guards, the Streltsi regiment, forced Peter to hasten home by the fast mail. He appointed himself executioner-in-chief and the Streltsi were hanged and quartered and killed to the last man. Sister Sophia, who had been the head of the rebellion, was locked up in a cloister and the rule of Peter began in earnest. This scene was repeated in the year 1716 when Peter had gone on his second western trip. That time the reactionaries followed the leadership of Peter's half-witted son, Alexis. Again the Tsar returned in great haste. Alexis was beaten to death in his prison cell and the friends of the old fashioned Byzantine ways marched thousands of dreary miles to their final destination in the Siberian lead mines. After that, no further outbreaks of popular discontent took place. Until the time of his death, Peter could reform in peace.

It is not easy to give you a list of his reforms in chronological order. The Tsar worked with furious haste. He followed no system. He issued his decrees with such rapidity that it is difficult to keep count. Peter seemed to feel that everything that had ever happened before was entirely wrong. The whole of Russia therefore must be changed within the shortest possible time. When he died he left behind a well-trained army of 200,000 men and a navy of fifty ships. The old system of government had been abolished over night. The Duma, or convention of Nobles, had been dismissed and in its stead, the Tsar had surrounded himself with an advisory board of state officials, called the Senate.

Russia was divided into eight large "governments" or provinces. Roads were constructed. Towns were built. Industries were created wherever it pleased the Tsar, without any regard for the presence of raw material. Canals were dug and mines were opened in the mountains of the east. In this land of illiterates, schools were founded and establishments of higher learning, together with Universities and hospitals and professional schools. Dutch naval engineers and tradesmen and artisans from all over the world were encouraged to move to Russia. Printing shops were established, but all books must be first read by the imperial censors. The duties of each class of society were carefully written down in a new law and the entire system of civil and criminal laws was gathered into a series of printed volumes. The old Russian costumes were abolished by Imperial decree, and policemen, armed with scissors, watching all the country roads, changed the long-haired Russian moujiks suddenly into a pleasing imitation of smooth-shaven west-Europeans.

In religious matters, the Tsar tolerated no division of power. There must be no chance of a rivalry between an Emperor and a Pope as had happened in Europe. In the year 1721, Peter made himself head of the Russian Church. The Patriarchate of Moscow was abolished and the Holy Synod made its appearance as the highest source of authority in all matters of the Established Church.

Since, however, these many reforms could not be success-

PETER THE GREAT BUILDS HIS NEW CAPITAL

ful while the old Russian elements had a rallying point in the town of Moscow, Peter decided to move his government to a new capital. Amidst the unhealthy marshes of the Baltic Sea the Tsar built this new city. He began to reclaim the land in the year 1703. Forty thousand peasants worked for years to lay the foundations for this Imperial city. The Swedes attacked Peter and tried to destroy his town and illness and misery killed tens of thousands of the peasants. But the work was continued, winter and summer, and the ready-made town soon began to grow. In the year 1712, it was officially de-

MOSCOW

clared to be the "Imperial Residence." A dozen years later it had 75,000 inhabitants. Twice a year the whole city was flooded by the Neva. But the terrific will-power of the Tsar created dykes and canals and the floods ceased to do harm. When Peter died in 1725 he was the owner of the largest city in northern Europe.

Of course, this sudden growth of so dangerous a rival had been a source of great worry to all the neighbours. From his side, Peter had watched with interest the many adventures of his Baltic rival, the kingdom of Sweden. In the year 1654, Christina, the only daughter of Gustavus Adolphus, the hero of the Thirty Years War, had renounced the throne and had gone to Rome to end her days as a devout Catholic. A Protestant nephew of Gustavus Adolphus had succeeded the last Queen of the House of Vasa. Under Charles X and Charles XI, the new dynasty had brought Sweden to its highest point of development. But in 1697, Charles XI died suddenly and was succeeded by a boy of fifteen, Charles XII.

This was the moment for which many of the northern states had waited. During the great religious wars of the seventeenth century, Sweden had grown at the expense of her neighbours. The time had come, so the owners thought, to balance the account. At once war broke out between Russia, Poland, Denmark and Saxony on the one side, and Sweden on the other. The raw and untrained armies of Peter were disastrously beaten by Charles in the famous battle of Narva in November of the year 1700. Then Charles, one of the most interesting military geniuses of that century, turned against his other enemies and for nine years he hacked and burned his way through the villages and cities of Poland, Saxony, Denmark and the Baltic provinces, while Peter drilled and trained his soldiers in distant Russia.

As a result, in the year 1709, in the battle of Poltawa, the Moscovites destroyed the exhausted armies of Sweden. Charles continued to be a highly picturesque figure, a wonderful hero of romance, but in his vain attempt to have his revenge, he ruined his own country. In the year 1718, he was accidentally killed or assassinated (we do not know which) and when peace was made in 1721, in the town of Nystadt, Sweden had lost all of her former Baltic possessions except Finland. The new Russian state, created by Peter, had become the leading power of northern Europe. But already a new rival was on the way. The Prussian state was taking shape.

THE RISE OF PRUSSIA

THE EXTRAORDINARY RISE OF A LITTLE STATE IN A DREARY PART OF NORTHERN GERMANY, CALLED PRUSSIA

THE history of Prussia is the history of a frontier district. In the ninth century, Charlemagne had transferred the old centre of civilisation from the Mediterranean to the wild regions of northwestern Europe. His Frankish soldiers had pushed the frontier of Europe further and further towards the east. They had conquered many lands from the heathenish Slavs and Lithuanians who were living in the plain between the Baltic Sea and the Carpathian Mountains, and the Franks administered those outlying districts just as the United States used to administer her territories before they achieved the dignity of statehood.

The frontier state of Brandenburg had been originally founded by Charlemagne to defend his eastern possessions against raids of the wild Saxon tribes. The Wends, a Slavic tribe which inhabited that region, were subjugated during the tenth century and their market-place, by the name of Brennabor, became the centre of and gave its name to the new province of Brandenburg.

During the eleventh, twelfth, thirteenth and fourteenth centuries, a succession of noble families exercised the functions of imperial governor in this frontier state. Finally in the fifteenth century, the House of Hohenzollern made its appearance, and as Electors of Brandenburg, commenced to change a sandy and forlorn frontier territory into one of the most efficient empires of the modern world.

These Hohenzollerns, who have just been removed from the historical stage by the combined forces of Europe and America, came originally from southern Germany. They were of very humble origin. In the twelfth century a certain Frederick of Hohenzollern had made a lucky marriage and had been appointed keeper of the castle of Nuremberg. His descendants had used every chance and every opportunity to improve their power and after several centuries of watchful grabbing, they had been appointed to the dignity of Elector, the name given to those sovereign princes who were supposed to elect the Emperors of the old German Empire. During the Reformation, they had taken the side of the Protestants and the early seventeenth century found them among the most powerful of the north German princes.

During the Thirty Years War, both Protestants and Catholics had plundered Brandenburg and Prussia with equal zeal. But under Frederick William, the Great Elector, the damage was quickly repaired and by a wise and careful use of all the economic and intellectual forces of the country, a state was founded in which there was practically no waste.

Modern Prussia, a state in which the individual and his wishes and aspirations have been entirely absorbed by the interests of the community as a whole—this Prussia dates back to the father of Frederick the Great. Frederick William I was a hard working, parsimonious Prussian sergeant, with a great love for bar-room stories and strong Dutch tobacco, an intense dislike of all frills and feathers, (especially if they were of French origin,) and possessed of but one idea. That idea was Duty. Severe with himself, he tolerated no weakness in his subjects, whether they be generals or common soldiers. The relation between himself and his son Frederick was never cordial, to say the least. The boorish manners of the father offended the finer spirit of the son. The son's love for French manners, literature, philosophy and music was rejected by the father as a manifestation of sissy-ness. There followed a terrible outbreak between these two strange temperaments. Frederick tried to escape to England. He was caught and court-martialed and forced to witness the decapitation of his best friend who had tried to help him. Thereupon as part of his punishment, the young prince was sent to a little fortress somewhere in the provinces to be taught the details of his future business of being a king. It proved a blessing in disguise. When Frederick came to the throne in 1740, he knew how his country was managed from the birth certificate of a pauper's son to the minutest detail of a complicated annual Budget.

As an author, especially in his book called the "Anti-Macchiavelli," Frederick had expressed his contempt for the political creed of the ancient Florentine historian, who had advised his princely pupils to lie and cheat whenever it was necessary to do so for the benefit of their country. The ideal ruler in Frederick's volume was the first servant of his people, the enlightened despot after the example of Louis XIV. In practice, however, Frederick, while working for his people twenty hours a day, tolerated no one to be near him as a counsellor. His ministers were superior clerks. Prussia was his private possession, to be treated according to his own wishes. And nothing was allowed to interfere with the interest of the state.

In the year 1740 the Emperor Charles VI, of Austria, died. He had tried to make the position of his only daughter, Maria Theresa, secure through a solemn treaty, written black on white, upon a large piece of parchment. But no sooner had the old emperor been deposited in the ancestral crypt of the Habsburg family, than the armies of Frederick were marching towards the Austrian frontier to occupy that part of Silesia for which (together with almost everything else in central Europe) Prussia clamored, on account of some ancient and very doubtful rights of claim. In a number of wars, Frederick conquered all of Silesia, and although he was often very near defeat, he maintained himself in his newly acquired territories against all Austrian counter-attacks.

Europe took due notice of this sudden appearance of a very powerful new state. In the eighteenth century, the Germans were a people who had been ruined by the great religious wars and who were not held in high esteem by any one. Frederick, by an effort as sudden and quite as terrific as that of Peter of Russia, changed this attitude of contempt into one of fear. The internal affairs of Prussia were arranged so skillfully that the subjects had less reason for complaint than elsewhere. The treasury showed an annual surplus instead of a deficit. Torture was abolished. The judiciary system was improved. Good roads and good schools and good universities, together with a scrupulously honest administration, made the people feel that whatever services were demanded of them, they (to speak the vernacular) got their money's worth.

After having been for several centuries the battle field of the French and the Austrians and the Swedes and the Danes and the Poles, Germany, encouraged by the example of Prussia, began to regain self-confidence. And this was the work of the little old man, with his hook-nose and his old uniforms covered with snuff, who said very funny but very unpleasant things about his neighbours, and who played the scandalous game of eighteenth century diplomacy without any regard for the truth, provided he could gain something by his lies. This in spite of his book, "Anti-Macchiavelli." In the year 1786 the end came. His friends were all gone. Children he had never had. He died alone, tended by a single servant and his faithful dogs, whom he loved better than human beings because, as he said, they were never ungrateful and remained true to their friends.

THE MERCANTILE SYSTEM

HOW THE NEWLY FOUNDED NATIONAL OR DYNASTIC STATES OF EUROPE TRIED TO MAKE THEMSELVES RICH AND WHAT WAS MEANT BY THE MERCANTILE SYSTEM

WE have seen how, during the sixteenth and the seventeenth centuries, the states of our modern world began to take shape. Their origins were different in almost every case. Some had been the result of the deliberate effort of a single king. Others had happened by chance. Still others had been the result of favourable natural geographic boundaries. But once they had been founded, they had all of them tried to strengthen their internal administration and to exert the greatest possible influence upon foreign affairs. All this of course had cost a great deal of money. The mediæval state with its lack of centralised power did not depend upon a rich treasury. The king got his revenues from the crown domains and his civil service paid for itself. The modern centralised state was a more complicated affair. The old knights disappeared and hired government officials or bureaucrats took their place. Army, navy, and internal administration demanded millions. The question then became—where was this money to be found?

Gold and silver had been a rare commodity in the middle ages. The average man, as I have told you, never saw a gold piece as long as he lived. Only the inhabitants of the large

317

THE VOYAGE OF THE PILGRIMS

cities were familiar with silver coin. The discovery of America and the exploitation of the Peruvian mines changed all this. The centre of trade was transferred from the Mediterranean to the Atlantic seaboard. The old "commercial cities" of Italy lost their financial importance. New "commercial nations" took their place and gold and silver were no longer a curiosity.

Through Spain and Portugal and Holland and England, precious metals began to find their way to Europe. The sixteenth century had its own writers on the subject of political economy and they evolved a theory of national wealth which seemed to them entirely sound and of the greatest possible benefit to their respective countries. They reasoned that both gold and silver were actual wealth. Therefore they believed that the country with the largest supply of actual cash in the vaults of its treasury and its banks was at the same time the richest country. And since money meant armies, it followed that the richest country was also the most powerful and could rule the rest of the world.

We call this system the "mercantile system," and it was accepted with the same unquestioning faith with which the early Christians believed in Miracles and many of the present-day American business men believe in the Tariff. In practice, the Mercantile system worked out as follows: To get the largest surplus of precious metals a country must have a favourable balance of export trade. If you can export more to your neighbour than he exports to your own country, he will owe you money and will be obliged to send you some of his gold. Hence you gain and he loses. As a result of this creed, the economic program of almost every seventeenth century state was as follows:

1. Try to get possession of as many precious metals as you can.

2. Encourage foreign trade in preference to domestic trade.

3. Encourage those industries which change raw materials into exportable finished products.

4. Encourage a large population, for you will need workmen for your factories and an agricultural community does not raise enough workmen.

5. Let the State watch this process and interfere whenever it is necessary to do so.

Instead of regarding International Trade as something akin to a force of nature which would always obey certain natural laws regardless of man's interference, the people of the sixteenth and seventeenth centuries tried to regulate their commerce by the help of official decrees and royal laws and financial help on the part of the government.

In the sixteenth century Charles V adopted this Mercantile System (which was then something entirely new) and introduced it into his many possessions. Elizabeth of England flattered him by her imitation. The Bourbons, especially King Louis XIV, were fanatical adherents of this doctrine and Colbert, his great minister of finance, became the prophet of Mercantilism to whom all Europe looked for guidance.

The entire foreign policy of Cromwell was a practical application of the Mercantile System. It was invariably directed against the rich rival Republic of Holland. For the Dutch shippers, as the common-carriers of the merchandise of Europe, had certain leanings towards free-trade and therefore had to be destroyed at all cost.

It will be easily understood how such a system must affect the colonies. A colony under the Mercantile System became merely a reservoir of gold and silver and spices, which was to be tapped for the benefit of the home country. The Asiatic, American and African supply of precious metals and the raw materials of these tropical countries became a monopoly of the state which happened to own that particular colony. No outsider was ever allowed within the precincts and no native was permitted to trade with a merchant whose ship flew a foreign flag.

Undoubtedly the Mercantile System encouraged the development of young industries in certain countries where there never had been any manufacturing before. It built roads

HOW EUROPE CONQUERED THE WORLD

and dug canals and made for better means of transportation. It demanded greater skill among the workmen and gave the merchant a better social position, while it weakened the power of the landed aristocracy.

On the other hand, it caused very great misery. It made the natives in the colonies the victims of a most shameless exploitation. It exposed the citizens of the home country to an even more terrible fate. It helped in a great measure to turn

SEA POWER

every land into an armed camp and divided the world into little bits of territory, each working for its own direct benefit, while striving at all times to destroy the power of its neighbours and get hold of their treasures. It laid so much stress upon the importance of owning wealth that "being rich" came to be regarded as the sole virtue of the average citizen. Economic systems come and go like the fashions in surgery and in the clothes of women, and during the nineteenth century the Mercantile System was discarded in favor of a system of free and open competition. At least, so I have been told.

THE AMERICAN REVOLUTION

AT THE END OF THE EIGHTEENTH CENTURY EUROPE HEARD STRANGE REPORTS OF SOMETHING WHICH HAD HAPPENED IN THE WILDERNESS OF THE NORTH AMERICAN CONTINENT. THE DESCENDANTS OF THE MEN WHO HAD PUNISHED KING CHARLES FOR HIS INSISTENCE UPON HIS "DIVINE RIGHTS" ADDED A NEW CHAPTER TO THE OLD STORY OF THE STRUGGLE FOR SELF-GOVERNMENT

FOR the sake of convenience, we ought to go back a few centuries and repeat the early history of the great struggle for colonial possessions.

As soon as a number of European nations had been created upon the new basis of national or dynastic interests, that is to say, during and immediately after the Thirty Years War, their rulers, backed up by the capital of their merchants and the ships of their trading companies, continued the fight for more territory in Asia, Africa and America.

THE FIGHT FOR LIBERTY

823

The Spaniards and the Portuguese had been exploring the
Indian Sea and the Pacific Ocean for more than a century ere
Holland and England appeared upon the stage. This proved
an advantage to the latter. The first rough work had already
been done. What is more, the earliest navigators had so often
made themselves unpopular with the Asiatic and American and
African natives that both the English and the Dutch were
welcomed as friends and deliverers. We cannot claim any

THE PILGRIMS

superior virtues for either of these two races. But they were
merchants before everything else. They never allowed religious
considerations to interfere with their practical common sense.
During their first relations with weaker races, all European nations have behaved with shocking brutality. The English and
the Dutch, however, knew better where to draw the line. Provided they got their spices and their gold and silver and their

HOW THE WHITE MAN SETTLED IN NORTH AMERICA

taxes, they were willing to let the native live as it best pleased him.

It was not very difficult for them therefore to establish themselves in the richest parts of the world. But as soon as this had been accomplished, they began to fight each other for still further possessions. Strangely enough, the colonial wars were never settled in the colonies themselves. They were decided three thousand miles away by the navies of the contending countries. It is one of the most interesting principles of ancient and modern warfare (one of the few reliable laws of history) that "the nation which commands the sea is also the nation which commands the land." So far this law has never failed to work, but the modern airplane may have changed it. In the eighteenth century, however, there were no flying machines and it was the British navy which gained for England her vast American and Indian and African colonies.

The series of naval wars between England and Holland in the seventeenth century does not interest us here. It ended as all such encounters between hopelessly ill-matched powers will end. But the warfare between England and France (her other rival) is of greater importance to us, for while the superior British fleet in the end defeated the French navy, a great deal of the preliminary fighting was done on our own American continent. In this vast country, both France and England claimed everything which had been discovered and a lot more which the eye of no white man had ever seen. In 1497 Cabot had landed in the northern part of America and twenty-seven years later, Giovanni Verrazano had visited these coasts. Cabot had flown the English flag. Verrazano had sailed under the French flag. Hence both England and France proclaimed themselves the owners of the entire continent.

During the seventeenth century, some ten small English colonies had been founded between Maine and the Carolinas. They were usually a haven of refuge for some particular sect of English dissenters, such as the Puritans, who in the year 1620 went to New England, or the Quakers, who settled in

THE BLOCKHOUSE IN THE WILDERNESS

Pennsylvania in 1681. They were small frontier communities, nestling close to the shores of the ocean, where people had gathered to make a new home and begin life among happier surroundings, far away from royal supervision and interference.

The French colonies, on the other hand, always remained a possession of the crown. No Huguenots or Protestants were

IN THE CABIN OF THE *MAYFLOWER*

allowed in these colonies for fear that they might contaminate the Indians with their dangerous Protestant doctrines and would perhaps interfere with the missionary work of the Jesuit fathers. The English colonies, therefore, had been founded upon a much healthier basis than their French neighbours and rivals. They were an expression of the commercial energy of the English middle classes, while the French settlements were inhabited by people who had crossed the ocean as servants of the king and who expected to return to Paris at the first possible chance.

Politically, however, the position of the English colonies was far from satisfactory. The French had discovered the mouth of the Saint Lawrence in the sixteenth century. From the region of the Great Lakes they had worked their way southward, had descended the Mississippi and had built several fortifications along the Gulf of Mexico. After a century of exploration, a line of sixty French forts cut off the English settlements along the Atlantic seaboard from the interior.

THE FRENCH EXPLORE THE WEST

The English land grants, made to the different colonial companies had given them "all land from sea to sea." This sounded well on paper, but in practice, British territory ended where the line of French fortifications began. To break through this barrier was possible but it took both men and money and caused a series of horrible border wars in which both sides murdered their white neighbours, with the help of the Indian tribes.

As long as the Stuarts had ruled England there had been no danger of war with France. The Stuarts needed the Bourbons in their attempt to establish an autocratic form of government and to break the power of Parliament. But in 1689 the last of the Stuarts had disappeared from British soil and Dutch

William, the great enemy of Louis XIV succeeded him. From
that time on, until the Treaty of Paris of 1763, France and
England fought for the possession of India and North America.

During these wars, as I have said before, the English navies
invariably beat the French. Cut off from her colonies, France
lost most of her possessions, and when peace was declared, the
entire North American continent had fallen into British hands
and the great work of exploration of Cartier, Champlain, La
Salle, Marquette and a score of others was lost to France.

THE FIRST WINTER IN NEW ENGLAND

Only a very small part of this vast domain was inhabited.
From Massachusetts in the north, where the Pilgrims (a sect
of Puritans who were very intolerant and who therefore had
found no happiness either in Anglican England or Calvinist
Holland) had landed in the year 1620, to the Carolinas and
Virginia (the tobacco-raising provinces which had been founded entirely for the sake of profit) stretched a thin line of
sparsely populated territory. But the men who lived in this
new land of fresh air and high skies were very different from
their brethren of the mother country. In the wilderness they
had learned independence and self-reliance. They were the
sons of hardy and energetic ancestors. Lazy and timourous
people did not cross the ocean in those days. The American

colonists hated the restraint and the lack of breathing space which had made their lives in the old country so very unhappy. They meant to be their own masters. This the ruling classes of England did not seem to understand. The government annoyed the colonists and the colonists, who hated to be bothered in this way, began to annoy the British government.

Bad feeling caused more bad feeling. It is not necessary to repeat here in detail what actually happened and what might have been avoided if the British king had been more intelligent than George III or less given to drowsiness and indifference than his minister, Lord North. The British colonists, when they understood that peaceful arguments would not settle the difficulties, took to arms. From being loyal subjects, they turned rebels, who exposed themselves to the punishment of death when they were captured by the German soldiers, whom George hired to do his fighting after the pleasant custom of that day, when Teutonic princes sold whole regiments to the highest bidder.

The war between England and her American colonies lasted seven years. During most of that time, the final success of the rebels seemed very doubtful. A great number of the people, especially in the cities, had remained loyal to their king. They were in favour of a compromise, and would have been willing to sue for peace. But the great figure of Washington stood guard over the cause of the colonists

Ably assisted by a handful of brave men, he used his steadfast but badly equipped armies to weaken the forces of the king Time and again when defeat seemed unavoidable, his strategy turned the tide of battle. Often his men were ill-fed. During the winter they lacked shoes and coats and were forced to live in unhealthy dug-outs. But their trust in their great leader was absolute and they stuck it out until the final hour of victory.

But more interesting than the campaigns of Washington or the diplomatic triumphs of Benjamin Franklin who was in Europe getting money from the French government and the Amsterdam bankers, was an event which occurred early in the revolution. The representatives of the different colonies had gathered in Philadelphia to discuss matters of common importance. It was the first year of the Revolution. Most of the big towns of the sea coast were still in the hands of the British. Reinforcements from England were arriving by the ship load. Only men who were deeply convinced of the righteousness of their cause would have found the courage to take the momentous decision of the months of June and July of the year 1776.

GEORGE WASHINGTON

In June, Richard Henry Lee of Virginia proposed a motion to the Continental Congress that "these united colonies are, and of right ought to be, free and independent states, that they are absolved from all allegiance to the British crown, and that all political connection between them and the state of Great Britain is and ought to be, totally dissolved."

The motion was seconded by John Adams of Massachusetts. It was carried on July the second and on July fourth, it was followed by an official Declaration of Independence, which was the work of Thomas Jefferson, a serious and exceedingly capable student of both politics and government and

THE MAIN EVENTS IN THE STRUGGLE FOR AMERICAN INDEPENDENCE

CANADA

QUEBEC

MONTREAL

ST LAWRENCE

NOVA SCOTIA

LAKE ONTARIO

BURGOYNE'S EXPEDITION

LAKE CHAMPLAIN

HALIFAX

LAKE ERIE

TICONDEROGA

LEXINGTON

BOSTON

WILDERNESS

SARATOGA 3

WASHINGTON DRIVES THE BRITISH OUT OF BOSTON

I

HUDSON RIVER

1
BATTLE OF LEXINGTON APRIL 19 1775 CONTINENTAL ARMY UNDER WASHINGTON BESIEGES BOSTON FROM JULY 1775 TO MARCH 17 OF THE YEAR 1776 THE BRITISH RETIRE TO HALIFAX

WASHINGTON SAVES HIS ARMY FROM DESTRUCTION

II

NEW YORK

3

LONG ISLAND

PRINCETON
TRENTON
PHILADELPHIA

JULY 4 1776 DECLARATION OF INDEPENDENCE

III
BALTIMORE

2

WASHINGTON DEFEATS CORNWALLIS

YORKTOWN

5

CHARLESTON

5

5

3
AFTER THE FAILURE OF THE NORTHERN CAMPAIGN THE BRITISH TAKE NEW YORK ON SEPT. 15 1776 BUT FAIL TO DESTROY THE FORCES OF WASHINGTON. TO CUT THE COLONIES IN TWO A BRITISH ARMY COMING FROM CANADA FORCED ITS WAY PAST TICONDEROGA. THESE TROOPS HOWEVER WERE NOT TRAINED FOR WILDERNESS-WARFARE AND AS A RESULT BURGOYNE AND ALL HIS MEN SURRENDER NEAR SARATOGA OCT. 17 OF THE YEAR 1777

5
AFTER THE FAILURE OF THE CENTRAL CAMPAIGN THE ENGLISH TROOPS ARE TAKEN SOUTH. THEY CAPTURE CHARLESTON MAY 12, 1780 AND THEN BEGIN THEIR MARCH TOWARDS THE NORTH. THIS EXPEDITION ENDS ON OCT. 19 OF THE YEAR 1781 WHEN CORNWALLIS AND ALL HIS MEN SURRENDER AT YORKTOWN IN VIRGINIA. THAT WAS THE END.

4
AFTER THE SURRENDER OF BURGOYNE FRANCE RECOGNIZES THE U.S. FEB. 8 1778 IN JUNE OF 1778 A FRENCH FLEET WITH 4000 MEN ARRIVES.

THE GREAT AMERICAN REVOLUTION

destined to be one of the most famous of our American presidents.

When news of this event reached Europe, and was followed by the final victory of the colonists and the adoption of the famous Constitution of the year 1787 (the first of all written constitutions) it caused great interest. The dynastic system of the highly centralised states which had been developed after the great religious wars of the seventeenth century had reached the height of its power. Everywhere the palace of the king had grown to enormous proportions, while the cities of the royal realm were being surrounded by rapidly growing acres of slums. The inhabitants of those slums were showing signs of restlessness. They were quite helpless. But the higher classes, the nobles and the professional men, they too were beginning to have certain doubts about the economic and political conditions under which they lived. The success of the American colonists showed them that many things were possible which had been held impossible only a short time before.

According to the poet, the shot which opened the battle of Lexington was "heard around the world." That was a bit of an exaggeration. The Chinese and the Japanese and the Russians (not to speak of the Australians and the Hawaiians who had just been re-discovered by Captain Cook, whom they had killed for his trouble) never heard of it at all. But it carried across the Atlantic Ocean. It landed in the powder house of European discontent and in France it caused an explosion which rocked the entire continent from Petrograd to Madrid and buried the representatives of the old statecraft and the old diplomacy under several tons of democratic bricks.

THE FRENCH REVOLUTION

THE GREAT FRENCH REVOLUTION PROCLAIMS THE PRINCIPLES OF LIBERTY, FRATERNITY AND EQUALITY UNTO ALL THE PEOPLE OF THE EARTH

BEFORE we talk about a revolution it is just as well that we explain just what this word means. In the terms of a great Russian writer (and Russians ought to know what they are talking about in this field) a revolution is "a swift overthrow, in a few years, of institutions which have taken centuries to root in the soil, and seem so fixed and immovable that even the most ardent reformers hardly dare to attack them in their writings. It is the fall, the crumbling away in a brief period, of all that up to that time has composed the essence of social, religious, political and economic life in a nation."

Such a revolution took place in France in the eighteenth century when the old civilisation of the country had grown stale. The king in the days of Louis XIV had become EVERYTHING and was the state. The Nobility, formerly the civil servant of the federal state, found itself without any duties and became a social ornament of the royal court.

This French state of the eighteenth century, however, cost incredible sums of money. This money had to be produced in the form of taxes. Unfortunately the kings of France had not been strong enough to force the nobility and the clergy to pay their share of these taxes. Hence the taxes were paid entirely by the agricultural population. But the peasants living in dreary hovels, no longer in intimate contact with their former landlords, but victims of cruel and incompetent land agents, were going from bad to worse. Why should they work and exert themselves? Increased returns upon their land merely meant more taxes and nothing for themselves and therefore they neglected their fields as much as they dared.

Hence we have a king who wanders in empty splendour through the vast halls of his palaces, habitually followed by hungry office seekers, all of whom live upon the revenue obtained from peasants who are no better than the beasts of the fields. It is not a pleasant picture, but it is not exaggerated. There was, however, another side to the so-called "Ancien Régime" which we must keep in mind.

A wealthy middle class, closely connected with the nobility (by the usual process of the rich banker's daughter marrying the poor baron's son) and a court composed of all the most entertaining people of France, had brought the polite art of graceful living to its highest development. As the best brains of the country were not allowed to occupy themselves with questions of political economics, they spent their idle hours upon the discussion of abstract ideas.

As fashions in modes of thought and personal behaviour are quite as likely to run to extremes as fashion in dress, it was natural that the most artificial society of that day should take a tremendous interest in what they considered "the simple life." The king and the queen, the absolute and unquestioned proprietors of France, and all its colonies and dependencies, together with their courtiers, went to live in funny little country houses all dressed up as milk-maids and stable-boys and played at being shepherds in a happy vale of ancient Hellas. Around them, their courtiers danced attendance, their court-musicians composed lovely minuets, their court barbers devised more and more elaborate and costly headgear, until from sheer boredom and lack of real jobs, this whole artificial world of Versailles (the great show place which Louis XIV had built far away from his noisy and restless city) talked of nothing but those subjects which were furthest removed from their own lives, just as a man who is starving will talk of nothing except food.

When Voltaire, the courageous old philosopher, play-wright, historian and novelist, and the great enemy of all religious and political tyranny, began to throw his bombs of criticism at everything connected with the Established Order of Things, the whole French world applauded him and his theatrical pieces played to standing room only. When Jean Jacques Rousseau waxed sentimental about primitive man and gave his contemporaries delightful descriptions of the happiness of the original inhabitants of this planet, (about whom he knew as little as he did about the children, upon whose education he was the recognised authority,) all France ᵣead his "Social Contract" and this society in which the king and the state were one, wept bitter tears when they heard Rous-seau's appeal for a return to the blessed days when the real sovereignty had lain in the hands of the people and when the king had been merely the servant of his people.

When Montesquieu published his "Persian Letters" in which two distinguished Persian travellers turn the whole ex-isting society of France topsy-turvy and poke fun at every-thing from the king down to the lowest of his six hundred pastry cooks, the book immediately went through four editions and assured the writer thousands of readers for his famous discussion of the "Spirit of the Laws" in which the noble Baron compared the excellent English system with the backward system of France and advocated instead of an abso-lute monarchy the establishment of a state in which the Execu-tive, the Legislative and the Judicial powers should be in separate hands and should work independently of each other. When Lebreton, the Parisian book-seller, announced that Messieurs Diderot, d'Alembert, Turgot and a score of other distinguished writers were going to publish an Encyclopædia which was to contain "all the new ideas and the new science and the new knowledge," the response from the side of the public was most satisfactory, and when after twenty-two years the last of the twenty-eight volumes had been finished, the somewhat belated interference of the police could not repress the enthusiasm with which French society received this most important but very dangerous contribution to the discussions of the day.

Here, let me give you a little warning. When you read a novel about the French revolution or see a play or a movie, you will easily get the impression that the Revolution was the work of the rabble from the Paris slums. It was nothing of the kind. The mob appears often upon the revolutionary stage, but invariably at the instigation and under the leadership of those middle-class professional men who used the hungry multitude as an efficient ally in their warfare upon the king and his court. But the fundamental ideas which caused the revolution were invented by a few brilliant minds, and they were at first introduced into the charming drawing-rooms of the "Ancien Régime" to provide amiable diversion for the much-bored ladies and gentlemen of his Majesty's court. These pleasant but careless people played with the dangerous fireworks of social criticism until the sparks fell through the cracks of the floor, which was old and rotten just like the rest of the building. Those sparks unfortunately landed in the basement where age-old rubbish lay in great confusion. Then there was a cry of fire. But the owner of the house who was interested in everything except the management of his property, did not know how to put the small blaze out. The flame spread rapidly and the entire edifice was consumed by the conflagration, which we call the Great French Revolution.

THE GUILLOTINE

For the sake of convenience, we can divide the French Revolution into two parts. From 1789 to 1791 there was a more or less orderly attempt to introduce a constitutional monarchy. This failed, partly through lack of good faith and stupidity on the part of the monarch himself, partly through circumstances over which nobody had any control.

From 1792 to 1799 there was a Republic and a first effort to establish a democratic form of government. But the actual outbreak of violence had been preceded by many years of unrest and many sincere but ineffectual attempts at reform.

When France had a debt of 4000 million francs and the treasury was always empty and there was not a single thing upon which new taxes could be levied, even good King Louis (who was an expert locksmith and a great hunter but a very poor statesman) felt vaguely that something ought to be done. Therefore he called for Turgot, to be his Minister of Finance. Anne Robert Jacques Turgot, Baron de l'Aulne, a man in the early sixties, a splendid representative of the fast disappearing class of landed gentry, had been a successful governor of a province and was an amateur political economist of great ability. He did his best. Unfortunately, he could not perform miracles. As it was impossible to squeeze more taxes out of the ragged peasants, it was necessary to get the necessary funds from the nobility and clergy who had never paid a centime. This made Turgot the best hated man at the court of Versailles. Furthermore he was obliged to face the enmity of Marie Antoinette, the queen, who was against everybody who dared to mention the word "economy" within her hearing. Soon Turgot was called an "unpractical visionary" and a "theoretical professor" and then of course his position became untenable. In the year 1776 he was forced to resign.

After the "professor" there came a man of Practical Business Sense. He was an industrious Swiss by the name of Necker who had made himself rich as a grain speculator and the partner in an international banking house. His ambitious wife had pushed him into the government service that she might establish a position for her daughter who afterwards as the wife of the Swedish minister in Paris, Baron de Staël, became a famous literary figure of the early nineteenth century.

Necker set to work with a fine display of zeal just as Turgot had done. In 1781 he published a careful review of the French finances. The king understood nothing of this "Compte Rendu." He had just sent troops to America to help the colonists against their common enemies, the English. This expedition proved to be unexpectedly expensive and Necker was asked to find the necessary funds. When instead of producing revenue, he published more figures and made statistics and began to use the dreary warning about "necessary economies" his days were numbered. In the year 1781 he was dismissed as an incompetent servant.

After the Professor and the Practical Business Man came the delightful type of financier who will guarantee everybody 100 per cent. per month on their money if only they will trust his own infallible system.

LOUIS XVI

He was Charles Alexandre de Calonne, a pushing official, who had made his career both by his industry and his complete lack of honesty and scruples. He found the country heavily indebted, but he was a clever man, willing to oblige everybody, and he invented a quick remedy. He paid the old debts by contracting new ones. This method is not new. The result since time immemorial has been disastrous. In less than three years more than 800,000,000 francs had been added to the French debt by this charming Minister of Finance who never worried and smilingly signed his name to every demand that was made by His Majesty and by his lovely

Queen, who had learned the habit of spending during the days of her youth in Vienna.

At last even the Parliament of Paris (a high court of justice and not a legislative body) although by no means lacking in loyalty to their sovereign, decided that something must be done. Calonne wanted to borrow another 80,000,000 francs. It had been a bad year for the crops and the misery and hunger in the country districts were terrible. Unless something sensible were done, France would go bankrupt. The King as always was unaware of the seriousness of the situation. Would it not be a good idea to consult the representatives of the people? Since 1614 no Estates General had been called together. In view of the threatening panic there was a demand that the Estates be convened. Louis XVI however, who never could take a decision, refused to go as far as that.

To pacify the popular clamour he called together a meeting of the Notables in the year 1787. This merely meant a gathering of the best families who discussed what could and should be done, without touching their feudal and clerical privilege of tax-exemption. It is unreasonable to expect that a certain class of society shall commit political and economic suicide for the benefit of another group of fellow-citizens. The 127 Notables obstinately refused to surrender a single one of their ancient rights. The crowd in the street, being now exceedingly hungry, demanded that Necker, in whom they had confidence, be reappointed. The Notables said "No." The crowd in the street began to smash windows and do other unseemly things. The Notables fled. Calonne was dismissed.

A new colourless Minister of Finance, the Cardinal Loménie de Brienne, was appointed and Louis, driven by the violent threats of his starving subjects, agreed to call together the old Estates General as "soon as practicable." This vague promise of course satisfied no one.

No such severe winter had been experienced for almost a century. The crops had been either destroyed by floods or had been frozen to death in the fields. All the olive trees of Provence had been killed. Private charity tried to do something but could accomplish little for eighteen million starving people. Everywhere bread riots occurred. A generation before these would have been put down by the army. But the work of the new philosophical school had begun to bear fruit. People began to understand that a shotgun is no effective remedy for a hungry stomach and even the soldiers (who came from among the people) were no longer to be depended upon. It was absolutely necessary that the king should do something definite to regain the popular goodwill, but again he hesitated.

Here and there in the provinces, little independent Republics were established by followers of the new school. The cry of "no taxation without representation" (the slogan of the American rebels a quarter of a century before) was heard among the faithful middle classes. France was threatened with general anarchy. To appease the people and to increase the royal popularity, the government unexpectedly suspended the former very strict form of censorship of books. At once a flood of ink descended upon France. Everybody, high or low, criticised and was criticised. More than 2000 pamphlets were published. Loménie de Brienne was swept away by a storm of abuse. Necker was hastily called back to placate, as best he could, the nation-wide unrest. Immediately the stock market went up thirty per cent. And by common consent, people suspended judgment for a little while longer. In May of 1789 the Estates General were to assemble and then the wisdom of the entire nation would speedily solve the difficult problem of recreating the kingdom of France into a healthy and happy state.

This prevailing idea, that the combined wisdom of the people would be able to solve all difficulties, proved disastrous. It lamed all personal effort during many important months. Instead of keeping the government in his own hands at this critical moment, Necker allowed everything to drift. Hence there was a new outbreak of the acrimonious debate upon the best ways to reform the old kingdom. Everywhere the power of the police weakened. The people of the Paris suburbs,

under the leadership of professional agitators, gradually began to discover their strength, and commenced to play the rôle
which was to be theirs all through the years of the great unrest,
when they acted as the brute force which was used by the actual
leaders of the Revolution to secure those things which could
not be obtained in a legitimate fashion.

As a sop to the peasants and the middle class, Necker de-

THE BASTILLE

cided that they should be allowed a double representation in
the Estates General. Upon this subject, the Abbé Siéyès then
wrote a famous pamphlet, "To what does the Third Estate
Amount?" in which he came to the conclusion that the Third
Estate (a name given to the middle class) ought to amount to
everything, that it had not amounted to anything in the past,
and that it now desired to amount to something. He expressed

the sentiment of the great majority of the people who had the best interests of the country at heart.

Finally the elections took place under the worst conditions imaginable. When they were over, 308 clergymen, 285 noblemen and 621 representatives of the Third Estate packed their trunks to go to Versailles. The Third Estate was obliged to carry additional luggage. This consisted of voluminous reports called "cahiers" in which the many complaints and grievances of their constituents had been written down. The stage was set for the great final act that was to save France.

The Estates General came together on May 5th, 1789. The king was in a bad humour. The Clergy and the Nobility let it be known that they were unwilling to give up a single one of their privileges. The king ordered the three groups of representatives to meet in different rooms and discuss their grievances separately. The Third Estate refused to obey the royal command. They took a solemn oath to that effect in a squash court (hastily put in order for the purpose of this illegal meeting) on the 20th of June, 1789. They insisted that all three Estates, Nobility, Clergy and Third Estate, should meet together and so informed His Majesty. The king gave in.

As the "National Assembly," the Estates General began to discuss the state of the French kingdom. The King got angry. Then again he hesitated. He said that he would never surrender his absolute power. Then he went hunting, forgot all about the cares of the state and when he returned from the chase he gave in. For it was the royal habit to do the right thing at the wrong time in the wrong way. When the people clamoured for A, the king scolded them and gave them nothing. Then, when the Palace was surrounded by a howling multitude of poor people, the king surrendered and gave his subjects what they had asked for. By this time, however, the people wanted A plus B. The comedy was repeated. When the king signed his name to the Royal Decree which granted his beloved subjects A and B they were threatening to kill the entire royal family unless they received A plus B plus C. And so on through the whole alphabet and up to the scaffold.

Unfortunately the king was always just one letter behind. He never understood this. Even when he laid his head under the guillotine, he felt that he was a much-abused man who had received a most unwarrantable treatment at the hands of people whom he had loved to the best of his limited ability.

Historical "ifs," as I have often warned you, are never of any value. It is very easy for us to say that the monarchy might have been saved "if" Louis had been a man of greater energy and less kindness of heart. But the king was not alone. Even "if" he had possessed the ruthless strength of Napoleon, his career during these difficult days might have been easily ruined by his wife who was the daughter of Maria Theresa of Austria and who possessed all the characteristic virtues and vices of a young girl who had been brought up at the most autocratic and mediæval court of that age.

She decided that some action must be taken and planned a counter-revolution. Necker was suddenly dismissed and loyal troops were called to Paris. The people, when they heard of this, stormed the fortress of the Bastille prison, and on the fourteenth of July of the year 1789, they destroyed this familiar but much-hated symbol of Autocratic Power which had long since ceased to be a political prison and was now used as the city lock-up for pickpockets and second-story men. Many of the nobles took the hint and left the country. But the king as usual did nothing. He had been hunting on the day of the fall of the Bastille and he had shot several deer and felt very much pleased.

The National Assembly now set to work and on the 4th of August, with the noise of the Parisian multitude in their ears, they abolished all privileges. This was followed on the 27th of August by the "Declaration of the Rights of Man," the famous preamble to the first French constitution. So far so good, but the court had apparently not yet learned its lesson. There was a wide-spread suspicion that the king was again trying to interfere with these reforms and as a result, on the 5th of October, there was a second riot in Paris. It spread to Versailles and the people were not pacified until they had brought the king back to his palace in Paris. They did not trust him in Versailles. They liked to have him where they could watch him and control his correspondence with his relatives in Vienna and Madrid and the other courts of Europe.

In the Assembly meanwhile, Mirabeau, a nobleman who had become leader of the Third Estate, was beginning to put order into chaos. But before he could save the position of the king he died, on the 2nd of April of the year 1791. The king, who now began to fear for his own life, tried to escape on the 21st of June. He was recognised from his picture on a coin, was stopped near the village of Varennes by members of the National Guard, and was brought back to Paris.

In September of 1791, the first constitution of France was accepted, and the members of the National Assembly went home. On the first of October of 1791, the legislative assembly came together to continue the work of the National Assembly. In this new gathering of popular representatives there were many extremely revolutionary elements. The boldest among these were known as the Jacobins, after the old Jacobin cloister in which they held their political meetings. These young men (most of them belonging to the professional classes) made very violent speeches and when the newspapers carried these orations to Berlin and Vienna, the King of Prussia and the Emperor decided that they must do something to save their good brother and sister. They were very busy just then dividing the kingdom of Poland, where rival political factions had caused such a state of disorder that the country was at the mercy of anybody who wanted to take a couple of provinces. But they managed to send an army to invade France and deliver the king.

Then a terrible panic of fear swept throughout the land of France. All the pent-up hatred of years of hunger and suffering came to a horrible climax. The mob of Paris stormed the palace of the Tuileries. The faithful Swiss bodyguards tried to defend their master, but Louis, unable to make up his mind, gave order to "cease firing" just when the crowd was retiring. The people, drunk with blood and noise and cheap wine, murdered the Swiss to the last man, then invaded the palace, and went after Louis who had escaped into the meeting hall of the Assembly, where he was immediately suspended of his office, and from where he was taken as a prisoner to the old castle of the Temple.

But the armies of Austria and Prussia continued their advance and the panic changed into hysteria and turned men and women into wild beasts. In the first week of September of the year 1792, the crowd broke into the jails and murdered all the prisoners. The government did not interfere. The Jacobins, headed by Danton, knew that this crisis meant either the success or the failure of the revolution, and that only the most brutal audacity could save them. The Legislative Assembly was closed and on the 21st of September of the year 1792, a new National Convention came together. It was a body composed almost entirely of extreme revolutionists. The king was formally accused of high treason and was brought before the Convention. He was found guilty and by a vote of 361 to 360 (the extra vote being that of his cousin the Duke of Orleans) he was condemned to death. On the 21st of January of the year 1793, he quietly and with much dignity suffered himself to be taken to the scaffold. He had never understood what all the shooting and the fuss had been about. And he had been too proud to ask questions.

Then the Jacobins turned against the more moderate element in the convention, the Girondists, called after their southern district, the Gironde. A special revolutionary tribunal was instituted and twenty-one of the leading Girondists were condemned to death. The others committed suicide. They were capable and honest men but too philosophical and too moderate to survive during these frightful years.

In October of the year 1793 the Constitution was suspended by the Jacobins "until peace should have been declared." All power was placed in the hands of a small committee of Public Safety, with Danton and Robespierre as its leaders. The Christian religion and the old chronology were abolished. The "Age of Reason" (of which Thomas Paine had

THE STORY OF MANKIND

The dangerous position of France, however, made it necessary that the government remain in the hands of a few strong men, until the many enemies of the revolution should have been driven from the soil of the French fatherland. While the half-clad and half-starved revolutionary armies fought their desperate battles of the Rhine and Italy and Belgium and Egypt, and defeated every one of the enemies of the Great Revolution, five Directors were appointed, and they ruled France for four years. Then the power was vested in the hands of a successful general by the name of Napoleon Bonaparte, who became "First Consul" of France in the year 1799. And during the next fifteen years, the old European continent became the laboratory of a number of political experiments, the like of which the world had never seen before.

written so eloquently during the American Revolution) had come and with it the "Terror" which for more than a year killed good and bad and indifferent people at the rate of seventy or eighty a day.

The autocratic rule of the King had been destroyed. It was succeeded by the tyranny of a few people who had such a passionate love for democratic virtue that they felt compelled to kill all those who disagreed with them. France was turned

THE FRENCH REVOLUTION
INVADES HOLLAND

into a slaughter house. Everybody suspected everybody else. No one felt safe. Out of sheer fear, a few members of the old Convention, who knew that they were the next candidates for the scaffold, finally turned against Robespierre, who had already decapitated most of his former colleagues. Robespierre, "the only true and pure Democrat," tried to kill himself but failed. His shattered jaw was hastily bandaged and he was dragged to the guillotine. On the 27th of July, of the year 1794 (the 9th Thermidor of the year II, according to the strange chronology of the revolution), the reign of Terror came to an end, and all Paris danced with joy.

NAPOLEON

NAPOLEON was born in the year 1769, the third son
of Carlo Maria Buonaparte, an honest notary public of
the city of Ajaccio in the island of Corsica, and his good
wife, Letizia Ramolino. He therefore was not a Frenchman,
but an Italian whose native island (an old Greek, Carthaginian and Roman colony in the Mediterranean Sea) had
for years been struggling to regain its independence,
first of all from the Genoese, and after the middle of the
eighteenth century from the French, who had kindly offered
to help the Corsicans in their struggle for freedom and had
then occupied the island for their own benefit.

During the first twenty years of his life, young Napoleon
was a professional Corsican patriot—a Corsican Sinn Feiner,
who hoped to deliver his beloved country from the yoke of the
bitterly hated French enemy. But the French revolution had
unexpectedly recognised the claims of the Corsicans and gradually Napoleon, who had received a good training at the military
school of Brienne, drifted into the service of his adopted country. Although he never learned to spell French correctly or
to speak it without a broad Italian accent, he became a Frenchman. In due time he came to stand as the highest expression
of all French virtues. At present he is regarded as the symbol
of the Gallic genius.

Napoleon was what is called a fast worker. His career

does not cover more than twenty years. In that short span of time he fought more wars and gained more victories and marched more miles and conquered more square kilometers and killed more people and brought about more reforms and generally upset Europe to a greater extent than anybody (including Alexander the Great and Jenghis Khan) had ever managed to do.

He was a little fellow and during the first years of his life his health was not very good. He never impressed anybody by his good looks and he remained to the end of his days very clumsy whenever he was obliged to appear at a social function. He did not enjoy a single advantage of breeding or birth or riches. For the greater part of his youth he was desperately poor and often he had to go without a meal or was obliged to make a few extra pennies in curious ways.

He gave little promise as a literary genius. When he competed for a prize offered by the Academy of Lyons, his essay was found to be next to the last and he was number 15 out of 16 candidates. But he overcame all these difficulties through his absolute and unshakable belief in his own destiny, and in his own glorious future. Ambition was the main-spring of his life. The thought of self, the worship of that capital letter "N" with which he signed all his letters, and which recurred forever in the ornaments of his hastily constructed palaces, the absolute will to make the name Napoleon the most important thing in the world next to the name of God, these desires carried Napoleon to a pinnacle of fame which no other man has ever reached.

When he was a half-pay lieutenant, young Bonaparte was very fond of the "Lives of Famous Men" which Plutarch, the Greek historian, had written. But he never tried to live up to the high standard of character set by these heroes of the older days. Napoleon seems to have been devoid of all those considerate and thoughtful sentiments which make men different from the animals. It will be very difficult to decide with any degree of accuracy whether he ever loved anyone besides himself. He kept a civil tongue to his mother, but

Letizia had the air and manners of a great lady and after the fashion of Italian mothers, she knew how to rule her brood of children and command their respect. For a few years he was fond of Josephine, his pretty Creole wife, who was the daughter of a French officer of Martinique and the widow of the Vicomte de Beauharnais, who had been executed by Robespierre when he lost a battle against the Prussians. But the Emperor divorced her when she failed to give him a son and heir and married the daughter of the Austrian Emperor, because it seemed good policy.

During the siege of Toulon, where he gained great fame as commander of a battery, Napoleon studied Macchiavelli with industrious care. He followed the advice of the Florentine statesman and never kept his word when it was to his advantage to break it. The word "gratitude" did not occur in his personal dictionary. Neither, to be quite fair, did he expect it from others. He was totally indifferent to human suffering. He executed prisoners of war (in Egypt in 1798) who had been promised their lives, and he quietly allowed his wounded in Syria to be chloroformed when he found it impossible to transport them to his ships. He ordered the Duke of Enghien to be condemned to death by a prejudiced court-martial and to be shot contrary to all law on the sole ground that the "Bourbons needed a warning." He decreed that those German officers who were made prisoner while fighting for their country's independence should be shot against the nearest wall, and when Andreas Hofer, the Tyrolese hero, fell into his hands after a most heroic resistance, he was executed like a common traitor.

In short, when we study the character of the Emperor, we begin to understand those anxious British mothers who used to drive their children to bed with the threat that "Bonaparte, who ate little boys and girls for breakfast, would come and get them if they were not very good." And yet, having said these many unpleasant things about this strange tyrant, who looked after every other department of his army with the utmost care, but neglected the medical service, and who ruined his uniforms with Eau de Cologne because he could not stand the smell of his poor sweating soldiers; having said all these unpleasant things and being fully prepared to add many more, I must confess to a certain lurking feeling of doubt.

Here I am sitting at a comfortable table loaded heavily with books, with one eye on my typewriter and the other on Licorice the cat, who has a great fondness for carbon paper, and I am telling you that the Emperor Napoleon was a most contemptible person. But should I happen to look out of the window, down upon Seventh Avenue, and should the endless procession of trucks and carts come to a sudden halt, and should I hear the sound of the heavy drums and see the little man on his white horse in his old and much-worn green uniform, then I don't know, but I am afraid that I would leave my books and the kitten and my home and everything else to follow him wherever he cared to lead. My own grandfather did this and Heaven knows he was not born to be a hero. Millions of other people's grandfathers did it. They received no reward, but they expected none. They cheerfully gave legs and arms and lives to serve this foreigner, who took them a thousand miles away from their homes and marched them into a barrage of Russian or English or Spanish or Italian or Austrian cannon and stared quietly into space while they were rolling in the agony of death.

If you ask me for an explanation, I must answer that I have none. I can only guess at one of the reasons. Napoleon was the greatest of actors and the whole European continent was his stage. At all times and under all circumstances he knew the precise attitude that would impress the spectators most and he understood what words would make the deepest impression. Whether he spoke in the Egyptian desert, before the backdrop of the Sphinx and the pyramids, or addressed his shivering men on the dew-soaked plains of Italy, made no difference. At all times he was master of the situation. Even at the end, an exile on a little rock in the middle of the Atlantic, a sick man at the mercy of a dull and intolerable British governor, he held the centre of the stage.

After the defeat of Waterloo, no one outside of a few trusted friends ever saw the great Emperor. The people of Europe knew that he was living on the island of St. Helena— they knew that a British garrison guarded him day and night —they knew that the British fleet guarded the garrison which guarded the Emperor on his farm at Longwood. But he was never out of the mind of either friend or enemy. When illness and despair had at last taken him away, his silent eyes continued to haunt the world. Even to-day he is as much of a force in the life of France as a hundred years ago when people fainted at the mere sight of this sallow-faced man who stabled his horses in the holiest temples of the Russian Kremlin, and who treated the Pope and the mighty ones of this earth as if they were his lackeys.

To give you a mere outline of his life would demand a couple of volumes. To tell you of his great political reform of the French state, of his new codes of laws which were adopted in most European countries, of his activities in every field of public activity, would take thousands of pages. But I can explain in a few words why he was so successful during the first part of his career and why he failed during the last ten years. From the year 1789 until the year 1804, Napoleon was the great leader of the French revolution. He was not merely fighting for the glory of his own name. He defeated Austria and Italy and England and Russia because he, himself, and his soldiers were the apostles of the new creed of "Liberty, Fraternity and Equality" and were the enemies of the courts while they were the friends of the people.

But in the year 1804, Napoleon made himself Hereditary Emperor of the French and sent for Pope Pius VII to come and crown him, even as Leo III, in the year 800 had crowned that other great King of the Franks, Charlemagne, whose example was constantly before Napoleon's eyes.

Once upon the throne, the old revolutionary chieftain became an unsuccessful imitation of a Habsburg monarch. He forgot his spiritual Mother, the Political Club of the Jacobins. He ceased to be the defender of the oppressed. He became the chief of all the oppressors and kept his shooting squads ready to execute those who dared to oppose his imperial will. No one had shed a tear when in the year 1806 the sad remains of the Holy Roman Empire were carted to the historical dustbin and when the last relic of ancient Roman glory was destroyed by the grandson of an Italian peasant. But when the Napoleonic armies had invaded Spain, had forced the Spaniards to recognise a king whom they detested, had massacred the poor Madrilenes who remained faithful to their old rulers, then public opinion turned against the former hero of Marengo and Austerlitz and a hundred other revolutionary battles. Then and only then, when Napoleon was no longer the hero of the revolution but the personification of all the bad traits of the Old Régime, was it possible for England to give direction to the fast-spreading sentiment of hatred which was turning all honest men into enemies of the French Emperor.

The English people from the very beginning had felt deeply disgusted when their newspapers told them the gruesome details of the Terror. They had staged their own great revolution (during the reign of Charles I) a century before. It had been a very simple affair compared to the upheaval of Paris. In the eyes of the average Englishman a Jacobin was a monster to be shot at sight and Napoleon was the Chief Devil. The British fleet had blockaded France ever since the year 1798. It had spoiled Napoleon's plan to invade India by way of Egypt and had forced him to beat an ignominious retreat, after his victories along the banks of the Nile. And finally, in the year 1805, England got the chance it had waited for so long.

Near Cape Trafalgar on the southwestern coast of Spain, Nelson annihilated the Napoleonic fleet, beyond a possible chance of recovery. From that moment on, the Emperor was landlocked. Even so, he would have been able to maintain himself as the recognised ruler of the continent had he understood the signs of the times and accepted the honourable peace which the powers offered him. But Napoleon had been blinded by the blaze of his own glory. He would recognise no equals.

He could tolerate no rivals. And his hatred turned against Russia, the mysterious land of the endless plains with its inex‧haustible supply of cannon-fodder.

As long as Russia was ruled by Paul I, the half-witted son of Catherine the Great, Napoleon had known how to deal with the situation. But Paul grew more and more irresponsible until his exasperated subjects were obliged to murder him, (lest they all be sent to the Siberian lead-mines) and the son of

THE RETREAT FROM MOSCOW

Paul, the Emperor Alexander, did not share his father's affec‧tion for the usurper whom he regarded as the enemy of man‧kind, the eternal disturber of the peace. He was a pious man who believed that he had been chosen by God to deliver the world from the Corsican curse. He joined Prussia and Eng‧land and Austria and he was defeated. He tried five times and five times he failed. In the year 1812 he once more taunted Napoleon until the French Emperor, in a blind rage, vowed that he would dictate peace in Moscow. Then, from far and wide, from Spain and Germany and Holland and Italy and Portugal, unwilling regiments were driven northward, that the wounded pride of the great Emperor might be duly avenged. The rest of the story is common knowledge. After a march of two months, Napoleon reached the Russian capital and established his headquarters in the holy Kremlin. On the night of September 15 of the year 1812, Moscow caught fire. The town burned four days. When the evening of the fifth day came, Napoleon gave the order for the retreat. Two weeks later it began to snow. The army trudged through mud and sleet until November the 26th when the river Berezina was reached. Then the Russian attacks began in all seriousness. The Cossacks swarmed around the "Grande Armée" which was no longer an army but a mob. In the middle of December the first of the survivors began to be seen in the German cities of the East.

Then there were many rumours of an impending revolt. "The time has come," the people of Europe said, "to free ourselves from this insufferable yoke." And they began to look for old shotguns which had escaped the eye of the ever-present French spies. But ere they knew what had happened, Napoleon was back with a new army. He had left his defeated soldiers and in his little sleigh had rushed ahead to Paris, making a final appeal for more troops that he might defend the sacred soil of France against foreign invasion.

Children of sixteen and seventeen followed him when he moved eastward to meet the allied powers. On October 16, 18, and 19 of the year 1813, the terrible battle of Leipzig took place where for three days boys in green and boys in blue fought each other until the Elster ran red with blood. On the afternoon of the 17th of October, the massed reserves of Russian infantry broke through the French lines and Napoleon fled.

Back to Paris he went. He abdicated in favour of his small son, but the allied powers insisted that Louis XVIII, the brother of the late king Louis XVI, should occupy the French throne, and surrounded by Cossacks and Uhlans, the dull-eyed Bourbon prince made his triumphal entry into Paris.

As for Napoleon, he was made the sovereign ruler of the

little island of Elba in the Mediterranean where he organised his stable boys into a miniature army and fought battles on a chess board.

But no sooner had he left France than the people began to realise what they had lost. The last twenty years, however costly, had been a period of great glory. Paris had been the capital of the world. The fat Bourbon king who had learned nothing and had forgotten nothing during the days of his exile disgusted everybody by his indolence.

On the first of March of the year 1815, when the representatives of the allies were ready to begin the work of unscrambling the map of Europe, Napoleon suddenly landed near Cannes. In less than a week the French army had deserted the Bourbons and had rushed southward to offer their swords and bayonets to the "little Corporal." Napoleon marched straight to Paris where he arrived on the twentieth of March. This time he was more cautious. He offered peace, but the allies insisted upon war. The whole of Europe arose against the "perfidious Corsican." Rapidly the Emperor marched northward that he might crush his enemies before they should be able to unite their forces. But Napoleon was no longer his old self. He felt sick. He got tired easily. He slept when he ought to have been up directing the attack of his advance-guard. Besides, he missed many of his faithful old generals. They were dead.

Early in June his armies entered Belgium. On the 16th of that month he defeated the Prussians under Blücher. But a subordinate commander failed to destroy the retreating army as he had been ordered to do.

Two days later, Napoleon met Wellington near Waterloo. It was the 18th of June, a Sunday. At two o'clock of the afternoon, the battle seemed won for the French. At three a speck of dust appeared upon the eastern horizon. Napoleon believed that this meant the approach of his own cavalry who would now turn the English defeat into a rout. At four o'clock he knew better. Cursing and swearing, old Blücher drove his deathly tired troops into the heart of the fray. The shock

broke the ranks of the guards. Napoleon had no further re=
serves. He told his men to save themselves as best they could,
and he fled.

For a second time, he abdicated in favor of his son. Just
one hundred days after his escape from Elba, he was making
for the coast. He intended to go to America. In the year
1803, for a mere song, he had sold the French colony of

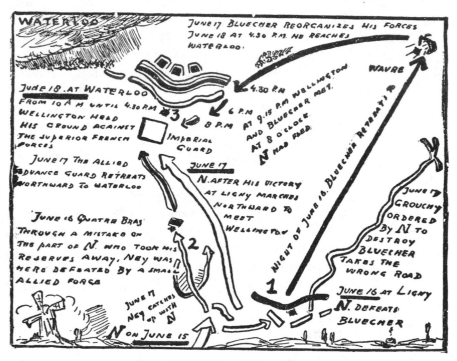

THE BATTLE OF WATERLOO

Louisiana (which was in great danger of being captured by
the English.) to the young American Republic. "The Americans," so he said, "will be grateful and will give me a little bit
of land and a house where I may spend the last days of my life
in peace and quiet." But the English fleet was watching all
French harbours. Caught between the armies of the Allies
and the ships of the British, Napoleon had no choice. The
Prussians intended to shoot him. The English might be more

OFF FOR TRAFALGAR

generous. At Rochefort he waited in the hope that something
might turn up. One month after Waterloo, he received orders
from the new French government to leave French soil inside
of twenty-four hours. Always the tragedian, he wrote a letter
to the Prince Regent of England (George III, the king, was
in an insane asylum) informing His Royal Highness of his
intention to "throw himself upon the mercy of his enemies and
like Themistocles, to look for a welcome at the fireside of his
foes . . ."

NAPOLEON GOES INTO EXILE

On the 15th of July he went on board the *"Bellerophon,"*
and surrendered his sword to Admiral Hotham. At Plymouth
he was transferred to the "Northumberland" which carried him
to St. Helena. There he spent the last seven years of his
life. He tried to write his memoirs, he quarrelled with his
keepers and he dreamed of past times. Curiously enough he
returned (at least in his imagination) to his original point of
departure. He remembered the days when he had fought the
battles of the Revolution. He tried to convince himself that
he had always been the true friend of those great principles of
"Liberty, Fraternity and Equality" which the ragged soldiers
of the convention had carried to the ends of the earth. He
liked to dwell upon his career as Commander-in-Chief and
Consul. He rarely spoke of the Empire. Sometimes he

thought of his son, the Duke of Reichstadt, the little eagle, who lived in Vienna, where he was treated as a "poor relation" by his young Habsburg cousins, whose fathers had trembled at the very mention of the name of Him. When the end came, he was leading his troops to victory. He ordered Ney to attack with the guards. Then he died.

But if you want an explanation of this strange career, if you really wish to know how one man could possibly rule so many people for so many years by the sheer force of his will, do not read the books that have been written about him. Their authors either hated the Emperor or loved him. You will learn many facts, but it is more important to "feel history" than to know it. Don't read, but wait until you have a chance to hear a good artist sing the song called "The Two Grenadiers." The words were written by Heine, the great German poet who lived through the Napoleonic era. The music was composed by Schumann, a German, who saw the Emperor, the enemy of his country, whenever he came to visit his imperial father-in-law. The song therefore is the work of two men who had every reason to hate the tyrant.

Go and hear it. Then you will understand what a thousand volumes could not possibly tell you.

THE HOLY ALLIANCE

AS SOON AS NAPOLEON HAD BEEN SENT TO ST. HELENA THE RULERS WHO SO OFTEN HAD BEEN DEFEATED BY THE HATED "CORSICAN" MET AT VIENNA AND TRIED TO UNDO THE MANY CHANGES THAT HAD BEEN BROUGHT ABOUT BY THE FRENCH REVOLUTION

THE Imperial Highnesses, the Royal Highnesses, their Graces the Dukes, the Ministers Extraordinary and Plenipotentiary, together with the plain Excellencies and their army of secretaries, servants and hangers-on, whose labours had been so rudely interrupted by the sudden return of the terrible Corsican (now sweltering under the hot sun of St. Helena) went back to their jobs. The victory was duly celebrated with dinners, garden parties and balls at which the new and very shocking "waltz" was danced to the great scandal of the ladies and gentlemen who remembered the minuet of the old Régime.

For almost a generation they had lived in retirement. At last the danger was over. They were very eloquent upon the subject of the terrible hardships which they had suffered. And they expected to be recompensed for every penny they had lost at the hands of the unspeakable Jacobins who had dared to kill their anointed king, who had abolished wigs and who had discarded the short trousers of the court of Versailles for the ragged pantaloons of the Parisian slums.

You may think it absurd that I should mention such a detail. But, if you please, the Congress of Vienna was one long succession of such absurdities and for many months the question of "short trousers vs. long trousers" interested the delegates more than the future settlement of the Saxon or Spanish problems. His Majesty the King of Prussia went so far as to order a pair of short ones, that he might give public evidence of his contempt for everything revolutionary.

Another German potentate, not to be outdone in this noble hatred for the revolution, decreed that all taxes which his subjects had paid to the French usurper should be paid a second time to the legitimate ruler who had loved his people from afar while they were at the mercy of the Corsican ogre. And so on. From one blunder to another, until one gasps and exclaims "but why in the name of High Heaven did not the people object?" Why not indeed? Because the people were utterly exhausted, were desperate, did not care what happened or how or where or by whom they were ruled, provided there was peace. They were sick and tired of war and revolution and reform.

In the eighties of the previous century they had all danced around the tree of liberty. Princes had embraced their cooks and Duchesses had danced the Carmagnole with their lackeys in the honest belief that the Millennium of Equality and Fraternity had at last dawned upon this wicked world. Instead of the Millennium they had been visited by the Revolutionary commissary who had lodged a dozen dirty soldiers in their parlor and had stolen the family plate when he returned to Paris to report to his government upon the enthusiasm with which the "liberated country" had received the Constitution, which the French people had presented to their good neighbours.

When they had heard how the last outbreak of revolutionary disorder in Paris had been suppressed by a young officer, called Bonaparte, or Buonaparte, who had turned his guns upon the mob, they gave a sigh of relief. A little less liberty, fraternity and equality seemed a very desirable thing. But ere long, the young officer called Buonaparte or Bonaparte became one of the three consuls of the French Republic, then sole consul and finally Emperor. As he was much more efficient than any ruler that had ever been seen before, his hand pressed heavily upon his poor subjects. He showed them no mercy. He impressed their sons into his armies, he married their daughters to his generals and he took their pictures and their statues to enrich his own museums. He turned the whole of Europe into an armed camp and killed almost an entire generation of men.

Now he was gone, and the people (except a few professional military men) had but one wish. They wanted to be let alone. For awhile they had been allowed to rule themselves, to vote for mayors and aldermen and judges. The system had been a terrible failure. The new rulers had been inexperienced and extravagant. From sheer despair the people turned to the representative men of the old Régime. "You rule us," they said, "as you used to do. Tell us what we owe you for taxes and leave us alone. We are busy repairing the damage of the age of liberty."

The men who stage-managed the famous congress certainly did their best to satisfy this longing for rest and quiet. The Holy Alliance, the main result of the Congress, made the policeman the most important dignitary of the State and held out the most terrible punishment to those who dared criticise a single official act.

Europe had peace, but it was the peace of the cemetery.

The three most important men at Vienna were the Emperor Alexander of Russia, Metternich, who represented the interests of the Austrian house of Habsburg, and Talleyrand, the erstwhile bishop of Autun, who had managed to live through the different changes in the French government by the sheer force of his cunning and his intelligence and who now travelled to the Austrian capital to save for his country whatever could be saved from the Napoleonic ruin. Like the gay young man of the limerick, who never knew when he was slighted, this unbidden guest came to the party and ate just as heartily as if he had been really invited. Indeed, before long,

THE SPECTRE WHICH FRIGHTENED THE HOLY ALLIANCE

he was sitting at the head of the table entertaining everybody with his amusing stories and gaining the company's good will by the charm of his manner.

Before he had been in Vienna twenty-four hours he knew that the allies were divided into two hostile camps. On the one side were Russia, who wanted to take Poland, and Prussia, who wanted to annex Saxony; and on the other side were Austria and England, who were trying to prevent this grab because it was against their own interest that either Prussia or Russia should be able to dominate Europe. Talleyrand played the two sides against each other with great skill and it was due to his efforts that the French people were not made to suffer for the ten years of oppression which Europe had endured at the hands of the Imperial officials. He argued that the French people had been given no choice in the matter. Napoleon had forced them to act at his bidding. But Napoleon was gone and Louis XVIII was on the throne. "Give him a chance," Talley-rand pleaded. And the Allies, glad to see a legitimate king upon the throne of a revolutionary country, obligingly yielded and the Bourbons were given their chance, of which they made such use that they were driven out after fifteen years.

The second man of the triumvirate of Vienna was Metternich, the Austrian prime minister, the leader of the foreign policy of the house of Habsburg. Wenzel Lothar, Prince of Metternich-Winneburg, was exactly what the name suggests. He was a Grand Seigneur, a very handsome gentleman with very fine manners, immensely rich, and very able, but the product of a society which lived a thousand miles away from the sweating multitudes who worked and slaved in the cities and on the farms. As a young man, Metternich had been studying at the University of Strassburg when the French Revolution broke out. Strassburg, the city which gave birth to the Marseillaise, had been a centre of Jacobin activities. Metternich remembered that his pleasant social life had been sadly interrupted, that a lot of incompetent citizens had suddenly been called forth to perform tasks for which they were not fit, that the mob had celebrated the dawn of the new liberty by the murder of perfectly innocent persons. He had failed to see the honest enthusiasm of the masses, the ray of hope in the eyes of women and children who carried bread and water to the ragged troops of the Convention, marching through the city on their way to the front and a glorious death for the French Fatherland.

The whole thing had filled the young Austrian with disgust. It was uncivilised. If there were any fighting to be done it must be done by dashing young men in lovely uniforms, charging across the green fields on well-groomed horses. But to turn an entire country into an evil-smelling armed camp where tramps were overnight promoted to be generals, that was both wicked and senseless. "See what came of all your fine ideas," he would say to the French diplomats whom he met at a quiet little dinner given by one of the innumerable Austrian grand-dukes. "You wanted liberty, equality and fraternity and you got Napoleon. How much better it would have been if you had been contented with the existing order of things." And he would explain his system of "stability." He would advocate a return to the normalcy of the good old days before the war, when everybody was happy and nobody talked nonsense about "everybody being as good as everybody else." In this attitude he was entirely sincere and as he was an able man of great strength of will and a tremendous power of persuasion, he was one of the most dangerous enemies of the Revolutionary ideas. He did not die until the year 1859, and he therefore lived long enough to see the complete failure of all his policies when they were swept aside by the revolution of the year 1848. He then found himself the most hated man of Europe and more than once ran the risk of being lynched by angry crowds of outraged citizens. But until the very last, he remained steadfast in his belief that he had done the right thing.

He had always been convinced that people preferred peace to liberty and he had tried to give them what was best for them. And in all fairness, it ought to be said that his efforts to establish universal peace were fairly successful. The great powers did not fly at each other's throat for almost forty years, indeed not until the Crimean war between Russia and England, France and Italy and Turkey, in the year 1854. That means a record for the European continent.

The third hero of this waltzing congress was the Emperor Alexander. He had been brought up at the court of his grand-

THE REAL CONGRESS OF VIENNA

mother, the famous Catherine the Great. Between the lessons of this shrewd old woman, who taught him to regard the glory of Russia as the most important thing in life, and those of his private tutor, a Swiss admirer of Voltaire and Rousseau, who filled his mind with a general love of humanity, the boy grew up to be a strange mixture of a selfish tyrant and a sentimental revolutionist. He had suffered great indignities during the life of his crazy father, Paul I. He had been obliged to wit-

ness the wholesale slaughter of the Napoleonic battle-fields.
Then the tide had turned. His armies had won the day for the
Allies. Russia had become the saviour of Europe and the Tsar
of this mighty people was acclaimed as a half-god who would
cure the world of its many ills.

But Alexander was not very clever. He did not know
men and women as Talleyrand and Metternich knew them.
He did not understand the strange game of diplomacy. He
was vain (who would not be under the circumstances?) and
loved to hear the applause of the multitude and soon he had
become the main "attraction" of the Congress while Metternich and Talleyrand and Castlereagh (the very able British
representative) sat around a table and drank a bottle of Tokay
and decided what was actually going to be done. They needed
Russia and therefore they were very polite to Alexander, but
the less he had personally to do with the actual work of the
Congress, the better they were pleased. They even encouraged
his plans for a Holy Alliance that he might be fully occupied
while they were engaged upon the work at hand.

Alexander was a sociable person who liked to go to parties
and meet people. Upon such occasions he was happy and gay
but there was a very different element in his character. He
tried to forget something which he could not forget. On the
night of the 23rd of March of the year 1801 he had been sitting
in a room of the St. Michael Palace in Petersburg, waiting for
the news of his father's abdication. But Paul had refused to
sign the document which the drunken officers had placed before him on the table, and in their rage they had put a scarf
around his neck and had strangled him to death. Then they
had gone downstairs to tell Alexander that he was Emperor of
all the Russian lands.

The memory of this terrible night stayed with the Tsar
who was a very sensitive person. He had been educated in
the school of the great French philosophers who did not believe in God but in Human Reason. But Reason alone could
not satisfy the Emperor in his predicament. He began to
hear voices and see things. He tried to find a way by which

he could square himself with his conscience. He became very pious and began to take an interest in mysticism, that strange love of the mysterious and the unknown which is as old as the temples of Thebes and Babylon.

The tremendous emotion of the great revolutionary era had influenced the character of the people of that day in a strange way. Men and women who had lived through twenty years of anxiety and fear were no longer quite normal. They jumped whenever the door-bell rang. It might mean the news of the "death on the field of honour" of an only son. The phrases about "brotherly love" and "liberty" of the Revolution were hollow words in the ears of sorely stricken peasants. They clung to anything that might give them a new hold on the terrible problems of life. In their grief and misery they were easily imposed upon by a large number of impostors who posed as prophets and preached a strange new doctrine which they dug out of the more obscure passages of the Book of Revelations.

In the year 1814, Alexander, who had already consulted a large number of wonder-doctors, heard of a new seeress who was foretelling the coming doom of the world and was exhorting people to repent ere it be too late. The Baroness von Krüdener, the lady in question, was a Russian woman of uncertain age and similar reputation who had been the wife of a Russian diplomat in the days of the Emperor Paul. She had squandered her husband's money and had disgraced him by her strange love affairs. She had lived a very dissolute life until her nerves had given way and for a while she was not in her right mind. Then she had been converted by the sight of the sudden death of a friend. Thereafter she despised all gaiety. She confessed her former sins to her shoemaker, a pious Moravian brother, a follower of the old reformer John Huss, who had been burned for his heresies by the Council of Constance in the year 1415.

The next ten years the Baroness spent in Germany making a specialty of the "conversion" of kings and princes. To convince Alexander, the Saviour of Europe, of the error of his ways was the greatest ambition of her life. And as Alexander, in his misery, was willing to listen to anybody who brought him a ray of hope, the interview was easily arranged. On the evening of the fourth of June of the year 1815, she was admitten to the tent of the Emperor. She found him reading his Bible. We do not know what she said to Alexander, but when she left him three hours later, he was bathed in tears, and vowed that "at last his soul had found peace." From that day on the Baroness was his faithful companion and his spiritual adviser. She followed him to Paris and then to Vienna and the time which Alexander did not spend dancing he spent at the Krüdener prayer-meetings.

You may ask why I tell you this story in such great detail? Are not the social changes of the nineteenth century of greater importance than the career of an ill-balanced woman who had better be forgotten? Of course they are, but there exist any number of books which will tell you of these other things with great accuracy and in great detail. I want you to learn something more from this history than a mere succession of facts. I want you to approach all historical events in a frame of mind that will take nothing for granted. Don't be satisfied with the mere statement that "such and such a thing happened then and there." Try to discover the hidden motives behind every action and then you will understand the world around you much better and you will have a greater chance to help others, which (when all is said and done) is the only truly satisfactory way of living.

I do not want you to think of the Holy Alliance as a piece of paper which was signed in the year 1815 and lies dead and forgotten somewhere in the archives of state. It may be forgotten but it is by no means dead. The Holy Alliance was directly responsible for the promulgation of the Monroe Doctrine, and the Monroe Doctrine of America for the Americans has a very distinct bearing upon your own life. That is the reason why I want you to know exactly how this document happened to come into existence and what the real motives were underlying this outward manifestation of piety and Christian devotion to duty.

The Holy Alliance was the joint labour of an unfortunate man who had suffered a terrible mental shock and who was trying to pacify his much-disturbed soul, and of an ambitious woman who after a wasted life had lost her beauty and her attraction and who satisfied her vanity and her desire for notoriety by assuming the rôle of self-appointed Messiah of a new and strange creed. I am not giving away any secrets when I tell you these details. Such sober minded people as Castlereagh, Metternich and Talleyrand fully understood the limited abilities of the sentimental Baroness. It would have been easy for Metternich to send her back to her German estates. A few lines to the almighty commander of the imperial police and the thing was done.

But France and England and Austria depended upon the good-will of Russia. They could not afford to offend Alexander. And they tolerated the silly old Baroness because they had to. And while they regarded the Holy Alliance as utter rubbish and not worth the paper upon which it was written, they listened patiently to the Tsar when he read them the first rough draft of this attempt to create the Brotherhood of Men upon a basis of the Holy Scriptures. For this is what the Holy Alliance tried to do, and the signers of the document solemnly declared that they would "in the administration of their respective states and in their political relations with every other government take for their sole guide the precepts of that Holy Religion, namely the precepts of Justice, Christian Charity and Peace, which far from being applicable only to private concerns must have an immediate influence on the councils of princes, and must guide all their steps as being the only means of consolidating human institutions and remedying their imperfections." They then proceeded to promise each other that they would remain united "by the bonds of a true and indissoluble fraternity, and considering each other as fellow-countrymen, they would on all occasions and in all places lend each other aid and assistance." And more words to the same effect.

Eventually the Holy Alliance was signed by the Emperor of Austria, who did not understand a word of it. It was signed by the Bourbons who needed the friendship of Napoleon's old enemies. It was signed by the King of Prussia, who hoped to gain Alexander for his plans for a "greater Prussia," and by all the little nations of Europe who were at the mercy of Russia. England never signed, because Castlereagh thought the whole thing buncombe. The Pope did not sign because he resented this interference in his business by a Greek-Orthodox and a Protestant. And the Sultan did not sign because he never heard of it.

The general mass of the European people, however, soon were forced to take notice. Behind the hollow phrases of the Holy Alliance stood the armies of the Quintuple Alliance which Metternich had created among the great powers. These armies meant business. They let it be known that the peace of Europe must not be disturbed by the so-called liberals who were in reality nothing but disguised Jacobins, and hoped for a return of the revolutionary days. The enthusiasm for the great wars of liberation of the years 1812, 1813, 1814 and 1815 had begun to wear off. It had been followed by a sincere belief in the coming of a happier day. The soldiers who had borne the brunt of the battle wanted peace and they said so.

But they did not want the sort of peace which the Holy Alliance and the Council of the European powers had now bestowed upon them. They cried that they had been betrayed. But they were careful lest they be heard by a secret-police spy. The reaction was victorious. It was a reaction caused by men who sincerely believed that their methods were necessary for the good of humanity. But it was just as hard to bear as if their intentions had been less kind. And it caused a great deal of unnecessary suffering and greatly retarded the orderly progress of political development.

THE GREAT REACTION

THEY TRIED TO ASSURE THE WORLD AN ERA
OF UNDISTURBED PEACE BY SUPPRESS-
ING ALL NEW IDEAS. THEY MADE THE
POLICE-SPY THE HIGHEST FUNCTIONARY
IN THE STATE AND SOON THE PRISONS
OF ALL COUNTRIES WERE FILLED WITH
THOSE WHO CLAIMED THAT PEOPLE
HAVE THE RIGHT TO GOVERN THEM-
SELVES AS THEY SEE FIT

To undo the damage done by the great Napoleonic flood
was almost impossible. Age-old fences had been washed away.
The palaces of two score dynasties had been damaged to such
an extent that they had to be condemned as uninhabitable.
Other royal residences had been greatly enlarged at the expense of less fortunate neighbours. Strange odds and ends
of revolutionary doctrine had been left behind by the receding
waters and could not be dislodged without danger to the entire
community. But the political engineers of the Congress did
the best they could and this is what they accomplished.

France had disturbed the peace of the world for so many
years that people had come to fear that country almost in-
stinctively. The Bourbons, through the mouth of Talleyrand,
had promised to be good, but the Hundred Days had taught
Europe what to expect should Napoleon manage to escape for
a second time. The Dutch Republic, therefore, was changed

into a Kingdom, and Belgium (which had not joined the Dutch struggle for independence in the sixteenth century and since then had been part of the Habsburg domains, first under Spanish rule and thereafter under Austrian rule) was made part of this new kingdom of the Netherlands. Nobody wanted this union either in the Protestant North or in the Catholic South, but no questions were asked. It seemed good for the peace of Europe and that was the main consideration.

Poland had hoped for great things because a Pole, Prince Adam Czartoryski, was one of the most intimate friends of Tsar Alexander and had been his constant advisor during the war and at the Congress of Vienna. But Poland was made a semi-independent part of Russia with Alexander as her king. This solution pleased no one and caused much bitter feeling and three revolutions.

Denmark, which had remained a faithful ally of Napoleon until the end, was severely punished. Seven years before, an English fleet had sailed down the Kattegat and without a declaration of war or any warning had bombarded Copenhagen and had taken away the Danish fleet, lest it be of value to Napoleon. The Congress of Vienna went one step further. It took Norway (which since the union of Calmar of the year 1397 had been united with Denmark) away from Denmark and gave it to Charles XIV of Sweden as a reward for his betrayal of Napoleon, who had set him up in the king business. This Swedish king, curiously enough, was a former French general by the name of Bernadotte,who had come to Sweden as one of Napolean's adjutants, and had been invited to the throne of that good country when the last of the rulers of the house of Hollstein-Gottorp had died without leaving either son or daughter. From 1815 until 1844 he ruled his adopted country (the language of which he never learned) with great ability. He was a clever man and enjoyed the respect of both his Swedish and his Norwegian subjects, but he did not succeed in joining two countries which nature and history had put asunder. The dual Scandinavian state was never a success and in 1905, Norway, in a most peaceful and orderly manner, set up as an independent kingdom and the Swedes bade her "good speed" and very wisely let her go her own way.

The Italians, who since the days of the Renaissance had been at the mercy of a long series of invaders, also had put great hopes in General Bonaparte. The Emperor Napoleon, however, had grievously disappointed them. Instead of the United Italy which the people wanted, they had been divided into a number of little principalities, duchies, republics and the Papal State, which (next to Naples) was the worst governed and most miserable region of the entire peninsula. The Congress of Vienna abolished a few of the Napoleonic republics and in their place resurrected several old principalities which were given to deserving members, both male and female, of the Habsburg family.

The poor Spaniards, who had started the great nationalistic revolt against Napoleon, and who had sacrificed the best blood of the country for their king, were punished severely when the Congress allowed His Majesty to return to his domains. This vicious creature, known as Ferdinand VII, had spent the last four years of his life as a prisoner of Napoleon. He had improved his days by knitting garments for the statues of his favourite patron saints. He celebrated his return by re-introducing the Inquisition and the torture-chamber, both of which had been abolished by the Revolution. He was a disgusting person, despised as much by his subjects as by his four wives, but the Holy Alliance maintained him upon his legitimate throne and all efforts of the decent Spaniards to get rid of this curse and make Spain a constitutional kingdom ended in bloodshed and executions.

Portugal had been without a king since the year 1807 when the royal family had fled to the colonies in Brazil. The country had been used as a base of supply for the armies of Wellington during the Peninsula war, which lasted from 1808 until 1814. After 1815 Portugal continued to be a sort of British province until the house of Braganza returned to the throne, leaving one of its members behind in Rio de Janeiro as Emperor of Brazil, the only American Empire which lasted.

for more than a few years, and which came to an end in 1889 when the country became a republic.

In the east, nothing was done to improve the terrible conditions of both the Slavs and the Greeks who were still subjects of the Sultan. In the year 1804 Black George, a Servian swineherd, (the founder of the Karageorgevich dynasty) had started a revolt against the Turks, but he had been defeated by his enemies and had been murdered by one of his supposed friends, the rival Servian leader, called Milosh Obrenovich, (who became the founder of the Obrenovich dynasty) and the Turks had continued to be the undisputed masters of the Balkans.

The Greeks, who since the loss of their independence, two thousand years before, had been subjects of the Macedonians, the Romans, the Venetians and the Turks, had hoped that their countryman, Capo d'Istria, a native of Corfu, and together with Czartoryski, the most intimate personal friend of Alexander, would do something for them. But the Congress of Vienna was not interested in Greeks, but was very much interested in keeping all "legitimate" monarchs, Christian, Moslem and otherwise, upon their respective thrones. Therefore nothing was done.

The last, but perhaps the greatest blunder of the Congress was the treatment of Germany. The Reformation and the Thirty Years War had not only destroyed the prosperity of the country, but had turned it into a hopeless political rubbish heap, consisting of a couple of kingdoms, a few grand-duchies, a large number of duchies and hundreds of margravates, principalities, baronies, electorates, free cities and free villages, ruled by the strangest assortment of potentates that was ever seen off the comic opera stage. Frederick the Great had changed this when he created a strong Prussia, but this state had not survived him by many years.

Napoleon had blue-penciled the demand for independence of most of these little countries, and only fifty-two out of a total of more than three hundred had survived the year 1806. During the years of the great struggle for independence, many

a young soldier had dreamed of a new Fatherland that should
be strong and united. But there can be no union without a
strong leadership, and who was to be this leader?

There were five kingdoms in the German speaking lands.
The rulers of two of these, Austria and Prussia, were kings by
the Grace of God. The rulers of three others, Bavaria, Saxony
and Wurtemberg, were kings by the Grace of Napoleon, and
as they had been the faithful henchmen of the Emperor, their
patriotic credit with the other Germans was therefore not very
good.

The Congress had established a new German Confederation, a league of thirty-eight sovereign states, under the chairmanship of the King of Austria, who was now known as the
Emperor of Austria. It was the sort of make-shift arrangement which satisfied no one. It is true that a German Diet,
which met in the old coronation city of Frankfort, had been
created to discuss matters of "common policy and importance."
But in this Diet, thirty-eight delegates represented thirty-eight
different interests and as no decision could be taken without a
unanimous vote (a parliamentary rule which had in previous
centuries ruined the mighty kingdom of Poland), the famous
German Confederation became very soon the laughing stock
of Europe and the politics of the old Empire began to resemble
those of our Central American neighbours in the forties and
the fifties of the last century.

It was terribly humiliating to the people who had sacrificed
everything for a national ideal. But the Congress was not
interested in the private feelings of "subjects," and the debate
was closed.

Did anybody object? Most assuredly. As soon as the first
feeling of hatred against Napoleon had quieted down—as soon
as the enthusiasm of the great war had subsided—as soon as
the people came to a full realisation of the crime that had been
committed in the name of "peace and stability" they began to
murmur. They even made threats of open revolt. But what
could they do? They were powerless. They were at the mercy

of the most pitiless and efficient police system the world had ever seen.

The members of the Congress of Vienna honestly and sincerely believed that "the Revolutionary Principle had led to the criminal usurpation of the throne by the former emperor Napoleon." They felt that they were called upon to eradicate the adherents of the so-called "French ideas" just as Philip II had only followed the voice of his conscience when he burned Protestants or hanged Moors. In the beginning of the sixteenth century a man who did not believe in the divine right of the Pope to rule his subjects as he saw fit was a "heretic" and it was the duty of all loyal citizens to kill him. In the beginning of the nineteenth century, on the continent of Europe, a man who did not believe in the divine right of his king to rule him as he or his Prime Minister saw fit, was a "heretic," and it was the duty of all loyal citizens to denounce him to the nearest policeman and see that he got punished.

But the rulers of the year 1815 had learned efficiency in the school of Napoleon and they performed their task much better than it had been done in the year 1517. The period between the year 1815 and the year 1860 was the great era of the political spy. Spies were everywhere. They lived in palaces and they were to be found in the lowest gin-shops. They peeped through the key-holes of the ministerial cabinet and they listened to the conversations of the people who were taking the air on the benches of the Municipal Park. They guarded the frontier so that no one might leave without a duly viséd passport and they inspected all packages, that no books with dangerous "French ideas" should enter the realm of their Royal masters. They sat among the students in the lecture hall and woe to the Professor who uttered a word against the existing order of things. They followed the little boys and girls on their way to church lest they play hookey.

In many of these tasks they were assisted by the clergy. The church had suffered greatly during the days of the revolution. The church property had been confiscated. Several priests had been killed and the generation that had learned its cathechism from Voltaire and Rousseau and the other French philosophers had danced around the Altar of Reason when the Committee of Public Safety had abolished the worship of God in October of the year 1793. The priests had followed the "émigrés" into their long exile. Now they returned in the wake of the allied armies and they set to work with a vengeance.

Even the Jesuits came back in 1814 and resumed their former labours of educating the young. Their order had been a little too successful in its fight against the enemies of the church. It had established "provinces" in every part of the world, to teach the natives the blessings of Christianity, but soon it had developed into a regular trading company which was for ever interfering with the civil authorities. During the reign of the Marquis de Pombal, the great reforming minister of Portugal, they had been driven out of the Portuguese lands and in the year 1773 at the request of most of the Catholic powers of Europe, the order had been suppressed by Pope Clement XIV. Now they were back on the job, and preached the principles of "obedience" and "love for the legitimate dynasty" to children whose parents had hired shopwindows that they might laugh at Marie Antoinette driving to the scaffold which was to end her misery.

But in the Protestant countries like Prussia, things were not a whit better. The great patriotic leaders of the year 1812, the poets and the writers who had preached a holy war upon the usurper, were now branded as dangerous "demagogues." Their houses were searched. Their letters were read. They were obliged to report to the police at regular intervals and give an account of themselves. The Prussian drill master was let loose in all his fury upon the younger generation. When a party of students celebrated the tercentenary of the Reformation with noisy but harmless festivities on the old Wartburg, the Prussian bureaucrats had visions of an imminent revolution. When a theological student, more honest than intelligent, killed a Russian government spy who was operating in Germany, the

universities were placed under police-supervision and professors were jailed or dismissed without any form of trial.

Russia, of course, was even more absurd in these anti-revo-
lutionary activities. Alexander had recovered from his attack
of piety. He was gradually drifting toward melancholia. He
well knew his own limited abilities and understood how at
Vienna he had been the victim both of Metternich and the
Krüdener woman. More and more he turned his back upon the
west and became a truly Russian ruler whose interests lay in
Constantinople, the old holy city that had been the first teacher
of the Slavs. The older he grew, the harder he worked and the
less he was able to accomplish. And while he sat in his study,
his ministers turned the whole of Russia into a land of military barracks.

It is not a pretty picture. Perhaps I might have shortened
this description of the Great Reaction. But it is just as well
that you should have a thorough knowledge of this era. It was
not the first time that an attempt had been made to set the
clock of history back. The result was the usual one.

NATIONAL INDEPENDENCE

THE LOVE OF NATIONAL INDEPENDENCE,
HOWEVER WAS TOO STRONG TO BE DE-
STROYED IN THIS WAY. THE SOUTH
AMERICANS WERE THE FIRST TO REBEL
AGAINST THE REACTIONARY MEASURES
OF THE CONGRESS OF VIENNA, GREECE
AND BELGIUM AND SPAIN AND A LARGE
NUMBER OF OTHER COUNTRIES OF THE
EUROPEAN CONTINENT FOLLOWED SUIT
AND THE NINETEENTH CENTURY WAS
FILLED WITH THE RUMOUR OF MANY
WARS OF INDEPENDENCE

IT will serve no good purpose to say "if only the Congress
of Vienna had done such and such a thing instead of taking
such and such a course, the history of Europe in the nineteenth
century would have been different." The Congress of Vienna
was a gathering of men who had just passed through a great
revolution and through twenty years of terrible and almost
continuous warfare. They came together for the purpose of
giving Europe that "peace and stability" which they thought
that the people needed and wanted. They were what we call
reactionaries. They sincerely believed in the inability of the
mass of the people to rule themselves. They re-arranged the
map of Europe in such a way as seemed to promise the greatest
possibility of a lasting success. They failed, but not through

381

any premeditated wickedness on their part. They were, for the greater part, men of the old school who remembered the happier days of their quiet youth and ardently wished a return of that blessed period. They failed to recognise the strong hold which many of the revolutionary principles had gained upon the people of the European continent. That was a misfortune but hardly a sin. But one of the things which the French Revolution had taught not only Europe but America as well, was the right of people to their own "nationality."

Napoleon, who respected nothing and nobody, was utterly ruthless in his dealing with national and patriotic aspirations. But the early revolutionary generals had proclaimed the new doctrine that "nationality was not a matter of political frontiers or round skulls and broad noses, but a matter of the heart and soul." While they were teaching the French children the greatness of the French nation, they encouraged Spaniards and Hollanders and Italians to do the same thing. Soon these people, who all shared Rousseau's belief in the superior virtues of Original Man, began to dig into their past and found, buried beneath the ruins of the feudal system, the bones of the mighty races of which they supposed themselves the feeble descendants.

The first half of the nineteenth century was the era of the great historical discoveries. Everywhere historians were busy publishing mediæval charters and early mediæval chronicles and in every country the result was a new pride in the old fatherland. A great deal of this sentiment was based upon the wrong interpretation of historical facts. But in practical politics, it does not matter what is true, but everything depends upon what the people believe to be true. And in most countries both the kings and their subjects firmly believed in the glory and fame of their ancestors.

The Congress of Vienna was not inclined to be sentimental. Their Excellencies divided the map of Europe according to the best interests of half a dozen dynasties and put "national aspirations" upon the Index, or list of forbidden books, together with all other dangerous "French doctrines."

But history is no respecter of Congresses. For some reason or other (it may be an historical law, which thus far has escaped the attention of the scholars) "nations" seemed to be necessary for the orderly development of human society and the attempt to stem this tide was quite as unsuccessful as the Metternichian effort to prevent people from thinking.

Curiously enough the first trouble began in a very distant part of the world, in South America. The Spanish colonies of that continent had been enjoying a period of relative independence during the many years of the great Napoleonic wars. They had even remained faithful to their king when he was taken prisoner by the French Emperor and they had refused to recognise Joseph Bonaparte, who had in the year 1808 been made King of Spain by order of his brother.

Indeed, the only part of America to get very much upset by the Revolution was the island of Haiti, the Espagnola of Columbus' first trip. Here in the year 1791 the French Convention, in a sudden outburst of love and human brotherhood, had bestowed upon their black brethren all the privileges hitherto enjoyed by their white masters. Just as suddenly they had repented of this step, but the attempt to undo the original promise led to many years of terrible warfare between General Leclerc, the brother-in-law of Napoleon, and Toussaint l'Ouverture, the negro chieftain. In the year 1801, Toussaint was asked to visit Leclerc and discuss terms of peace. He received the solemn promise that he would not be molested. He trusted his white adversaries, was put on board a ship and shortly afterwards died in a French prison. But the negroes gained their independence all the same and founded a Republic. Incidentally they were of great help to the first great South American patriot in his efforts to deliver his native country from the Spanish yoke.

Simon Bolivar, a native of Caracas in Venezuela, born in the year 1783, had been educated in Spain, had visited Paris where he had seen the Revolutionary government at work, had lived for a while in the United States and had returned to his native land where the widespread discontent against Spain, the mother country, was beginning to take a definite form. In the year 1811, Venezuela declared its independence and Bolivar became one of the revolutionary generals. Within two months, the rebels were defeated and Bolivar fled.

For the next five years he was the leader of an apparently lost cause. He sacrificed all his wealth and he would not have been able to begin his final and successful expedition without the support of the President of Haiti. Thereafter the revolt spread all over South America and soon it appeared that Spain was not able to suppress the rebellion unaided. She asked for the support of the Holy Alliance.

This step greatly worried England. The British shippers had succeeded the Dutch as the Common Carriers of the world and they expected to reap heavy profits from a declaration of independence on the part of all South America. They had hopes that the United States of America would interfere but the Senate had no such plans and in the House, too, there were many voices which declared that Spain ought to be given a free hand.

Just then, there was a change of ministers in England. The Whigs went out and the Tories came in. George Canning became secretary of State. He dropped a hint that England would gladly back up the American government with all the might of her fleet, if said government would declare its disapproval of the plans of the Holy Alliance in regard to the rebellious colonies of the southern continent. President Monroe thereupon, on the 2nd of December of the year 1823, addressed Congress and stated that: "America would consider any attempt on the part of the allied powers to extend their system to any portion of this western hemisphere as dangerous to our peace and safety," and gave warning that "the American government would consider such action on the part of the Holy Alliance as a manifestation of an unfriendly disposition toward the United States." Four weeks later, the text of the "Monroe Doctrine" was printed in the English newspapers and the members of the Holy Alliance were forced to make their choice.

Metternich hesitated. Personally he would have been willing to risk the displeasure of the United States (which had allowed both its army and navy to fall into neglect since the end

THE MONROE DOCTRINE

of the Anglo-American war of the year 1812.)   But Canning's
threatening attitude and trouble on the continent forced him
to be careful.   The expedition never took place and South
America and Mexico gained their independence.

As for the troubles on the continent of Europe, they were
coming fast and furious.   The Holy Alliance had sent French
troops to Spain to act as guardians of the peace in the year
1820.   Austrian troops had been used for a similar purpose in
Italy when the "Carbonari" (the secret society of the Charcoal
Burners) were making propaganda for a united Italy and had
caused a rebellion against the unspeakable Ferdinand of
Naples.

Bad news also came from Russia where the death of Alexander had been the sign for a revolutionary outbreak in St.
Petersburg, a short but bloody upheaval, the so-called Deka-
berist revolt (because it took place in December,) which ended
with the hanging of a large number of good patriots who had
been disgusted by the reaction of Alexander's last years and
had tried to give Russia a constitutional form of government.

But worse was to follow.   Metternich had tried to assure
himself of the continued support of the European courts by a
series of conferences at Aix-la-Chapelle, at Troppau, at
Laibach, and finally at Verona.   The delegates from the
different powers duly travelled to these agreeable watering
places where the Austrian prime minister used to spend
his summers.   They always promised to do their best
to suppress revolt but they were none too certain of their
success.   The spirit of the people was beginning to be ugly and
especially in France the position of the king was by no means
satisfactory.

The real trouble however began in the Balkans, the gate-
way to western Europe through which the invaders of that
continent had passed since the beginning of time.   The first
outbreak was in Moldavia, the ancient Roman province of
Dacia which had been cut off from the Empire in the third
century.   Since then, it had been a lost land, a sort of Atlantis,
where the people had continued to speak the old Roman tongue

and still called themselves Romans and their country Roumania. Here in the year 1821, a young Greek, Prince Alexander Ypsilanti, began a revolt against the Turks. He told his followers that they could count upon the support of Russia. But Metternich's fast couriers were soon on their way to St. Petersburg and the Tsar, entirely persuaded by the Austrian arguments in favor of "peace and stability," refused to help. Ypsilanti was forced to flee to Austria where he spent the next seven years in prison.

In the same year, 1821, trouble began in Greece. Since 1815 a secret society of Greek patriots had been preparing the way for a revolt. Suddenly they hoisted the flag of independence in the Morea (the ancient Peloponnesus) and drove the Turkish garrisons away. The Turks answered in the usual fashion. They took the Greek Patriarch of Constantinople, who was regarded as their Pope both by the Greeks and by many Russians, and they hanged him on Easter Sunday of the year 1821, together with a number of his bishops. The Greeks came back with a massacre of all the Mohammedans in Tripolitsa, the capital of the Morea and the Turks retaliated by an attack upon the island of Chios, where they murdered 25,000 Christians and sold 45,000 others as slaves into Asia and Egypt.

Then the Greeks appealed to the European courts, but Metternich told them in so many words that they could "stew in their own grease," (I am not trying to make a pun, but I am quoting His Serene Highness who informed the Tsar that this "fire of revolt ought to burn itself out beyond the pale of civilisation") and the frontiers were closed to those volunteers who wished to go to the rescue of the patriotic Hellenes. Their cause seemed lost. At the request of Turkey, an Egyptian army was landed in the Morea and soon the Turkish flag was again flying from the Acropolis, the ancient stronghold of Athens. The Egyptian army then pacified the country "à la Turque," and Metternich followed the proceedings with quiet interest, awaiting the day when this "attempt against the peace of Europe" should be a thing of the past.

Once more it was England which upset his plans. The greatest glory of England does not lie in her vast colonial possessions, in her wealth or her navy, but in the quiet heroism and independence of her average citizen. The Englishman obeys the law because he knows that respect for the rights of others marks the difference between a dog-kennel and civilised society. But he does not recognize the right of others to interfere with his freedom of thought. If his country does something which he believes to be wrong, he gets up and says so and the government which he attacks will respect him and will give him full protection against the mob which to-day, as in the time of Socrates, often loves to destroy those who surpass it in courage or intelligence. There never has been a good cause, however unpopular or however distant, which has not counted a number of Englishmen among its staunchest adherents. The mass of the English people are not different from those in other lands. They stick to the business at hand and have no time for unpractical "sporting ventures." But they rather admire their eccentric neighbour who drops everything to go and fight for some obscure people in Asia or Africa and when he has been killed they give him a fine public funeral and hold him up to their children as an example of valor and chiv alry.

Even the police spies of the Holy Alliance were powerless against this national characteristic. In the year 1824, Lord Byron, a rich young Englishman who wrote the poetry over which all Europe wept, hoisted the sails of his yacht and started south to help the Greeks. Three months later the news spread through Europe that their hero lay dead in Missolonghi, the last of the Greek strongholds. His lonely death caught the imagination of the people. In all countries, societies were formed to help the Greeks. Lafayette, the grand old man of the American revolution, pleaded their cause in France. The king of Bavaria sent hundreds of his officers. Money and supplies poured in upon the starving men of Missolonghi.

In England, George Canning, who had defeated the plans of the Holy Alliance in South America, was now prime minister. He saw his chance to checkmate Metternich for a second time. The English and Russian fleets were already in the Mediterranean. They were sent by governments which dared no longer suppress the popular enthusiasm for the cause of the Greek patriots. The French navy appeared because France, since the end of the Crusades, had assumed the rôle of the defender of the Christian faith in Mohammedan lands. On October 20 of the year 1827, the ships of the three nations attacked the Turkish fleet in the bay of Navarino and destroyed it. Rarely has the news of a battle been received with such general rejoicing. The people of western Europe and Russia who enjoyed no freedom at home consoled themselves by fighting an imaginary war of liberty on behalf of the oppressed Greeks. In the year 1829 they had their reward. Greece became an independent nation and the policy of reaction and stability suffered its second great defeat.

It would be absurd were I to try, in this short volume, to give you a detailed account of the struggle for national independence in all other countries. There are a large number of excellent books devoted to such subjects. I have described the struggle for the independence of Greece because it was the first successful attack upon the bulwark of reaction which the Congress of Vienna had erected to "maintain the stability of Europe." That mighty fortress of suppression still held out and Metternich continued to be in command. But the end was near.

In France the Bourbons had established an almost unbearable rule of police officials who were trying to undo the work of the French revolution, with an absolute disregard of the regulations and laws of civilised warfare. When Louis XVIII died in the year 1824, the people had enjoyed nine years of "peace" which had proved even more unhappy than the ten years of war of the Empire. Louis was succeeded by his brother, Charles X.

Louis had belonged to that famous Bourbon family which, although it never learned anything, never forgot anything. The recollection of that morning in the town of Hamm. when

news had reached him of the decapitation of his brother, remained a constant warning of what might happen to those
kings who did not read the signs of the times aright. Charles,
on the other hand, who had managed to run up private debts of
fifty million francs before he was twenty years of age, knew
nothing, remembered nothing and firmly intended to learn
nothing. As soon as he had succeeded his brother, he established a government "by priests, through priests and for
priests," and while the Duke of Wellington, who made this re-
mark, cannot be called a violent liberal, Charles ruled in such
a way that he disgusted even that trusted friend of law and
order. When he tried to suppress the newspapers which dared
to criticise his government, and dismissed the Parliament because it supported the Press, his days were numbered.

On the night of the 27th of July of the year 1830, a revolution took place in Paris. On the 30th of the same month, the
king fled to the coast and set sail for England. In this way
the "famous farce of fifteen years" came to an end and the
Bourbons were at last removed from the throne of France.
They were too hopelessly incompetent. France then might
have returned to a Republican form of government, but such
a step would not have been tolerated by Metternich.

The situation was dangerous enough. The spark of rebellion had leaped beyond the French frontier and had set fire to
another powder house filled with national grievances. The new
kingdom of the Netherlands had not been a success. The Belgian and the Dutch people had nothing in common and their
king, William of Orange (the descendant of an uncle of William the Silent), while a hard worker and a good business man,
was too much lacking in tact and pliability to keep the peace
among his uncongenial subjects. Besides, the horde of priests
which had descended upon France, had at once found its way
into Belgium and whatever Protestant William tried to do was
howled down by large crowds of excited citizens as a fresh attempt upon the "freedom of the Catholic church." On the 25th
of August there was a popular outbreak against the Dutch
authorities in Brussels. Two months later, the Belgians

declared themselves independent and elected Leopold of Co-
burg, the uncle of Queen Victoria of England, to the throne.
That was an excellent solution of the difficulty. The two countries, which never ought to have been united, parted their
ways and thereafter lived in peace and harmony and behaved
like decent neighbours.

News in those days when there were only a few short railroads, travelled slowly, but when the success of the French
and the Belgian revolutionists became known in Poland there
was an immediate clash between the Poles and their Russian
rulers which led to a year of terrible warfare and ended with a
complete victory for the Russians who "established order along
the banks of the Vistula" in the well-known Russian fashion.
Nicholas the First, who had succeeded his brother Alexander in
1825, firmly believed in the Divine Right of his own family,
and the thousands of Polish refugees who had found shelter
in western Europe bore witness to the fact that the principles
of the Holy Alliance were still more than a hollow phrase in
Holy Russia.

In Italy too there was a moment of unrest. Marie Louise,
Duchess of Parma and wife of the former Emperor Napoleon, whom she had deserted after the defeat of Waterloo, was
driven away from her country, and in the Papal state the exasperated people tried to establish an independent Republic.
But the armies of Austria marched to Rome and soon everything was as of old. Metternich continued to reside at the Ball
Platz, the home of the foreign minister of the Habsburg
dynasty, the police spies returned to their job, and peace
reigned supreme. Eighteen more years were to pass before a
second and more successful attempt could be made to deliver
Europe from the terrible inheritance of the Vienna Congress.

Again it was France, the revolutionary weather-cock of
Europe, which gave the signal of revolt. Charles X had been
succeeded by Louis Philippe, the son of that famous Duke of
Orleans who had turned Jacobin, had voted for the death of his
cousin the king, and had played a rôle during the early days

of the revolution under the name of "Philippe Egalité" or "Equality Philip." Eventually he had been killed when Robespierre tried to purge the nation of all "traitors," (by which name he indicated those people who did not share his own views) and his son had been forced to run away from the revolutionary army. Young Louis Philippe thereupon had wandered far and wide. He had taught school in Switzerland and had spent a couple of years exploring the unknown "far west" of America. After the fall of Napoleon he had returned to Paris. He was much more intelligent than his Bourbon cousins. He was a simple man who went about in the public parks with a red cotton umbrella under his arm, followed by a brood of children like any good housefather. But France had outgrown the king business and Louis did not know this until the morning of the 24th of February, of the year 1848, when a crowd stormed the Tuileries. and drove his Majesty away and proclaimed the Republic.

When the news of this event reached Vienna, Metternich expressed the casual opinion that this was only a repetition of the year 1793 and that the Allies would once more be obliged to march upon Paris and make an end to this very unseemly democratic row. But two weeks later his own Austrian capital was in open revolt. Metternich escaped from the mob through the back door of his palace, and the Emperor Ferdinand was forced to give his subjects a constitution which embodied most of the revolutionary principles which his Prime Minister had tried to suppress for the last thirty-three years.

This time all Europe felt the shock. Hungary declared itself independent, and commenced a war against the Habsburgs under the leadership of Louis Kossuth. The unequal struggle lasted more than a year. It was finally suppressed by the armies of Tsar Nicholas who marched across the Carpathian mountains and made Hungary once more safe for autocracy. The Habsburgs thereupon established extraordinary court-martials and hanged the greater part of the Hungarian patriots whom they had not been able to defeat in open battle.

As for Italy, the island of Sicily declared itself independent from Naples and drove its Bourbon king away. In the Papal states the prime minister, Rossi, was murdered and the Pope was forced to flee. He returned the next year at the head of a French army which remained in Rome to protect His Holiness against his subjects until the year 1870. Then it was called back to defend France against the Prussians, and Rome became the capital of Italy. In the north, Milan and Venice rose against their Austrian masters. They were supported by king Albert of Sardinia, but a strong Austrian army under old Radetzky marched into the valley of the Po, defeated the Sardinians near Custozza and Novara and forced Albert to abdicate in favour of his son, Victor Emanuel, who a few years later was to be the first king of a united Italy.

In Germany the unrest of the year 1848 took the form of a great national demonstration in favour of political unity and a representative form of government. In Bavaria, the king who had wasted his time and money upon an Irish lady who posed as a Spanish dancer—(she was called Lola Montez and lies buried in New York's Potter's Field) —was driven away by the enraged students of the university. In Prussia, the king was forced to stand with uncovered head before the coffins of those who had been killed during the street fighting and to promise a constitutional form of government. And in March of the year 1849, a German parliament, consisting of 550 delegates from all parts of the country came together in Frankfort and proposed that king Frederick William of Prussia should be the Emperor of a United Germany.

Then, however, the tide began to turn. Incompetent Ferdinand had abdicated in favour of his nephew Francis Joseph. The well-drilled Austrian army had remained faithful to their war-lord. The hangman was given plenty of work and the Habsburgs, after the nature of that strangely cat-like family, once more landed upon their feet and rapidly strengthened their position as the masters of eastern and western Europe. They played the game of politics very adroitly and used the jealousies of the other German states to prevent the elevation of the Prussian king to the Imperial dignity. Their long training in the art of suffering defeat had taught them the value of patience. They knew how to wait. They bided their time and while the liberals, utterly untrained in practical politics, talked and talked and talked and got intoxicated by their own fine speeches, the Austrians quietly gathered their forces, dismissed the Parliament of Frankfort and re-established the old and impossible German confederation which the Congress of Vienna had wished upon an unsuspecting world.

But among the men who had attended this strange Parliament of unpractical enthusiasts, there was a Prussian country squire by the name of Bismarck, who had made good use of his eyes and ears. He had a deep contempt for oratory. He knew (what every man of action has always known) that nothing is ever accomplished by talk. In his own way he was a sincere patriot. He had been trained in the old school of diplomacy and he could outlie his opponents just as he could outwalk them and outdrink them and outride them.

Bismarck felt convinced that the loose confederation of little states must be changed into a strong united country if it would hold its own against the other European powers. Brought up amidst feudal ideas of loyalty, he decided that the house of Hohenzollern, of which he was the most faithful servant, should rule the new state, rather than the incompetent Habsburgs. For this purpose he must first get rid of the Austrian influence, and he began to make the necessary preparations for this painful operation.

Italy in the meantime had solved her own problem, and had rid herself of her hated Austrian master. The unity of Italy was the work of three men, Cavour, Mazzini and Garibaldi. Of these three, Cavour, the civil-engineer with the short-sighted eyes and the steel-rimmed glasses, played the part of the careful political pilot. Mazzini, who had spent most of his days in different European garrets, hiding from the Austrian police, was the public agitator, while Garibaldi, with his band of red-shirted rough-riders, appealed to the popular imagination.

Mazzini and Garibaldi were both believers in the Republican form of government. Cavour, however, was a monarchist, and the others who recognised his superior ability in such matters of practical statecraft, accepted his decision and sacrificed their own ambitions for the greater good of their beloved Fatherland.

Cavour felt towards the House of Sardinia as Bismarck did towards the Hohenzollern family. With infinite care and great shrewdness he set to work to jockey the Sardinian King into a position from which His Majesty would be able to assume the leadership of the entire Italian people. The unsettled political conditions in the rest of Europe greatly helped him in his plans and no country contributed more to the independence of Italy than her old and trusted (and often distrusted) neighbour, France.

GIUSEPPE MAZZINI

In that turbulent country, in November of the year 1852, the Republic had come to a sudden but not unexpected end. Napoleon III the son of Louis Bonaparte the former King of Holland, and the small nephew of a great uncle, had re-established an Empire and had made himself Emperor "by the Grace of God and the Will of the People."

This young man, who had been educated in Germany and who mixed his French with harsh Teutonic gutturals (just as the first Napoleon had always spoken the language of his adopted country with a strong Italian accent) was trying very hard to use the Napoleonic tradition for his own benefit. But he had many enemies and did not feel very certain of his hold upon his ready-made throne. He had gained the friendship of Queen Victoria but this had not been a difficult task, as the good Queen was not particularly brilliant and was very susceptible to flattery. As for the other European sovereigns, they treated the French Emperor with insulting haughtiness and sat up nights devising new ways in which they could show their upstart "Good Brother" how sincerely they despised him.

Napoleon was obliged to find a way in which he could break this opposition, either through love or through fear. He well knew the fascination which the word "glory" still held for his subjects. Since he was forced to gamble for his throne he decided to play the game of Empire for high stakes. He used an attack of Russia upon Turkey as an excuse for bringing about the Crimean war in which England and France combined against the Tsar on behalf of the Sultan. It was a very costly and exceedingly unprofitable enterprise. Neither France nor England nor Russia reaped much glory.

But the Crimean war did one good thing. It gave Sardinia a chance to volunteer on the winning side and when peace was declared it gave Cavour the opportunity to lay claim to the gratitude of both England and France.

Having made use of the international situation to get Sardinia recognised as one of the more important powers of Europe, the clever Italian then provoked a war between Sardinia and Austria in June of the year 1859. He assured himself of the support of Napoleon in exchange for the provinces of Savoy and the city of Nice, which was really an Italian town. The Franco-Italian armies defeated the Austrians at Magenta and Solferino, and the former Austrian provinces and duchies were united into a single Italian kingdom. Florence became the capital of this new Italy until the year 1870 when the French recalled their troops from Rome to defend France against the Germans. As soon as they were gone, the Italian troops entered the eternal city and the House of Sardinia took up its residence in the old Palace of the Quirinal which an ancient Pope had built on the ruins of the baths of the Emperor Constantine.

The Pope, however, moved across the river Tiber and hid behind the walls of the Vatican, which had been the home of many of his predecessors since their return from the exile of Avignon in the year 1377. He protested loudly against this high-handed theft of his domains and addressed letters of appeal to those faithful Catholics who were inclined to sympathise with him in his loss. Their number, however, was small, and it has been steadily decreasing. For, once delivered from the cares of state, the Pope was able to devote all his time to questions of a spiritual nature. Standing high above the petty quarrels of the European politicians, the Papacy assumed a new dignity which proved of great benefit to the church and made it an international power for social and religious progress which has shown a much more intelligent appreciation of modern economic problems than most Protestant sects.

In this way, the attempt of the Congress of Vienna to settle the Italian question by making the peninsula an Austrian province was at last undone.

The German problem however remained as yet unsolved. It proved the most difficult of all. The failure of the revolution of the year 1848 had led to the wholesale migration of the more energetic and liberal elements among the German people. These young fellows had moved to the United States of America, to Brazil, to the new colonies in Asia and America. Their work was continued in Germany but by a different sort of men.

In the new Diet which met at Frankfort, after the collapse of the German Parliament and the failure of the Liberals to establish a united country, the Kingdom of Prussia was represented by that same Otto von Bismarck from whom we parted a few pages ago. Bismarck by now had managed to gain the complete confidence of the king of Prussia. That was all he asked for. The opinion of the Prussian parliament or of the Prussian people interested him not at all. With his own eyes he had seen the defeat of the Liberals. He knew that he would not be able to get rid of Austria without a war and he began by strengthening the Prussian army. The Landtag, exasperated at his high-handed methods, refused to give him the necessary credits. Bismarck did not even bother to discuss the matter. He went ahead and increased his army with the help of funds which the Prussian house of Peers and the king placed at his disposal. Then he looked for a national cause

which could be used for the purpose of creating a great wave
of patriotism among all the German people.

In the north of Germany there were the Duchies of Schleswig and Holstein which ever since the middle ages had been a
source of trouble. Both countries were inhabited by a certain
number of Danes and a certain number of Germans, but although they were governed by the King of Denmark, they
were not an integral part of the Danish State and this led to
endless difficulties. Heaven forbid that I should revive this
forgotten question which now seems settled by the acts of the
recent Congress of Versailles. But the Germans in Holstein
were very loud in their abuse of the Danes and the Danes in
Schleswig made a great ado of their Danishness, and all Europe was discussing the problem and German Männerchors
and Turnvereins listened to sentimental speeches about the
"lost brethren" and the different chancelleries were trying to
discover what it was all about, when Prussia mobilised her
armies to "save the lost provinces." As Austria, the official
head of the German Confederation, could not allow Prussia
to act alone in such an important matter, the Habsburg troops
were mobilised too and the combined armies of the two great
powers crossed the Danish frontiers and after a very brave resistance on the part of the Danes, occupied the two duchies.
The Danes appealed to Europe, but Europe was otherwise
engaged and the poor Danes were left to their fate.

Bismarck then prepared the scene for the second number
upon his Imperial programme. He used the division of the
spoils to pick a quarrel with Austria. The Habsburgs fell into
the trap. The new Prussian army, the creation of Bismarck and
his faithful generals, invaded Bohemia and in less than six
weeks, the last of the Austrian troops had been destroyed at
Königgrätz and Sadowa and the road to Vienna lay open. But
Bismarck did not want to go too far. He knew that he would
need a few friends in Europe.   He offered the defeated
Habsburgs very decent terms of peace, provided they would
resign their chairmanship of the Confederation. He was less
merciful to many of the smaller German states who had taken

the side of the Austrians, and annexed them to Prussia. The greater part of the northern states then formed a new organisation, the so-called North German Confederacy, and victorious Prussia assumed the unofficial leadership of the German people.

Europe stood aghast at the rapidity with which the work of consolidation had been done. England was quite indifferent but France showed signs of disapproval. Napoleon's hold upon the French people was steadily diminishing. The Crimean war had been costly and had accomplished nothing.

A second adventure in the year 1863, when a French army had tried to force an Austrian Grand-Duke by the name of Maximilian upon the Mexican people as their Emperor, had come to a disastrous end as soon as the American Civil War had been won by the North. For the Government at Washington had forced the French to withdraw their troops and this had given the Mexicans a chance to clear their country of the enemy and shoot the unwelcome Emperor.

It was necessary to give the Napoleonic throne a new coat of glory-paint. Within a few years the North German Confederation would be a serious rival of France. Napoleon decided that a war with Germany would be a good thing for his dynasty. He looked for an excuse and Spain, the poor victim of endless revolutions, gave him one.

Just then the Spanish throne happened to be vacant. It had been offered to the Catholic branch of the house of Hohenzollern. The French government had objected and the Hohenzollerns had politely refused to accept the crown. But Napoleon, who was showing signs of illness, was very much under the influence of his beautiful wife, Eugénie de Montijo, the daughter of a Spanish gentleman and the grand-daughter of William Kirkpatrick, an American consul at Malaga, where the grapes come from. Eugénie, although shrewd enough, was as badly educated as most Spanish women of that day. She was at the mercy of her spiritual advisers and these worthy gentlemen felt no love for the Protestant King of Prussia. "Be bold," was the advice of the Empress to her husband, but she omitted to add the second half of that famous Persian proverb which admonishes the hero to "be bold but not too bold." Napoleon, convinced of the strength of his army, addressed himself to the king of Prussia and insisted that the king give him assurances that "he would never permit another candidature of a Hohenzollern prince to the Spanish crown." As the Hohenzollerns had just declined the honour, the demand was superfluous, and Bismarck so informed the French government. But Napoleon was not satisfied.

It was the year 1870 and King William was taking the waters at Ems. There one day he was approached by the French minister who tried to re-open the discussion. The king answered very pleasantly that it was a fine day and that the Spanish question was now closed and that nothing more remained to be said upon the subject. As a matter of routine, a report of this interview was telegraphed to Bismarck, who handled all foreign affairs. Bismarck edited the dispatch for the benefit of the Prussian and French press. Many people have called him names for doing this. Bismarck however could plead the excuse that the doctoring of official news, since time immemorial, had been one of the privileges of all civilised governments. When the "edited" telegram was printed, the good people in Berlin felt that their old and venerable king with his nice white whiskers had been insulted by an arrogant little Frenchman and the equally good people of Paris flew into a rage because their perfectly courteous minister had been shown the door by a Royal Prussian flunkey.

And so they both went to war and in less than two months, Napoleon and the greater part of his army were prisoners of the Germans. The Second Empire had come to an end and the Third Republic was making ready to defend Paris against the German invaders. Paris held out for five long months. Ten days before the surrender of the city, in the nearby palace of Versailles, built by that same King Louis XIV who had been such a dangerous enemy to the Germans, the King of Prussia was publicly proclaimed German Emperor and a loud booming of guns told the hungry Parisians that a new German Empire had taken the place of the old harmless Confederation of Teutonic states and statelets.

In this rough way, the German question was finally settled. By the end of the year 1871, fifty-six years after the memorable gathering at Vienna, the work of the Congress had been entirely undone. Metternich and Alexander and Talleyrand had tried to give the people of Europe a lasting peace. The methods they had employed had caused endless wars and revolutions and the feeling of a common brotherhood of the eighteenth century was followed by an era of exaggerated nationalism which has not yet come to an end.

THE AGE OF THE ENGINE

BUT WHILE THE PEOPLE OF EUROPE WERE
FIGHTING FOR THEIR NATIONAL INDE-
PENDENCE, THE WORLD IN WHICH THEY
LIVED HAD BEEN ENTIRELY CHANGED
BY A SERIES OF INVENTIONS, WHICH HAD
MADE THE CLUMSY OLD STEAM ENGINE
OF THE 18TH CENTURY THE MOST FAITH-
FUL AND EFFICIENT SLAVE OF MAN

THE greatest benefactor of the human race died more than
half a million years ago. He was a hairy creature with a low
brow and sunken eyes, a heavy jaw and strong tiger-like teeth.
He would not have looked well in a gathering of modern scientists, but they would have honoured him as their master. For
he had used a stone to break a nut and a stick to lift up a heavy
boulder. He was the inventor of the hammer and the lever, our
first tools, and he did more than any human being who came
after him to give man his enormous advantage over the other
animals with whom he shares this planet.

Ever since, man has tried to make his life easier by the use
of a greater number of tools. The first wheel (a round disc
made out of an old tree) created as much stir in the communities of 100,000 B.C. as the flying machine did only a few years
ago.

In Washington, the story is told of a director of the Patent
Office who in the early thirties of the last century suggested

that the Patent Office be abolished, because "everything that possibly could be invented had been invented." A similar feeling must have spread through the prehistoric world when the first sail was hoisted on a raft and the people were able to move from place to place without rowing or punting or pulling from the shore.

Indeed one of the most interesting chapters of history is the effort of man to let some one else or something else do his work for him, while he enjoyed his leisure, sitting in the sun or painting pictures on rocks, or training young wolves and little tigers to behave like peaceful domestic animals.

Of course in the very olden days, it was always possible to enslave a weaker neighbour and force him to do the unpleasant tasks of life. One of the reasons why the Greeks and Romans, who were quite as intelligent as we are, failed to devise more interesting machinery, was to be found in the widespread existence of slavery. Why should a great mathematician waste his time upon wires and pulleys and cogs and fill the air with noise and smoke when he could go to the market-place and buy all the slaves he needed at a very small expense?

And during the middle-ages, although slavery had been abolished and only a mild form of serfdom survived, the guilds discouraged the idea of using machinery because they thought this would throw a large number of their brethren out of work. Besides, the Middle-Ages were not at all interested in producing large quantities of goods. Their tailors and butchers and carpenters worked for the immediate needs of the small community in which they lived and had no desire to compete with their neighbours, or to produce more than was strictly necessary.

During the Renaissance, when the prejudices of the Church against scientific investigations could no longer be enforced as rigidly as before, a large number of men began to devote their lives to mathematics and astronomy and physics and chemistry. Two years before the beginning of the Thirty Years War, John Napier, a Scotchman, had published his little book which described the new invention of logarithms. During the war it-

self, Gottfried Leibnitz of Leipzig had perfected the system of
infinitesimal calculus. Eight years before the peace of Westphalia, Newton, the great English natural philosopher, was
born, and in that same year Galileo, the Italian astronomer,
died. Meanwhile the Thirty Years War had destroyed the prosperity of central Europe and there was a sudden but very general interest in "alchemy," the strange pseudo-science of the
middle-ages by which people hoped to turn base metals into
gold. This proved to be impossible but the alchemists in their
laboratories stumbled upon many new ideas and greatly helped
the work of the chemists who were their successors.

The work of all these men provided the world with a solid
scientific foundation upon which it was possible to build even
the most complicated of engines, and a number of practical
men made good use of it. The Middle-Ages had used wood for
the few bits of necessary machinery. But wood wore out
easily. Iron was a much better material, but iron was scarce
except in England. In England therefore most of the smelting was done. To smelt iron, huge fires were needed. In the
beginning, these fires had been made of wood, but gradually
the forests had been used up. Then "stone coal" (the petrified trees of prehistoric times) was used. But coal as you
know has to be dug out of the ground and it has to be transported to the smelting ovens and the mines have to be kept
dry from the ever invading waters.

These were two problems which had to be solved at once.
For the time being, horses could still be used to haul the coal-
wagons, but the pumping question demanded the application
of special machinery. Several inventors were busy trying to
solve the difficulty. They all knew that steam would have to
be used in their new engine. The idea of the steam engine was
very old. Hero of Alexandria, who lived in the first century
before Christ, has described to us several bits of machinery
which were driven by steam. The people of the Renaissance
had played with the notion of steam-driven war chariots. The
Marquis of Worcester, a contemporary of Newton, in his book
of inventions, tells of a steam engine. A little later, in the year

1698, Thomas Savery of London applied for a patent for a pumping engine. At the same time, a Hollander, Christian Huygens, was trying to perfect an engine in which gun-powder was used to cause regular explosions in much the same way as we use gasoline in our motors.

All over Europe, people were busy with the idea. Denis Papin, a Frenchman, friend and assistant of Huygens, was making experiments with steam engines in several countries. He invented a little wagon that was driven by steam, and a paddle-wheel boat. But when he tried to take a trip in his vessel, it was confiscated by the authorities on a complaint of the boatmen's union, who feared that such a craft would deprive them of their livelihood. Papin finally died in London in great poverty, having wasted all his money on his inventions. But at the time of his death, another mechanical enthusiast, Thomas Newcomen, was working on the problem of a new steam-pump. Fifty years later his engine was improved upon by James Watt, a Glasgow instrument maker. In the year 1777, he gave the world the first steam engine that proved of real practical value.

But during the centuries of experiments with a "heat-engine," the political world had greatly changed. The British people had succeeded the Dutch as the common-carriers of the world's trade. They had opened up new colonies. They took the raw materials which the colonies produced to England, and there they turned them into finished products, and then they exported the finished goods to the four corners of the world. During the seventeenth century, the people of Georgia and the Carolinas had begun to grow a new shrub which gave a strange sort of woolly substance, the so-called "cotton wool." After this had been plucked, it was sent to England and there the people of Lancashire wove it into cloth. This weaving was done by hand and in the homes of the workmen. Very soon a number of improvements were made in the process of weaving. In the year 1730, John Kay invented the "fly shuttle." In 1770, James Hargreaves got a patent on his "spinning jenny." Eli Whitney, an American, invented the cotton-gin which separated the cotton from its seeds, a job which had previously been done by hand at the rate of only a pound a day. Finally Richard Arkwright and the Reverend Edmund Cart·· wright invented large weaving machines, which were driven by water power. And then, in the eighties of the eighteenth century, just when the Estates General of France had begun those famous meetings which were to revolutionise the political system of Europe, the engines of Watt were arranged in such a way that they could drive the weaving machines of Arkwright, and this created an economic and social revolution which has changed human relationship in almost every part of the world.

As soon as the stationary engine had proved a success, the inventors turned their attention to the problem of propelling boats and carts with the help of a mechanical contrivance. Watt himself designed plans for a "steam locomotive," but ere he had perfected his ideas, in the year 1804, a locomotive made by Richard Trevithick carried a load of twenty tons at Pen-y-darran in the Wales mining district.

At the same time an American jeweller and portrait-painter by the name of Robert Fulton was in Paris, trying to convince Napoleon that with the use of his submarine boat, the "Nautilus," and his "steam-boat," the French might be able to destroy the naval supremacy of England.

Fulton's idea of a steamboat was not original. He had undoubtedly copied it from John Fitch, a mechanical genius of Connecticut whose cleverly constructed steamer had first navigated the Delaware river as early as the year 1787. But Napoleon and his scientific advisers did not believe in the practical possibility of a self-propelled boat, and although the Scotch-built engine of the little craft puffed merrily on the Seine, the great Emperor neglected to avail himself of this formidable weapon which might have given him his revenge for Trafalgar.

As for Fulton, he returned to the United States and, being a practical man of business, he organised a successful steam-boat company together with Robert R. Livingston, a signer of the Declaration of Independence, who was American Minister

THE MODERN CITY

to France when Fulton was in Paris, trying to sell his inven-
tion. The first steamer of this new company, the "Clermont,"
which was given a monopoly of all the waters of New York
State, equipped with an engine built by Boulton and Watt of
Birmingham in England, began a regular service between New
York and Albany in the year 1807.

As for poor John Fitch, the man who long before any one
else had used the "steam-boat" for commercial purposes, he
came to a sad death. Broken in health and empty of purse, he
had come to the end of his resources when his fifth boat, which

THE FIRST STEAMBOAT

was propelled by means of a screw-propeller, had been destroyed. His neighbours jeered at him as they were to laugh a
hundred years later when Professor Langley constructed his
funny flying machines. Fitch had hoped to give his country
an easy access to the broad rivers of the west and his countrymen preferred to travel in flat-boats or go on foot. In the year
1798, in utter despair and misery, Fitch killed himself by taking poison.

But twenty years later, the "Savannah," a steamer of 1850

tons and making six knots an hour, (the Mauretania goes just four times as fast,) crossed the ocean from Savannah to Liverpool in the record time of twenty-five days. Then there was an end to the derision of the multitude and in their enthusiasm the people gave the credit for the invention to the wrong man.

Six years later, George Stephenson, an Englishman, who had

THE ORIGIN OF THE STEAMBOAT

been building locomotives for the purpose of hauling coal from the mine-pit to smelting ovens and cotton factories, built his famous "travelling engine" which reduced the price of coal by almost seventy per cent and which made it possible to establish the first regular passenger service between Manchester and Liverpool, when people were whisked from city to city at the unheard-of speed of fifteen miles per hour. A dozen years later, this speed had been increased to twenty miles per hour.

At the present time, any well-behaved flivver (the direct descendant of the puny little motor-driven machines of Daimler and Levassor of the eighties of the last century) can do better than these early "Puffing Billies."

But while these practically-minded engineers were improving upon their rattling "heat engines," a group of "pure"

THE ORIGIN OF THE AUTOMOBILE

scientists (men who devote fourteen hours of each day to the study of those "theoretical" scientific phenomena without which no mechanical progress would be possible) were following a new scent which promised to lead them into the most secret and hidden domains of Nature.

Two thousand years ago, a number of Greek and Roman philosophers (notably Thales of Miletus and Pliny who was killed while trying to study the eruption of Vesuvius of the year 79 when Pompeii and Herculaneum were buried beneath the ashes) had noticed the strange antics of bits of straw and of feather which were held near a piece of amber which was being rubbed with a bit of wool. The schoolmen of the Middle Ages had not been interested in this mysterious "electric" power. But immediately after the Renaissance, William Gilbert, the private physician of Queen Elizabeth, wrote his famous treatise on the character and behaviour of Magnets. During the Thirty Years War Otto von Guericke, the burgomaster of Magdeburg and the inventor of the air-pump, constructed the first electrical machine. During the next century a large number of scientists devoted themselves to the study of electricity. Not less than three professors invented the famous Leyden Jar in the year 1795. At the same time, Benjamin Franklin, the most universal genius of America next to Benjamin Thomson (who after his flight from New Hampshire on account of his pro-British sympathies became known as Count Rumford) was devoting his attention to this subject. He discovered that lightning and the electric spark were manifestations of the same electric power and continued his electric studies until the end of his busy and useful life. Then came Volta with his famous "electric pile" and Galvani and Day and the Danish professor Hans Christian Oersted and Ampère and Arago and Faraday, all of them diligent searchers after the true nature of the electric forces.

They freely gave their discoveries to the world and Samuel Morse (who like Fulton began his career as an artist) thought that he could use this new electric current to transmit messages from one city to another. He intended to use copper wire and a little machine which he had invented. People laughed at him. Morse therefore was obliged to finance his own experiments and soon he had spent all his money and then he was very poor and people laughed even louder. He then asked Congress to help him and a special Committee on Commerce promised him their support. But the members of Congress were not at all interested and Morse had to wait twelve years before he was given a small congressional appropriation. He then built a "telegraph" between Baltimore and Washington. In the year 1837 he had shown his first successful "telegraph" in one of the lecture halls of New York University. Finally, on the 24th of May of the year 1844 the first long-distance message was sent from Washington to Baltimore and to-day the whole world is covered with telegraph wires and we can send news from Europe to Asia in a few seconds. Twenty-three years later Alexander Graham Bell used the electric current for his telephone. And half a century afterwards Marconi improved upon these ideas by inventing a system of sending messages which did away entirely with the old-fashioned wires.

While Morse, the New Englander, was working on his "telegraph," Michael Faraday, the Yorkshire-man, had constructed the first "dynamo." This tiny little machine was completed in the year 1831 when Europe was still trembling as a result of the great July revolutions which had so severely upset the plans of the Congress of Vienna. The first dynamo grew and grew and grew and to-day it provides us with heat and with light (you know the little incandescent bulbs which Edison, building upon French and English experiments of the forties and fifties, first made in 1878) and with power for all sorts of machines. If I am not mistaken the electric-engine will soon entirely drive out the "heat engine" just as in the olden days the more highly-organised prehistoric animals drove out their less efficient neighbours.

Personally (but I know nothing about machinery) this will make me very happy. For the electric engine which can be run by waterpower is a clean and companionable servant of mankind but the "heat-engine," the marvel of the eighteenth century, is a noisy and dirty creature for ever filling the world with ridiculous smoke-stacks and with dust and soot and asking that it be fed with coal which has to be dug out of mines at great inconvenience and risk to thousands of people.

And if I were a novelist and not a historian, who must stick to facts and may not use his imagination, I would describe the happy day when the last steam locomotive shall be taken to the Museum of Natural History to be placed next to the skeleton of the Dinosaur and the Pterodactyl and the other extinct creatures of a by gone age.

THE SOCIAL REVOLUTION

BUT THE NEW ENGINES WERE VERY EXPEN-
SIVE AND ONLY PEOPLE OF WEALTH
COULD AFFORD THEM. THE OLD CARPEN-
TER OR SHOEMAKER WHO HAD BEEN HIS
OWN MASTER IN HIS LITTLE WORKSHOP
WAS OBLIGED TO HIRE HIMSELF OUT TO
THE OWNERS OF THE BIG MECHANICAL
TOOLS, AND WHILE HE MADE MORE
MONEY THAN BEFORE, HE LOST HIS FOR-
MER INDEPENDENCE AND HE DID NOT
LIKE THAT

In the olden days the work of the world had been done by
independent workmen who sat in their own little workshops in
the front of their houses, who owned their tools, who boxed the
ears of their own apprentices and who, within the limits prescribed by their guilds, conducted their business as it pleased
them. They lived simple lives, and were obliged to work very
long hours, but they were their own masters. If they got up
and saw that it was a fine day to go fishing, they went fishing
and there was no one to say "no."

But the introduction of machinery changed this. A machine is really nothing but a greatly enlarged tool. A railroad train which carries you at the speed of a mile a minute is
in reality a pair of very fast legs, and a steam hammer which
flattens heavy plates of iron is just a terrible big fist, made of
steel.

413

But whereas we can all afford a pair of good legs and a good strong fist, a railroad train and a steam hammer and a cotton factory are very expensive pieces of machinery and they are not owned by a single man, but usually by a company of people who all contribute a certain sum and then divide the

MAN POWER AND MACHINE POWER

profits of their railroad or cotton mill according to the amount of money which they have invested.

Therefore, when machines had been improved until they were really practicable and profitable, the builders of those large tools, the machine manufacturers, began to look for customers who could afford to pay for them in cash.

During the early middle ages, when land had been almost the only form of wealth, the nobility were the only people who were considered wealthy. But as I have told you in a previous chapter, the gold and silver which they possessed was quite insignificant and they used the old system of barter, exchanging cows for horses and eggs for honey. During the crusades, the burghers of the cities had been able to gather riches from the reviving trade between the east and the west, and they had been serious rivals of the lords and the knights.

The French revolution had entirely destroyed the wealth of the nobility and had enormously increased that of the middle class or "bourgeoisie." The years of unrest which followed the Great Revolution had offered many middle-class people a chance to get more than their share of this world's goods. The estates of the church had been confiscated by the French Convention and had been sold at auction. There had been a terrific amount of graft. Land speculators had stolen thousands of square miles of valuable land, and during the Napoleonic wars, they had used their capital to "profiteer" in grain and gun-powder, and now they possessed more wealth than they needed for the actual expenses of their households and they could afford to build themselves factories and to hire men and women to work the machines.

This caused a very abrupt change in the lives of hundreds of thousands of people. Within a few years, many cities doubled the number of their inhabitants and the old civic centre which had been the real "home" of the citizens was surrounded with ugly and cheaply built suburbs where the workmen slept after their eleven or twelve hours, or thirteen hours, spent in the factories and from where they returned to the factory as soon as the whistle blew.

Far and wide through the countryside there was talk of the fabulous sums of money that could be made in the towns. The peasant boy, accustomed to a life in the open, went to the city. He rapidly lost his old health amidst the smoke and dust and dirt of those early and badly ventilated workshops, and the end, very often, was death in the poor-house or in the hospital.

Of course the change from the farm to the factory on the part of so many people was not accomplished without a certain amount of opposition. Since one engine could do as much work as a hundred men, the ninety-nine others who were thrown out of employment did not like it. Frequently they attacked the factory-buildings and set fire to the machines, but

THE FACTORY

Insurance Companies had been organised as early as the 17th century and as a rule the owners were well protected against loss.

Soon, newer and better machines were installed, the factory was surrounded with a high wall and then there was an end to the rioting. The ancient guilds could not possibly survive in this new world of steam and iron. They went out of existence and then the workmen tried to organise regular labour unions. But the factory-owners, who through their wealth could exercise great influence upon the politicians of the different countries, went to the Legislature and had laws passed which forbade the forming of such trade unions because they interfered with the "liberty of action" of the working man.

Please do not think that the good members of Parliament who passed these laws were wicked tyrants. They were the true sons of the revolutionary period when everybody talked of "liberty" and when people often killed their neighbours because they were not quite as liberty-loving as they ought to have been. Since "liberty" was the foremost virtue of man, it was not right that labour-unions should dictate to their members the hours during which they could work and the wages which they must demand. The workman must at all times, be "free to sell his services in the open market," and the employer must be equally "free" to conduct his business as he saw fit. The days of the Mercantile System, when the state had regulated the industrial life of the entire community, were coming to an end. The new idea of "freedom" insisted that the state stand entirely aside and let commerce take its course.

The last half of the 18th century had not merely been a time of intellectual and political doubt, but the old economic ideas, too, had been replaced by new ones which better suited the need of the hour. Several years before the French revolution, Turgot, who had been one of the unsuccessful ministers of finance of Louis XVI, had preached the novel doctrine of "economic liberty." Turgot lived in a country which had suffered from too much red-tape, too many regulations, too many officials trying to enforce too many laws. "Remove this official supervision," he wrote, "let the people do as they please, and everything will be all right." Soon his famous advice of "laissez faire" became the battle-cry around which the economists of that period rallied.

At the same time in England, Adam Smith was working on his mighty volumes on the "Wealth of Nations," which made another plea for "liberty" and the "natural rights of trade." Thirty years later, after the fall of Napoleon, when the reactionary powers of Europe had gained their victory at Vienna,

that same freedom which was denied to the people in their
political relations was forced upon them in their industrial
life.

The general use of machinery, as I have said at the beginning of this chapter, proved to be of great advantage to the
state. Wealth increased rapidly. The machine made it possible for a single country, like England, to carry all the burdens of the great Napoleonic wars. The capitalists (the people who provided the money with which machines were bought)
reaped enormous profits. They became ambitious and began
to take an interest in politics. They tried to compete with the
landed aristocracy which still exercised great influence upon
the government of most European countries.

In England, where the members of Parliament were still
elected according to a Royal Decree of the year 1265, and
where a large number of recently created industrial centres were
without representation, they brought about the passing of the
Reform Bill of the year 1832, which changed the electoral
system and gave the class of the factory-owners more influence upon the legislative body. This however caused great
discontent among the millions of factory workers, who were
left without any voice in the government. They too began
an agitation for the right to vote. They put their demands
down in a document which came to be known as the "People's
Charter." The debates about this charter grew more and
more violent. They had not yet come to an end when the revolutions of the year 1848 broke out. Frightened by the threat
of a new outbreak of Jacobinism and violence, the English
government placed the Duke of Wellington, who was now in
his eightieth year, at the head of the army, and called for Volunteers. London was placed in a state of siege and preparations were made to suppress the coming revolution.

But the Chartist movement killed itself through bad leadership and no acts of violence took place. The new class of
wealthy factory owners, (I dislike the word "bourgeoisie"
which has been used to death by the apostles of a new social

order,) slowly increased its hold upon the government, and the conditions of industrial life in the large cities continued to transform vast acres of pasture and wheat-land into dreary slums, which guard the approach of every modern European town.

EMANCIPATION

THE GENERAL INTRODUCTION OF MACHIN-
ERY DID NOT BRING ABOUT THE ERA OF
HAPPINESS AND PROSPERITY WHICH
HAD BEEN PREDICTED BY THE GENERA-
TION WHICH SAW THE STAGE COACH RE-
PLACED BY THE RAILROAD. SEVERAL
REMEDIES WERE SUGGESTED BUT NONE
OF THESE QUITE SOLVED THE PROBLEM

In the year 1831, just before the passing of the first Reform Bill Jeremy Bentham, the great English student of legislative methods and the most practical political reformer of that
day, wrote to a friend: "The way to be comfortable is to
make others comfortable. The way to make others comfortable is to appear to love them. The way to appear to love them
is to love them in reality." Jeremy was an honest man. He
said what he believed to be true. His opinions were shared by
thousands of his countrymen. They felt responsible for the
happiness of their less fortunate neighbours and they tried
their very best to help them. And Heaven knows it was time
that something be done!

The ideal of "economic freedom" (the "laissez faire" of
Turgot) had been necessary in the old society where mediæval
restrictions lamed all industrial effort. But this "liberty of
action" which had been the highest law of the land had led to
a terrible, yea, a frightful condition. The hours in the fac-

tory were limited only by the physical strength of the workers. As long as a woman could sit before her loom, without
fainting from fatigue, she was supposed to work. Children of
five and six were taken to the cotton mills, to save them from
the dangers of the street and a life of idleness. A law had
been passed which forced the children of paupers to go to work
or be punished by being chained to their machines. In returr
for their services they got enough bad food to keep them alive
and a sort of pigsty in which they could rest at night. Often
they were so tired that they fell asleep at their job. To keep
them awake a foreman with a whip made the rounds and beat
them on the knuckles when it was necessary to bring them back
to their duties. Of course, under these circumstances thousands
of little children died. This was regrettable and the employers,
who after all were human beings and not without a heart, sincerely wished that they could abolish "child labour." But since
man was "free" it followed that children were "free" too. Besides, if Mr. Jones had tried to work his factory without the
use of children of five and six, his rival, Mr. Stone, would have
hired an extra supply of little boys and Jones would have beer
forced into bankruptcy. It was therefore impossible for Jones
to do without child labour until such time as an act of Parliament should forbid it for all employers.

But as Parliament was no longer dominated by the old
landed aristocracy (which had despised the upstart factory-
owners with their money bags and had treated them with open
contempt), but was under control of the representatives from
the industrial centres, and as long as the law did not allow
workmen to combine in labour-unions, very little was accomplished. Of course the intelligent and decent people of that
time were not blind to these terrible conditions. They were
just helpless. Machinery had conquered the world by surprise and it took a great many years and the efforts of thousands of noble men and women to make the machine what it
ought to be, man's servant, and not his master.

Curiously enough, the first attack upon the outrageous
system of employment which was then common in all parts of

the world, was made on behalf of the black slaves of Africa
and America. Slavery had been introduced into the American continent by the Spaniards. They had tried to use the
Indians as labourers in the fields and in the mines, but the Indians, when taken away from a life in the open, had laid down
and died and to save them from extinction a kind-hearted priest
had suggested that negroes be brought from Africa to do the
work. The negroes were strong and could stand rough treatment. Besides, association with the white man would give
them a chance to learn Christianity and in this way, they would
be able to save their souls, and so from every possible point of
view, it would be an excellent arrangement both for the kindly
white man and for his ignorant black brother. But with the
introduction of machinery there had been a greater demand for
cotton and the negroes were forced to work harder than ever
before, and they too, like the Indians, began to die under the
treatment which they received at the hands of the overseers.

Stories of incredible cruelty constantly found their way to
Europe and in all countries men and women began to agitate
for the abolition of slavery. In England, William Wilberforce
and Zachary Macaulay, (the father of the great historian whose
history of England you must read if you want to know how
wonderfully interesting a history-book can be,) organised a
society for the suppression of slavery. First of all they got a
law passed which made "slave trading" illegal. And after the
year 1840 there was not a single slave in any of the British colonies. The revolution of 1848 put an end to slavery in the
French possessions. The Portuguese passed a law in the year
1858 which promised all slaves their liberty in twenty years
from date. The Dutch abolished slavery in 1863 and in the
same year Tsar Alexander II returned to his serfs that liberty
which had been taken away from them more than two centuries
before.

In the United States of America the question led to
grave difficulties and a prolonged war. Although the Declaration of Independence had laid down the principle that
"all men were created equal," an exception had been made for

those men and women whose skins were dark and who worked
on the plantations of the southern states. As time went on, the
dislike of the people of the North for the institution of slavery
increased and they made no secret of their feelings. The south-
erners however claimed that they could not grow their cotton
without slave-labour, and for almost fifty years a mighty debate raged in both the Congress and the Senate.

The North remained obdurate and the South would not give
in. When it appeared impossible to reach a compromise, the
southern states threatened to leave the Union. It was a most
dangerous point in the history of the Union. Many things
"might" have happened. That they did not happen was the
work of a very great and very good man.

On the sixth of November of the year 1860, Abraham Lincoln, an Illinois lawyer, and a man who had made his own intellectual fortune, had been elected president by the Republicans who were very strong in the anti-slavery states. He
knew the evils of human bondage at first hand and his shrewd
common-sense told him that there was no room on the northern
continent for two rival nations. When a number of southern
states seceded and formed the "Confederate States of America," Lincoln accepted the challenge. The Northern states
were called upon for volunteers. Hundreds of thousands of
young men responded with eager enthusiasm and there followed four years of bitter civil war. The South, better prepared and following the brilliant leadership of Lee and Jack-
son, repeatedly defeated the armies of the North. Then the
economic strength of New England and the West began to
tell. An unknown officer by the name of Grant arose from ob-
scurity and became the Charles Martel of the great slave war.
Without interruption he hammered his mighty blows upon the
crumbling defences of the South. Early in the year 1863,
President Lincoln issued his "Emancipation Proclamation"
which set all slaves free. In April of the year 1865 Lee surrendered the last of his brave armies at Appomattox. A few
days later, President Lincoln was murdered by a lunatic. But
his work was done. With the exception of Cuba which was

still under Spanish domination, slavery had come to an end in every part of the civilised world.

But while the black man was enjoying an increasing amount of liberty, the "free" workmen of Europe did not fare quite so well. Indeed, it is a matter of surprise to many contemporary writers and observers that the masses of workmen (the so-called proletariat) did not die out from sheer misery. They lived in dirty houses situated in miserable parts of the slums. They ate bad food. They received just enough schooling to fit them for their tasks. In case of death or an accident, their families were not provided for. But the brewery and distillery interests, (who could exercise great influence upon the Legislature,) encouraged them to forget their woes by offering them unlimited quantities of whisky and gin at very cheap rates.

The enormous improvement which has taken place since the thirties and the forties of the last century is not due to the efforts of a single man. The best brains of two generations devoted themselves to the task of saving the world from the disastrous results of the all-too-sudden introduction of machinery. They did not try to destroy the capitalistic system. This would have been very foolish, for the accumulated wealth of other people, when intelligently used, may be of very great benefit to all mankind. But they tried to combat the notion that true equality can exist between the man who has wealth and owns the factories and can close their doors at will without the risk of going hungry, and the labourer who must take whatever job is offered, at whatever wage he can get, or face the risk of starvation for himself, his wife and his children.

They endeavoured to introduce a number of laws which regulated the relations between the factory owners and the factory workers. In this, the reformers have been increasingly successful in all countries. To-day, the majority of the labourers are well protected; their hours are being reduced to the excellent average of eight, and their children are sent to the schools instead of to the mine pit and to the carding-room of the cotton mills.

But there were other men who also contemplated the sight

of all the belching smoke-stacks, who heard the rattle of the railroad trains, who saw the store-houses filled with a surplus of all sorts of materials, and who wondered to what ultimate goal this tremendous activity would lead in the years to come. They remembered that the human race had lived for hundreds of thousands of years without commercial and industrial competition. Could they change the existing order of things and do away with a system of rivalry which so often sacrificed human happiness to profits?

This idea—this vague hope for a better day—was not restricted to a single country. In England, Robert Owen, the owner of many cotton mills, established a so-called "socialistic community" which was a success. But when he died, the prosperity of New Lanark came to an end and an attempt of Louis Blanc, a French journalist, to establish "social workshops" all over France fared no better. Indeed, the increasing number of socialistic writers soon began to see that little individual communities which remained outside of the regular industrial life, would never be able to accomplish anything at all. It was necessary to study the fundamental principles underlying the whole industrial and capitalistic society before useful remedies could be suggested.

The practical socialists like Robert Owen and Louis Blanc and François Fournier were succeeded by theoretical students of socialism like Karl Marx and Friedrich Engles. Of these two, Marx is the best known. He was a very brilliant man whose family had for a long time lived in Germany. He had heard of the experiments of Owen and Blanc, and he began to interest himself in questions of labour and wages and unemployment. But his liberal views made him very unpopular with the police authorities of Germany, and he was forced to flee to Brussels and then to London, where he lived a poor and shabby life as the correspondent of the New York Tribune.

No one, thus far, had paid much attention to his books on economic subjects. But in the year 1864 he organized the first international association of working men and three years later, in 1867, he published the first volume of his well-known treatise called "Capital." Marx believed that all history was a long struggle between those who "have" and those who "don't have." The introduction and general use of machinery had created a new class in society, that of the capitalists who used their surplus wealth to buy the tools which were then used by the labourers to produce still more wealth, which was again used to build more factories and so on, until the end of time. Meanwhile, according to Marx, the third estate (the bourgeoisie) was growing richer and richer and the fourth estate (the proletariat) was growing poorer and poorer, and he predicted that in the end, one man would possess all the wealth of the world while the others would be his employees and dependent upon his good will.

To prevent such a state of affairs, Marx advised working men of all countries to unite and to fight for a number of political and economic measures which he had enumerated in a Manifesto in the year 1848, the year of the last great European revolution.

These views of course were very unpopular with the governments of Europe, many countries, especially Prussia, passed severe laws against the Socialists and policemen were ordered to break up the Socialist meetings and to arrest the speakers. But that sort of persecution never does any good. Martyrs are the best possible advertisements for an unpopular cause. In Europe the number of socialists steadily increased and it was soon clear that the Socialists did not contemplate a violent revolution but were using their increasing power in the different Parliaments to promote the interests of the labouring classes. Socialists were even called upon to act as Cabinet Ministers, and they co-operated with progressive Catholics and Protestants to undo the damage that had been caused by the Industrial Revolution and to bring about a fairer division of the many benefits which had followed the introduction of machinery and the increased production of wealth.

THE AGE OF SCIENCE

BUT THE WORLD HAD UNDERGONE ANOTHER CHANGE WHICH WAS OF GREATER IMPORTANCE THAN EITHER THE POLITICAL OR THE INDUSTRIAL REVOLUTIONS. AFTER GENERATIONS OF OPPRESSION AND PERSECUTION, THE SCIENTIST HAD AT LAST GAINED LIBERTY OF ACTION AND HE WAS NOW TRYING TO DISCOVER THE FUNDAMENTAL LAWS WHICH GOVERN THE UNIVERSE

THE PHILOSOPHER

THE Egyptians, the Babylonians, the Chaldeans, the Greeks and the Romans, had all contributed something to the first vague notions of science and scientific investigation. But the great migrations of the fourth century had destroyed the classical world of the Mediterranean, and the Christian Church, which was more interested in the life of the soul than in the life of the body, had regarded science as a manifestation of that human arrogance which wanted to pry into divine affairs which belonged to the realm of Almighty God, and which therefore was closely related to the seven deadly sins.

427

The Renaissance to a certain but limited extent had broken through this wall of Mediæval prejudices. The Reformation, however, which had overtaken the Renaissance in the early 16th century, had been hostile to the ideals of the "new civilisation," and once more the men of science were threatened with severe punishment, should they try to pass beyond the narrow limits of knowledge which had been laid down in Holy Writ.

Our world is filled with the statues of great generals, atop of prancing horses, leading their cheering soldiers to glorious victory. Here and there, a modest slab of marble announces that a man of science has found his final resting place. A thousand years from now we shall probably do these things differently, and the children of that happy generation shall know of the splendid courage and the almost inconceivable devotion to duty of the men who were the pioneers of that abstract knowledge, which alone has made our modern world a practical possibility.

Many of these scientific pioneers suffered poverty and contempt and humiliation. They lived in garrets and died in dungeons. They dared not print their names on the title-pages of their books and they dared not print their conclusions in the land of their birth, but smuggled the manuscripts to some secret printing shop in Amsterdam or Haarlem. They were exposed to the bitter enmity of the Church, both Protestant and Catholic, and were the subjects of endless sermons, inciting the parishioners to violence against the "heretics."

Here and there they found an asylum. In Holland, where the spirit of tolerance was strongest, the authorities, while regarding these scientific investigations with little favour, yet refused to interfere with people's freedom of thought. It became a little asylum for intellectual liberty where French and English and German philosophers and mathematicians and physicians could go to enjoy a short spell of rest and get a breath of free air.

In another chapter I have told you how Roger Bacon, the great genius of the thirteenth century, was prevented for years from writing a single word, lest he get into new troubles with the authorities of the church. And five hundred years later, the contributors to the great philosophic "Encyclopædia" were under the constant supervision of the French gendarmerie. Half a century afterwards, Darwin, who dared to question the story of the creation of man, as revealed in the Bible, was denounced from every pulpit as an enemy of the human race. Even to-day, the persecution of those who venture into the unknown realm of science has not entirely come to an end. And while I am writing this Mr. Bryan is addressing a vast multitude on the "Menace of Darwinism," warning his hearers against the errors of the great English naturalist.

GALILEO

All this, however, is a mere detail. The work that has to be done invariably gets done, and the ultimate profit of the discoveries and the inventions goes to the mass of those same people who have always decried the man of vision as an unpractical idealist.

The seventeenth century had still preferred to investigate the far off heavens and to study the position of our planet in relation to the solar system. Even so, the Church had disapproved of this unseemly curiosity, and Copernicus who first of all had proved that the sun was the centre of the universe, did not publish his work until the day of his death. Galileo spent the greater part of his life under the supervision of the clerical authorities, but he continued to use his telescope and provided Isaac Newton with a mass of practical observations, which greatly helped the English mathematician when he dis-

covered the existence of that interesting habit of falling objects which came to be known as the Law of Gravitation.

That, for the moment at least, exhausted the interest in the
Heavens, and man began to study the earth. The invention
of a workable microscope, (a strange and clumsy little thing,)
by Anthony van Leeuwenhoek during the last half of the 17th
century, gave man a chance to study the "microscopic" creatures who are responsible for so many of his ailments. It laid
the foundations of the science of "bacteriology" which in the
last forty years has delivered the world from a great number of
diseases by discovering the tiny organisms which cause the
complaint. It also allowed the geologists to make a more
careful study of different rocks and of the fossils (the petrified
prehistoric plants) which they found deep below the surface of
the earth. These investigations convinced them that the earth
must be a great deal older than was stated in the book of
Genesis and in the year 1830, Sir Charles Lyell published his
"Principles of Geology" which denied the story of creation as
related in the Bible and gave a far more wonderful description
of slow growth and gradual development.

At the same time, the Marquis de Laplace was working on
a new theory of creation, which made the earth a little blotch
in the nebulous sea out of which the planetary system had
been formed and Bunsen and Kirchhoff, by the use of the spec-
troscope, were investigating the chemical composition of the
stars and of our good neighbour, the sun, whose curious spots
had first been noticed by Galileo.

Meanwhile after a most bitter and relentless warfare with
the clerical authorities of Catholic and Protestant lands, the
anatomists and physiologists had at last obtained permission
to dissect bodies and to substitute a positive knowledge of our
organs and their habits for the guesswork of the mediæval
quack.

Within a single generation (between 1810 and 1840) more
progress was made in every branch of science than in all the
hundreds of thousands of years that had passed since man first
looked at the stars and wondered why they were there. It

THE AIRPLANE

must have been a very sad age for the people who had been educated under the old system. And we can understand their feeling of hatred for such men as Lamarck and Darwin, who did not exactly tell them that they were "descended from monkeys," (an accusation which our grandfathers seemed to regard as a personal insult,) but who suggested that the proud human race had evolved from a long series of ancestors who could trace the family-tree back to the little jelly-fishes who were the first inhabitants of our planet.

The dignified world of the well-to-do middle class, which dominated the nineteenth century, was willing to make use of the gas or the electric light, of all the many practical applications of the great scientific discoveries, but the mere investigator, the man of the "scientific theory" without whom no progress would be possible, continued to be distrusted until very recently. Then, at last, his services were recognised. To-day the rich people who in past ages donated their wealth for the building of a cathedral, construct vast laboratories where silent men do battle upon the hidden enemies of mankind and often sacrifice their lives that coming generations may enjoy greater happiness and health.

Indeed it has come to pass that many of the ills of this world, which our ancestors regarded as inevitable "acts of God," have been exposed as manifestations of our own ignorance and neglect. Every child nowadays knows that he can keep from getting typhoid fever by a little care in the choice of his drinking water. But it took years and years of hard work before the doctors could convince the people of this fact. Few of us now fear the dentist chair. A study of the microbes that live in our mouth has made it possible to keep our teeth from decay. Must perchance a tooth be pulled, then we take a sniff of gas, and go our way rejoicing. When the newspapers of the year 1846 brought the story of the "painless operation" which had been performed in America with the help of ether, the good people of Europe shook their heads. To them it seemed against the will of God that man should escape the pain which was the share of all mortals, and it took a long time before the practice of taking ether and chloroform for operations became general.

But the battle of progress had been won. The breach in the old walls of prejudice was growing larger and larger, and as time went by, the ancient stones of ignorance came crumbling down. The eager crusaders of a new and happier social order rushed forward. Suddenly they found themselves facing a new obstacle. Out of the ruins of a long-gone past, another citadel of reaction had been erected, and millions of men had to give their lives before this last bulwark was destroyed.

A CHAPTER OF ART

WHEN a baby is perfectly healthy and has had enough to eat and has slept all it wants, then it hums a little tune to show how happy it is. To grown-ups this humming means nothing. It sounds like "goo-zum, goo-zum, goo-o-o-o-o," but to the baby it is perfect music. It is his first contribution to art.

As soon as he (or she) gets a little older and is able to sit up, the period of mud-pie making begins. These mud-pies do not interest the outside world. There are too many million babies, making too many million mud-pies at the same time. But to the small infant they represent another expedition into the pleasant realm of art. The baby is now a sculptor.

At the age of three or four, when the hands begin to obey the brain, the child becomes a painter. His fond mother gives him a box of coloured chalks and every loose bit of paper is rapidly covered with strange pothooks and scrawls which represent houses and horses and terrible naval battles.

Soon however this happiness of just "making things" comes to an end. School begins and the greater part of the day is filled up with work. The business of living, or rather the business of "making a living," becomes the most important event in the life of every boy and girl. There is little time left for "art" between learning the tables of multiplication and the past participles of the irregular French verbs. And unless the desire for making certain things for the mere pleasure of creating them without any hope of a practical return be very strong, the child grows into manhood and forgets that the first five years of his life were mainly devoted to art.

Nations are not different from children. As soon as the cave-man had escaped the threatening dangers of the long and shivering ice-period, and had put his house in order, he began to make certain things which he thought beautiful, although they were of no earthly use to him in his fight with the wild animals of the jungle. He covered the walls of his grotto with pictures of the elephants and the deer which he hunted, and out of a piece of stone, he hacked the rough figures of those women he thought most attractive.

As soon as the Egyptians and the Babylonians and the Persians and all the other people of the east had founded their little countries along the Nile and the Euphrates, they began to build magnificent palaces for their kings, invented bright pieces of jewellery for their women and planted gardens which sang happy songs of colour with their many bright flowers.

Our own ancestors, the wandering nomads from the distant Asiatic prairies, enjoying a free and easy existence as fighters and hunters, composed songs which celebrated the mighty deeds of their great leaders and invented a form of poetry which has survived until our own day. A thousand years later, when they had established themselves on the Greek mainland, and had built their "city-states," they expressed their joy (and their sorrows) in magnificent temples, in statues, in comedies and in tragedies, and in every conceivable form of art.

The Romans, like their Carthaginian rivals, were too busy administering other people and making money to have much love for "useless and unprofitable" adventures of the spirit. They conquered the world and built roads and bridges but they borrowed their art wholesale from the Greeks. They invented certain practical forms of architecture which answered the demands of their day and age. But their statues and their histories and their mosaics and their poems were mere Latin imi-

tations of Greek originals. Without that vague and hard-to-
define something which the world calls "personality," there can
be no art and the Roman world distrusted that particular sort
of personality.   The Empire needed efficient soldiers and
tradesmen.   The business of writing poetry or making pictures was left to foreigners.

Then came the Dark Ages. The barbarian was the proverbial bull in the china-shop of western Europe. He had no use
for what he did not understand. Speaking in terms of the year
1921, he liked the magazine covers of pretty ladies, but threw
the Rembrandt etchings which he had inherited into the ash-
can. Soon he came to learn better. Then he tried to undo the
damage which he had created a few years before. But the ash-
cans were gone and so were the pictures.

But by this time, his own art, which he had brought with
him from the east, had developed into something very beautiful
and he made up for his past neglect and indifference by the so-
called "art of the Middle Ages" which as far as northern Europe is concerned was a product of the Germanic mind and had
borrowed but little from the Greeks and the Latins and nothing
at all from the older forms of art of Egypt and Assyria, not
to speak of India and China, which simply did not exist, as far
as the people of that time were concerned. Indeed, so little
had the northern races been influenced by their southern neighbours that their own architectural products were completely
misunderstood by the people of Italy and were treated by
them with downright and unmitigated contempt.

You have all heard the word Gothic. You probably asso-
ciate it with the picture of a lovely old cathedral, lifting its slender spires towards high heaven. But what does the word really
mean?

It means something "uncouth" and "barbaric"—something
which one might expect from an "uncivilised Goth," a rough
backwoods-man who had no respect for the established rules of
classical art and who built his "modern horrors" to please his
own low tastes without a decent regard for the examples of
the Forum and the Acropolis.

And yet for several centuries this form of Gothic architecture was the highest expression of the sincere feeling for art which inspired the whole northern continent. From a previous chapter, you will remember how the people of the late Middle Ages lived. Unless they were peasants and dwelt in villages, they were citizens of a "city" or "civitas," the old Latin name for a tribe. And indeed, behind their high walls and their deep moats, these good burghers were true tribesmen who shared the common dangers and enjoyed the common safety and prosperity which they derived from their system of mutual protection.

In the old Greek and Roman cities the market-place, where the temple stood, had been the centre of civic life. During the Middle Ages, the Church, the House of God, became such a centre. We modern Protestant people, who go to our church only once a week, and then for a few hours only, hardly know what a mediæval church meant to the community. Then, before you were a week old, you were taken to the Church to be baptised. As a child, you visited the Church to learn the holy stories of the Scriptures. Later on you became a member of the congregation, and if you were rich enough you built yourself a separate little chapel sacred to the memory of the Patron Saint of your own family. As for the sacred edifice, it was open at all hours of the day and many of the night. In a certain sense it resembled a modern club, dedicated to all the inhabitants of the town. In the church you very likely caught a first glimpse of the girl who was to become your bride at a great ceremony before the High Altar. And finally, when the end of the journey had come, you were buried beneath the stones of this familiar building, that all your children and their grandchildren might pass over your grave until the Day of Judgement.

Because the Church was not only the House of God but also the true centre of all common life, the building had to be different from anything that had ever been constructed by the hands of man. The temples of the Egyptians and the Greeks and the Romans had been merely the shrine of a local divinity. As no sermons were preached before the images of Osiris or Zeus or Jupiter, it was not necessary that the interior offer space for a great multitude. All the religious processions of the old Mediterranean peoples took place in the open. But in the north, where the weather was usually bad, most functions were held under the roof of the church.

During many centuries the architects struggled with this problem of constructing a building that was large enough. The Roman tradition taught them how to build heavy stone walls with very small windows lest the walls lose their strength. On the top of this they then placed a heavy stone roof. But in the twelfth century, after the beginning of the Crusades, when the architects had seen the pointed arches of the Mohammedan builders, the western builders discovered a new style which gave them their first chance to make the sort of building which those days of an intense religious life demanded. And then

GOTHIC ARCHITECTURE

they developed this strange style upon which the Italians bestowed the contemptuous name of "Gothic" or barbaric. They achieved their purpose by inventing a vaulted roof which was supported by "ribs." But such a roof, if it became too heavy, was apt to break the walls, just as a man of three hundred pounds sitting down upon a child's chair

will force it to collapse. To overcome this difficulty, certain
French architects then began to re-enforce the walls with
"buttresses" which were merely heavy masses of stone against
which the walls could lean while they supported the roof. And
to assure the further safety of the roof they supported the ribs
of the roof by so-called "flying buttresses," a very simple
method of construction which you will understand at once when
you look at our picture.

This new method of construction allowed the introduction
of enormous windows. In the twelfth century, glass was still
an expensive curiosity, and very few private buildings possessed glass windows. Even the castles of the nobles were
without protection and this accounts for the eternal drafts
and explains why people of that day wore furs in-doors as
well as out.

Fortunately, the art of making coloured glass, with which
the ancient people of the Mediterranean had been familiar,
had not been entirely lost. There was a revival of stained
glass-making and soon the windows of the Gothic churches
told the stories of the Holy Book in little bits of brilliantly
coloured window-pane, which were caught in a long frame-
work of lead.

Behold, therefore, the new and glorious house of God,
filled with an eager multitude, "living" its religion as no people
have ever done either before or since! Nothing is considered
too good or too costly or too wondrous for this House of God
and Home of Man. The sculptors, who since the destruction
of the Roman Empire have been out of employment, haltingly
return to their noble art. Portals and pillars and buttresses
and cornices are all covered with carven images of Our Lord
and the blessed Saints. The embroiderers too are set to work
to make tapestries for the walls. The jewellers offer their
highest art that the shrine of the altar may be worthy of complete adoration. Even the painter does his best. Poor man,
he is greatly handicapped by lack of a suitable medium.

And thereby hangs a story.

The Romans of the early Christian period had covered the

floors and the walls of their temples and houses with mosaics; pictures made of coloured bits of glass. But this art had been exceedingly difficult. It gave the painter no chance to express all he wanted to say, as all children know who have ever tried to make figures out of coloured blocks of wood. The art of mosaic painting therefore died out during the late Middle Ages except in Russia, where the Byzantine mosaic painters had found a refuge after the fall of Constantinople and continued to ornament the walls of the orthodox churches until the day of the Bolsheviki, when there was an end to the building of churches.

Of course, the mediæval painter could mix his colours with the water of the wet plaster which was put upon the walls of the churches. This method of painting upon "fresh plaster" (which was generally called "fresco" or "fresh" painting) was very popular for many centuries. To-day, it is as rare as the art of painting miniatures in manuscripts and among the hundreds of artists of our modern cities there is perhaps one who can handle this medium successfully. But during the Middle Ages there was no other way and the artists were "fresco" workers for lack of something better. The method however had certain great disadvantages. Very often the plaster came off the walls after only a few years, or dampness spoiled the pictures, just as dampness will spoil the pattern of our wall paper. People tried every imaginable expedient to get away from this plaster background. They tried to mix their colours with wine and vinegar and with honey and with the sticky white of egg, but none of these methods were satisfactory. For more than a thousand years these experiments continued. In painting pictures upon the parchment leaves of manuscripts the mediæval artists were very successful. But when it came to covering large spaces of wood or stone with paint which would stick, they did not succeed very well.

At last, during the first half of the fifteenth century, the problem was solved in the southern Netherlands by Jan and Hubert van Eyck. The famous Flemish brothers mixed their paint with specially prepared oils and this allowed them to use wood and canvas or stone or anything else as a background for their pictures.

But by this time the religious ardour of the early Middle Ages was a thing of the past. The rich burghers of the cities were succeeding the bishops as patrons of the arts. And as art invariably follows the full dinner-pail, the artists now began to work for these worldly employers and painted pictures for kings, for grand-dukes and for rich bankers. Within a very short time, the new method of painting with oil spread through Europe and in every country there developed a school of special painting which showed the characteristic tastes of the people for whom these portraits and landscapes were made.

In Spain, for example, Velasquez painted court-dwarfs and the weavers of the royal tapestry-factories, and all sorts of persons and subjects connected with the king and his court. But in Holland, Rembrandt and Frans Hals and Vermeer painted the barnyard of the merchant's house, and they painted his rather dowdy wife and his healthy but bumptious children and the ships which had brought him his wealth. In Italy on the other hand, where the Pope remained the largest patron of the arts, Michelangelo and Correggio continued to paint Madonnas and Saints, while in England, where the aristocracy was very rich and powerful and in France where the kings had become uppermost in the state, the artists painted distinguished gentlemen who were members of the government, and very lovely ladies who were friends of His Majesty.

The great change in painting, which came about with the neglect of the old church and the rise of a new class in society, was reflected in all other forms of art. The invention of printing had made it possible for authors to win fame and reputation by writing books for the multitudes. In this way arose the profession of the novelist and the illustrator. But the people who had money enough to buy the new books were not the sort who liked to sit at home of nights, looking at the ceiling or just sitting. They wanted to be amused. The few minstrels of the Middle Ages were not sufficient to cover the demand for entertainment. For the first time since the early Greek city-states of two thousand years before, the professional play-wright had a chance to ply his trade. The Middle Ages had known the theatre merely as part of certain church celebrations. The tragedies of the thirteenth and fourteenth centuries had told the story of the suffering of our Lord. But during the sixteenth century the worldly theatre made its reappearance. It is true that, at first, the position of the professional playwright and actor was not a very high one. William Shakespeare was regarded as a sort of circus-fellow who amused his neighbours with his tragedies and comedies. But when he died in the year 1616 he had begun to enjoy the respect of his neighbours and actors were no longer subjects of police supervision.

William's contemporary, Lope de Vega, the incredible Spaniard who wrote no less than 1800 worldly and 400 religious plays, was a person of rank who received the papal approval upon his work. A century later, Molière, the Frenchman, was deemed worthy of the companionship of none less than King Louis XIV.

Since then, the theatre has enjoyed an ever increasing affection on the part of the people. To-day a "theatre" is part of every well-regulated city, and the "silent drama" of the movies has penetrated to the tiniest of our prairie hamlets.

Another art, however, was to become the most popular of all. That was music. Most of the old art-forms demanded a great deal of technical skill. It takes years and years of practice before our clumsy hand is able to follow the commands of the brain and reproduce our vision upon canvas or in marble. It takes a lifetime to learn how to act or how to write a good novel. And it takes a great deal of training on the part of the public to appreciate the best in painting and writing and sculpture. But almost any one, not entirely tone-deaf, can follow a tune and almost everybody can get enjoyment out of some sort of music. The Middle Ages had heard a little music but it had been entirely the music of the church. The holy chants were subject to very severe laws of rhythm and harmony

and soon these became monotonous. Besides, they could not
well be sung in the street or in the market-place.

The Renaissance changed this. Music once more came
into its own as the best friend of man, both in his happiness and
in his sorrows.

The Egyptians and the Babylonians and the ancient Jews
had all been great lovers of music. They had even combined
different instruments into regular orchestras. But the Greeks
had frowned upon this barbaric foreign noise. They liked to
hear a man recite the stately poetry of Homer and Pindar.
They allowed him to accompany himself upon the lyre (the
poorest of all stringed instru-
ments). That was as far as any
one could go without incurring
the risk of popular disapproval.
The Romans on the other hand
had loved orchestral music at
their dinners and parties and
they had invented most of the
instruments which (in *very*
modified form) we use to-day.
The early church had despised
this music which smacked too
much of the wicked pagan
world which had just been destroyed. A few songs rendered
by the entire congregation were
all the bishops of the third and

THE TROUBADOUR

fourth centuries would tolerate. As the congregation was apt
to sing dreadfully out of key without the guidance of an instrument, the church had afterwards allowed the use of an
organ, an invention of the second century of our era which consisted of a combination of the old pipes of Pan and a pair of
bellows.

Then came the great migrations. The last of the Roman
musicians were either killed or became tramp-fiddlers going
from city to city and playing in the street, and begging for
pennies like the harpist on a modern ferry-boat.

But the revival of a more worldly civilisation in the cities of the late Middle Ages had created a new demand for musicians. Instruments like the horn, which had been used only as signal-instruments for hunting and fighting, were remodelled until they could reproduce sounds which were agreeable in the dance-hall and in the banqueting room. A bow strung with horse-hair was used to play the old-fashioned guitar and before the end of the Middle Ages this six-stringed instrument (the most ancient of all string-instruments which dates back to Egypt and Assyria) had grown into our modern four-stringed fiddle which Stradivarius and the other Italian violin-makers of the eighteenth century brought to the height of perfection.

And finally the modern piano was invented, the most widespread of all musical instruments, which has followed man into the wilderness of the jungle and the ice-fields of Greenland. The organ had been the first of all keyed instruments but the performer always depended upon the co-operation of some one who worked the bellows, a job which nowadays is done by electricity. The musicians therefore looked for a handier and less circumstantial instrument to assist them in training the pupils of the many church choirs. During the great eleventh century, Guido, a Benedictine monk of the town of Arezzo (the birthplace of the poet Petrarch) gave us our modern system of musical annotation. Some time during that century, when there was a great deal of popular interest in music, the first instrument with both keys and strings was built. It must have sounded as tinkly as one of those tiny children's pianos which you can buy at every toy-shop. In the city of Vienna, the town where the strolling musicians of the Middle Ages (who had been classed with jugglers and card sharps) had formed the first separate Guild of Musicians in the year 1288, the little monochord was developed into something which we can recognise as the direct ancestor of our modern Steinway. From Austria the "clavichord" as it was usually called in those days (because it had "claves" or keys) went to Italy. There it was perfected into the "spinet" which was so called after the inventor, Giovanni Spinetti of Venice. At last during the eighteenth century, some time between 1709 and 1720, Bartolomeo Cristofori made a "clavier" which allowed the performer to play both loudly and softly or as it was said in Italian, "piano" and "forte." This instrument with certain changes became our "pianoforte" or piano.

Then for the first time the world possessed an easy and convenient instrument which could be mastered in a couple of years and did not need the eternal tuning of harps and fiddles and was much pleasanter to the ears than the mediæval tubas, clarinets, trombones and oboes. Just as the phonograph has given millions of modern people their first love of music so did the early "pianoforte" carry the knowledge of music into much wider circles. Music became part of the education of every well-bred man and woman. Princes and rich merchants maintained private orchestras. The musician ceased to be a wandering "jongleur" and became a highly valued member of the community. Music was added to the dramatic performances of the theatre and out of this practice, grew our modern Opera. Originally only a few very rich princes could afford the expenses of an "opera troupe." But as the taste for this sort of entertainment grew, many cities built their own theatres where Italian and afterwards German operas were given to the unlimited joy of the whole community with the exception of a few sects of very strict Christians who still regarded music with deep suspicion as something which was too lovely to be entirely good for the soul.

By the middle of the eighteenth century the musical life of Europe was in full swing. Then there came forward a man who was greater than all others, a simple organist of the Thomas Church of Leipzig, by the name of Johann Sebastian Bach. In his compositions for every known instrument, from comic songs and popular dances to the most stately of sacred hymns and oratorios, he laid the foundation for all our modern music. When he died in the year 1750 he was succeeded by Mozart, who created musical fabrics of sheer loveliness which remind us of lace that has been woven out of harmony and rhythm. Then came Ludwig von Beethoven, the most tragic of men, who gave us our modern orchestra, yet heard none of his greatest compositions because he was deaf, as the result of a cold contracted during his years of poverty.

Beethoven lived through the period of the great French Revolution. Full of hope for a new and glorious day, he had dedicated one of his symphonies to Napoleon. But he lived to regret the hour. When he died in the year 1827, Napoleon was gone and the French Revolution was gone, but the steam engine had come and was filling the world with a sound that had nothing in common with the dreams of the Third Symphony.

Indeed, the new order of steam and iron and coal and large factories had little use for art, for painting and sculpture and poetry and music. The old protectors of the arts, the Church and the princes and the merchants of the Middle Ages and the seventeenth and eighteenth centuries no longer existed. The leaders of the new industrial world were too busy and had too little education to bother about etchings and sonatas and bits of carved ivory, not to speak of the men who created those things, and who were of no practical use to the community in which they lived. And the workmen in the factories listened to the drone of their engines until they too had lost all taste for the melody of the flute or fiddle of their peasant ancestry. The arts became the step-children of the new industrial era. Art and Life became entirely separated. Whatever paintings had been left, were dying a slow death in the museums. And music became a monopoly of a few "virtuosi" who took the music away from the home and carried it to the concert-hall.

But steadily, although slowly, the arts are coming back into their own. People begin to understand that Rembrandt and Beethoven and Rodin are the true prophets and leaders of their race and that a world without art and happiness resembles a nursery without laughter.

COLONIAL EXPANSION AND WAR

A CHAPTER WHICH OUGHT TO GIVE YOU A
GREAT DEAL OF POLITICAL INFORMA-
TION ABOUT THE LAST FIFTY YEARS, BUT
WHICH REALLY CONTAINS SEVERAL EX-
PLANATIONS AND A FEW APOLOGIES

IF I had known how difficult it was to write a History of
the World, I should never have undertaken the task. Of course,
any one possessed of enough industry to lose himself for half
a dozen years in the musty stacks of a library, can compile a
ponderous tome which gives an account of the events in every
land during every century. But that was not the purpose of
the present book. The publishers wanted to print a history
that should have rhythm—a story which galloped rather than
walked. And now that I have almost finished I discover that
certain chapters gallop, that others wade slowly through the
dreary sands of long forgotten ages—that a few parts do not
make any progress at all, while still others indulge in a veritable jazz of action and romance. I did not like this and I suggested that we destroy the whole manuscript and begin once
more from the beginning. This, however, the publishers would
not allow.

As the next best solution of my difficulties, I took the type-
written pages to a number of charitable friends and asked them
to read what I had said, and give me the benefit of their advice.
The experience was rather disheartening. Each and every

man had his own prejudices and his own hobbies and preferences. They all wanted to know why, where and how I dared to omit their pet nation, their pet statesman, or even their most beloved criminal. With some of them, Napoleon and Jenghiz Khan were candidates for high honours. I explained that I had tried very hard to be fair to Napoleon, but that in my estimation he was greatly inferior to such men as George Washington, Gustavus Wasa, Augustus, Hammurabi or Lincoln, and a score of others all of whom were obliged to

THE PIONEER

content themselves with a few paragraphs, from sheer lack of space. As for Jenghiz Khan, I only recognise his superior ability in the field of wholesale murder and I did not intend to give him any more publicity than I could help.

"This is very well as far as it goes," said the next critic, "but how about the Puritans? We are celebrating the ter-centenary of their arrival at Plymouth. They ought to have more space." My answer was that if I were writing a history of America, the Puritans would get fully one half of the first twelve chapters; that however this was a history of mankind and that the event on Plymouth rock was not a matter of far-reaching international importance until many centuries later; that the United States had been founded by thirteen colonies and not by a single one; that the most prominent leaders of the first twenty years of our history had been from Virginia, from Pennsylvania, and from the island of Nevis, rather than from Massachusetts; and that therefore the Puritans ought to content themselves with a page of print and a special map.

Next came the prehistoric specialist. Why in the name of the great Tyrannosaur had I not devoted more space to the wonderful race of Cro-Magnon men, who had developed such a high stage of civilisation 10,000 years ago?

Indeed, and why not? The reason is simple. I do not take as much stock in the perfection of these early races as some of our most noted anthropologists seem to do. Rousseau and the philosophers of the eighteenth century created the "noble savage" who was supposed to have dwelt in a state of perfect happiness during the beginning of time. Our modern scientists have discarded the "noble savage," so dearly beloved by our grandfathers, and they have replaced him by the "splendid savage" of the French Valleys who 35,000 years ago made an end to the universal rule of the low-browed and low-living brutes of the Neanderthal and other Germanic neighbourhoods. They have shown us the elephants the Cro-Magnon painted and the statues he carved and they have surrounded him with much glory.

I do not mean to say that they are wrong. But I hold that we know by far too little of this entire period to re-construct that early west-European society with any degree (however humble) of accuracy. And I would rather not state certain things than run the risk of stating certain things that were not so.

Then there were other critics, who accused me of direct unfairness. Why did I leave out such countries as Ireland and Bulgaria and Siam while I dragged in such other countries as Holland and Iceland and Switzerland? My answer was that I did not drag in any countries. They pushed themselves in by main force of circumstances, and I simply could not keep them out. And in order that my point may be understood, let me state the basis upon which active membership to this book of history was considered.

There was but one rule. "Did the country or the person in question produce a new idea or perform an original act without which the history of the entire human race would have been different?" It was not a question of personal taste. It was a matter of cool, almost mathematical judgment. No race ever played a more picturesque rôle in history than the Mongolians, and no race, from the point of view of achievement or intelligent progress, was of less value to the rest of mankind.

The career of Tiglath-Pileser, the Assyrian, is full of dramatic episodes. But as far as we are concerned, he might just as well never have existed at all. In the same way, the history of the Dutch Republic is not interesting because once upon a time the sailors of de Ruyter went fishing in the river Thames, but rather because of the fact that this small mud-bank along the shores of the North Sea offered a hospitable asylum to all sorts of strange people who had all sorts of queer ideas upon all sorts of very unpopular subjects.

It is quite true that Athens or Florence, during the hey-day of their glory, had only one tenth of the population of Kansas City. But our present civilisation would be very different had neither of these two little cities of the Mediterranean basin existed. And the same (with due apologies to the good people of Wyandotte County) can hardly be said of this busy metropolis on the Missouri River.

And since I am being very personal, allow me to state one other fact.

When we visit a doctor, we find out before hand whether he is a surgeon or a diagnostician or a homeopath or a faith healer, for we want to know from what angle he will look at our complaint. We ought to be as careful in the choice of our historians as we are in the selection of our physicians. We think, "Oh well, history is history," and let it go at that. But the writer who was educated in a strictly Presbyterian household somewhere in the backwoods of Scotland will look differently upon every question of human relationships from his neighbour who as a child, was dragged to listen to the brilliant exhortations of Robert Ingersoll, the enemy of all revealed Devils. In due course of time, both men may forget their early training and never again visit either church or lecture hall. But the influence of these impressionable years stays with them and they cannot escape showing it in whatever they write or say or do.

In the preface to this book, I told you that I should not be an infallible guide and now that we have almost reached the end, I repeat the warning. I was born and educated in an atmosphere of the old-fashioned liberalism which had followed the discoveries of Darwin and the other pioneers of the nineteenth century. As a child, I happened to spend most of my waking hours with an uncle who was a great collector of the books written by Montaigne, the great French essayist of the sixteenth century. Because I was born in Rotterdam and educated in the city of Gouda, I ran continually across Erasmus and for some unknown reason this great exponent of tolerance took hold of my intolerant self. Later I discovered Anatole France and my first experience with the English language came about through an accidental encounter with Thackeray's "Henry Esmond," a story which made more impression upon me than any other book in the English language.

If I had been born in a pleasant middle western city I probably should have a certain affection for the hymns which I had heard in my childhood. But my earliest recollection of music goes back to the afternoon when my Mother took me to hear nothing less than a Bach fugue. And the mathematical perfection of the great Protestant master influenced me to such an extent that I cannot hear the usual hymns of our prayer-meetings without a feeling of intense agony and direct pain.

Again, if I had been born in Italy and had been warmed by the sunshine of the happy valley of the Arno, I might love many colourful and sunny pictures which now leave me indifferent because I got my first artistic impressions in a country where the rare sun beats down upon the rain-soaked land with

almost cruel brutality and throws everything into violent con-
trasts of dark and light.

I state these few facts deliberately that you may know
the personal bias of the man who wrote this history and may
understand his point-of-view. The bibliography at the end of
this book, which represents all sorts of opinions and views, will
allow you to compare my ideas with those of other people.
And in this way, you will be able to reach your own final conclusions with a greater degree of fairness than would
otherwise be possible.

THE CONQUEST OF THE WEST

After this short but necessary excursion, we return to the
history of the last fifty years. Many things happened during
this period but very little occurred which at the time seemed
to be of paramount importance. The majority of the greater
powers ceased to be mere political agencies and became large
business enterprises. They built railroads. They founded and
subsidized steam-ship lines to all parts of the world. They
connected their different possessions with telegraph wires.
And they steadily increased their holdings in other continents.
Every available bit of African or Asiatic territory was claimed

by one of the rival powers. France became a colonial nation
with interests in Algiers and Madagascar and Annam and
Tonkin (in eastern Asia). Germany claimed parts of south-
west and east Africa, built settlements in Kameroon on the
west coast of Africa and in New Guinea and many of the
islands of the Pacific, and used the murder of a few missionaries
as a welcome excuse to take the harbour of Kiaochau on the
Yellow Sea in China. Italy tried her luck in Abyssinia, was
disastrously defeated by the soldiers of the Negus, and consoled herself by occupying the Turkish possessions in Tripoli
in northern Africa. Russia, having occupied all of Siberia,
took Port Arthur away from China. Japan, having defeated
China in the war of 1895, occupied the island of Formosa and
in the year 1905 began to lay claim to the entire empire of
Corea. In the year 1883 England, the largest colonial empire
the world has ever seen, undertook to "protect" Egypt. She
performed this task most efficiently and to the great material
benefit of that much neglected country, which ever since the
opening of the Suez canal in 1868 had been threatened with a
foreign invasion. During the next thirty years she fought a
number of colonial wars in different parts of the world and in
1902 (after three years of bitter fighting) she conquered the
independent Boer republics of the Transvaal and the Orange
Free State. Meanwhile she had encouraged Cecil Rhodes to
lay the foundations for a great African state, which reached
from the Cape almost to the mouth of the Nile, and had faithfully picked up such islands or provinces as had been left without a European owner.

The shrewd king of Belgium, by name Leopold, used
the discoveries of Henry Stanley to found the Congo Free
State in the year 1885. Originally this gigantic tropical empire was an "absolute monarchy." But after many years of
scandalous mismanagement, it was annexed by the Belgian
people who made it a colony (in the year 1908) and abolished
the terrible abuses which had been tolerated by this very unscrupulous Majesty, who cared nothing for the fate of the
natives as long as he got his ivory and rubber.

As for the United States, they had so much land that they desired no further territory. But the terrible misrule of Cuba, one of the last of the Spanish possessions in the western hemisphere, practically forced the Washington government to take action. After a short and rather uneventful war, the Spaniards were driven out of Cuba and Puerto Rico and the Philippines, and the two latter became colonies of the United States.

This economic development of the world was perfectly natural. The increasing number of factories in England and France and Germany needed an ever increasing amount of raw materials and the equally increasing number of European workers needed an ever increasing amount of food. Everywhere the cry was for more and for richer markets, for more easily accessible coal mines and iron mines and rubber plantations and oil-wells, for greater supplies of wheat and grain.

The purely political events of the European continent dwindled to mere insignificance in the eyes of men who were making plans for steamboat lines on Victoria Nyanza or for railroads through the interior of Shantung. They knew that many European questions still remained to be settled, but they did not bother, and through sheer indifference and carelessness they bestowed upon their descendants a terrible inheritance of hate and misery. For untold centuries the south-eastern corner of Europe had been the scene of rebellion and bloodshed. During the seventies of the last century the people of Serbia and Bulgaria and Montenegro and Roumania were once more trying to gain their freedom and the Turks (with the support of many of the western powers), were trying to prevent this.

After a period of particularly atrocious massacres in Bulgaria in the year 1876, the Russian people lost all patience. The Government was forced to intervene just as President McKinley was obliged to go to Cuba and stop the shooting-squads of General Weyler in Havana. In April of the year 1877 the Russian armies crossed the Danube, stormed the Shipka pass, and after the capture of Plevna, marched southward until they reached the gates of Constantinople. Turkey appealed for help to England. There were many English people who denounced their government when it took the side of the Sultan. But Disraeli (who had just made Queen Victoria Empress of India and who loved the picturesque Turks while he hated the Russians who were brutally cruel to the Jewish people within their frontiers) decided to interfere. Russia was forced to conclude the peace of San Stefano (1878) and the question of the Balkans was left to a Congress which convened at Berlin in June and July of the same year.

This famous conference was entirely dominated by the personality of Disraeli. Even Bismarck feared the clever old man with his well-oiled curly hair and his supreme arrogance, tempered by a cynical sense of humor and a marvellous gift for flattery. At Berlin the British prime-minister carefully watched over the fate of his friends the Turks. Montenegro. Serbia and Roumania were recognised as independent kingdoms. The principality of Bulgaria was given a semi-independent status under Prince Alexander of Battenberg, a nephew of Tsar Alexander II. But none of those countries were given the chance to develop their powers and their resources as they would have been able to do, had England been less anxious about the fate of the Sultan, whose domains were necessary to the safety of the British Empire as a bulwark against further Russian aggression.

To make matters worse, the congress allowed Austria to take Bosnia and Herzegovina away from the Turks to be "administered" as part of the Habsburg domains. It is true that Austria made an excellent job of it. The neglected provinces were as well managed as the best of the British colonies, and that is saying a great deal. But they were inhabited by many Serbians. In older days they had been part of the great Serbian empire of Stephan Dushan, who early in the fourteenth century had defended western Europe against the invasions of the Turks and whose capital of Uskub had been a centre of civilisation one hundred and fifty years before Columbus discovered the new lands of the west. The Serbians remembered their ancient glory as who would not?   They resented the presence of the Austrians in two provinces, which, so they felt, were theirs by every right of tradition.

And it was in Sarajevo, the capital of Bosnia, that the archduke Ferdinand, heir to the Austrian throne, was murdered on June 28 of the year 1914.   The assassin was a Serbian student who had acted from purely patriotic motives.

But the blame for this terrible catastrophe which was the immediate, though not the only cause of the Great World War did not lie with the half-crazy Serbian boy or his Austrian victim.   It must be traced back to the days of the famous Berlin Conference when Europe was too busy building a material civilisation to care about the aspirations and the dreams of a forgotten race in a dreary corner of the old Balkan peninsula.

A NEW WORLD

THE GREAT WAR WHICH WAS REALLY THE STRUGGLE FOR A NEW AND BETTER WORLD

THE Marquis de Condorcet was one of the noblest charac-ters among the small group of honest enthusiasts who were responsible for the outbreak of the great French Revolution. He had devoted his life to the cause of the poor and the unfor-tunate. He had been one of the assistants of d'Alembert and Diderot when they wrote their famous Encyclopédie. During the first years of the Revolution he had been the leader of the Moderate wing of the Convention.

His tolerance, his kindliness, his stout common sense, had made him an object of suspicion when the treason of the king and the court clique had given the extreme radicals their chance to get hold of the government and kill their opponents. Condorcet was declared "hors de loi," or outlawed, an outcast who was henceforth at the mercy of every true patriot. His friends offered to hide him at their own peril. Condorcet refused to accept their sacrifice. He escaped and tried to reach his home, where he might be safe. After three nights in the open, torn and bleeding, he entered an inn and asked for some food. The suspicious yokels searched him and in his pockets they found a copy of Horace, the Latin poet. This showed that their prisoner was a man of gentle breeding and had no business upon the highroads at a time when every educated person was regarded as an enemy of the Revolutionary state. They took Condorcet and they bound him and they gagged him and they threw him into the village lock-up, but in the morning when the soldiers came to drag him back to Paris and cut his head off, behold! he was dead.

This man who had given all and had received nothing had good reason to despair of the human race. But he has written a few sentences which ring as true to-day as they did one hundred and thirty years ago. I repeat them here for your benefit.

"Nature has set no limits to our hopes," he wrote, "and the picture of the human race, now freed from its chains and

WAR

marching with a firm tread on the road of truth and virtue and happiness, offers to the philosopher a spectacle which consoles him for the errors, for the crimes and the injustices which still pollute and afflict this earth."

The world has just passed through an agony of pain compared to which the French Revolution was a mere incident. The shock has been so great that it has killed the last spark of hope in the breasts of millions of men. They were chanting a hymn of progress, and four years of slaughter followed their prayers for peace. "Is it worth while," so they ask, "to work and slave for the benefit of creatures who have not yet passed beyond the stage of the earliest cave men?"

There is but one answer.

That answer is "Yes!"

The World War was a terrible calamity. But it did not mean the end of things. On the contrary it brought about the coming of a new day.

It is easy to write a history of Greece and Rome or the Middle Ages. The actors who played their parts upon that long-forgotten stage are all dead. We can criticize them with a cool head. The audience that applauded their efforts has dispersed. Our remarks cannot possibly hurt their feelings.

But it is very difficult to give a true account of contemporary events. The problems that fill the minds of the people with whom we pass through life, are our own problems, and they hurt us too much or they please us too well to be described with that fairness which is necessary when we are writing history and not blowing the trumpet of propaganda. All the same I shall endeavour to tell you why I agree with poor Condorcet when he expressed his firm faith in a better future.

Often before have I warned you against the false impression which is created by the use of our so-called historical epochs which divide the story of man into four parts, the ancient world, the Middle Ages, the Renaissance and the Reformation, and Modern Time. The last of these terms is the most dangerous. The word "modern" implies that we, the people of the twentieth century, are at the top of human achievement. Fifty years ago the liberals of England who followed the leadership of Gladstone felt that the problem of a truly representative and democratic form of government had been solved forever by the second great Reform Bill, which gave workmen an equal share in the government with their employers. When Disraeli and his conservative friends talked of a dangerous "leap in the dark" they answered "No." They felt certain of their cause and trusted that henceforth all classes of society would co-operate to make the government of their common country a success. Since then many things have happened, and the few liberals who are still alive begin to understand that they were mistaken.

There is no definite answer to any historical problem.

Every generation must fight the good fight anew or perish

as those sluggish animals of the prehistoric world have perished.

If you once get hold of this great truth you will get a new and much broader view of life. Then, go one step further and try to imagine yourself in the position of your own great-great-grandchildren who will take your place in the year 10,000. They too will learn history. But what will they think of those short four thousand years during which we have kept a written record of our actions and of our thoughts? They will think of Napoleon as a contemporary of Tiglath Pileser, the Assyrian conqueror. Perhaps they will confuse him with Jenghiz Khan or Alexander the Macedonian. The great war which has just come to an end will appear in the light of that long commercial conflict which settled the supremacy of the Mediterranean when Rome and Carthage fought during one hundred and twenty-eight years for the mastery of the sea. The Balkan troubles of the 19th century (the struggle for freedom of Serbia and Greece and Bulgaria and Montenegro) to them will seem a continuation of the disordered conditions caused by the Great Migrations. They will look at pictures of the Rheims cathedral which only yesterday was destroyed by German guns as we look upon a photograph of the Acropolis ruined two hundred and fifty years ago during a war between the Turks and the Venetians. They will regard the fear of death, which is still common among many people, as a childish superstition which was perhaps natural in a race of men who had burned witches as late as the year 1692. Even our hospitals and our laboratories and our operating rooms of which we are so proud will look like slightly improved workshops of alchemists and mediæval surgeons.

And the reason for all this is simple. We modern men and women are not "modern" at all. On the contrary we still belong to the last generations of the cave-dwellers. The foundation for a new era was laid but yesterday. The human race was given its first chance to become truly civilised when it took courage to question all things and made "knowledge and understanding" the foundation upon which to create a more reasonable and sensible society of human beings. The Great War was the "growing-pain" of this new world.

For a long time to come people will write mighty books to prove that this or that or the other person brought about the war. The Socialists will publish volumes in which they will ac-

THE STRENGTH OF THE IMPERIAL IDEA

SINCE 1876 the Kings of England are Emperors of India

After 1452 the imperial tradition of Eastern Rome was continued by the Russian grand dukes of Moscow. This lasted until 1918

10

In 1918 the imperial German eagle was deposited here

9

In 1870 the war between France and Germany took place. The French empire came to an end. A new German empire was founded.

In 1804 Napoleon was made emperor

8

7

In the fifth century the Roman empire was divided in two parts

The East Roman empire lasted until 1453

6

In 800 Charles king of the Franks was made emperor to unite and defend Christian Europe

5

From 962 until 1801 the Holy Roman empire of the German nation existed

4

In 48 B.C. Caesar was given the official title of Imperator. The Roman empire established by Augustus lasted five centuries

3

In 336 B.C. Alexander the Great got the imperial idea in Asia.

2

ASIA

In the valley of the Nile in 3000 B.C. the imperial idea seems to have originated.

1

PERSIA

THE SPREAD OF THE IMPERIAL IDEA

cuse the "capitalists" of having brought about the war for "commercial gain." The capitalists will answer that they lost infinitely more through the war than they made—that their children were among the first to go and fight and be killed—and they will show how in every country the bankers tried their very best to avert the outbreak of hostilities. French historians will go through the register of German sins from the days of Charlemagne until the days of William of Hohenzollern and German historians will return the compliment and will go through the list of French horrors from the days of Charlemagne until the days of President Poincaré. And then they will establish to their own satisfaction that the other fellow was guilty of "causing the war." Statesmen, dead and not yet dead, in all countries will take to their typewriters and they will explain how they tried to avert hostilities and how their wicked opponents forced them into it.

The historian, a hundred years hence, will not bother about these apologies and vindications. He will understand the real nature of the underlying causes and he will know that personal ambitions and personal wickedness and personal greed had very little to do with the final outburst. The original mistake, which was responsible for all this misery, was committed when our scientists began to create a new world of steel and iron and chemistry and electricity and forgot that the human mind is slower than the proverbial turtle, is lazier than the well-known sloth, and marches from one hundred to three hundred years behind the small group of courageous leaders.

A Zulu in a frock coat is still a Zulu. A dog trained to ride a bicycle and smoke a pipe is still a dog. And a human being with the mind of a sixteenth century tradesman driving a 1921 Rolls-Royce is still a human being with the mind of a sixteenth century tradesman.

If you do not understand this at first, read it again. It will become clearer to you in a moment and it will explain many things that have happened these last six years.

Perhaps I may give you another, more familiar, example. to show you what I mean. In the movie theatres, jokes and funny remarks are often thrown upon the screen. Watch the audience the next time you have a chance. A few people seem almost to inhale the words. It takes them but a second to read the lines. Others are a bit slower. Still others take from twenty to thirty seconds. Finally those men and women who do not read any more than they can help, get the point when the brighter ones among the audience have already begun to decipher the next cut-in. It is not different in human life, as I shall now show you.

In a former chapter I have told you how the idea of the Roman Empire continued to live for a thousand years after the death of the last Roman Emperor. It caused the establishment of a large number of "imitation empires." It gave the Bishops of Rome a chance to make themselves the head of the entire church, because they represented the idea of Roman world-supremacy. It drove a number of perfectly harmless barbarian chieftains into a career of crime and endless warfare because they were for ever under the spell of this magic word "Rome." All these people, Popes, Emperors and plain fighting men were not very different from you or me. But they lived in a world where the Roman tradition was a vital issue—something living—something which was remembered clearly both by the father and the son and the grandson. And so they struggled and sacrificed themselves for a cause which to-day would not find a dozen recruits.

In still another chapter I have told you how the great religious wars took place more than a century after the first open act of the Reformation and if you will compare the chapter on the Thirty Years War with that on Inventions, you will see that this ghastly butchery took place at a time when the first clumsy steam engines were already puffing in the laboratories of a number of French and German and English scientists. But the world at large took no interest in these strange contraptions, and went on with a grand theological discussion which to-day causes yawns, but no anger.

And so it goes. A thousand years from now, the historian will use the same words about Europe of the out-going nineteenth century, and he will see how men were engaged upon terrific nationalistic struggles while the laboratories all around them were filled with serious folk who cared not one whit for politics as long as they could force nature to surrender a few more of her million secrets.

You will gradually begin to understand what I am driving at. The engineer and the scientist and the chemist, within a single generation, filled Europe and America and Asia with their vast machines, with their telegraphs, their flying machines, their coal-tar products. They created a new world in which time and space were reduced to complete insignificance. They invented new products and they made these so cheap that almost every one could buy them. I have told you all this before but it certainly will bear repeating.

To keep the ever increasing number of factories going, the owners, who had also become the rulers of the land, needed raw materials and coal. Especially coal. Meanwhile the mass of the people were still thinking in terms of the sixteenth and seventeenth centuries and clinging to the old notions of the state as a dynastic or political organisation. This clumsy mediæval institution was then suddenly called upon to handle the highly modern problems of a mechanical and industrial world. It did its best, according to the rules of the game which had been laid down centuries before. The different states created enormous armies and gigantic navies which were used for the purpose of acquiring new possessions in distant lands. Wherever there was a tiny bit of land left, there arose an English or a French or a German or a Russian colony. If the natives objected, they were killed. In most cases they did not object, and were allowed to live peacefully, provided they did not interfere with the diamond mines or the coal mines or the oil mines or the gold mines or the rubber plantations, and they derived many benefits from the foreign occupation.

Sometimes it happened that two states in search of raw materials wanted the same piece of land at the same time. Then there was a war. This occurred fifteen years ago when Russia and Japan fought for the possession of certain territories which belonged to the Chinese people. Such conflicts, however, were the exception. No one really desired to fight. Indeed, the idea of fighting with armies and battleships and submarines began to seem absurd to the men of the early 20th century. They associated the idea of violence with the long-ago age of unlimited monarchies and intriguing dynasties. Every day they read in their papers of still further inventions, of groups of English and American and German scientists who were working together in perfect friendship for the purpose of an advance in medicine or in astronomy. They lived in a busy world of trade and of commerce and factories. But only a few noticed that the development of the state, (of the gigantic community of people who recognise certain common ideals,) was lagging several hundred years behind. They tried to warn the others. But the others were occupied with their own affairs.

I have used so many similes that I must apologise for bringing in one more. The Ship of State (that old and trusted expression which is ever new and always picturesque,) of the Egyptians and the Greeks and the Romans and the Venetians and the merchant adventurers of the seventeenth century had been a sturdy craft, constructed of well-seasoned wood, and commanded by officers who knew both their crew and their vessel and who understood the limitations of the art of navigating which had been handed down to them by their ancestors.

Then came the new age of iron and steel and machinery. First one part, then another of the old ship of state was changed. Her dimensions were increased. The sails were discarded for steam. Better living quarters were established, but more people were forced to go down into the stoke-hole, and while the work was safe and fairly remunerative, they did not like it as well as their old and more dangerous job in the rigging. Finally, and almost imperceptibly, the old wooden square-rigger had been transformed into a modern ocean liner. But the captain and the mates remained the same. They were appointed or elected in the same way as a hundred years before. They were taught the same system of navigation which had served the mariners of the fifteenth century. In their cabins hung the same charts and signal flags which had done service in the days of Louis XIV and Frederick the Great. In short, they were (through no fault of their own) completely incompetent.

The sea of international politics is not very broad. Wh_n those Imperial and Colonial liners began to try and outrun each other, accidents were bound to happen. They did happen. You can still see the wreckage if you venture to pass through that part of the ocean.

And the moral of the story is a simple one. The world is in dreadful need of men who will assume the new leadership— who will have the courage of their own visions and who will recognise clearly that we are only at the beginning of the voyage, and have to learn an entirely new system of seamanship.

They will have to serve for years as mere apprentices. They will have to fight their way to the top against every possible form of opposition. When they reach the bridge, mutiny of an envious crew may cause their death. But some day, a man will arise who will bring the vessel safely to port, and he shall be the hero of the ages.

AS IT EVER SHALL BE

"The more I think of the problems of our lives, the more I am
"persuaded that we ought to choose Irony and Pity for our
"assessors and judges as the ancient Egyptians called upon
"the Goddess Isis and the Goddess Nephtys on behalf of their
"dead.

"Irony and Pity are both of good counsel; the first with her
"smiles makes life agreeable; the other sanctifies it with her
"tears.

"The Irony which I invoke is no cruel Deity. She mocks
"neither love nor beauty. She is gentle and kindly disposed.
"Her mirth disarms and it is she who teaches us to laugh at
"rogues and fools, whom but for her we might be so weak as
"to despise and hate."

AFTER SEVEN YEARS

The treaty of Versailles was writ with the point of a bayonet. And however useful the invention of Colonel Fuysegur may have been in a close scrimmage, as an instrument of peace it has never been considered a success.

To make matters worse, the people who handled this deadly weapon were all of them old men. It is one thing when a band of young fellows get into a scrap. They will fight each other with a deadly hatred. But once they have got rid of their pent-up anger, they can return to the affairs of the day without any great personal resentment toward those who only a short while before were their enemies. But it is something very different when half a dozen smooth-shaven graybeards, filled with the futile rage of a lifetime of frustrated ambitions, sit down around a green table and make ready to judge half a dozen defenseless opponents who in the heyday of their victory disregarded every principle of law and international decency.

On such an occasion may Heaven have mercy upon us!

Alas! the Good Lord, whose name had been so terribly abused during the previous four years, was in no mood to extend his merciful hand to his undeserving children.

The carnage was of their own making. Now let them settle their difficulties as best they could!

What that "best" was, we have since then had occasion to learn. And the story of the last seven years is an almost uninterrupted recital of ignominious blunders, of greed, of cruelty and short-sighted meanness—an epoch of such hair-raising imbecility that it stands unique among the dreary annals of human

A WORLD IN FLAMES

stupidity, which (if I may be permitted this aside) is saying a great deal.

It is of course quite impossible to predict what the people of the year 2500 will have to say about the underlying causes of the great upheaval that destroyed the civilization of Europe and bestowed upon the unsuspecting American people the leadership of the human race. But in the light of what had gone before, ever since nations had become highly organized business organizations, they will probably come to the conclusion that an outbreak of some sort between the two great contending commercial factions was absolutely unavoidable, and was bound to occur sooner or later. In plain English, they will recognize that Germany had become too much of a menace to the prosperity of the British Empire to be allowed any further development as the general purveyor of the world's manifold wants and needs.

We who lived through the struggle find it much more difficult to estimate the events of the last decade at their true light, but now after seven years it is possible to draw a few fairly definite conclusions without causing too much commotion among our peaceful neighbors and friends.

The history of the last five hundred years is really the record of a gigantic struggle between the so-called "leading powers" and those who hoped to deprive them of their fortunate position and become their successors as the recognized masters of the seas. Spain came to glory across the dead bodies of the great Italian commercial republics and of Portugal. As soon as Spain had established that far-famed empire upon which the sun (for reasons of geography or honesty) was never known to set, Holland tried to rob her of her riches and in view of the difference in size of the two countries, the Dutch Republic achieved a very remarkable success. But no sooner had Holland acquired those parts of the world which then seemed to offer the biggest chance of immediate profit than France and England appeared upon the scene to despoil the Dutch people of their newly acquired possessions. When this had been accomplished, France and England fought for the spoils and after a long and costly struggle, England came out on top. Thereafter England dominated the world for more than a century. She brooked no rivalry. Small nations that came in her path were run under foot. Large ones which could not be tackled single handedly suddenly found themselves confronted by one of those mysterious political alliances of which the rulers of England (past masters in the craft of foreign politics) seemed to possess the secret.

In view of these well-known economic developments (faithfully described in every primary textbook of history) the policies which the rulers of Germany followed during the first two decades of the twentieth century seem little short of naïve.

SEA POWER

Some people claim that the former Kaiser was to blame and their argument deserves our close attention. William II was an honest man, of very restricted ability and a victim of that strange form of self-delusion which is so common among those who are by birth lifted into the seats of the mighty and who contemplate the rest of the world from such a high pinnacle of anointed superiority that they soon lose all touch with the ordinary run of humanity. This much is certain; that no man ever tried so hard to gain the good will of the British people and that no foreigner ever failed quite so ignominiously to understand the true nature of the English character.

That curious island on the other side of the North Sea lives by and of and for just one thing—trade. Those who do not interfere with British commerce are, if not exactly "friends," at least "tolerated strangers." Those on the other hand who, however remotely, might become a menace to the imperial hegemony are "enemies" and they must be destroyed at the first possible opportunity. And all the lovely speeches and all the obvious manifestations of good-will and friendship on the part of the anglophile Teuton emperor never even for a single moment made the average Englishman forget that the Germans were his most dangerous competitors and would sooner or later try to dump their own cheaper wares upon every part of the civilized and uncivilized world.

But that was only one side of the question. A most important one but not sufficient to account for the wholesale slaughter that was so characteristic of the late war.

In the happy days before the railroad and the telegraph, when each country was more or less of a definite entity which proceeded upon its own career with the plodding determina tion of an elephant pushing a circus truck, the quarrel between the two contending candidates for commercial supremacy would have proceeded slowly and the wily diplomats of the old school would probably have succeeded in localizing the quarrel. Unfortunately in the year 1914 the whole world was one large international workshop. A strike in the Argentine was apt to cause suffering in Berlin. A raise in the price of certain raw materials in London might spell disaster to tens of thousands of long-suffering Chinese coolies who never even had heard of the existence of the big city on the Thames. The invention of some obscure Privat-Dozent in a third-rate German university would often force dozens of Chilean banks to close their doors, while bad management on the part of an old commercial house in Gothenburg might deprive hundreds of little boys and girls in Australia of a chance to go to college.

Of course, not all nations had reached the same stage of industrial development. A few of them were still wholly agricultural and others were only just emerging from a state of

almost medieval feudalism. This, however, did not make them
undesirable allies in the eyes of their industrialized neighbors.
On the contrary. Such states, as a rule, are possessed of almost
unlimited reservoirs of man-power and as sheer cannon fodder
the Russian peasant had never had a rival.

How and in what way all these different and conflicting
interests were marshaled into one gigantic group of associated

MAN POWER

nations and why for more than four years they consented to
fight for a common purpose—these are questions the solution
of which we had better leave to our grandchildren. The world
will have to know a great deal more about the preliminaries of
the war than it does to-day before it can pass judgment upon
those misguided patriots who turned the continent of Europe
into one vast shambles.

All we can hope to do this hot day of August in the year of
Grace 1926 is to draw attention to one salient fact which is
almost invariably overlooked by those who call themselves historians, to wit: that the great European conflict which began
as a world-wide war ended as a world-wide revolution and that

it did not mean a short interruption of the normal development of affairs (as all the wars of the last three hundred years had done) but marked the beginning of an entirely new social and economic epoch. The old men who were responsible for the peace treaty of Versailles were too much a product of their own original surroundings to be able to recognize this.

They thought and talked and acted in terms of a bygone age.

That probably is the reason why their labors proved such a curse to the rest of humanity. But still one other element which contributed greatly to the disastrous outcome of the war for democracy and the rights of small nations was the belated participation in the struggle on the part of the United States of America.

As a nation the American people, feeling themselves safely entrenched behind three thousand miles of ocean, had never taken any deep interest in foreign politics. Accustomed to think in terms of slogans and captions and headlines and cheerfully ignorant of the historical development of Europe (or for that matter of any other part of the world) during the last two thousand years, the majority of President Wilson's fellow-citizens were obliged to get their historical information second-hand. Aided and abetted by certain colossal crimes on the part of the German military and naval leaders, it was an easy task for the manufacturers of allied propaganda to make their American friends see the war as a definite struggle between right and wrong, a clash between white and black, a duel to the death between the angels of Anglo-Saxon self-determination and the devils of Teutonic autocracy, until the American people, kind-hearted and sentimental (and therefore apt to run to certain curious extremes of emotionalism and cruelty) felt that they could not possibly keep out of the struggle without becoming unfaithful to all that was good and decent in their own manhood. A hot wave of a crusadelike zeal and eagerness swept across the country. Slowly but steadily the gigantic mills of American industry began to grind and ere long two million men were hastening to the battlefields of Europe to put a stop to the intolerable depravities of the Hun.

PROPAGANDA

Now it was only natural that these millions of serious-minded and earnest young men should try and revaluate their fighting ideals into terms that should be comprehensible to all of their fellow countrymen. Hence the slogan of "a war to end war." Hence the famous fourteen points of President Wilson—the new decalogue of international righteousness. Hence the enthusiasm for the self-determination of small nations, the hilariously expressed desire to "make the world safe for democracy."

To the Balfours and the Poincarés and the Churchills (not to mention the exiled leaders of the old Russian régime) such words must have sounded like rank heresy. If any of their own people had undertaken to parade such battle-cries they would have been sent before a firing-squad at very short notice. But the commander-in-chief of two million men, the trusted gatekeeper of all the treasures of the world, must be listened to with an outward semblance of respect. Hence the leaders of the different European nations, during the last year and a half of the war, fought for certain ideals for which they had no more use than for those fantastic economic innovations which were now being shouted in a hundred different tongues from the battlements of the old Kremlin. And as soon as the Germans, agreeably surprised by the reasonable terms of their much feared American antagonists, had thrown their emperor overboard, had changed the name of their country from an "Empire" to that of a "Republic," and adorned with red cockades and singing the popular song of international brotherhood had started upon their famous backward march to the Rhine, the allied chieftains hastened to rid themselves of those foolish and embarrassing American ideals and made ready to conclude a peace upon that well-known principle of "woe to the loser" which ever since the days of the caveman had been accepted as the logical conclusion to a well-regulated physical encounter.

Their task would have been a great deal less complicated if President Wilson had not hit upon the unfortunate plan of taking a direct and personal part in the diplomatic negotiations of the year 1919. Had he remained at home, the European powers would have concluded peace according to their own terms of right and wrong. From an American point of view they would have been wrong, but right or wrong, their decisions would have been an honest expression of a definite school of thought. How, however, American and European ideals (which never have mixed) got so horribly interwoven that nothing was definitely settled, that every one of the allies was left with a grievance, and that the peace proved infinitely more costly than the war.

But there was still another element which contributed greatly to the chaos caused by the Treaty of Versailles. President Wilson, himself the head of a federation of semi-independent nations, had visions of a federated world-state. The thing had proved possible on the American continent. For more than a century it had given an ever-increasing number of sovereign states a degree of political liberty and economic well-being which had made the nation as a whole the most prosperous and the richest country on the entire planet. Why should not the people of Europe learn the lesson which Virginia and Pennsylvania and Massachusetts had taken to heart in the year 1776?

Why not, indeed?

And so the allied leaders bowed low and listened respectfully when Mr. Wilson explained his scheme for a League of Nations. Under the press of circumstances they even agreed to incorporate the principles of a United States of the World into their treaty of peace. But just as soon as the Presidential ship had hoisted anchor and had set course for the western hemisphere, they began to undo the work that had been closest to the heart of the great president and returned to the old diplomatic ideals of secret treaties and surreptitious alliances.

Meanwhile a very definite revulsion of feeling had taken place in America itself. It is, of course, very easy to blame certain personal characteristics of Mr. Wilson for this changed attitude towards the League of Nations on the part of so many of his contemporaries. But other forces, infinitely more subtle, were at work.

In the first place, the soldiers who had taken part in the fight were returning to their homes. Their first-hand acquaintance with European conditions had not made them over-anxious to continue the close intimacy of the last two years.

In the second place, the peo- ple at large were beginning to recover from the mad fury of the war. They were no longer in fear for the lives of their be- loved sons and daughters and once more were able to think soberly. The traditional dis- trust of Europe began to re- assert itself. Soon it became clear that George Washing- ton's ominous warning against "entangling alliances" had as much of a hold upon the mass

AMERICA GOES ABROAD

of the people of the year 1918 as it had had a century before.

In the third place, after two years of parades and four- minute speeches and liberty loans, it was very pleasant to go back to the quiet routine of a profitable business career.

In short, the infant League of Nations which President Wilson had dumped so unceremoniously upon the threshold of Europe was now repudiated by its own spiritual parents. The child did not die. But it lived a precarious existence and grew up to be a weak and emaciated creature, too feeble to make its influence felt in any decisive way and merely irritating those who were its friends by an occasional futile scolding and the waving of a naughty, naughty finger.

Once more we are confronted by an ominous historical "if."
"If the League of Nations had really turned the whole of the civilized world into a successful United States of the World. . . ."
I don't know, but even under the most favorable circum-

stances, the plan of President Wilson had only a slender chance of success.

For the war, as we are now beginning to understand, was not so much a war as a revolution and it was a revolution in which the victory was carried away by an unsuspected third party, who since then has been identified as the grandson of one, James Watt, and who is coming to be known in wider and wider circles as "the Iron Man."

THE IRON MAN

Originally the steam engine (like his younger brother, the electric engine) had been a welcome addition to the family of civilized human beings because he was a willing slave and ever ready to lighten the tasks of man and beast.

But soon it became clear that this inanimate factotum was full of cunning and devilment and the war with its temporary suspension of all the decencies of life gave the iron contraption a chance to enslave those who in reality were meant to be his masters.

Here and there some wise men of science may have foreseen the danger that threatened the race from the side of this unruly servant but as soon as such an unfortunate prophet opened his mouth and issued a word of warning, he was denounced as an enemy of society, as a rank Bolshevik and a seditious radical and he was bade to hold his tongue or take the consequences. For the politicians and the diplomats who had been responsible for the war were now engaged upon the serious task of fabricating a suitable peace and they must not be interrupted in these holy endeavors. Unfortunately, as a class such worthies are almost always completely ignorant of those elementary principles of natural science and political economy which happen to dominate our present industrialized and mechanical form of society and they are less fit to handle complicated modern problems than any other group of men of whom I can think at the present moment. The plenipotentiaries of Paris were no exception. They met in the shadow of the Iron Man, they talked of a world that was dominated by the Iron Man, yet never became aware of his presence and until the very end talked in words and symbols that represented the mentality of the eighteenth century but not that of the twentieth.

The result was inevitable. It is impossible to think in terms of the year 1719 and prosper in terms of the year 1919. But that, it is becoming increasingly evident, is exactly what the old men of Versailles did.

Now behold the world as it has been left in the wake of this orgy of hatred and unreason—a crazy quilt of phantastic new nationalities that may possess some value as historical curiosities but that will never be able to hold their own in a world dominated by coal and oil and water-power and wholesale credits—a continent divided by artificial frontiers which look pretty enough upon a children's atlas but bear no relation whatsoever to the urgent necessities of modern civilization—a vast armed camp of people in yellow and green and purple uniforms masquerading as feeble imitations of their mythical ancestors but of less practical use to our contemporary society than any little cash-girl that works in the basement of a ten-cent store.

This may sound like a brutal condemnation of a state of affairs that still fills the souls of millions of honest European patriots with gratitude and pride.

I am sorry but not until the statesmen of Europe shall be willing to leave the solution of modern problems to people with modern minds can there be any lasting improvement. Meanwhile in their agony and distress the people will turn to the cure-alls offered by Bolshevism and Fascism.

Incidentally this outburst of rhetoric will explain the most dangerous and regrettable of all recent political developments —the rapidly increasing dislike between the people of Europe and those of America. Since I am trying to write for the children of all races and not merely for those who live on the fortunate patch of land that stretches from the Atlantic to the Pacific, this apparent waving of the stars and stripes may be considered as an exhibition of very doubtful taste. But this is a time for plain speech and even at the risk of being mistaken for a hundred per cent patriot (the very last honor to which I aspire) I shall try to make my point clear.

I do not for a moment claim that man for man and woman for woman the Americans as a nation are superior to any of their cousins of the old world. But fortunately for themselves they have little consciousness of the past and therefore they are more able to approach the problems of the present with an open eye towards the future than the members of almost any other race. As a result they have accepted the modern world without any reservations and having accepted it with all its good and all its evil, they are rapidly reaching a "modus vivendi" whereby animate man and his inanimate servant shall be able to exist on terms of peace and mutual respect. It sounds absurd yet it is true that the country which has achieved the greatest mechanical perfection is also the first to bring the Iron Man to terms. In order to do this the American people have been forced to throw overboard a great deal of ancestral ballast. They have sacrificed hundreds of ideas and prejudices and ideals that served a highly useful purpose two hundred or two thousand years ago but which to-day are of no more value than a stagecoach or a miracle-working image. As far as I can see there will be no hope for Europe until the mass of Germans and Englishmen and Spaniards and Heaven-only-knows-what-they-are-called do likewise.

In a chapter like this it would be so easy to deliver noble harangues upon the accomplishments of Locarno; the unfeasibility of a Marxian program of applied economics; to discuss the follies of those small-town French politicians who have not yet learned that the days of Louis XIV and Napoleon have long since been relegated to the era of the Stone Age. But it would be a waste of energy and printer's ink.

The misery that has come over the world during the last ten years (hastened along by the Great War but by no means caused by that sanguinary conflict) is in reality due to a profound change in the economic and social structure of the entire world. But Europe, steeped in the lore of the past, has thus far been unwilling or unable to realize this fact.

The peace of Versailles, the last great gesture of the old régime, was meant as a final stronghold against the inevitable approach of the modern era. In less than eight years it has become an obsolete ruin. It would have been considered a sublime piece of statecraft in the year of Grace 1700. To-day not one out of ten thousand people has ever bothered to read it. For the twentieth century is dominated by certain economic and industrial principles which recognize no political boundaries and tend with absolute inevitableness to turn the entire world into a single large and prosperous workshop regardless of language, race or previous condition of ancestral glory.

What eventually will come out of this workshop, what form of civilization will be developed by an intelligent and willing co-operation between man and his machines—that I do not know and it really does not matter so very much. Life means change and this is not the first time that the human race has been faced by a similar emergency.

Our remote and our less-distant ancestors have lived through such crises.

No doubt our children and grandchildren will do the same.

But for us, who are alive to-day, the one and only serious problem is a world-wide reorganization along economic rather than worn-out political lines.

Seven years ago, our ears deafened by the noise of the big guns, our eyes blinded by the flash of the searchlights, we were still too dazed to understand whither the great upheaval had carried us. At that moment any fairly honorable and sincere man who pretended that he could guide us back to the happy days of 1914 was welcomed as a leader and was assured of our willing loyalty.

To-day we know better.

We have begun to understand that the comfortable old world in which we dwelled so unsuspectingly until the outbreak of the war had in reality outlived its usefulness by several decades.

This does not mean that we are absolutely certain about the road that now lies before us. Most likely we will follow a dozen wrong tracks before we find the right direction. And in the meantime we are fast learning one very important lesson —that the future belongs to the living and that the dead ought to mind their own business.

THE UNITED STATES COMES
OF AGE

BEING THE FIRST OF SEVERAL CHAPTERS ON
CURRENT HISTORY WRITTEN BY THEIR
UNCLE WILLEM FOR PIET, JAN, DIRK AND
JANE VAN LOON AND THEIR CONTEM-
PORARIES

LIKE most busy men, your grandfather left a lot of work
unfinished. "The Story of Mankind" had been written for your
father and myself when we were small boys. He had always
planned to make it your book too by bringing it up to date.
But up to what date? That was the question.

If you were trying to describe something very big, something like, let us say, an ocean storm, you would sit on a high
hill from where you could see far in every direction. In this
way you would be able to view things "in their true perspec-
tive." If, on the other hand, you were out on the sea in a boat
you could only describe those waves that were bouncing you
about.

The same applies to writing about history. The past we
can view from the high hill of the present. We can see "the
whole picture." But as for current history—and by current I
mean the history of the past twenty or thirty years—there we
are still very much "at sea." While trying to steer a safe
course our "Ship of State" is being buffeted by wind and waves
from every side. We don't know how big a storm it is or when
it will be over. We can simply try to take our bearings and
hope for the best.

People used to speak of "lulls" in history, periods when "nothing happened." Today we know better. These lulls were, like the weather, purely local. Prior to the development of the telegraph, the telephone and the radio, such major historical events as wars, revolutions and changes of government could take place in one country without even its neighbors knowing much about them. This is no longer the case. Thanks to modern communications and our free press, every turn in events in Lhasa, Rome or Cape Town can be known the very next day by every citizen of Kansas City, New Orleans or Vancouver. I say *can* be. There are, of course, those who do not wish to be informed.

The last time the people of the United States deliberately tried to ignore the rumblings of history elsewhere on this planet was after World War I. (This was the lull in which the "Story of Mankind" was written as a word of warning.) Having helped our erstwhile Allies win the war against Germany we felt we had done all that could be expected of us. Still blithely unaware of the responsibility that history was to toss into our lap we turned our backs on the League of Nations and left Europe to stew in its own juices.

The "Roaring Twenties" were upon us. Under President Harding's slogan of "a return to normalcy" this country embarked on a wild scramble to exploit all forms of enterprise. Wastefulness, lawlessness and corruption were to be found in high places as well as low. Harding's sudden death, under ambiguous circumstances, gave rise to the rumor that, had he lived, he would have faced impeachment. Although the present generation chooses to look upon this "Jazz Age" with rose-colored glasses, the picture it painted of prosperity was on very rotten canvas.

If it seems odd that I should mention such a purely local development in what is essentially a history of the world, I do so with a purpose. Just as it takes a long time for a person or a nation to build up a reputation, so it also takes a long time for them to live one down. Although the 1920's saw us grow immensely rich and powerful our prestige as a nation of responsible citizens sank calamitously low.   While many were paying little or no attention to developments beyond our borders, the eyes and ears of the rest of the world were focused on us.

Novelists like Sinclair Lewis and Theodore Dreiser, whose works mirrored the American scene, were being widely translated and much discussed.   American plays found a new audience abroad and, even more important, there was that new great export commodity, the "movies."   No history of America's role in world affairs can overlook the Judas kiss given this country by our motion pictures.   By portraying and glorifying our riches and our free-and-easy ways these pictures built in the minds of the common people everywhere an exaggerated concept of America that was to come home to roost.   Just one example will show you what I mean.   In every foreign language today you will find at least one American word: "Gangster."

Nobody was interested when in 1922 the former editor of the Socialist paper "Avanti" marched on Rome carrying a banner bearing the "Fasces," an ax enclosed in a bundle of rods which was the symbol of authority in ancient Rome.   When this same Benito Mussolini became "Dictator" of Italy, Americans simply said, "Thank goodness, now the Italian trains will run on time."   This was true.   They did.   The thousands of tourists who now flocked to Rome, Florence, Venice and Naples often had to stop at the street corners while a phalanx of black-shirted youths went marching along singing "Giovinezza." But these sightseers never stopped to realize what those singing boys and their bull-necked little "Duce" were up to.   (See Chapter 24).

Nor did the world pay much attention to an unfortunate incident which took place on the Odeonsplatz in Munich in 1923.   There a strangely assorted group of men calling themselves the National Socialist German Workers Party tried to stage a "Putsch" to overthrow the Bavarian government.   They were fired on by the police.   Since one of these "Nazis," as they later came to be known, was old General Erich Friederich

Wilhelm Ludendorff, everyone felt most apologetic. The Nazi ringleader, an Austrian of uncertain profession, was sentenced to five years in Landsberg prison but served only nine months. He put this time to good use. Having both unlimited supplies of paper and a devoted cell-mate and secretary named Rudolf Hess, this irascible little man dictated a book. Not being a man of much education his German usage was embarrassingly bad. Ghost writers soon remedied this and "Mein Kampf" (My Battle) by Adolf Hitler was translated for all the world to read.

Few people troubled to see what was in this dull, bombastic work. It is a pity they didn't. If they had they might have paid more attention to the efforts of a Frenchman named Aristide Briand and a German named Gustav Stresemann. As representatives of their two countries they signed a very conciliatory pact. In 1926 they were jointly awarded the Nobel Peace Prize. That was that.

Then there was Russia. It was easy not to know much about Russia. The Russians wanted it that way. They always had. Their distrust of the West, from which they had borrowed everything including the art of ballet dancing, existed even under the Tsars. This, like many other things, the Soviet Government saw no reason to change. On the contrary, if it was important that outsiders not know how well, or how poorly, each successive Soviet Five Year Plan was faring, it was even more important that the citizens of the Soviet Union learn as little as possible about the outside world.

Nevertheless, observant readers could note the gradual disappearance of the name Trotsky in all Soviet news reports and its replacement by the name Joseph Stalin. That this also meant a shift in the policy and aims of this potentially powerful nation was clear to those interested in the foreign news section of their daily papers. The others hopped from the murders on page 1 to the stock market reports and there settled down to do some serious reading. But on October 29, 1929 the stock market hit the front page.

The big Wall Street pot that had been bubbling so merrily

finally boiled over and put out the flame. The roar of the Twenties became a panic-stricken shriek. Harding's successor, "Cautious Cal" Coolidge, a president who prided himself on his ability to say nothing and do less, stepped down and made way for Herbert Hoover. In his attempts to rekindle the financial flame even this great economist was as helpless as a city-ite on a picnic trying to light wet wood without matches. He applied every known formula but unemployment and hysteria only increased.

The stock market crash did not bring an era to an end. This era, the era of exploitation, had died quite some time before and the crash simply revealed to what extent rot had set in. In America, the nineteenth century had lasted till 1929.

Unfortunately, few of the men who had waxed prosperous and influential in this period ever found time to read their history books. If they had they would have learned that those who wish to enjoy greater privilege must also assume greater responsibility. Otherwise the national apple-cart overturns. Such an incident is usually followed by a revolution. We had our "revolution" and it was known as "The Depression."

During the next few years we were far too preoccupied with our own troubles to notice what explosions our financial crack-up had set off elsewhere. But certain events were taking place which were to shift global responsibilities onto our youthful shoulders. Whether it liked it or not, the United States had come of age.

THE "AXIS" PARTNERS

THE "CRASH THAT WAS FELT AROUND THE WORLD" HASTENS THE COLLAPSE OF A PEACE THAT WAS BUILT ON MEDIEVAL FOUNDATIONS

ONE day, many years ago, someone wanted to borrow a great deal of money. In return he offered the money-lender or "banker" some "shares of stock" in his business. The banker, being a bit of a gambler, decided to auction off these stocks to the highest bidder. Thus he became a "stock-broker." Such stock markets, of which the Bourse in Paris is one of the oldest, at first did business on a small local scale. Then a broker got the idea of employing couriers to carry "quotations" from one town to another. Finally, with the coming of the telegraph, stock market transactions became international. Today every important bid made on Wall Street sets ticker tape machines going in London, Cape Town and Buenos Aires.

During this final boom of the 1920's, stock prices on Wall Street went up and up. A gambling fever gripped the nation. By 1929 many important companies had over-expanded. Suddenly they went bankrupt. Their stocks became worthless. Some banks which had speculated in these stocks went bankrupt too. Many people whose money was invested in these banks became destitute.

Now place dominoes on end, one in front, two behind the two, four behind the three, etc. Push the front one over and as it falls it knocks the next two over. Soon they will have all gone down. This will explain what happened all over the world in 1929. One bank failed, then two, then three. Everywhere, in America, in Europe, in Asia, banks began to close their doors. The smaller ones went first, then the bigger ones. Because business had become international the disaster was universal. In 1931 the powerful Austrian Credit-Anstalt collapsed. But worse was yet to come.

For centuries the English pound sterling had been accepted as the standard and all other currencies were valued accordingly. But on September 21, 1931, the Bank of England, that symbol of British prosperity and reliability, slipped off the gold standard. You will have to read a book on banking to know exactly what that means. Till then you must take my word for it that this was a severe jolt to the stability of national economy everywhere. It was also the first real crack in the structure of the British Empire.

There were other signs which pointed to a general dissolution of "the Empire on which the sun never sets." In India a soft-spoken Hindu named Mohandas Karamchand Gandhi, and called the "Mahatma" or "Great Souled" by his followers, was repeatedly imprisoned by British authorities. He kept urging his countrymen to achieve home rule through "passive resistance."

And then there was Palestine. The British had taken it away from the Turks after World War I. By the Balfour Declaration of 1917 they designated it as a Jewish homeland. The sudden increase in Jewish migration was met by severe opposition on the part of the local Arabs. Unfortunately it was also important to England to be on good terms with the Arabs. It was they who controlled the land close to the Suez Canal, and the great oil fields of the Near East which were then beginning to be exploited. With a change of heart the British took steps to stem the flow of Zionists to their Biblical homeland. How completely they failed in this is proven by the existence of the State of Israel today.

If you will now spin the globe around half way (something everyone should do once in a while), you will observe a relatively small string of islands off the China coast. That is the Empire of Japan. Said to have been founded by Emperor Jimmu Tenno in the year 660 B.C., little of Japan's early history is definitely known. Accidentally discovered by the Portuguese in 1542, Japan was openly hostile to Western traders and the missionaries they brought with them. In 1663 she closed her ports to all except the Dutch. Then in 1853 Commodore Matthew Perry, bearing a letter from President Fillmore, sailed into Tokyo Bay. Six years later Japan signed a commercial treaty first with the United States and then with other nations. Seemingly overnight this feudal empire became a modern industrial and military power.

In 1895 Japan took Formosa from China; in 1905 she won a brief war with Russia for port and rail rights in Manchuria; in 1910 she annexed Korea. Japan was now ready to embark on one of the greatest schemes of Asiatic imperialism since the days of Genghis Khan. She had everything that was needed for such an exploit—wealth, industry, vast man power reserves due to over-population and a religion in which the Emperor was God and to die for him was an honor. Cannily she bided her time.

With American prestige at a low ebb and most of Europe in a state of financial and political turmoil, Japan chose 1931 as the year in which to send her troops across the Korean border into Manchuria. It was a quick victory. The League of Nations sent out a commission to investigate the "Manchukuo Incident" and the United States refused to recognize the Japanese puppet state under Emperor Henry Pu-Yi. Feigning hurt feelings, Japan indignantly withdrew from the League but continued to do business with the U.S.A. The "incident" was closed.

One man was watching Japan's defiance of the League of Nations with interest. He was the author of "Mein Kampf" and runner-up in the recent German presidential elections. His name was Adolf Hitler.

The Weimar Republic, although culturally one of the most brilliant periods in history, was a political failure. Unused to the privilege of forming their own political parties, the German people found themselves split up into as many as 125 different, and very weak, factions. Under these circumstances it was almost impossible to elect a president. The German Republic had only two: Friederich Ebert, by profession a saddle-maker, and Paul Ludwig Hans Anton von Benackendorf und von Hindenburg, a twice retired general.

Seventy-eight when he took office in 1925, the venerable hero of both the Franco-Prussian War and World War I looked excellent on postage stamps but was no longer the man for the job. Although reelected in 1932, defeating Adolf Hitler at the polls, the aged field marshal was no match for the upstart ex-corporal and his Nazi Party. With bankruptcy jitters shaking the young German Republic to its foundations, Hitler made the most of the situation. His only serious rivals were the German Communists. Their tactics and his were far too similar for comfort. In 1933 the Nazis secretly set fire to the Berlin Reichstag building and "framed" an ex-Communist, Marinus van der Lubbe, as arsonist. This time the "Putsch" succeeded. With his own son a Nazi, Hindenburg yielded to pressure and named Adolf Hitler Chancellor.

On Hindenburg's death in 1934, Hitler became both Chancellor and President of Germany. Following the example of Italy's Mussolini, who had dubbed himself "Il Duce" (The Commander), Hitler became the "Führer" or Leader of the German people.

How can one explain Hitler's astonishing rise to power? He, or in any event his advisers, possessed an uncanny knowledge of "popular psychology." To the German military clique, smarting under the provisions of the Versailles Treaty, Hitler promised rehabilitation. To the man-in-the-street he promised the return of German power and prestige. From Nordic mythology and the writings of Friederich Nietzsche he concocted the theory of a so-called "Herrenrasse" or Germanic Master Race. But if they were so strong, why then had the Germans taken such a licking in the World War? They had been betrayed! By whom? Hitler needed a scape-goat.

Taking an example from the Slavic countries, where discontent of any sort was apt to end in a pogrom, he pointed to
the Jews. Although they formed less than one per cent of the
total population, Hitler maintained that the Jewish minority
had caused the downfall of peace-loving, hard-working,
"Aryan" Germany.

Did people actually believe this nonsense? Unfortunately,
yes. Nor were all of Hitler's supporters within Germany itself.
Like Mussolini before him, Hitler was widely hailed as the
man-of-the-people who had established order out of chaos. Still
ignorant of the unthinkable excesses to which Hitler's "Master
Race" theories would lead, everyone seemed quite willing to let
him make the Third Reich into an arsenal. He was fulfilling
his promise to provide the world with a convenient bulwark
against Communism.

Once in the saddle Hitler wasted no time. He rode rough-
shod over any individual or group which stood in his way. The
old military clique, now seeking its reward for supporting him,
found itself by-passed in the remobilization program. Needing
the cooperation of German industry Hitler wooed the tradi-
tionally conservative industrialists by "purging" the more radically socialistic of his followers. With Machiavellian thorough-
ness he used a trumped-up plot against his life as the excuse to
murder General von Schleicher, Ernst Röhm and other former
friends. The Enabling Act, passed in 1934, took from the German people those democratic freedoms they had enjoyed under
the Weimar Republic but apparently had never appreciated.
Instead they were permitted to take part in an all-out campaign
against Jews, Catholics, intellectuals and Communists.

Future generations may wonder at Hitler's campaign
against the Communists. "Weren't Nazism and Communism
both related ideologies?" they will ask. "Wasn't Germany the
land of the National *Socialists* and Russia the Union of Soviet
Socialist Republics?"

Similar ideologies do not prevent conflicts any more than
divergent ones bring them about. The real issues in history lie
deeper. Germany under Hitler was still Germany and Russia

under Stalin was still Russia. The age-old power struggle between them had never ceased. On the contrary. In Hitler's opinion it had now been given a logical and "scientific" basis. That basis he found in geopolitics.

Proclaiming to have established a definite interrelation between politics and geography, geopoliticians divide the Eurasian land mass into "heart-land" and "rim-land." According to their teachings, whoever dominates the heart-land and gains access to the sea, will dominate the world. This heart-land is in Russia. With Germany's leading geopolitician, Karl Haushofer, as his political advisor, Hitler pointed to the danger of a world dominated by Russia through Communism. But in point of truth he coveted the Russian heart-land himself and set his sights accordingly.

It is therefore understandable that Soviet Russia took a dim view of the events in 1933. Already nervous about the Japanese activity, the Soviets had concluded non-aggression pacts with Poland, the Baltic States and France. Now, with the Nazi landslide in Germany, the Soviets began looking around for new friends. When Hitler, in his first test of strength, undid the work of Stresemann by withdrawing from the League of Nations, the Soviet Union became a member.

Although Mussolini undoubtedly joined his countrymen in their traditional contempt for the barbarians to the north, he reached a paternal hand to Hitler and bade him welcome. There followed any number of short diplomatic courtesy calls by both their foreign ministers until finally in 1934, amid an atmosphere of well-rehearsed enthusiasm, Hitler traveled to Rome. Despite the parades and banquets the visit resulted in friction, for someone kept bringing up the thorny question of Austria.

The crash of 1929 had not left Italy unscathed. Fear of bankruptcy caused Mussolini to impose increasingly rigid controls. The enthusiastic cheers with which Il Duce's first proclamations had been received took on a hollow ring. Mussolini diagnosed the symptoms of dissatisfaction correctly. The time had come to create a new cause, a diversion.

He too had been watching the League of Nations falter and took note. Italy, Il Duce pondered, was only a Kingdom. Rome had been an Empire. What was the most defenseless country he could find some reason to attack? His acquisitive eye fell on Abyssinia.

By always minding its own business, "the mysterious kingdom of Prester John" (see page 231) had managed to survive almost sixteen centuries of human progress. Its rugged terrain and its even more rugged fighters were legendary. They served as a deterrent to would-be empire builders. Not only did these dark-skinned Christians throw a lethal spear but they also had a habit of mutilating their prisoners of war. Italy, as you read on page 452, had once before attempted to annex Abyssinia, or Ethiopia as it is now called. She had suffered a humiliating defeat at Adua in 1887, a defeat she may have forgiven but never forgot. Both countries signed a solemn treaty of friendship in 1928.

In December 1934, Italian and Ethiopian troops clashed at Ualual, on the disputed frontier of Italian Somaliland. Mussolini, pretending outrage, demanded reparations and refused to arbitrate. The Ethiopian Negus, Haile Selassie, laid his case before the League of Nations. Just as Mussolini expected, the League listened attentively and did nothing. Then Mussolini let it be known that he would arbitrate after all. The ruse worked.

As soon as he was ready, Mussolini invaded Ethiopia. With naked feet and armed with spears Haile Selassie's troops displayed the courage for which they were famous. They were no match for Italy's tanks, machine guns and bombing planes. Italy's fliers, among them the Duce's own son, gloatingly reported what "good sport" it was to achieve a direct hit on unarmed Ethiopians and watch the burst "open up like a flower."

The League of Nations, in a final effort, branded Italy an "aggressor" and voted to apply sanctions. But England was loath to close the Suez Canal to Italy, lest this "precipitate a war." On May 9, 1936, Mussolini was able to proclaim the

King of Italy Emperor of Ethiopia and the League of Nations was as good as dead.

The next move was Hitler's. Having already violated the Versailles Treaty by reinstituting military conscription, he now scrapped the Stresemann-Briand Locarno Pact and sent German troops into the Rhineland. The stage was set for the Führer and the Duce to act in unison. The scene was Spain.

In 1936 death came to Antonia Mercé, a Spanish dancer known as "La Argentina." Through her superb artistry and dignity of bearing this Argentine-born woman seemed, to all who saw her, a living symbol of the glory that was Spain. Spain's only other public symbol, her king, had in the meantime been doing his best to create just the opposite impression. Like many another Bourbon before him, Alfonso XIII was not very bright.

Preferring dalliance abroad to duties at home, Alfonso had left the running of his government to the Marqués de Estella, also called Primo de Rivera. In 1925 this nobleman assumed the powers of a dictator and, by jamming the lid down hard, managed to preserve a semblance of order. But he antagonized his fellow aristocrats and in 1930 they persuaded the king to get rid of him. In 1931 the Spanish people also got rid of their king. Spain became a "Worker's Republic." But the Spaniards, like the Germans, had neither the education nor the patience necessary for self-government. They soon were split up into many impotent factions and the social unrest which followed everywhere in the wake of our depression swept over Spain.

In July 1936, the news spotlight jumped from Abyssinia to Melilla in Spanish Morocco. Here a group of generals, among them the former governor of the Canary Islands, Francisco Franco, fomented a revolt against the recently formed *Frente Popular*. This leftist coalition had achieved a peaceful victory in the Cortes, or Parliament, over the Monarchists, Republicans and Clerics.

The struggle which followed lasted almost three years. When it ended Spain's treasury was bankrupt, her citizens exhausted and her cities shattered by Europe's first taste of bomb warfare. Emerging victorious, General Franco became Dictator or "El Caudillo." The resemblance to Hitler and Mussolini was no accident. What had began as a Civil War between "Nationalists" and "Loyalists" had become, through armed intervention, the first test of strength between Berlin and Rome on one side and Moscow on the other. And Berlin and Rome had won.

Again I must ask you to forget "ideologies" and study geography. Then it will become more apparent to you what a "Loyalist" (meaning Communist) victory in Spain would have meant. A sudden projection of Soviet influence into this key spot of Western Europe would have, come at a time when France was corrupt and weak, and England, following the abdication of Edward VIII, decidedly shaken. Therefore both countries welcomed Franco's victory as the lesser of two evils. The 1937 Neutrality Act, which was aimed at keeping the Western Hemisphere out of European conflicts, still permitted the United States to sell arms to Portugal. These arms then conveniently found their way into Franco's hands.

Lack of modern equipment and military discipline hamstrung the Loyalists from the start. Aided by Soviet strategists and an international group of volunteers (the "Lincoln Brigade" was composed of Americans), these unfortunate pawns on the chess board of European power politics quickly lost ground but put up a spirited defense of Madrid and Valencia against Nazi bombing and "Fifth Column" strategy.

While some newspapers were trying to warn the world that the tactical lessons learned by the intervening powers in the "Spanish manoeuvres" might soon be applied elsewhere, others were reporting on the activity, or lack thereof, of a Non-intervention Committee composed of twenty-one nations, among them Germany, Italy and the Soviet Union.

It was against this background that the Axis came into being.

If anyone believed that Hitler's racial theories were more than a trumped-up expedient, the events of November 26, 1936 must have given him a serious shock. For on this date Nazi Germany welcomed the Japanese people (to whom Kaiser Wilhelm had once referred as "the Yellow Peril") as "honorary Aryans" and allies. Known as the Anti-Comintern or Anti-Communist Pact this scrap of paper created the Berlin-Tokyo arm of the Axis. The following year Japan embarked on an undeclared but all-out war against the Chinese.

In 1937 Mussolini also signed this document. The handwriting of history was on the wall for anyone who cared to read.

ISOLATIONISM AND APPEASEMENT

HOW THE AXIS PARTNERS BEGAN TO DIVIDE THE WORLD AMONG THEMSELVES AND WHY THEY GOT AS FAR AS THEY DID

WORLD WAR I had not actually been a global struggle. It was called a "World War" at the time mainly because improved communications had brought the struggle in Europe and the Near East to the attention of everyone capable of reading a newspaper. It was also the first conflict in which an American Expeditionary Force had gone into battle on European soil.

The fighting had been going on for almost three years when the United States came to the aid of the Allies, England, France and Belgium; and American troops moved into the trenches under the slogan "To make the world safe for Democracy." (See page 475.)

Hardly had the last shot been fired when the emptiness of this became apparent. The European Allies, republics and kingdoms alike, were little concerned with ideological aims. Maintaining the European "balance of power" was the sole issue which interested them. They thanked the United States for its aid and promised in return to go on doing business with us.

In the interest of honest historical reporting that is all we should have expected, for that is all we actually went into the war to achieve. But some Americans seemed loath to take such a realistic or, as they called it, "cynical" attitude. Hence they were disillusioned. They felt themselves betrayed and duped. Loudly they inveighed against any further "foreign entanglements." Thus "isolationism" in America became a political issue.

Undoubtedly patriotic in their motives, these isolationists were soon to find themselves duped and betrayed in earnest. From the time he came to power in 1933, Hitler made use of America's isolationist sentiment to assure himself a free hand in Europe. His Propaganda Ministry, under Joseph Göbbels, used every medium at its disposal to dissuade the United States, burdened with its own internal affairs, from "meddling" in those of Germany. Several Congressmen and members of such organizations as "The German-American Bund," "The America First Organization" and the Ku Klux Klan willingly joined in echoing this sentiment. (In homage to Hitler the Klan added anti-Semitism to its roster of "desirable American attributes.")

The United States did have troubles, that is true. Replacing Hoover as president in 1932, Franklin D. Roosevelt fell heir to the task of legislating the country out of economic chaos. By declaring a "bank holiday" and by passage of the Glass-Steagall Banking Act, the National Industrial Recovery Act (declared unconstitutional in 1935) and other unprecedented measures, Roosevelt finally managed to bring the depression to an end.

These new laws were bitter medicine to a people unused to any sort of government control in private enterprise. But the world was then, and still is, in the grip of that Social Revolution which began when man made himself master of the machine. (See page 413.) Like trees in a hurricane, old, rigid governments were toppled by it while others bowed before the storm but did not break. What had brought Communism to Russia, Fascism to Central Europe and unrest to Asia, Africa and South America brought only social legislation to the United States. For that we must be very grateful. The restrictions this country now felt were simply those everyone feels the day he finds out he is "growing up." And as we have said before, the United States had come of age.

One of the surest signs of our growing maturity was the fact that, for the first time in its history, the United States began to take an interest in that vast continent in the Southern Hemisphere to which ours is linked by name, history and geography. Despite their political independence, the majority of the Central and South American countries still maintain the language and many of the traditions of their Spanish motherland. (Brazil, the one exception, is similarly bound to Portugal.) The Civil War in Spain was therefore destined to have serious repercussions from Tierra del Fuego to the Rio Grande.

Hard hit by the depression of the thirties, the Latin American republics had suffered economic unrest, which was followed by increased political activity. Just as in Spain, two major factions eventually formed, each seeking to gain full control of their country's government. Though never identical, the line-up usually looked much the same. On one side was a "Worker's Party," whose members made up for their lack of education, discipline and financial backing by their vast enthusiasm for the achievements of the Soviet Union. Opposing them was a faction that was "Nationalist" (sometimes "National-Socialist") in character. Headed by conservative politicians, army men and industrialists, this party had everything its rival lacked, with one exception. Both parties had an equal disposition to brutality and lack of scruple.

For a while each side would jockey for position. In some countries the outcome of the contest almost seemed in doubt. But the Nationalist parties nearly always managed to out-manoeuvre and "out-putsch" their adversaries, and a strong man stepped from the wings and took the center of the stage.

If one of these men had let his admiration for Franco mislead him into lending the Insurgents military aid, the Western Hemisphere would have become entangled in what was still, theoretically, a Civil War in Spain. In order to forestall such a move President Roosevelt suggested a meeting of the Americas in Buenos Aires. It was here that the 1937 Neutrality Pact was signed. In the next few years several other agreements were signed which drew North and South America together for the first time.

In Europe meanwhile the Axis program was going ahead on schedule. Basing his audacity on the premise that "people don't like to get excited about things till they have to and by that time it is usually too late," Hitler was meeting with marked success. The fact that his anti-Communism, anti-Semitism and anti-Intellectualism was sending Germany's leading scientists, musicians and writers elsewhere, and *not* as enthusiastic spokesmen for the Fatherland, seemingly slipped his mind. The loss of men like Thomas Mann, Stefan Zweig, Kurt Weill and Arnold Schönberg was not a matter of concern to one of Hitler's limited education. But that Albert Einstein was also among the exiles should have given him pause. Along with Einstein went the formula which was to place the atomic bomb in American and not in German hands.

Having Germany well in hand, the time had come for Hitler's "logical expansion." (*"Heute gehört uns Deutschland, Morgen die ganze Welt"*—"Today Germany is ours, tomorrow the world.") The annexation of Austria, or *Anschluss* (attempted first in 1934 but blocked by Mussolini), was planned and carried out with cold-blooded precision.

The Austrian Chancellor, Dr. Kurt Schuschnigg, was invited to be a guest at Hitler's home in Berchtesgaden. Within twenty-four hours this confident statesman had been reduced to political helplessness. Exposed to every form of psychological intimidation, Schuschnigg agreed to legalize the Austrian Nazi Party, pardon imprisoned Nazis, appoint Artur von Seyss-Inquart as Minister of Public Safety and attach one hundred German officers to the Austrian Army.

Once back at home Schuschnigg regretted his timidity and twelve days later defied Hitler and demanded a plebiscite. This "act of perfidy" was just the excuse Hitler had been waiting for. When he massed troops at the Austrian border, Schuschnigg resigned and fled the country. On March 13, 1938 Seyss-Inquart proclaimed the *Anschluss* an established fact. On March 14 Hitler marched into Vienna.

Next on his list was Czechoslovakia.

Now flanked on three sides by "Grossdeutschland," this fortress state with its munitions works, its wealth of resources and its strategic location was a tempting morsel. It was also easy prey. Along Czechoslovakia's northern border, in the Sudetenland, lived almost three million people of German origin. "Suddenly" they developed a great desire for stationary repatriation. That is to say, they felt the Reich should expand and envelop them. Thus was the "Fifth Column" tactic of the Spanish War coming into its own.

Under the leadership of Konrad Henlein these Sudeten Germans took advantage of the freedom granted them by Czech democracy to form their own military organizations, whose similarity to those of the Nazis was obvious. Finally on April 24, 1938, in the Karlsbad Declaration, Henlein openly demanded autonomy for the Sudeten Germans.

Again the historic "if." IF those governments which helped create the Czech Republic after World War I had really been interested in its survival, could they not have saved it? Could Hitler have been stopped before he became too strong? The answer is very probably yes. We know now that in 1938 Hitler was bluffing, that he was not prepared to back his demands with a full scale war. But neither at the time were France and England ready for armed conflict. The United States was a neutral and Russia, though bound diplomatically to France, was unwelcome to England as an ally. Therefore England and France adopted a policy of "appeasement."

On September 12, after a summer of uncertainty punctuated by diplomatic activity, increased French mobilization and the expansion of the British fleet, Hitler flatly demanded self-determination for the Sudeten Germans. Rioting broke out in Czechoslovakia and martial law was proclaimed.

It was then that Britain's Prime Minister traveled to Berchtesgaden. Carrying his well-known umbrella, which newspaper cartoonists later used as a symbol of appeasement, Neville Chamberlain agreed that Czechoslovakia had no right to demand arbitration. Like Schuschnigg before him, Chamberlain did not realize till he returned home what had been put over on him. But it was too late. Having won this first concession, Hitler now demanded not only the surrender of the Sudeten territory with factories and military establishments intact, but a plebiscite to be held by November for those areas of Czechoslovakia with a large German minority. This time Chamberlain and France's Premier Edouard Daladier did confer with Russia while the United States appealed to Hitler for a meeting of European powers. At the eleventh hour Mussolini came up with a plan for a four-power meeting, held in Munich.

One of the most shameful betrayals in history was cheered at the time by millions with sighs of relief. Chamberlain, returning from the meeting where he had joined Daladier in selling out Czechoslovakia, stepped from the plane which brought him home and announced, "I believe it is peace for our time."

Hitler's "last territorial demand" was soon carried out. While Germany annexed Czechoslovakia's well-fortified western frontier, Poland and Hungary chewed off chunks in the east. In March 1939 the remaining core of this short-lived republic placed itself under "German protection."

Japanese troops meanwhile were sweeping across great areas of Chinese territory. To the "incidents" of Lukuchiao and Shanghai were added those of Soochow, Nanking and Hangchow. Under Generalissimo Chiang Kai-shek the well-trained Chinese army fought a dogged and defensive battle against an even better trained and ruthless adversary. And here, as in Spain and Ethiopia, it was the unarmed civilian population which suffered. Although civilian suffering was as old as warfare itself, never before had it been inflicted with such impersonal and mechanized brutality—nor had it ever been so thoroughly documented. This documentation, in the form of newsreels and on-the-spot reports, was not only condoned but encouraged by the Axis partners with the idea of striking fear in the heart of anyone who might seek to oppose them. To a certain extent this plan succeeded. But in many countries this "terror propaganda" had just the opposite effect. Shown in the United States, the Japanese newsreels, coupled with reports of renewed Nazi anti-Semitic activity, went a long way toward enabling President Roosevelt to combat American complacency and inaugurate his 1938 preparedness program. By 1939, "isolationism" in the United States was a dying issue. In Europe "appeasement" was also soon to die in the only way it could, by violence.

THE ATLANTIC CHARTER

HOW THE "WAR OF NERVES" GAVE WAY TO "TOTAL WAR" AND HOW HITLER MADE SOME SERIOUS MISCALCULATIONS

On March 22, 1939, Hitler demanded the Baltic port of Memel: it had been ceded by Germany to Lithuania after World War 1. The city was immediately yielded. Turning now to his former ally, Poland, Hitler demanded the city of Danzig and the right to build a motor highway and a railroad across the "Polish Corridor." Poland demurred and looked to Britain and France to back her up. Realizing, at long last, the outcome of appeasement, Britain and France pledged mutual aid to Poland in the event of German aggression.

Poland now also hoped for the Soviet Government's support. But the Soviet Union suddenly began to shift her course. The first hint of this came when Foreign Minister Vyacheslav Molotov opened a verbal attack on Britain. Then, in August 1939, the unimaginable happened. Even Communist sympathizers were speechless with astonishment when Nazi Germany and the Soviet Union signed mutual trade and non-aggression pacts. (One of the stipulations the Nazis made, and which Stalin granted, was that the Soviet Union surrender to Hitler those former German Communists who had fled to Russia in 1933.)

With German "volunteers" already marching into Danzig and creating "border incidents," the British government was voted wartime powers. On August 31, 1939, Hitler announced that the Poles had rejected *his* sixteen-point peace proposal, a document which in reality they never saw. At dawn Nazi troops crossed the Polish frontier.

That day Albert Forster, leader of the Nazi Fifth Column in Poland, proclaimed the return of Danzig to the German Reich. With Nazi tanks rolling across Poland and the "Luftwaffe" (Air Force) displaying its startling, new "Blitzkrieg" (Lightning War) tactics, England and France sent Hitler an ultimatum demanding the withdrawal of German troops from Polish soil. Hitler rejected it. On September 2, 1939, Britain and France made a joint declaration of war. The "war of nerves" was over and in its stead began that global struggle called World War II.

With the Western powers unable to lend immediate aid, Poland was carved up on schedule. On September 12 Soviet troops marched across her eastern border. The battered city of Warsaw surrendered to the Nazis.

For about six months, Western Europe now experienced "the phony war," one of those deceptive lulls of which we spoke before. Having sent an Expeditionary Force to cool its heels in France, the English dug shelters at home and waited. None the less pressure was brought to bear on the other members of the British Empire. Australia, New Zealand and India declared war on Germany immediately. On September 5, when Jan Christian Smuts became Prime Minister, the Union of South Africa defeated a proposal to remain neutral. Canada joined England on September 12. Only Ireland, remembering past grievances, remained "neutral" and provided a cooperative and convenient listening-post for Hitler's espionage.

In France the "Maginot mentality" still prevailed. Following the advice of her Minister of War, André Maginot, France had built massive and supposedly tank-proof fortifications along her eastern borders. Costing two million dollars a mile this Maginot Line was never completed and thereby rendered useless. (The money appropriated to extend the fortifications along the Belgian frontier found its way into certain politicians' pockets.) Despite this fact a large portion of the French

Army manned the pill-boxes and lived for months in moist subterranean barracks.

Across the Rhine Hitler's answer to M. Maginot had been the "Siegfried Line." From here his troops did little that winter but use loudspeakers to hurl insults at their ancient enemies while the French retaliated in kind.

On the high seas, however, Nazi submarines were very active. Their threat to world shipping caused the Pan-American Conference, held in Panama, to declare a "safety zone" around the Western Hemisphere. The United States forbade its ships to enter belligerent waters but Roosevelt repealed the arms embargo and placed exports to belligerents on a cash-and-carry basis.

In Eastern Europe the Soviet Union had quietly gone about securing fortified bases in Estonia, Latvia and Lithuania. Now the same demand was made of the Finns. When the Finns balked Soviet troops attacked.

Thus Europe was faced with the spectacle of a "war within a war." Italy considered itself sufficiently neutral to join Britain and France in sending planes, supplies and technical advisers to the aid of General von Mannerheim and his brave little army. Also neutral, the United States lent Finland 10 million dollars. For a while it seemed as if Finland would be able to hold off the invaders indefinitely. But after three months of intense winter warfare Finland's "Mannerheim Line" was breached. In March 1940, Finland sued for peace and yielded ten per cent of its territory, including the Karelian Isthmus, to the Soviet Union.

What was the reason for this seemingly arbitrary move on Soviet Russia's part? Again I must refer you to your map. If you look at it closely you will discover that, despite their treaty with Hitler, the Soviet leaders were providing themselves with "buffer territory" all along the frontier. History was to prove them very wise indeed.

With the arrival of spring a new song was becoming popular in Germany. It was called "Wir fahren gegen England" ("We go against England"). As a first step toward the realization of this plan, Hitler ordered the invasion of Denmark and Norway. In this way he hoped to outflank England and secure bases and ports in the North Sea. Denmark was quickly overrun. Norway, despite extensive propaganda and Fifth Column preparation, put up a stiff fight. Now, too, for the first time English and French troops went into action. The Germans were driven out of Bergen and Trondheim. But in Norway's rugged terrain only one factor counted, air superiority. The Germans had it. When, on June 7, 1940, King Haakon fled to London, a Norwegian Nazi named Vidkun Quisling was made Minister President and a new word for "traitor" found its way into every language of the world.

Tragic as it was, the debacle in Norway had one fortunate result. At No. 10 Downing Street, traditional residence of British Prime Ministers, Neville Chamberlain's appeasing umbrella made way for Winston Churchill's defiant cigar. Long called a "war-monger," this great statesman and leader of Britain's Conservative Party now was hailed as "the man of the hour." An eloquent orator and man of letters, Churchill promised the British people nothing but "blood, sweat and tears" and summed up the new British policy and goal with the words, "Victory—victory at all costs, victory in spite of all terror, victory no matter how long and hard the road may be; for without victory there is no survival." (By coincidence the opening measures of Beethoven's Fifth Symphony were found to have the same rhythmic beat as the letter "V" in Morse Code. Aired over the BBC for the first time on July 20, 1941, this became the symbol of victory for all who opposed the Axis.)

The darkest days for England were yet to come. On May 10, 1940, the day Churchill became Prime Minister, Hitler outflanked the Maginot Line by invading Belgium, Luxembourg and the Netherlands. Despite the arrival of French and British troops Holland surrendered in four days and Belgium in eighteen. Outnumbered and outmanoeuvred, the Allies retreated towards the vicinity of Dunkerque where the Nazis encircled them and drove them literally into the sea. But

Hitler had not reckoned with Britain's sea-going citizenry. In one of the most heroic rescues ever undertaken a fleet of 900 destroyers, launches, fishing craft, river tugs and pleasure yachts braved the Blitzkrieg and took three-fourths of the British army off the beaches.

Hitler's air force having rendered the Maginot Line as obsolete as the cross-bow, France crumbled quickly. To protect it from bombing, Paris was declared an open city. When the government quit Paris and fled to Tours and finally to Bordeaux it reflected the panic which had seized the French as a whole. Goaded by Nazi Fifth Columnists, civilians clogged the radial roads leading out of Paris and impeded the movement of troops going towards the front. On June 10, Mussolini dropped his mask of neutrality and, in the words of President Roosevelt, "plunged the dagger into the back of his neighbor." On June 15 the Nazis entered Paris. A week later Hitler performed a little dance of triumph in the Forest of Compiègne for the benefit of the newsreels. Then, in the same railway car in which the Armistice of 1918 had been signed, France surrendered. Germany occupied two-thirds of France, and the remaining territory was ruled by a puppet government in Vichy under Marshal Henri Pétain. Britain now stood alone.

For once Hitler's schedule was wrong. France fell almost two months sooner than he had expected. He was not yet ready for the next and logical step, the invasion of the British Isles. The necessary invasion barges and other equipment were on order but were not completed till August. But by that time the era of German air superiority had passed. Hitler's hopes of finishing up in the West before turning to the East were to be shattered by "*The Few.*"

In August of 1940 the "Battle of Britain" began. Wave upon wave of German planes flew across the English channel, displaying over Coventry, Manchester and London the same skill and precision they had shown over Warsaw, Oslo and Rotterdam. Much to their surprise a handful of British planes rose to meet them. These were "The Few," those RAF flyers who in that fateful winter manifested a courage matched only by that of Britain's civilian population. These were the days when one city after another was being "Coventryized," and Hitler boasted that not even U. S. aid could save England from her fate. But as more and more Nazi planes were destroyed and as RAF bombers began their raids over Germany, the invaders' hopes grew dimmer. Then, beginning in 1942, the American Eighth Air Force joined the RAF and the embattled island became an "unsinkable aircraft carrier."

Again an "if." If the British Isles had become a Nazi air base, would American cities have felt the Nazi Blitz? Knowing what we do now of Germany's pioneer work in guided missiles and jet propulsion, the answer is undoubtedly yes. Fortunately in December 1940 Roosevelt called for full air aid to England and termed the United States the "Arsenal of Democracy." In March 1941 he signed his name to a bill numbered HR 1776 and Lend-Lease came into being. In August of that same year, meeting aboard American and British warships anchored off Newfoundland, Roosevelt and Churchill drew up the Atlantic Charter. This eight-point document finally placed the United States squarely behind Great Britain in her battle with the Axis and in so doing gave the world the basic tenets of the future United Nations Charter.

While this Anglo-American friendship was prospering the Italian-German one was running into difficulties. Whereas Roosevelt and Churchill had both repudiated all desire for territorial expansion, Mussolini was finding his Axis partner far more expert at land-grabbing than he had bargained for. Then too, although Italy had annexed Albania in 1939, on every subsequent move Mussolini was forced to rely on Hitler to help him out.

Setting out from Libya in September 1940, the Italians pushed eastward along the coast into Egypt before the English had a chance to strike back. When they did, they threatened to make short work of Mussolini's half-hearted conquerors. It was then that the German Afrika Korps, under the leadership of General Erwin Rommel, arrived on the scene, recaptured Tobruk and pushed the British back to El Alamein.

The Italian fiasco in Greece was also no doubt prompted by Mussolini's urge to emulate his more successful Axis partner. Late in October 1940 he sent his troops from Albania into Greece. By mid-November they were soundly trounced. This Greek victory not only dealt a stunning blow to Axis prestige but also gave Britain the excuse she needed to come to Greece's aid and enter Europe by "the back door of the Balkans." In Hitler's anticipated eastward thrust an Allied army marching north could have caught him from the flank. Although the necessity for protecting Italy delayed his impending invasion of Soviet Russia for one fatal month, Hitler headed south. German instead of Italian tanks rolled into Athens in April 1941.

That Hitler had his eye on the Balkans had long been obvious. In June 1940, Soviet Russia again anticipated a German move and seized Bessarabia from Rumania. By August the remainder of the country was demobilizing and the Nazis walked in. Thus Hungary and Bulgaria joined the Axis. But when the same action was taken by the Yugoslav government, rioting broke out and King Peter was forced to flee. This was Hitler's cue to march. Nor did he stop till he had taken Greece and surprised the British by an airborne invasion of the island of Crete. The date was May 20, 1941. To make Mussolini's ignominy all the more complete, British troops were in possession of Ethiopia, which they had liberated the day before.

That same month Rudolf Hess, Germany's third Deputy Führer, parachuted to earth in Scotland in the hope of achieving, through personal contacts, what Hitler's bombing strategy had failed to bring about, an end to the German war with England. Hess was made prisoner of war but the reason for his mission soon became obvious. On June 22 Hitler invaded the U.S.S.R.

The Soviet Union was not completely taken by surprise. For three weeks the two huge, well-matched armies clashed at the border. Then the "Stalin Line" broke and the Germans fanned out. Now Hitler made the greatest mistake of his career. He allowed his "Master Race" theories to cost him a victory

Many Russians looked upon the invading Germans as liberators. Under the leadership of the Russian General Andrei Vlassov six anti-Communist divisions placed themselves at Hitler's disposal. Ready to join them were two million men to whom the overthrow of the Kremlin meant the fulfillment of a dream. But according to Alfred Rosenberg, Hitler's racial theorist, the Russians were "Untermenschen" in the Nazi scheme of things, a people fit only for slave labor in the nefarious Organization Todt. Hitler was out to conquer Russia, not to liberate it. He thereby sealed his doom. Passionate nationalists, the Russians loved their country more than they disliked the Politburo. Disgusted with Hitler they deserted Vlassov's cause.

Having committed themselves, the others fought on with him, retreated with the Germans and were finally captured in Germany. Handed over to the Soviets by the Americans, Vlassov and his followers met traitors' deaths in 1945.

Heading north, Hitler besieged Leningrad in September 1941, and in November he overran the Crimea and attacked Sevastopol. Regardless of losses, the embittered Russians made the Germans pay for every inch of ground. Then, on the road to Moscow, the month that Hitler had lost in taking Greece caught up with him. His troops ran into Russia's eternal ally, "General Winter." Undernourished because of the Soviet "scorched earth" policy and lacking adequate winter clothing, the German army was brought to a standstill outside Moscow and was forced to wait till spring. By then two things had changed; the Russians had a new ally and the Wehrmacht a new Commander-in-Chief. The latter, who now conducted the war by "intuition," was none other than the ex-corporal Adolf Hitler who had promoted himself to the rank of Field Marshal. Russia's new ally was the United States.

Between Japan and the United States relations had been growing increasingly strained. A full Axis partner since September 1940, Japan had suffered a curtailment in American war materials. Japanese assets in America were frozen. One by one the more cautious elements in the Japanese Government were replaced by men of the temper of General Hideki Tojo, who became Premier on October 16, 1941.

On December 7, while the Japanese peace envoy Saburo Kurusu was in Washington to continue negotiations, Japanese planes made a surprise attack on Pearl Harbor in the Hawaiian Islands.

GLOBAL WAR

HOW THE AXIS WAS DEFEATED IN THE "BATTLE OF PRODUCTION" BUT FINAL VICTORY WAS SCORED BY AMERICAN AND BRITISH SCIENTISTS AND A NEW ERA DAWNED FOR ALL MANKIND

THE more you look at the map the more incredible it seems. In December 1941 the Japanese held northeastern China. By June of 1942 they had also overrun the Philippines, Guam and the Netherlands East Indies. They dominated French Indo-China and Thailand and threatened India by way of Burma. They landed on Attu in the Aleutians. At Pearl Harbor their bombers had crippled a major portion of the U. S. Pacific Fleet.

This was indeed the "year of agony" for those who opposed the Axis. Yet in one respect it was a year of triumph too. Twenty-six nations, many of them represented by "governments-in-exile," committed themselves to the principles of the Atlantic Charter and thereby formed the nucleus of what was to become the United Nations.

When the American declaration of war on Japan was followed by counter-declarations on the part of Germany and Italy, the United States geared its entire industrial capacity for war. In this era of highly mechanized warfare it was necessary not only to outfight but also to outproduce the enemy. As in other countries, women now joined the men in the defense factories and were inducted as auxiliaries into the Army, the

Navy and the Marine Corps. Every technical skill, every branch of science and medicine was brought into play. Radar, penicillin, plastic materials are but a few of the discoveries whose development was hastened by the "defense effort." Overnight, trans-oceanic flying became commonplace. And now too the United States government allotted millions of dollars for research into a hitherto obscure branch of science, that of atomic fission.

The first all-American bombing raids over Germany did not take place till 1943. But on November 8, 1942, barely two weeks after General Sir Bernard Montgomery's decisive victory over Rommel at El Alamein, U. S. and British forces landed in French North Africa. Germany immediately occupied all of France yet failed to secure the French fleet. Part of it set sail for North Africa. The rest was scuttled in the harbor of Toulon.

That autumn was a crucial one on every front. In September the Red Army dealt a crushing defeat to the Germans at Stalingrad and thereby blocked their thrust towards the Caspian oil fields. In November the Japanese, still smarting under the April bombing of Tokyo and Yokohama by carrier-based U. S. planes, suffered their first defeat at sea. A three day naval engagement in the Solomon Islands ended in victory for the United States.

It was in a spirit of optimism that Churchill and Roosevelt met at Casablanca in January 1943. With Stalin unable to attend and France represented by the rival Free French leaders, Giraud and de Gaulle, the Allies felt certain enough of victory to press for the "unconditional surrender" of the Axis partners.

The next few months brought that victory nearer. In all of Russia the German forces had now begun a slow retreat. In the Pacific, General Douglas MacArthur reported a hard-won victory over the Japanese on Guadalcanal in the Solomons. Under General Dwight D. Eisenhower, the American Second Army, moving eastward along North Africa, met the British Eighth Army in Tunisia. A month later, on May 12, 1943, the last remnants of the once-proud **Afrika Korps** surrendered at Cape Bon.

With the Allied victory in North Africa, Mussolini's prestige collapsed. An Allied landing on Sicily was followed by the overthrow of Mussolini and his imprisonment. The Italian government, now headed by King Victor Emmanuel III and Marshal Pietro Badoglio surrendered unconditionally on September 8. But a week later Mussolini was rescued by German troops and taken to northern Italy where he proclaimed the establishment of a Republican Fascist Party. Fighting in Italy continued until 1945 with German troops retreating inch by inch the length of the peninsula. The destruction of the beautiful Monte Cassino monastery which the Germans used as an observation post, the bombing of German-held Rome, the havoc wrought by the Allied landing at Anzio, the demolition of the bridges of Florence, these were Mussolini's legacy. His friendship with the Führer ended in making Italy a German "buffer-territory." Disguised in a Wehrmacht uniform the one-time Duce attempted to escape to Germany in April 1945. He was captured by partisans and shot.

The Second World War was the war of global conferences. Air travel made it possible for the wartime leaders and their aides to meet and discuss informally the problems of mutual concern. Twice Churchill crossed the Atlantic to meet Roosevelt, once in Washington in 1941, once in Quebec in 1943. Late in November of that year Generalissimo Chiang Kai-shek flew to Cairo to confer with Roosevelt and Churchill on Far Eastern strategy and two days later the British and the American leaders met with Premier Stalin at Teheran.

With the exception of those troops on occupation duty in Nazi-held territories and those facing the Allies in Italy, the bulk of Hitler's armies was deployed along the eastern front. To relieve this pressure it is understandable that the Soviet Union clamored for the opening of a "second front." On June 6, 1944, with the invasion of Normandy, their wish was realized. D-Day had arrived.

As a result of the daring strategy, detailed planning and

precise coordination achieved by the Supreme Headquarters of the Allied Expeditionary Force (SHAEF), the troops which crossed the channel or parachuted from the skies to storm the heavily defended Atlantic Wall were able to capture both Cherbourg and Caen within a month.   Under the leadership of General Eisenhower the liberation of France soon became a reality.   On August 15 another landing was made, this one on the Riviera.   Ten days later the other allies halted outside of Paris to accord French troops the honor of joining the underground as French Forces of the Interior in the job of clearing the last remaining Germans from the French capital. Sweeping south of Paris the American Third Army, under the command of General George S. Patton, made a swift armored thrust towards the river Rhine.   But to the north, in Belgium and Holland, geography and the weather aided the Germans in making one last determined stand.

Allied airborne troops dropped at Arnhem failed to receive the ground support they needed from the south.   They were encircled and all but wiped out.   Breaking the dikes to flood the low-lying country was undertaken by German and Allies alike, thereby turning much of the land in the Rhine delta into impassable swamps.   This prevented German troops from sweeping south as they had done in 1940.   It also prevented an Allied northward thrust to outflank the West Wall.   The Allies stopped to consolidate their gains.   Then came the "Battle of the Bulge."

The amazing thing about this last great German counter-attack was its degree of success.   That, in turn, was due to the fact that the Allies were taken by surprise.   No one, not even the German generals themselves, believed their armies still capable of taking such a stand.   But Field Marshal Karl R. G. von Rundstedt who commanded the German forces in the West had received an order from the Führer.   He was in no position to quibble.   Since the events of July 1944 Wehrmacht generals were expendable.

Friction between Hitler and the German general staff had been of long standing.   Out of the nucleus of Hitler's personal pre-1933 bodyguard had come the "SS," short for "Schutz-staffel" or Protective Echelon. Again and again Hitler had promised the Wehrmacht hierarchy that the SS would not be armed. Then he had promptly turned around and formed SS divisions, providing them with the finest equipment and such high sounding names as "Totenkopf" (Death's Head), "Leib-standarte Adolf Hitler" and so on. When Wehrmacht soldiers faltered, SS officers would be sent in to keep them in line. But Hitler's self-appointment as Commander-in-Chief of the Armed Forces was the last straw. The Wehrmacht plotted a revolt. On July 20 a bomb planted in a briefcase injured Hitler only slightly, and his escape convinced him more than ever of his league with Destiny. After General von Witzleban and several co-plotters had been brutally strangled Hitler held the reins firmly in his hand. It was he who ordered a German break-through to the sea.

Coming at a time when Brussels, Antwerp and Aachen were already in Allied hands, the attack by twenty-four divisions began on December 16 and lasted eight days. Under orders to take no prisoners, the SS and Wehrmacht troops swarmed over an area of about 100 square miles. At Bastogne the American 101st Airborne Division was encircled and its sur-render demanded. As answer the Germans received from General McAuliffe the now classic monosyllable, "Nuts." Elements of the Third Army lifted the seige of Bastogne. On December 24 a raid by 7,000 planes brought the Germans to a halt. It was not until early the following February that the last of them were driven from Belgian soil.

While the Allies were preparing to cross the Rhine in force, American troops luckily discovered an undestroyed rail-way bridge at Remagen, south of Bonn. Other crossings by boat brought the bulk of the Allied armies over the river in March.

From the east meanwhile the Soviet advance was steadily progressing. Finland, which had sided with Germany in 1941, suffered a second Soviet attack shortly after D-Day. In the south the Red Army reached the Rumanian border by March of 1944. The invasion of Hungary and Czechoslovakia followed, and with the ultimate surrender of Budapest in February 1945, the Soviet conquest of the Balkans was complete.

In April 1943 the Soviet Government had broken off diplomatic relations with the Polish government-in-exile. In the capture of Warsaw in January 1945 the reflection of a new but as yet veiled pattern of power politics could be seen. Later that month the Red Army crossed the river Oder and on February 7 was rolling towards the outskirts of Berlin.

On that day Stalin was playing host to Churchill and Roosevelt at Yalta in the Crimea. From this, their last meeting, came the Yalta Agreement, post-war plans for Germany and Austria and an arrangement for the Soviet participation in the war against Japan.

Elected for a fourth term of office in 1944, Roosevelt was not a well man when he went to Yalta. Two months later, on April 12, 1945, he died at Warm Springs, Georgia and his vice president, Harry S. Truman, was sworn into office that afternoon. The following day the Red Army marched into Vienna and at the first United Nations parley in San Francisco on April 25 came the announcement that Soviet and American troops had met on the river Elbe. Before the signing of the United Nations Charter brought the two-month session to a close the war in Europe was over. On May 1 an announcement was made by Grand Admiral Karl von Dönitz that Hitler had committed suicide in his bomb-shelter beneath the ruined Chancellery in Berlin. A week later came the German unconditional surrender at Rheims. V-E Day was May 7, 1945.

Anti-German feeling ran high as Stalin met with Truman and Churchill in Potsdam in July to discuss the post-war plans. British ire had been particularly aroused by the sudden appearance of jet-propelled long range bombs and rockets which the Germans launched after D-Day from the French, Belgian and Dutch coasts. (Known as "V-Weapons," the "V" was the Nazi answer to the "V for Victory" of the Allies. In German it stood for "Vergeltung" or retaliation.) The Soviet Union, as has been mentioned, deeply resented the wholesale deportation of its citizens to work as slave labor in the Organization Todt. World-wide indignation was aroused by the discovery of the Nazi concentration camps where Jews, political prisoners and all "enemies of the state" were herded together to die of disease and starvation, or in the highly efficient gas chambers.

For their wanton "war-crimes" those Nazi leaders who had not followed their Führer into death were tried before a Four Power Tribunal in Nürnberg. One, Martin Bormann, was never captured and was condemned *in absentia.* Two died awaiting trial, three were acquitted, seven imprisoned for life and ten hanged. On the eve of the hanging Hermann Göring committed suicide in his cell.

During the Potsdam Conference a British election swept the Socialist leader Clement Attlee into office. As the new Prime Minister he took Winston Churchill's place at the conference table. Now, with two of the Axis partners defeated, the Allies turned their entire interest to the war with Japan.

A possible Japanese invasion of Australia had been forestalled in 1942. Over a vast expanse of ocean, much of it 3,500 miles from Japan itself, American, British, Australian and Philippine troops began a new kind of amphibious warfare known as "island hopping."

Initiating a concerted offensive in July 1943, the Allies by-passed certain of the larger Japanese-held islands completely and attacked those which could provide air bases from which planes could harass the Japanese shipping of supplies. In this way it was possible to starve the Japanese from many islands without a fight. But a look at the map will show you the magnitude of this operation. If only one island in every hundred was invaded you can still see why the Pacific War took such a terrific toll of lives.

The offensive began with the taking of tiny Rendova island in the Solomons. By the year's end Bougainville Island and the air base at Munda on New Georgia Island had been secured. On New Guinea Salamaua had fallen and the Japanese in Lae were encircled. The Allies now struck out towards the Gilbert Islands and began a great encircling move.

In the year 1944 the Japanese discovered how difficult it was to chew what they had bitten off. Though many of these islands were no more than coral atolls their possession by the Allies was a vital necessity. In an outer arc, landings were made at Kwajalein and Einewetok in the Marshall group and a bold thrust was made into the Marianas. With the recapture of the by-passed island of Guam in August the Allies had a base from which superfortresses could bomb Kyushu, the southernmost of the Japanese islands. Moving up the New Guinea coast Aitape and then Hollandia were taken as well as Admiralty and Schouten Island. Landings were also made in the Carolines and the Moluccas. On October 19 General Douglas MacArthur was able to fulfill a promise when he stepped ashore at Leyte in the Philippines.

On the Asiatic continent, meanwhile, Chiang Kai-shek's troops were scoring victories and the Japanese had been driven out of India. With the Burma Road to China still in Japanese hands a regular Allied air-freight service had been initiated from India over "the hump" to Chiang Kai-shek's provisional capital at Chungking. Then began the grueling but successful campaign to force the Japanese out of the Burmese jungle.

The last phase of the Pacific War began late in 1944 when Saipan in the Marianas became the base for an all-out air offensive against Japanese industrial targets. It was an extremely hazardous undertaking: Japan was still more than 1,000 miles away. In March 1945 the month-long battle for the fortress island of Iwo Jima gave American bombers a base within 750 miles of Yokohama. This was followed in April by the invasion of Okinawa. Coinciding with the defeat of Germany, the greatest air offensive of the war could be unleashed on cities only 325 miles away. In southeast Asia, meanwhile, Admiral Lord Louis Mountbatten was able to announce a complete victory of British, American and Chinese forces over the no longer "Banzai-ing" Japanese.

Already aghast at the toll of lives the war had taken, the Allies knew that the contemplated invasion of Japan itself would take still more. While re-deployed troops were on their way from the European battlefronts, science stepped in to bring the war to a speedy and terrifying conclusion.

Physicists the world over had long been aware that the atom was not, as the Greeks had believed, a basic and unchanging entity. Research into the problem of converting "matter" into "energy" by splitting the atom had been hampered only by the need for securing "fissionable" material in sufficient quantities to make experimentation possible. The basic or key formula on which these experiments would be based was, as you know, carried from Germany to America in the head of the exiled German scientist, Albert Einstein.

The Allies knew that the Nazis had appropriated large sums of money to continue research along atomic lines. A daring British sabotage raid on a "heavy water" plant at Rjukan in Nazi-held Norway was made with this knowledge in mind. It was now clear to such scientists as Enrico Fermi, Lisa Meitner and to Einstein himself that the discovery of atomic energy could place a powerful weapon in the hands of those who came upon it first. The urgency of this matter was pressed upon President Roosevelt and in greatest secrecy an atomic laboratory—which became a town in itself—was set up at Oak Ridge in Tennessee.

Working together, British and American scientists were able to witness, on July 16, 1945, the first atomic explosion ever seen by man. It took place in the desert at White Sands, New Mexico. On August 6, a second explosion took place, this one over the Japanese city of Hiroshima. In one devastating blast three-fifths of the city was destroyed, many thousands of people killed and as many injured. Three days later a third and even more devastating atom bomb was dropped at Nagasaki.

These events, coupled with a Soviet declaration of war upon Japan and a simultaneous invasion of Manchuria, brought Japan to her knees. Assured that their emperor, Hirohito, could remain, the Japanese surrendered formally aboard the U. S. battleship Missouri anchored in Tokyo Bay. This was V-J Day, September 2, 1945.

The nightmare of global war was over. Yet, as detailed reports of what had taken place in Hiroshima and Nagasaki filled the news, all mankind realized that a new and disturbing era had begun. What had been discovered could not be kept a secret by the United States and Great Britain for ever. What was to be the future of the world now that this terrifying force was at man's disposal? For an answer the world now turned to the United Nations.

THE UNITED NATIONS

HOW THE UNITED STATES FELL HEIR TO WORLD LEADERSHIP AND PLAYED HOST TO THE PARTICIPANTS IN A GREAT EXPERIMENT IN INTERNATIONAL RELATIONS

OSCAR WILDE once quipped, "As long as war is regarded as wicked it will always have its fascination. When it is looked upon as vulgar, it will cease to be popular." If he had substituted the word "unprofitable" for "vulgar" he would have come even closer to the truth. Armies march not only "on their stomachs," as the saying goes, but on hope; the hope of a victor's recompense—riches, new territory, a better life or, ironically, peace. Take away this hope and armies will cease to march.

The havoc wrought by World War I seemed to have done just that. Calling it "the war to end war," optimists maintained that another such mechanized slaughter would be totally unfeasible and unprofitable even for the winner. But mankind is a creature of habit and slow to learn by his mistakes. Two decades later another war broke out. Those who started it hoped for a quick, violent and profitable victory. Instead they were defeated and their cities suffered great destruction and their governments bankruptcy. But the victors suffered as much if not more. Large portions of the Soviet Union lay in ruins. China was wracked with internal strife. The British Empire partially disintegrated and its burden of leadership

shifted to the United States. In order to maintain its economy
and have nations to do business with, the United States had to
begin lending financial support to former allies and enemies
alike. (This aid soon served another and almost more vital
purpose, of which more later.)

The mushroom-shaped atomic cloud over Nagasaki had
done more than bring Japan's dream of an Asiatic "Co-
prosperity Sphere" to an abrupt end. Like a finger pointing
to the sky it seemed to warn that warfare with atomic weapons
would spell out "Winner take nothing." The alternative was
arbitration of some new kind.

Even before the atom bomb was dropped, Winston Churchill
had suggested that the United States, the British Common-
wealth and the U.S.S.R. band together to create an organization as unprecedented in history as had been the creation of the
United States of America itself. The urgency was so great
that, despite the fiasco of the League of Nations, the idea took
hold.

Anticipating the havoc and the misery the war would leave,
the United Nations Relief and Rehabilitation Administration
held its first session in Atlantic City in November 1943 and a
second one in Montreal the following September. (UNRRA,
as it was known, became the International Refugee Organization in 1947.)

In April 1944 the formation of a U.N. Organization for
Educational and Cultural Reconstruction was proposed at a
meeting of Allied Ministers in London. At the Bretton Woods
Conference in July of that year forty-four nations participated in the first U.N. Monetary and Financial Conference,
aimed at improving world-wide economic conditions through
the creation of an International Monetary Fund and an International Bank for Reconstruction and Development.

Finally, after the Dumbarton Oaks Conference held in
October, the "Big Three" published the proposals for a permanent international organization to be called the United
Nations. This proposal was endorsed by Churchill, Roosevelt
and Stalin at Yalta and worked out in detail in San Francisco

in 1945. The Charter of the United Nations provided for the representation of all peace-loving nations in a General Assembly, and for a more powerful Security Council comprising five permanent members—the United States, Great Britain, the U.S.S.R., China and France—plus six other members elected for a term of two years each. Also there were created an Economic and Social Council and an International Court of Justice. The administrative work was to be undertaken by the Secretariat headed by a Secretary-General. The first man to hold this post was the Norwegian Trygve Lie.

The question of how the Security Council members were to vote created difficulties from the start. As finally arranged at the Crimea Conference, a negative vote or "veto" by one of the five permanent members would be enough to defeat any proposal except one concerning procedure.

Through making excessive use of the veto the Soviet Union soon displayed its former truculence and its proverbial distrust of the Western world. It became evident that the U.S.S.R. had little intention of attempting an honest settlement of the post-war problems in which it was involved. Whereas in 1943 the Soviet Union had voluntarily dissolved the "Comintern"—its international propaganda organization—as a gesture of friendship to its "fellow democracies," its delegates now accused their recent allies of "economic imperialism," thereby seeking to mask the Soviets' own increasingly imperialistic intentions. These, however, were rapidly becoming obvious.

At the Potsdam Conference it had been agreed to partition Germany and Austria. The capital cities of these two countries, although now both within the zones accorded the Soviets, were themselves divided into four parts. At the time when the U.S.S.R. lowered an "Iron Curtain" between its territories and those held by the other three occupying powers, England, France and the United States still maintained Military Government headquarters in Vienna and Berlin. This arrangement the Soviet Union found irksome. In order to force the Allies out of Berlin, in 1948 the Soviet government adopted the policy of blocking all road, rail and canal traffic from the West. The

American answer to this was the "airlift," an air shuttle service from Frankfurt to Berlin that provided the French, British and American sectors with such vital necessities as food and coal. After a year and a half of mounting tension, during which the matter was referred to the United Nations, the Soviet Union lifted the blockade in May 1949. Instead of withdrawing from those Balkan countries they had overrun, the Soviets drew them closer and closer into their orbit. Finally, by means of a neatly staged *coup d'état,* they placed Czechoslovakia behind the Iron Curtain in 1948.

Elsewhere in Europe Soviet strong-arm tactics were meeting with less success. In Italy King Victor Emmanuel III stepped down in favor of his son, Umberto. He, in turn, bowed to a referendum held in 1946 and Italy became a republic. Amid the existing chaos of this disillusioned, impoverished country the threat of a Communist "Putsch" loomed large on the horizon. It was then that American Marshall Plan aid, under the European Recovery Program, yielded its first benefits. This plan, suggested by the wartime Chief of Staff and later Secretary of State, General George C. Marshall, was designed to lend financial aid to those countries not under Communist control—thus becoming America's realistic answer to Soviet expansion. Emerging from World War II as a powerful champion of the cause of self-government, the United States became the logical protector of those countries resisting totalitarian domination.

The American policy of "Soviet containment" also helped curb the spread of Soviet influence in France. Following a substantial gain by the Communist faction in the French national elections in 1946, France was in turmoil. For the next few years French governments rose and fell. Still, during this time the Council of Europe was formed, consisting of the Benelux countries (Belgium, the Netherlands and Luxembourg), France, Italy, England and Ireland and the three Scandinavian kingdoms. By 1950, thanks to the Marshall Plan, France was once more in a condition stable enough so that it no longer feared Communism, and put forward the

"Schumann Plan" which called for a pooling of West European coal and steel production. Britain, invited to join in this, held herself aloof.

In one of the Balkan countries Joseph Stalin now met with unexpected resistance. Under Marshal Tito, the wartime guerrilla leader, Yugoslavia at first seemed content to become just another Soviet satellite. Suddenly, in 1948, Tito bolted and established himself as a Communist dictator without benefit of the Soviet Union. Though Tito did not openly turn to the Western Powers for support they welcomed the breach he had made in the Iron Curtain. Late in 1950 Yugoslavia received substantial Marshall Plan aid from the United States.

To the south, Greece was the only European country where liberation did not bring the fighting to an end. When the British overcame the Nazi invaders in 1944, pro-Communist resistance forces immediately attacked the liberators in order to forestall the restoration of the monarchy. When in 1946 a plebiscite brought about the recall of King George II, anti-Royalist guerrillas, aided by Communists infiltrating from the north, increased their depredations by way of protest. On King George's death in 1947 his brother Paul came to the throne. That same year the United States appropriated 300 million dollars for Greek aid, and U. S. supplies enabled the Greek forces to bring hostilities to an end in 1949.

With the Zionists insisting on the creation of an independent Jewish state in Palestine, and with the newly formed Arab League threatening to meet such a move with armed resistance, in April of 1947 Great Britain handed the problem over to the United Nations. On May 15, 1949 the British mandate over Palestine ended and the new Republic of Israel was proclaimed. War broke out immediately, but the Arab League was no match for the Israeli forces. A temporary truce was arranged through the Swedish U.N. mediator Count Folke Bernadotte, the same man who had acted as go-between in arranging the German surrender in 1945. After Bernadotte was assassinated at the hands of a political extremist, Dr. Ralph Bunche, an American, continued the mediation. He succeeded in obtaining an Israeli-Egyptian armistice. For the first time in two thousand years the Jewish people had a nation and a flag of their own. In 1949 Israel was voted into the U.N.

In India too nationalism had long been asserting itself. Independence had been one condition demanded of the British in return for participation in the war against Japan. Now, however, the Moslem League under Mohammed Ali Jinnah sought the creation of a separate Moslem state of Pakistan. The Hindus opposed this plan firmly and Great Britain became more and more reluctant to take sides. Bringing matters to a head, early in 1947 the English announced the imminent transfer of authority to "responsible Indian hands" and bade the Hindus and Moslems reach an understanding. Yet despite the partition of British India into the Republics of Pakistan and India, religious strife and bloodshed followed the actual withdrawal of the British in August 1949. Mahatma Gandhi, the Hindu lawyer whose doctrine of "passive resistance" had contributed so much toward Indian independence, was assassinated in 1948. His disciple Pandit Nehru soon placed India in a position of leadership in Asiatic affairs. Both India and Pakistan are members of the U.N.

Elsewhere in the East the Japanese war-cry of "Asia for the Asiatics" had aroused many a nationalistic echo. Abiding by its promise, the United States granted the Philippines their independence in 1947. In the Netherlands East Indies a revolt broke out which ended only when, through U.N. intervention, the United States of Indonesia was formed. Similar rebellions faced the British in Burma and Malaya, and the French in Indo-China found themselves embroiled in a full-scale jungle war against well-armed guerrillas from the province of Viet Nam.

It was no coincidence that all these insurrections bore a similar, Communist stamp. The spread of Soviet influence, though momentarily checked in Europe, was made easy in the Orient by the exploitation suffered at the hands of Western empire-builders by the native populations. Although they had much to be thankful for in the field of medical help and education, in their eagerness to throw off the yoke of the West they failed to realize that by merely exchanging one form of imperialism for another they had less to gain than to lose.

The most tragic example of this was China. Though the war with Japan had temporarily healed old political antagonisms, its end brought a new eruption of them. Chiang Kai-shek's reactionary and dictatorial government relied on the support of its Western allies to keep it in power, but at a crucial moment it failed. Soviet-backed Communist forces under the veteran Communist leader Mao Tse-tung attacked the Nationalist forces in October 1945. Chiang appealed to the United States for aid and was rebuffed. He was forced to give ground and finally, in January 1949, he resigned and fled to the island of Formosa. There he proceeded to build the largest anti-Communist force in all Asia.

Once in control of the Chinese mainland, the Chinese Communists established a new capital at Peiping. Afterwards, their forces invaded the province of Tibet, high in the Himalayas. India, which had seemed friendly toward Mao Tse-tung, viewed this latest move with great concern. In French Indo-China, Chinese Communist aid to the Vietminh troops now caused the French to withdraw their forces from frontier positions. It was against this troubled background that the Korean War was waged.

As agreed at Yalta, Korea was divided at the 38th parallel into two zones, the northern to be occupied by the Soviet Union, the southern by the United States. Friction between these two rival powers was reflected in the violence which broke out during the elections held in 1946 and 1948 in the American Zone. After the creation there of the Democratic Republic of Korea both sides mobilized, the South Koreans with the aid of American officers, the North Koreans with Soviet aid. On June 25, 1950, without warning or provocation, the North Korean army marched across the 38th parallel. Taken by surprise the South Koreans fell back. Then, for the first time, the United Nations flag went into battle. Using Japan as a spring-board, General

Douglas MacArthur took command of the U.N. forces fighting in Korea.

With amazing speed American troops in Korea were augmented by others called from Japanese occupation duty and from the United States. They were soon joined by contingents from England, Australia, Canada, the Philippines, France and Turkey. The U.N. forces succeeded in driving the North Koreans back across the 38th parallel and reached the Manchurian border in November 1950. Then Communist China intervened. Severely outnumbered, the U.N. troops fell back along the road they had come. At the port of Hungnam the largest troop evacuation since Dunkerque was successfully carried out and the troops were put ashore further down the peninsula, ready to fight again. The bitter Korean winter seemed to agree with the Chinese troops even less than it did with the U.N. forces, and by spring the Chinese were retreating once more toward the north.

Realizing now that the Soviet government would be deterred from further aggression only by a show of strength, the United States initiated a program of full-scale mobilization and war-production. At the same time it promised close support and cooperation to the twelve European nations that had signed the North Atlantic Pact in 1949. On an American proposal to rearm Western Germany, bitter opposition was voiced by France. On the other hand, Konrad Adenauer, Chancellor of the newly formed Bonn Republic, made use of the strong bargaining position of Western Germany to insist that rearmament be accompanied by full equality of Western Germany with the other Atlantic Pact nations.

Then on December 19, 1950, the twelve Atlantic Pact nations met in Brussels and appointed General Dwight D. Eisenhower as Supreme Commander of the proposed Western European Army.

A TURBULENT PEACE

HOW THE COLD WAR HAS DEVELOPED IN EUROPE AS OPEN CONFLICT ERUPTS IN OTHER LANDS

The Korean War did not end the way that wars usually end, with a victory and a peace treaty. After many months of confused and bitter fighting between the forces of the United Nations and those of the Communists, armistice negotiations were begun on July 5th, 1951. These talks dragged on for more than two years while the fighting continued intermittently. The stumbling block which caused most of the trouble was the repatriation of prisoners. The representatives of the United Nations wanted a program of voluntary repatriation, but the North Koreans insisted that all prisoners should be returned to their native countries whether they wanted to go or not. This would have resulted in the executions of many thousands of unwilling Communist returnees. Finally, however, compromises were worked out and, on July 27th, 1953, an armistice was formally concluded and political conditions reverted to what they had been before the aggression began.

The war had been unpopular in the United States (which had supplied the great majority of the men for the fifteen-nation forces of the United Nations) and it had been costly— billions of dollars had been expended and almost two million casualties had been suffered. What had really been accomplished? For the first time in history, an armed force representing an international group of nations had succeeded in turning back a military thrust against a peaceful country. The United Nations had passed its first great test. To the multitudes of Asia though, something even more remarkable had taken place. These millions, subjected to indignities by Europeans for centuries, saw the conflict as a blunting of American imperialist desires in the Far East by an emerging China. Western power and influence had been frustrated by an oriental power awakened from a sleep of centuries. Whether for good or evil, out of the ashes of Korea had emerged a "new" force in world politics and things would never again be quite the same. Today, the embattled nation of Korea remains a divided and potentially dangerous area where no permanent peace agreement has ever been effected.

While the fighting along the 38th Parallel in Korea had continued, the nations which had created the North Atlantic Treaty Organization carried out their plans to secure western Europe from Communist attack. The original twelve signatories to the pact (Belgium, Canada, Denmark, France, Iceland, Italy, Luxembourg, the Netherlands, Norway, Portugal, the United Kingdom, and the United States) were joined, by 1954, by Greece, Turkey and West Germany. The war in Korea had heightened American fears of Russian expansion and the United States had taken the lead in advocating a rearming of West Germany. The French, however, showed considerable anxiety over the rearming of their recent conqueror and also voiced displeasure at the rather lukewarm British commitment to the organization. Despite these internal difficulties, the Western European Union came into existence in 1954 as an indication of the determination of the nations of the West to oppose further Soviet expansion. The Russians could not view these moves with anything but alarm. They countered by creating, in 1955, the Warsaw Treaty Organization in an attempt to imitate the Western program. The eight members of this pact (Albania, Bulgaria, Czechoslovakia, East Germany, Hungary, Poland, Rumania and the USSR) have shown considerable differences of opinion on many issues and revealed severe internal stresses—political, economic and ideological. The disagreements between the members of the two groups that do exist cannot hide the fact that Europe is once again, as so often before, divided into armed camps. But, hopefully, other forces are at work which might, in the somewhat distant future, put an end to the nationalistic bickerings and squabblings which have been the bane of European life for so many centuries.

On August 10th, 1952, a proposal developed by Jean Monnet and Robert Schumann of France was put into operation. This was the Schumann Plan by which six industrial nations (Belgium, France, Italy, Luxembourg, the Netherlands and West Germany) banded together to form a European Coal and Steel Community to make possible a pooling of their mineral resources. This arrangement was quite successful and the cooperative agencies which had been set up to supervise its workings became the basis for further cooperation between these nations. On January 1, 1958, the European Economic Community, or Common Market, was formed. The goals of this organization include: a plan to develop economic activities throughout the European community by eliminating tariff barriers; the establishment of a free movement of labor and capital across political borders; and the hope that eventual political unity can be achieved through economic cooperation. The structure has been a great success even though Great Britain's bid for membership was blocked several times by France. These were only temporary delays, however, and Great Britain was finally accepted for membership in 1971. With all this economic cooperation, Western Europe slowly moves toward the day when individual nations would forget their differences in a common cause.

Twenty years after the most horrible of wars, Europe was (thanks in great part to American aid) more prosperous than it had ever been. It was still far from complete political unity and it had to live with the American-Soviet rivalry which could explode into war at any time. Even so, Western Europe was more optimistic and aware of its responsibilities and opportunities than ever before. Nineteenth-century autocrats like Napoleon I and Tsar Alexander I had dreamed of uniting Europe by conquering the other nations but had failed. Now there was a chance that the twentieth-century statesmen, elected to their offices and responsible to their electors, could succeed where their predecessors had failed. Who would dare compare Robert Schumann to the great Corsican and yet, someday when there is something like a United States of Europe, might not the name of the first be as famous as that of the second? Stranger things have happened.

It is recorded that on the tomb of Timur the Lame (whom we call Tamerlane) there is an inscription, "If I were alive, you would tremble." The terror that this man inspired in his lifetime shines through this awful warning. Only a few men who have lived in the centuries since Timur have used fear so effectively as he did. One such man was Josif Vissarionovich Dzhugashvili, whom the world calls Stalin, the "man of steel." This one-time theological student from Georgia near the Black Sea ended his life as the terror of millions. When, on March 5th, 1953, a strange death ended his thirty-year rule as all-powerful leader of the Soviets, few tears were shed over his passing. Once he was safely dead, the usual power-struggle took place and Georgi Malenkov became the leader of Russia. Since that time, Russia's attitude toward the West, and especially the United States, has been characterized by rapid changes of policy which, while confusing and irritating, have added up to an improvement over the inflexibility of Stalin. If the world has been kept in a state of tension, it has been less charged with danger than before, and we can perhaps begin to think of the possibility that competition and "peaceful coexistence" will someday replace fear. The "thaw" in the Cold War that has developed has not resulted in any major Soviet concessions to the West, but it has been evidence of the fact that the Soviets no longer follow the "hard" Stalin line which taught that war between them and the West was inevitable. They seemed to believe that they could conquer the world by "peaceful" means and were willing to try to do so with political and economic instead of military tools.

Malenkov, who concentrated upon increasing the flow of consumer goods to the Russian people at the expense of war production, was ousted from office on February 8th, 1955, when these policies did not find favor with certain of the ruling elements.   He was followed in office by Nikolai Bulganin, a Marshal of the Soviet Army, and Nikita Khrushchev, a party functionary and one of the most remarkable political figures of this century.   Bulganin, who was a rather drab figure, was gradually eased from power by the clever Khrushchev, who remained as the Russian leader until his overthrow in 1964.   It is worth noting that neither Malenkov nor Bulganin was executed.   They were simply "demoted."   This is, in itself, representative of the quite remarkable change that has come over Russia since the death of Stalin.   For almost a decade, Khrushchev occupied the center of the world stage and gave a truly memorable (if sometimes a bit incredible) performance.   Whatever his faults and idiosyncrasies, he was responsible, in great measure, for the fact that relations between Russia and the Western nations at the end of his tenure of office were much better than they ever could have been under Stalin.   Perhaps he recognized that inflexibility was not the easy road to success.   Stalin had believed it was.   Or perhaps he believed that it was really possible for the Communist system to outdo the capitalist nations in open economic competition.   We don't know what went on in his mind.   It may have been for another reason entirely.

The first crack in the Communist monolith had appeared as early as the defection of Tito in 1948.   When, on June 28th of that year, Yugoslavia was expelled from the Cominform, it was evident that all was not well in the Communist bloc.   Unrest, chiefly caused by nationalistic feelings antagonistic to Soviet directives that all must look to Moscow as the final loyalty, was near the surface in many places.   On June 17th, 1953, workers in East Berlin rioted against conditions in their sector of the divided city.   All too obvious to their eyes was the fact that life in Western-occupied West Berlin was superior in every way to life in Soviet-occupied East Berlin.   The

West Germans had, with generous American help, performed the miracle of rebuilding their shattered land and now enjoyed a standard of living equal to that of any other European nation, and Berlin was a kind of shining light in the darkness of East Germany. The drab and regimented existence of the East Berliners showed up and contributed greatly to the discontent of the people. Trouble broke out. For several days an incredulous world was treated to scenes of fighting between stone-throwing German youths and massive Russian tanks but, and inevitably, the tanks won out. Order, if not contentment, was restored. Again, on June 28th, 1956, similar riots broke out in the Polish city of Poznan. Here long-standing resentment against Russian occupation was coupled with Roman Catholic protests over state interference with religious affairs and together they produced an explosive situation. After some angry demonstrations an uneasy truce was effected and Poland has remained within the Russian orbit (although its ties to the West have been considerably strengthened in recent years). Even these Russian difficulties with the satellites were dwarfed by the revolt that began in Budapest on October 24th, 1956. Thousands of Hungarians, led by Imre Nágy, participated in a nation-wide uprising, centered in Budapest, against the Russian masters of their country. An amazed world watched as Russian puppets were hurled out of office and revolutionary officers installed. The Russian occupying army had withdrawn to observe the progress of the revolution and to determine whether or not it could be quelled by the Hungarian police and army. On November 4th they had decided that things could not be allowed to continue in the direction in which they were going and the Red Army returned to Budapest, and crushed the revolt. Thousands were killed and thousands more were imprisoned, placed in internment camps or deported to Siberia. Almost a quarter of a million Hungarians fled their homeland to take refuge in the West. The revolt, though unsuccessful, showed plainly the degree of dissatisfaction that existed in the satellite nations and left many wondering whether the puppets of eastern Europe might not turn out to be millstones instead of jewels about the Russians' necks. The revolt also showed that the new "peaceful co-existence" policy of the Kremlin could be pushed only so far and no further. When the anti-Stalinist, Wladyslaw Gomulka, had come to power as a result of the Polish unrest, Khrushchev had not intervened directly because he saw the difficulties only as an extension of Polish nationalism and independence and he accepted Gomulka as an alternative to armed intervention. But Hungary was a different story. There, the threat of a complete overthrow of the Red regime brought down the Russian wrath. Gomulka remained in power until the riots in 1970, while Nágy was treacherously murdered. Thus, though all has not been well for the Russians in these unhappy areas, there have been no further successful defections from Communist rule. Yugoslavia remains a "Communist neutral" and has maintained a precarious national communism; Albania no longer serves as the mouthpiece of Red China and remains isolated; Catholic Poland is the only Communist nation to give legal recognition to the Common Market; Rumania has closer economic ties to France than she does to her neighbors; and so on. Even so, no man or nation can live in the shadow of the Red Army and be completely independent of Russian influence, but the events in the satellites have shown that even rigid adherence to Marxist principles has not been enough to stifle completely the independence of mind that makes Man the highest of the animals.

Russia is not the only center of communism. The growing part in international affairs that Red China has been playing since Chiang fled to Formosa at the end of 1949 has been mentioned before. Neither the despots of antiquity nor the dictators of the modern world succeeded in imposing the degree of control upon their peoples that Chairman Mao and his followers have accomplished. Family life, so dear to Chinese civilization, has been almost obliterated and replaced by unquestioning loyalty to the state. A program of forced communization was begun that dwarfed the efforts of the Russians in this direction a quarter of a century before. Too, the Chinese began to play more and more of a part in the affairs of Asia. Their intervention in Korea was only the first of many such adventures. Tibet, which they had long claimed, was invaded and crushed in 1951. Indian territory was annexed in 1959 and again in 1962. To millions of people in the underdeveloped areas of the world who have long been accustomed to the aggressive moves of the white man, similar actions on the part of the Chinese have been accepted and even applauded. To these people, the Chinese revolution, based as it is on the uprising of the peasants (as contrasted with the Russian emphasis upon the industrial working class), has had a considerable attraction. Their needs and their desires are met by the beliefs and actions of Mao (or so they profess to believe) and China has taken its place as a leader of world politics to a degree exceeded only by the USSR and the United States. This rise to eminence has been accompanied by terrible suffering. Families have been uprooted and whole cities have been moved or recreated without regard for human life. Internally, opposition to the new programs has usually meant death. Chairman Mao admitted in 1958 that 800,000 "enemies of the Revolution" had been liquidated, but experts in the United Nations calculated the number of executions at an even higher figure. In 1956, Mao gave a celebrated speech in which he ordered that China should, "Let one hundred flowers bloom. Let one hundred schools of thought contend." He did not foresee that his invitation to more intellectual freedom would result in widespread denunciation of the excesses of his regime. When this happened, the old curbs were returned and they have remained since. Although much hardship and many reverses have been suffered, the face of China has been redone. A tottering nation has become a giant, albeit one with enormous difficulties to overcome. China exhibited a fanatical anti-Westernism especially in the late Sixties during "the Cultural Revolution." Other developments have shown that serious differences between China and the Soviet Union also exist. As early as 1956, it became clear that all was not well in Sino-Soviet relations. The reason for this trouble (besides the ideological difference already mentioned) include the rivalry for leadership of the Communist world between the two Red giants and a Chinese belief in the inevitability of atomic war with the West which the Russians, with their hard-won industrial progress at stake, will not accept. There have been small battles along the border, and the future may well see a complete split between the Communist leaders but whether this will bode good or evil for the world is impossible to see. Meanwhile, a nation in which one-fifth of the population of the world lives is engaged in a rapid industrialization that will, with its virtually unlimited resources of people and minerals, make it one of the world's leaders for many years to come. The Chinese have, despite much hardship and the reverses suffered during the excesses of the Great Leap Forward, as they called their industrial movement in 1958, made great industrial advances, including the production of nuclear weapons.

Although China finally joined the United Nations in 1971, her exact destiny is still unclear. Yet it is certain that this huge country is awake and will play a major role in the future of mankind.

Another power has also risen again in the Far East. The damage done by Japan's utter defeat—symbolized by the atomic fire balls of Hiroshima and Nagasaki—was repaired under the firm guidance of General MacArthur. The Emperor of Japan has divested himself of his former "divinity," the Mitsubishi and other big business dynasties were dissolved, and a new constitution was put into effect which permitted the establishment of strong labor unions and democratic political institutions. Whether or not this democratization will be permanent remains to be seen.

Japan was soon making giant strides toward economic recovery and economic expansion through co-operation with the West. Thanks to "the Japanese Economic Miracle," the hardworking, intelligent Japanese people were again making goods that were sold throughout the world. Tokyo became the most populous city in the world, and Japan became a place where old ways crossed and blended with the new. Cherry blossoms, kimonas, and Shinto shrines remained, but, in the large cities, a forest of television antennas appeared above the roofs of quaint Japanese houses. Automobiles crowded the narrow streets. Billboards and neon signs advertised everything from the latest

American motion picture to the newest Toyota automobile to come off the Japanese assembly line. Japanese guitar-playing cowboys strummed in night spots while modern Japanese department stores in Tokyo's shopping district—the Ginza—displayed English ties and French gowns.

The greatest changes may have taken place in Japanese social life. Women play a greater role in business, education and political life. The modern democratic family is replacing the all-powerful father. Perhaps these changes are but a prelude to the dimming, if not the destruction, of the old military values which the Japanese people have inherited from their feudal past.

The continued position of the United States as the world's greatest power has been one of the realities of the world picture since the capitulation of the Axis partners in 1945. Except for the Soviet Union, no nation on earth has ever dared to challenge seriously the military power of the United States. Prosperous as no other nation has ever been (though they are but one-twentieth of the world's population, Americans enjoy almost one-third of the world's estimated income), its citizens believe themselves committed to the protection of the free world. America's participation in the Korean venture had shown her determination to fill the requirements of this new role. The old spirit of isolation (or neutrality) was gone forever. As early as 1949, the United States had helped to create NATO as a bulwark against Russian expansion in Europe and in doing so had pledged herself to a constant involvement in European affairs. A similar commitment was made in Asiatic affairs when, on September 8th, 1954, the South East Asia Treaty Organization (SEATO) was formed. This agreement, sometimes referred to as the Manila Pact, included Australia, France, Great Britain, New Zealand, Pakistan, the Philippine Republic and the United States as members. This pact was signed only a year after the conservative Dwight Eisenhower had taken over the reins of American government from Harry Truman, and was an indication that no fundamental change in American foreign policy had taken place. Eisenhower, who could speak from a position of incredible military strength because the United States had added the most powerful of all weapons, the hydrogen bomb, to its arsenal on November 1, 1952, carried out the policy of "containment" of Communism that his predecessors had inaugurated with the Truman Doctrine. A pact guaranteeing the safety of Formosa was signed in 1955 and a program to combat Red inroads in the Middle East (the Eisenhower Doctrine) was announced on January 5, 1957. While pursuing these policies which were aimed at stopping Communism's spread, Eisenhower also attempted to improve diplomatic relations between the United States and Russia. In the summer of 1955 he met with the Soviet leaders in a "Summit Conference" at Geneva, Switzerland. Later, in 1959, he played host to the first visit of a Russian ruler to the United States as Nikita Khrushchev and American Vice-President Richard Nixon exchanged visits. The furthering of understanding that took place as a result of these meetings was shattered on May 5, 1960, when an American reconnaissance plane was shot down deep over Russian home territory (the U-2 Incident). The handling of the affair by the administration (the United States claimed at first that the craft was merely a weather ship that had strayed off-course and this crude attempt at a cover-up was gleefully exploited by the wily Khrushchev) resulted in a considerable loss of American prestige. America did not regain "face" until October 1962 when the new President, John F. Kennedy, instituted a naval blockade of Cuba to prevent the Soviet government from supplying "offensive" rockets to Cuba's revolutionary leader, Fidel Castro. The resolute and courageous fashion in which this explosive affair was handled evoked admiration and confidence in the American nation and its new leader. Tragically, President Kennedy was murdered on November 22, 1963, and the Presidency passed into the hands of Lyndon B. Johnson.

In 1956 there were only three independent nations in Africa south of the Sahara (Liberia, Ethiopia and the Union of South Africa). After the passage of a decade there were thirty-seven. This emergence of the African areas into the world's political arena has been a phenomenon of great importance. "Uhuru," a Swahili word meaning freedom or independence, has resounded throughout the continent since the terrible Mau Mau uprising in British Kenya that began in 1952. The first of the new African states to become free was the former British colony of the Gold Coast, which achieved independence as Ghana on March 6th, 1957. It was soon followed by Guinea, Nigeria, Gabon, the Ivory Coast and, eventually, more than thirty others. Some of the periods of transition from colony to independent nation were marked by relative tranquillity (as in most of the former British colonies where some degree of native participation in government had been encouraged). In other areas, this was not the case. The great Belgian colony in the Congo, for example, was granted independence on July 1st, 1960. Within hours, an army revolt began that soon turned into anarchy and atrocity. Europeans fled for their lives and only the intervention of United Nations' troops, mostly from the African nations, prevented what could have become disastrous civil war. However, so weak and inept was the new Congolese government and so strong were the ancient tribal divisions within the country that the tensions were not eased for several years. The experience in the Congo illustrated the new nations' lack of many of the characteristics of government that provide economic and political stability and these needs will continue to exist for years to come. The emerging areas are handicapped by religious and tribal disunity and are sorely lacking in trained and responsible leadership. Too often, political adventurers possessed of charisma (that indefinable attraction which made Hendrik van Loon's grandfather forget his Dutch hatred for the French and follow the banner of Napoleon) have caused great harm to their nations by reckless or misguided actions. Kwame Nkrumah, the dictatorial first leader of Ghana, and Patrice Lumumba, the rather unstable leftist who led the Congo until his abduction and murder six months after the achieving of independence, are prime examples of this kind of irresponsible leadership. The more farsighted African leaders have tried to build a federated Africa and, although the problems to be found in such a project are immense, a start has been made. In 1961, an Inter-Africa and Malagasy Organization was formed to promote African unity. This group was succeeded by the Organization of African Unity in 1963. The purposes of these organizations have been to promote the unity and development of Africa and to attempt to erase the traces of European colonialism. Today, however, everywhere in Africa there is dictatorship, corruption and inefficiency—the heritages of a European colonialism much more interested in economic gain than in the social or cultural advancement of the subject peoples. Too, everywhere there is an awareness of the developing power of the black man and an interest in his problems no matter where they exist. Pride in the Black heritage has been continually stressed by leaders such as Julius Nyerere of Tanzania and leads many Africans to become interested in racial and civil rights problems in the United States. It is not too much to say that every movement in American race relations is followed by the residents of Nairobi, Lagos and Conakry. Nor is it too much to say that racial discord in the United States might have a definite bearing on the outcome of the contest between the United States and the Soviet Union for political favor in Black Africa. However this problem is resolved, we can only hope that the peoples of Africa will accept cautious long-range programs for their own betterment and will not fall prey to Utopian schemes offered to them by self-interested leaders and agitators from the outside.

North of the Sahara, there have been problems, too. Many Palestinian Arabs, who had lived on lands out of which Israel had been carved, were refugees living in the Gaza Strip along the Mediterranean Sea or on the west bank of the Jordan River. The impoverished refugees, who endured wretched conditions in refugee camps, plotted to destroy Israel so that they could return to their former homes, and were a source of serious concern to the Israelis. Indeed, the Arab nations of the Middle East and of North Africa refused to recognize the new Jewish state, and vowed to drive the Israelis back to the sea. Egypt (which was renamed the United Arab Republic in 1958) assumed a leading role in the Arab world. Egypt's leader in this venture was Gamal Abdel Nasser, who had been one of the leaders of the 1952 revolt which overthrew the corrupt reign of the notorious King Farouk.

Although the first Arab-Israeli War (1948) had been stopped by United Nations action, tensions continued to mount in the Middle East. Under an agreement with Egypt, Great Britain had guarded the Suez Canal for many years. In 1956, the British troops withdrew. In the same year, Nasser seized the canal and closed it to Israeli shipping. Israel sent an army to take over the canal, and British and French troops landed in the canal area in order to keep it open to ships of all nations. When the United Nations met, both the United States and the Soviet Union supported a United Nations condemnation of the military actions, and Great Britain, France and Israel withdrew their forces. In recompense for Israel's withdrawal to her old borders, the United States guaranteed free passage for Israeli ships into the Red Sea through the previously blockaded Strait of Tiran.

Until his death in 1970, Nasser was the undisputed leader of the Arab world. He had successfully removed the Suez Canal from foreign control in 1956 and, as a result, his prestige and potential as a leader was almost unlimited. After the Israeli-Egyptian War of 1956, the bitter dispute over Israel's right to exist and occasional raids continued. When the Egyptians reimposed the blockade of the Straits of Tiran, the Israelis realized that eventual war was inevitable. The Israelis took the initiative and powerful Israeli forces waged campaigns simultaneously against Egypt, Jordan and Syria, winning resounding victories. After six days of combat, a cease-fire left the Israelis occupying all of the Sinai Peninsula, the Gaza Strip, the east bank of the Suez Canal, all of the west bank of Jordan, and the strategic Golen heights in western Syria. After the six day war, the Arab nations were more bitter than ever and began sending trained guerrilla fighters into Israel, and the

Israelis continued to strike back. In 1969, while guerrilla activity continued, Prime Minister Levi Eshkol died. He was succeeded by Mrs. Golda Meir, who, in her younger years, had taught school in the United States.

Why is the Middle East such a tinder box where a single spark could ignite a conflict that might possibly become the dreaded World War III?

Israel began as a neutral nation, willing to accept aid from the Communists as well as from the West. The Soviet Union, however, soon turned from Israel to the Arabs with a covetous eye toward the Arabs' oil and the possibility of establishing its naval power in the Mediterranean Sea. The United States, and many other western nations, do not want Russia's hopes of dominating the area to become a reality. Hence the United States, which tried to help both the Arabs and the Israelis, was forced to become Israel's firmest supporter among the great powers.

The Arabs say that oil is often mixed with blood and sand. This is sadly true. The area is divided into two armed camps, and at stake are the great oil fields of the Arabian peninsula and North Africa, the control of the Suez Canal, and military dominance in the Mediterranean basin.

These nations of the Middle East and Africa, both Arab and Negro, have much in common with their Asiatic and our Latin American neighbors. They share the terrible problem of overpopulation. It is estimated, for instance, that the populations of the United Arab Republic and Costa Rica will double in less than twenty years and China adds between fifteen and twenty-five million people to her masses every year. All suffer from want of capital and skilled workers. The differences in the living standards of these underdeveloped areas and the highly industrialized nations of the West are immense. While the per capita income in the United States was over $3000 in the mid-Sixties, the average Bolivian worker earned about $130 and the average Indian worker received $55 for his year's labor. The gulf between these peoples is obviously great. Programs to aid these nations, such as the Alliance For Progress that is

sponsored by the United States in Latin America, are trying to remedy the effects of centuries of exploitation but the
problems, despite tremendous expenditure, remain acute. $500,-
000,000 in American aid goes to the nations of Africa every
year, and double that is given annually to help the people of
Latin America. The French, the British and the Russians have
also contributed aid to these new countries and will continue to
compete for the favor of the former colonies. These new nations have understood all too clearly their advantages and disadvantages in this political tug-of-war between East and West
and have been quite content to accept aid from both sides without committing themselves politically to either. Money and
goods flow to these new nations in much greater amounts than
they ever received while they were colonies and we can observe
the spectacle of the former masters competing for the favors of
peoples who were their virtual slaves only a decade ago.

Europe's recovery from World War II has been almost
complete. Britain no longer rules the waves but she is still a
force in European politics and her Commonwealth is a major
factor in the world's economy. France, which was suffering
from domestic ills and colonial uprisings in 1951, has righted
herself. Charles de Gaulle, who helped to create the Fifth
French Republic and bring order out of chaos in 1958, returned
France to prominence. Her colonies are gone—some by bloody
revolt (Algeria and Indo-China) and some by amicable parting of the ways (the members of the French Community
such as Chad and Gabon)—but France's stature has returned.
De Gaulle convinced Frenchmen that theirs is a mighty destiny
and he led the difficult way to economic stability and international prestige. By the time de Gaulle retired from politics in
1969 France had become one of the world's nuclear powers and
now sees herself as the leader of a new Europe where she hopes
to replace the United States as the determining factor in politics. Many Frenchmen suffered agonies over the losses of
Algeria and Indo-China, but these losses had to be endured.
France is a better nation because of them.

In 1963, France and West Germany signed a treaty of mutual friendship. With this declaration, signed by de Gaulle and Konrad Adenauer, some of the hatred and distrust of centuries was removed. Of all the strange and wonderful events of the recent past this is certainly one of the most encouraging. Perhaps it is not too much to hope that other men and other nations, profiting by the example of these two ancient foes, might resolve their differences in ways other than war.

The world today is threatened as never before with total destruction. The spark to set off World War III might come from an incident in divided Berlin (divided by an actual wall since 1961!) or from another Israeli-Arab clash. It could come from one of the periodic battles between Pakistan and India; the latest Indian victory over Pakistan and the creation of Bangla Desh in 1972 certainly stirred up Moslem-Hindu hatred. Or it might come from Cuba or Cyprus or the Soviet-Chinese border. Or it might come from Viet Nam or elsewhere in Southeast Asia. With all these potentially explosive situations, it is obvious that the United Nations has not solved all of the world's problems. But it has accomplished much—aggressions have been stopped in Korea and in the Middle East; order has been brought out of disorder in the Congo and on Cyprus; and much has been accomplished of a humanitarian nature. It is a far-from-perfect body, but it remains, in the words of the American President John Kennedy, "The last hope of the world."

AN OLD ORDER GIVES WAY

AS MEMORIES OF THE WARS OF THE FIRST HALF OF THE TWENTIETH CENTURY FADE AWAY, NEW GENERATIONS STRIVE "TO TAME THE SAVAGENESS OF MAN AND MAKE GENTLE THE LIFE OF THE WORLD"

By 1971, all of the great leaders of World War II—Franklin D. Roosevelt, Winston Churchill, Dwight D. Eisenhower, Charles de Gaulle and Douglas MacArthur—were dead. The torch, in the words of John Fitzgerald Kennedy, had been passed to a new generation born in this century, tempered by war, and disciplined by a hard and bitter peace. The younger generation, vigorous and impatient, looked at old problems with critical eyes.

To many of the people of the world John Kennedy represented the new activism and high idealism that marked the troubled Sixties. In January 1961, the youthful Kennedy took over the burdens of the Presidency from the fatherly and very popular Dwight David Eisenhower. He devoted his brief inaugural address to explaining his country's role in a hungry and divided world. The United States, he said, had been summoned "to bear the burden of a long twilight struggle . . . against the common enemies of man: tyranny, poverty, disease, and war itself." He pleaded with both parties in the Cold War to "begin anew the quest for peace, before the dark powers of destruction unleashed by science engulf all humanity

in planned or accidental destruction." On numerous other occasions, he said: "It's time to get America moving again. We
can do better, we must do better . . ."

Surrounded by bright young men, President Kennedy saw a
"New Frontier" both at home and abroad, and Americans were
thrilled by his idealism. "Ask not what your country can do
for you," he said, "ask what you can do for your country."
Inspired by his words, thousands of young Americans—and
many older ones too—joined the Peace Corps or as "Freedom Riders" aided impoverished and unschooled people in
the Deep South or in Appalachia, where, among other things,
they taught the forgotten men and women to exercise their
right as American citizens to vote.

To bring equality of opportunity and more freedom to his
people, Dr. Martin Luther King, Jr., a young, black Baptist
minister, fought segregation in buses in Montgomery, Alabama;
and in school, jobs, and housing all over the nation. He told us
about his "dream of equality of opportunity . . . a dream of a
land where men will not argue that the color of a man's skin
determines the content of his character."

Discrimination was not a new problem. In the 1940's,
President Truman made civil rights a national issue. During
his administration, a historic report, "To Secure These Rights,"
denounced religious and racial discrimination as twin evils frus-
trating the achievement of the ideal of American democracy.
And, in the 1950's, President Eisenhower had completed desegregation of the armed forces, and vigorously enforced the
Supreme Court's school desegregation decision in a dramatic
confrontation in Little Rock, Arkansas.

After President Kennedy's untimely death, Lyndon Johnson pledged to carry on the New Frontier policies. Indeed, the
new President assured the nation in his State of the Nation
Address that, if the social needs of the nation were met, the
"Great Society" would emerge. In the "Great Society," President Johnson felt, it was the responsibility of the federal government to plan for and cope with national problems such as
poverty, discrimination, inadequate medical care, the problems

of the cities and so on. He especially wanted to make life in the cities more livable, to provide good educations for all the children and job opportunities for everyone. Until the dream of the Great Society was obliterated by the war in Vietnam, he made some progress toward his goals by securing the passage of civil rights and voting rights acts and inaugurating his war on poverty.

There was an ugly side to the decade of the 1960s, too. The political assassinations of Dr. King and the two Kennedy brothers, John F. and Robert, and the riots and campus unrest, not to mention several vicious wars in Asia and Africa—all cast a shadow over the decade's accomplishments. Life in our large cities became more dangerous, unhealthful and unpleasant by the day. Tons of pollution were dumped into our skies and our waters; crime and the drug menace threatened our lives; slums grew dirtier and increasingly unsafe.

During his brief "thousand days" in office, President Kennedy had shown the way to meet these challenges from home and abroad. In foreign policy he set the style for himself and his successors when he said: "Let us never negotiate out of fear. But let us never fear to negotiate." He also attempted to promote better understanding through personal contacts with heads of states. He found Nikita Khrushchev a "hard nut to crack." After a two day session in Vienna President Kennedy described the difficulties he encountered in negotiating with the Russians in the following words. "The Soviets and ourselves give totally different meanings to the same words: war, peace, democracy, and popular will. We have different views of right and wrong, of what is an internal affair, and of what is aggression. And above all, we have totally different concepts of where the world is and where it is going." Despite such difficulties, however, the United States and the Soviet Union took a first step toward preventing nuclear war by negotiating a treaty to prevent the spread of nuclear weapons to other nations. The treaty was badly needed. Communist China and France were already manufacturing and testing nuclear weapons and other nations like Israel and India were thinking of doing the same.

The treaty was drawn up by the Johnson Administration and approved by the United States Senate shortly after Richard Nixon became President. Most of the nations of the world would have signed it.

To slow down the arms race, which was not only monstrously expensive but dangerous as well (on the theory that if a little boy has a fire cracker he will be tempted to explode it), the two super-powers negotiated the Limited Nuclear Test Ban Treaty in 1963 by which they agreed to stop the testing of nuclear weapons in the air, under the water, or in space. In 1968, the United States and the Soviet Union joined with other nations in banning the use of nuclear weapons in space. Finally, President Nixon sent representatives to Helsinki, Finland, to begin discussions known as SALT (Strategic Arms Limitation Talks).

In the Sixties men and women of this century had grappled with old problems and had met with some success. Yet, during these years, mankind became aware of some very grave problems that had been scarcely noticed at the start of the decade.

SPACESHIP EARTH

WE MUST MAINTAIN THE EARTH'S LIFE-SUPPORT SYSTEMS OR PAY THE PENALTY

In the Space Age, twentieth-century man is probing the unknown with the same curiosity and spirit of adventure as did his ancestors during the Age of Discovery. Like the explorers of the sixteenth century, spacemen take great risks, seek fame, court disaster and are rewarded by being the first to see whole new worlds "swim into their ken." But there is a big difference, too. Whereas months, often years, passed before discoveries became generally known four centuries ago, instant communication by television, press and wire make it possible today for the whole world to see as they occur the fiery take-offs of spaceships, men walking in space, space-vehicles docking and men actually landing on the Moon.

On April 12, 1961, in a craft named Vostok I, a Russian named Yuri Gagarin became the first man to enter the great realm of outer space. For as long as man has lived on this planet, he dreamed of leaving to explore the heavens above him. This dream became a reality as Gagarin's ship soared to an altitude of 203 miles above the earth at a speed of more than 17,000 miles per hour. This flight was a milestone in the race for space leadership between the Soviet Union and the United States that had been accelerated when the Russians launched heir first artificial satellite, Sputnik I, on October 4, 1957. The eyes of men are now on the stars in a way different than they have ever been before. When World War II ended, man was still tied to the Earth. Now the whole universe beckons to us.

When Gherman Titov, the second of Russia's "cosmonauts" to orbit the earth, was in flight around the globe, he called back to earth, "I am an eagle! I am an eagle!" The exhilaration he felt is shared by many of us as we realize that, although the awful threat of nuclear war is constantly with us, our potential as creators of our destinies has only begun to be tapped. We stand on the threshold of wonders our ancestors never dreamed of attaining. The world is indeed a most wonderful and dangerous place.

Putting a man on the Moon was the ultimate triumph of "the Iron Man," the term Hendrik van Loon applied to the Industrial Revolution. The feat was accomplished by courageous men and the technical skill of "ground control." But there was more to it than this. Actually the tiny spaceship, with its closed life-support system, was backed up by America's mighty industrial power. In a sense, too, the round-trip to the Moon, accomplished by Neil A. Armstrong, Edwin E. Aldrin, Jr. and Michael Collins, was motivated by national pride and possible military and commercial advantages that accrue from "getting there first."

Yet, as exciting as their fantastic adventures in the heavens are, all cosmonauts and astronauts must inevitably return to Earth from whence they were rocketed into space.

Until very recently, we have taken it for granted that the capacity of the Earth's life-support systems was limitless. Since we have started monitoring them, however, we have learned to our dismay that we are in deep trouble. Scientists throughout the world are warning us that, unless we stop abusing its vital life-support systems, the Earth's future is grim indeed. Astronauts contrast the awesome beauty of the Earth spinning in the velvet blackness of space with the cold grayness of the Moon. From space, the surface of the Earth is alive with color of incredible beauty—vivid blues, bright greens and swirly whites. From Earth, on closer scrutiny, our landscape is scarred and marred, mutilated over the years by the thoughtless excesses of its human inhabitants.

According to Genesis, God told man: "Be fruitful and multiply and replenish the earth and subdue it; and have dominion over the fish of the sea and the fowl of the air and over every living thing that moveth upon the earth." This is one commandment that man has obeyed faithfully and greatly to his peril. In a sense, the whole story of mankind has been the story of how man has been changing his surroundings to suit his growing physical and spiritual needs. He killed deer for food and wolves for safety; he felled forests for shelter, cropland and building materials; he mined the Earth for fuels and metals; he dammed and diverted rivers for irrigation, and he used chemicals to combat pests and disease and to lessen the toil of farming. Eventually man's efforts to tame nature and to shape his needs seriously affected the earth's ecology. (Ecology is the relationship of all living things to their surroundings and to other forms of life.)

The problems of ecology began in the Garden of Eden. When Adam cast aside the first apple core, he began the process of despoiling "the good earth." Until quite recently, the earth's resources of water, air and soil seemed inexhaustible. From the dawn of civilization, the life-support systems of Earth had kept its air, pressure and temperature in delicate balance so that life could be maintained. While men lived in traditional societies, their lives were bound by custom and limited by the primitive tools at their disposal. Under such circumstances, mankind lacked the power to destroy its environment on a global level. Nonetheless, men did make a desert out of much of the "Fertile Crescent"—valleys of the Euphrates, the Tigris and the Nile, which had served as "cradles of civilization" at the dawn of recorded history. Like the early settlers in the New World, men could always escape the consequences of their ignorance, however, by moving on to greener pastures and to untouched lands.

There is no Garden of Eden on earth today. The careless days of innocence and plenty are now over. Man's power today is such that he can—and, indeed, he is—destroying or at least very seriously impairing his environment on a global scale. Today we are gathering in the bitter fruit of unplanned development, ruthless exploitation of natural resources and just plain ignorance. Once clear, pure streams are now rainbow colored, reflecting not the glow of the sky after a shower, but the oily film formed by wastes dumped into them. We are slicing up woodlands for freeways, paving over farmlands for shopping center parking lots, fouling lakes and rivers, disturbing the balance of life in those waters on which human welfare depends. Even more insidious and dangerous is a new and horrifying threat unleashed by man's genius, the power of atomic energy not only to annihilate but also to pollute and destroy life—human, animal and inanimate.

The problems of environment are worldwide. On the arid plain of Castile in Spain, there is a magnificent park of ancient oak trees. The wood is one of the few left of the immense oak forests that once grew in Spain. It has survived because it was the hunting preserve of Spanish kings. The harsh, dry plains of Spain, and of the entire Mediterranean Basin for that matter, are a tragic example of what happens when people ignore ecology. In Greece, Italy, as well as Spain, wealthy sheep owners turned their huge flocks loose on the countryside during the Middle Ages, and thus upset the delicate balance of nature. In India, polluted water annually causes 2 million deaths and 50 million serious illnesses.

Now man is beginning to understand that each advance to a better life has almost invariably come at the expense of his environment. Automobiles have enabled us to travel short and long distances comfortably, but automobile exhausts poison the air. Pesticides improve crop yields, and chemical weed killers eliminate back-breaking hand labor, but they also pollute the streams and the atmosphere.

We can never get rid of all pollution. To return our natural surroundings to their original purity would involve a return to stone age living conditions. Man can, however, improve the quality of his surroundings if he is willing to pay the costs involved. He may have to forego rapid growth; his taxes may rise; and some of the products he buys, now produced cheaply at the expense of his environment, will cost more. At present, our ever-growing population and the increasing quantity of goods produced put "altered resources" or pollutants back into our skies, waterways, and lands at a rate so fast that they cannot be assimilated without creating harmful effects.

Another global worry is the increase in the world's population. The population of the earth, now 3.6 billion persons, is growing at a rate that will double the number of persons inhabiting this earth in thirty years. Our own population of 205 million will be more than 305 million in that same period of time. With at least one-third of the world undernourished, ill-housed and poorly clothed now, starvation and universal misery become a stark possibility. Population growth will—indeed, must—end soon because Spaceship Earth, to which humanity is clinging, is a sphere only 8,000 miles in diameter shrouded in a thin film of air and clouds.

In the first century, A.D., when Augustus was the Roman Emperor, the population of the world was estimated to be 250 million people. Sixteen hundred years were required to double that figure. Today, the more than three billion people on earth will double in thirty years time, and the world's population will then be increasing at the rate of an additional billion every eight years. Your little brother, born in 1972, living into his seventies, would know a world of 15 billion inhabitants. His grandson might share Spaceship Earth with 60 billion fellow humans. Even now half of humanity is hungry. There is actually less food per person on the planet today than during the Great Depression of the 1930's. Thousands of people are dying each year of malnutrition, if not outright starvation, right now.

In short, scientists have warned us that we are following a

primrose path leading to the imminent collapse of civilization because we are destroying the life-support systems of Spaceship Earth by doubling the number of passengers (the world population) every thirty years, by increasing our demands on our limited natural resources and by polluting the planet in the process.

THE EARTH AS A GLOBAL VILLAGE

HOW THE MARVELS OF SCIENCE AND TECHNOLOGY HAVE MADE OUR PLANET A SHRINKING WORLD AND ALL MEN BROTHERS

What can one say about the gloomy predictions of the world's scientific prophets of doom? Should we dismiss their findings and warnings about population and pollution as scientific fiction?

Perhaps it is best to remember that people have always thought that no previous generation had ever seen so many awful or wonderful events as they did. We are no different from our ancestors in this respect. We believe that we are living in a world whose threats are more terrible and whose promises are greater than any that have existed before. We forget that the atomic holocaust is no more terrifyingly real to us than were the hordes of Atilla to frightened peoples of fifth-century Europe and that the material blessings of our civilization seem no more fabulous to us than those of China did to the contemporaries of Li-Po many centuries before Christ was born. On an occasion when the dark clouds of war had lifted just a wee bit, Winston Churchill remarked that, perhaps after all, mankind might soon be "moving along a broad, smooth causeway of peace and plenty, instead of roaming and peering around the rim of hell."

Indeed, the United States and other highly industrialized nations are moving into a more humane post-industrial age.

More people are engaged in providing services for their fellow-men in fields such as teaching, medicine and recreation. It is estimated that per capita incomes in post-industrial societies will be fifty times greater than in pre-industrial economies. In the future there will probably be guaranteed minimum incomes and basic welfare services for all people. In post-industrial lands education will be a life-long process. Throughout your mature years, you will probably undergo periodic retraining for other careers, perhaps as many as four in a lifetime. This will be essential because increased leisure will open up new opportunities for self-fulfillment.

The success of the Apollo 11 Mission made the Moon man's province. But, psychologically it did more. People now believe that nothing should be allowed to stand in the way of achieving a better world with all of the Earth's inhabitants enjoying "the good life," that is, more leisure, economic security, social justice and a clean, healthful environment. Of course, the technological and scientific skills that put men on the Moon cannot be converted to working similar miracles with human beings who cannot be programmed mathematically. But many people now think that a country that is able to explore the Moon is also certainly capable of making life on Earth safe, comfortable and more satisfying.

Today, many people are worrying less about the scarcity of material goods and more about the quality of their lives. The quality of one's life is determined by beauty and cleanliness of one's natural surroundings and one's freedom to pursue leisure-time pleasures even at the expense of lost income and reduced production. Workers are looking forward to a shorter work week so that they can enjoy more leisure hours in doing what they like to do. We have seen the many technological miracles of the past generation: television, space exploration, computer science, the conquest of some diseases and space-age technology.

Of the many achievements of the Industrial Revolution, the progress made in electronics may well be the most significant for world civilization. It made the Space Age possible. Starting in the mid-nineteenth century, the human voice was amplified by telegraph, telephone and radio until it could reach every corner of the Earth. After photography was invented, photographs could also be sent by wire, made to move, and, by means of television, to record events as they were taking place. Without the persuasive spoken words pouring from radio loudspeakers, the new nationalism of Black Africans, the Southeast Asians, or the Arabs would have been greatly hindered.

With the development of communications satellites, starting with Early Bird in 1965, the world for the first time can be bound together by spoken words. Hitherto such instant news existed only on the level of the village. Farseeing men think that instantaneous communication will, in fact, bring about a global village, and that national boundaries will ultimately fade away and become obsolete. The problems of other countries will become so intimate as to appear to be one's own. Differences among men, which create suspicion and hostility, will tend to lessen. Indeed, soon we may all be speaking a second global language. The benefits of education, news events, even symphonies played in great urban centers, can be shared by people from the Arctic to the tropics.

It seems clear that while the world is threatened as never before, mankind does have the means to work together to avert any great disaster—a new world war, over-population or irreparable pollution. The alarm has been sounded in the United Nations and carried by our modern means of communications to the four corners of the world. With courage and determination Man will prevail.

APPROACHING THE YEAR 2000

THE PERILS AND HOPES OF OUR AGE

PEOPLE living in any age probably insist that their era is the most dramatic, exciting, and challenging in the long story of Mankind. The landing on the moon in July 1969 seemed to mark a new stage in human ingenuity and triumph. The 1960s had been, for the most part, a period of great optimism; the 1970s were not. In the 1970s and early 1980s, even our greatest scientific achievements seemed to be a mixed blessing. And some of the perpetual problems of the human condition have obstinately refused to disappear. The deterrence of nuclear war and the protection of our environment may be the greatest challenges mankind has ever faced.

There seems no limit to the astonishing advances that science has brought technologically advanced countries and people who can afford them. The space exploration programs of the United States and the Soviet Union have continued at great cost. Both powers sent spaceships far into our universe. In 1970, a dramatic rescue operation occurred far away in space when an explosion in an oxygen tank aboard the *Apollo 13* spaceship risked the lives of the astronauts. Several years later, an unmanned craft transmitted close photos of Saturn, revealing some of the secrets of its rings. These spaceships can travel as fast as 50,000 miles per hour. *Viking I* landed on Mars in 1976, sending back pictures for nightly television news. So many satellites circulate in outer space that those of us left back on earth may soon have to worry about "space

RACE FOR SPACE

junk" falling to our planet. Advances in the space programs of the United States and the Soviet Union may have been made with another purpose in mind: the waging of war, which could bring the popular "Star Wars" movie series and the computerized video games of amusement arcades into a terrifying reality.

Back on *terra firma*, the electronics revolution, the most recent stage of the Industrial Revolution, has made an incredible impact on our lives, from how we bank to how we cook our food. A computer that twenty years ago would virtually fill an entire room has been reduced to pocket size. The age of the "personal computer" is upon us. Knowledge of computers ("Computer literacy") may very well become mandatory for students in college, high school, and even some grade schools. Computerized video games became the rage in the late 1970s. Airplanes now can practically fly themselves. Instant telecommunications and word processors have modernized business and education, leading to bitter economic struggles between the giant IBM corporation and its competitors, and between Japan and the United States. When people first learned about computers in the 1950s, there was talk that the era of the "push-button" might eventually cause our bodies to waste away from inactivity. Only our fingers might get exercise pushing buttons. Now, more than ever, computers have replaced manual labor in some fields. Computerized robots almost bring to life early science fiction novels as they take their place on the assembly lines of auto factories in Detroit and Japan. While few would disagree that computers have contributed greatly to making many aspects of our lives easier, there have been some costs to humans as well. The computer revolution has created a new level of white-collar personnel trained in computer skills. But the number of jobs in industries has been reduced because of the computer, contributing in some measure to the higher unemployment rates in certain industries. The computer has "dehumanized" business, reducing personal contact. While greatly increasing productivity in some industries, computers have contributed to increasing economic power in the hands of a few giant companies, as only the largest can afford to keep up with the rapid and expensive advances in computer technology. Those less able to compete fall behind. Advances in electronics technology are also apt to widen further the gap between rich and poor nations. And some people worry, with a degree of justification, about the use to which the government could put the computer—collecting information on citizens at the push of a button. It may be difficult to safeguard computerized information stored by governments, companies, universities, and hospitals. What happens when a rival company or a foreign power is able to tap into someone else's computer? Can laws be rewritten to punish for stealing computerized information just as they do for breaking and entering a home or a store? The computer has been, so far, the friend of Mankind, but it also could become its foe if citizens were arbitrarily subjected to what an expert has called the "quiet violence" of the computer.

PUSH-BUTTON AGE

The development of genetic science has made astonishing progress, allowing scientists to understand as never before the makeup of the human body. Some possibilities may be both reassuring and unsettling. As we come to understand human genes, it seems possible to predict which people may inherit certain diseases or be particularly susceptible to contracting them later on in life. At the same time, doctors can determine the genetic makeup of babies before they are born; learning the sex of the baby and the presence of certain forms of mental retardation are only the first steps. Soon it may be possible to know if an infant will be susceptible later to diseases such as muscular dystrophy and hepatitis. Such prenatal "screening" for genetic defects becomes ever more sophisticated.

Yet as scientists push toward understanding more about the origins and genetic characteristics of the diseases that afflict Mankind, certain ethical questions inevitably follow. Should doctors be able to alter some aspects of the nature of Mankind? Could families be tempted to terminate the pregnancy of an unborn child whom doctors find might risk developing a disease forty years later? Could someone be turned down for a job because scientists had determined that his or her genetic makeup suggested the possibility of disease sometime in the future? The manipulation of genes has already developed an oversized mouse; what would be the implication of such alterations on Mankind in the distant future?

Other major advances in science and technology have posed threats. In 1979 radioactive water leaked from a nuclear power plant at Three Mile Island in Pennsylvania, threatening the safety of the entire vicinity. For several days, specialists sought to cool the nuclear generator to prevent "meltdown," an overheating of the nuclear facility that would have spread radioactive materials over hundreds of miles of heavily populated areas. Residents of towns near the plant waited anxiously, ready to flee their homes in case of disaster. Luckily, experts were able to avert such a catastrophe. But the near-accident raised new questions about the safety and practicality of atomic energy as a feasible alternative to oil. Several years later, policymakers began to wrestle with the problem of what would be done to dismantle nuclear plants when they were obsolete, something those who originally built them may never have considered.

The nuclear arms race remains an even greater danger to our planet, particularly as that race no longer involves just two powers, the United States and the Soviet Union. Great Britain, France, and China certainly have the capacity to wage nuclear warfare. So probably do India, Pakistan (the two are bitter enemies), Israel, South Africa, and perhaps Argentina. Every year the survivors of the atomic bombs in Hiroshima and Nagasaki in 1945 gather to remind the world of what incredible horrors might again take place. One can only hope that mankind has learned a lesson.

The environment in the United States and other countries as well did not fare well in the 1970s. The dumping of toxic chemicals and other hazardous waste materials in many cities was discovered to pose grave health risks; making it necessary to evacuate many people, even whole towns. Recently the Environmental Protection Agency, originally established to protect the United States, permitted big companies to continue to pollute the environment. "Acid rain" became a diplomatic issue between Canada and the United States, as pollutants produced in the latter country were carried to Canada and fell as contaminated rain, killing fish and plants in distant lakes. Even supersonic air travel posed a similar dilemma between technological advance and human needs. In 1976, the first supersonic airliner, the *Concorde*, a joint venture of France and Great Britain, cut almost in half the time it takes to travel across the Atlantic. The *Concorde* links Paris and London with New York and Washington, and the flight takes little more than three hours. But many people were worried about the ecological consequences of supersonic transport. Furthermore, the cost of tickets on the *Concorde* was prohibitively expensive for almost everyone. For these reasons, the Congress of the United States refused to approve funds for an American supersonic transport.

The French were responsible for the most impressive improvement in rail travel. Japan had long since had a "bullet" train running between its largest cities when the French inaugurated their TGV ("train of great speed") in September 1981. The French train was even faster, able to travel safely at speeds of up to 220

ACID RAIN

miles per hour. The TGV has cut the travel time for the 275-mile trip from Paris to Lyon, France's second-largest city, to less than two hours, an average speed of almost 150 miles per hour. This train carries thousands of people each day, and its speed allows it to compete successfully with the airplane.

Acid rain, toxic waste, and air and noise pollution are relatively new problems. During the 1970s, the world's oldest problem, hunger, remained as grave as ever. At the end of 1974, the world's reserves of grain reached a twenty-six-year low. It was then estimated that half a billion poeple throughout the world did not have enough to eat. About ten thousand people perished each week in Africa, Asia, and Latin America. In West Bengal, experts estimated that fifteen million people were starving to death. The so-called Green Revolution had increased agriculture yields and brought more land under cultivation in many parts of the world. But even this good news was not enough to meet the world's food needs in the face of rapid population increases and shifts in the world's weather.

The population of our planet has continued to grow by about 200,000 people per day, or 7.5 million per year. In January 1984 there were approximately 4.7 billion people on earth. It was estimated that the same rate of population growth would double the world's population by the end of this century, no longer so far away. Cities such as Singapore, Mexico City, Calcutta, and Rio, whose resources were already straining under enormous populations, were inundated with thousands of poor migrants from the countryside, many living in shanty towns propped up on the outskirts of the burgeoning metropolises. Despite some reduction in population growth over the past few years—for example, in China, India, Russia, and some Western countries—food resources are increasingly strained by an ever-expanding population. Compounding this terrible problem, the world's weather began to change in about 1970. Harsh winters and burning droughts became commonplace throughout much of the world. Some ocean currents changed, with disastrous results. For example, when the currents shifted off of the coast of Peru, the small anchovy fish was almost wiped out. The anchovy is a source of protein for animal feed. The result was a reduction in meat supply. For the first time in twenty years, the total production of food in the world fell, declining by an estimated 33 million tons.

Changes in weather, however minor they may seem on a chart, had a dramatic and disastrous impact on the growing season in some nations. Since the 1940s, for example, the average world temperature has fallen by 1 degree Fahrenheit. Such a drop in temperature reduced the growing season by as much as ten days in many of the countries lying in the middle latitudes of the earth, our most productive regions. Wheat and rice, those crops most associated with the Green Revolution, are particularly vulnerable to changes in weather. A drop in moisture reduces crop yields. An increase in the icy winds that whip around our planet from top to bottom prevented the moisture-laden equatorial winds that bring rain to many regions from forming. West Africa and India suffered terrible droughts. On the other hand, growing pollution of the atmosphere may be causing a "greenhouse" effect, heating up parts of the earth. If the giant polar ice field begins to melt, the level of the oceans could rise dangerously, perhaps submerging some of the world's coastal cities.

Population growth, changes in weather, and limitations of the Green Revolution contributed to increase the gap between rich and poor nations. People began to speak of differences between "North and South" instead of just "East and West," contrasting the wealthier northern nations of the world to their less developed southern neighbors.

Hunger threatened to become a source of global conflict. People sometimes referred to those nations that were not industrial and capitalist or Communist as the Third World, although, as time has passed, many of these countries have chosen one camp or the other. Differences between countries in economic growth have led some economists to subdivide the Third World with its population of two billion people into three parts: the "third world," with enough raw material to attract foreign investments and technology (nations such as Zaire, Morocco, and Brazil); the "fourth world," with some raw materials but without capital (such as Peru and the Dominican Republic), and the "fifth world," those nations without raw materials and unable even to grow enough food to allow their own people to survive. These countries, such as Chad and Ethiopia in Africa and Bangladesh in Asia, all suffered deadly droughts during much of the 1970s. The plight of these impoverished lands has been made even worse by internal wars.

As if this were not enough, the temporary refusal of the Arab nations to sell oil to the West, the oil embargo of October 1973, began a period when the price of energy skyrocketed in much of the world. During the next ten years, the price of gasoline quadrupled, rising in the United States from about thirty cents per gallon to a peak of more than one dollar forty cents, although still far less than the price in Western Europe. The embargo had an immediate impact in the United States and led to long lines at gas stations. The speed limit was reduced from 70 to 55 miles per hour to save fuel. Americans took fewer trips in their cars and in airplanes, as the cost of airline tickets rose with the rapidly mounting price of fuel. Many cities and companies started "carpool" programs to encourage riders to share energy use and costs.

GAS SHORTAGES

Americans who had always owned large cars now bought smaller and more fuel-efficient models, an increasing proportion of which were made in Japan. Over the next years, people adjusted to higher energy costs by keeping their houses and offices at cooler temperatures during winter. Some Americans reacted to these deprivations with bitterness, blaming the oil-producing nations, particularly the Arabs, for changing the American way of life. "We're like a castle," observed an expert on the energy crisis, "a brilliant medieval castle, defending itself against foreign at-tackers. Then we suddenly discover that the water supply was outside the castle." The British discovered oil in the North Sea; Mexico and Venezuela prospered as oil-producing countries, at least until oil prices slid back in the early 1980s. Average Amer-icans and also Europeans had to accept some alterations in their lifestyles. They envied the oil that lies under the sands of the Middle East. The question of oil and energy, which put the

United States at a comparative disadvantage with the Soviet Union—which had access to more oil reserves—came to affect the diplomatic policies of American presidents and the domestic decisions of ordinary people confronted with the rising fuel costs and cold winters.

The Iranian Revolution of 1978–79 brought a second period of higher oil prices. The price of a barrel of oil rose to more than ten times what it had been before the first price rises and the original embargo. But consumption, too, fell, as Americans cut back their use of energy. The United States' share of the total consumption of oil in the world fell from 31 percent in 1970 to 25 percent in 1982. The average American home in 1983 used one-fifth less energy than at the time of the embargo. Government controls on the oil industry were ended, which increased production and gave the oil companies enormous "windfall profits." At the same time, weaker controls on pollution allowed the burning of other fuels, notably coal, still a vast resource of the United States. In 1977, the 7.7-billion-dollar Alaska pipeline opened to bring oil from that large, mineral-rich state. At the same time, automobile companies proved they could develop cars that were more fuel efficient. Between 1973 and 1983, the average car's mileage per gallon doubled.

In 1983, a relative "glut," or oversupply, of oil occurred; oil prices stabilized and even temporarily fell; some oil-producing but relatively poor nations, such as Venezuela, Mexico, and Nigeria, that had been given considerable credit found themselves unable to pay their national debts, causing fear of an international financial crisis. But the economic costs of the oil shortage have stayed with us. The oil crisis and higher energy costs short-circuited progress in many underdeveloped countries lacking energy sources of their own. On the other hand, the oil-rich countries of the Middle East found themselves with more money—particularly American dollars—than they knew what to do with. Kuwait's oil supply has made it the richest country in the world of any size in per capita income. Large amounts of real estate in Europe and the United States were purchased by Arabs with U.S. dollars. For many Europeans and Americans, the world seemed to be stood on its head, as the Western World became a "bargain basement" for the oil-rich nations. The energy crisis eroded the confidence of the United States, making Americans wonder if all things were still possible. The nation's position in the world economy also changed. The American steel industry and the automobile and electronic industries faltered against stiff competition from abroad, as Japanese- and German-made products, often technologically superior and produced less expensively, flooded the American market.

In foreign policy no other conflict has so burdened the soul of the American people as the war in Vietnam. Formal American involvement in that troubled land began during the 1950s. The Communist forces of Ho Chi Minh had defeated the French, who had colonized the country, at the battle of Dien Bien Phu in May 1954. At a conference in Geneva, Switzerland, Vietnam was divided into two parts, North and South, with Ho Chi Minh founding a Communist government in the north. Ngo Dinh Diem became the premier of South Vietnam, backed by the United States. In 1955, the possibility of reunification ended when the United States went along with Diem's decision to refuse to agree to elections that could have led to a united Vietnam. Guerilla warfare in the south between supporters of the Communists and the government of South Vietnam became an increasingly familiar scene. Several American military advisers were killed in July of 1959.

Four years later, Diem's dictatorial government faced waves of protests. He was overthrown as Americans stepped aside, and then executed. Thirteen governments in nineteen months followed, as the Vietcong—the South Vietnamese Communists— grew in strength in the countryside and launched a full-fledged war against the government of South Vietnam.

The involvement of the United States in the Vietnam civil war "escalated"—one of those words that came to symbolize the 1960s. In 1964, President Lyndon Johnson asked Congress to pass a resolution calling on him to take "all necessary steps" in Southeast Asia. He alleged that North Vietnamese ships had attacked American destroyers in the Gulf of Tonkin. By 1965, American marines were sent to Vietnam. Another *coup d'état* in South Vietnam, this one by the South Vietnamese Army, left General Nguyen Van Thieu as head of state and Marshal Nguyen Cao Ky as Premier. Some 150,000 American troops were brought to Vietnam by the end of 1965. Three years later, U.S. forces in Vietnam had risen in number to well over half a million.

The United States thus found itself fighting an undeclared war on the other side of the world that an increasingly large number of its citizens did not believe was necessary, moral, or worth its enormous cost in lives and money. The first open discussions about and against the war ("teach-ins") took place on university campuses as early as the spring of 1965. Students burned their draft cards defiantly. As fighting spread to the demilitarized zone between the North and South in 1967, waves of American aircraft began to bomb the North. But neither bombs from the air nor troops on the ground could destroy the Vietcong, aided by troops from the North. On January 30, 1968, they launched the Tet offensive, attacking virtually all important cities in the South. Despite the eventual defeat of the Tet offensive, the Communist

VIETNAM

forces dealt a major blow to South Vietnam. They proved that they could mount a major military campaign in the South as well as continue to strike in guerilla fashion against the South Vietnamese and Americans. The Tet offensive also gave the world one of the most awful images in the war, a picture seen by millions of people on their television screens. The director of the South Vietnamese National Police was captured forever on film as he fired his pistol into the temple of a prisoner. An even more gripping image was a terrified peasant woman with a child hideously disfigured by a burning chemical solution called napalm dropped by American planes.

In America, President Johnson announced he would not run for a second term in 1968, and truce talks finally opened in Paris between representatives of the United States and North Vietnam. Senator Eugene McCarthy ran for the Democrat nomination as President, with opposition to the war his number one issue. Richard Nixon, who defeated Hubert Humphrey, presidential candidate of the Democrats, emphasized secret negotiations in the Paris talks and sought "Vietnamization" of the fighting. But anti-war protests spread in the United States, particularly in the fall of 1969.

In April of 1970, President Nixon sent troops into Cambodia to attack areas where the Vietcong had been relatively secure across the border. Massive bombing killed thousands of villagers. In the United States, waves of protest, especially among college students, followed, one climaxing in the shooting of four unarmed students at Kent State University by the National Guard. In the spring of 1972, the Communists launched another major offensive. Nixon then ordered American ships to mine Haiphong Harbor and other major ports. But already secret talks were pointing toward an American withdrawal from combat. In June 1972, the same month that the Watergate break-in began to cast an enormous shadow over President Nixon and American political life, most American troops were withdrawn from Vietnam.

A peace agreement was signed in January 1973, but the war—for the Vietnamese—was far from over. Both sides violated the cease-fire. The South Vietnamese Army, facing a cutoff of military funds from the United States and weakened by corruption

and indifference, gradually abandoned the highlands. The Vietcong took over cities in the South one by one. In 1975, South
Vietnam fell to Communist forces. Once again, television cameras
caught the most memorable moments of that disastrous war, as
Americans and South Vietnamese civilians desperately pushed
their way into helicopters to get out as Saigon "fell," or "was
liberated" (depending on one's point of view—once again history
often seems to be a question of "whose ox has been gored"). By
the end of 1976, Cambodia and Laos were Communist as well.

The United States' longest war was over. More than 56,000
Americans had died in Vietnam, far fewer than the approximately
1,250,000 Vietnamese who were killed. Vietnam left many marks
on the America of the 1970s and early 1980s. For one thing, it had
been brought by television into American living rooms. And the
costs were enormous. Over 140 billion dollars had been spent, a
sum that fueled inflation at home. Other costs were large, as well.
The war helped alienate many among those of college age in the
late 1960s and early 1970s. Some students evaded the draft by
going to Canada, registering as conscientious objectors, or even
going to prison for their beliefs that the war, and war in general, was
wrong. American campuses exploded in anger, rocked by protests
and, sometimes, violence. Some hardcore protesters sought to
"bring the war home." An explosion set by an anti-war activist
killed a researcher in one American university in 1970. But the
war touched the conscience of America. An American army
lieutenant was convicted of mass murder for his actions in a
massacre of civilians in My Lai, Vietnam, in 1968. The savage
Christmas bombing of North Vietnam in 1972—just after Secretary of State Henry Kissinger had promised, before the election of
that November, that peace was "at hand"—angered many Americans. What is more, the war caused great strains on America's
relations with its allies. American embassies in almost every
country in the world were scenes of demonstrations. Daniel
Ellsberg, who revealed the contents of the "Pentagon Papers,"
telling of a secret American war in supposedly "neutral" Cambodia, forced the country to confront the morality of its own
policies. Yet, despite the carnage, American citizens helped bring

the war to a close. The Vietnam experience forced the United States to reexamine its role in the world.

Gravely shaken by the Vietnam War, American self-confidence was further weakened by what came to be called the Watergate scandal. Richard Nixon, Dwight Eisenhower's vice-president from 1952 to 1960, had never succeeded in completely overcoming his reputation as "Tricky Dick," which went back to his early political life. Victor over Hubert Humphrey in the 1968 election, the Republican Nixon was elected by a landslide over George McGovern in 1972. Few people paid much attention earlier that year in June to the arrest of five men caught planting listening devices in the headquarters of the Democratic National Committee at the Watergate building in Washington, D.C. The fact that these five "burglars" were linked to the CIA and to Nixon's reelection committee had little influence on the election.

Yet the trial of these Watergate burglars revealed that they were "taking the rap" for highly placed people. As the Watergate scandal came to occupy public attention, the responsibility for the seedy affair moved closer to Nixon himself. His former counsel, John Dean, named the President as a conspirator in the cover-up of the Watergate affair. It became known that Nixon had taped conversations held in his Oval Office. The President tried to keep the tapes from scrutiny and asked Attorney General Elliot Richardson to fire the special prosecutor for the Watergate affair, Archibald Cox. Richardson refused and then resigned. Nixon's bold effort to subvert the judicial process, known as the Saturday Night Massacre, brought increasing demands for Nixon's resignation or impeachment. When the tapes were finally turned over to the Watergate prosecutor, one had a gap of over eighteen minutes long. It turned out that the Watergate burglary was merely the "tip of the iceberg," just one of a whole host of dirty tricks and illegal activities by Nixon administration officials, including accepting illegal campaign contributions from big business. The tapes themselves revealed a large dark side to Nixon's presidency. Some of the men who had surrounded him and been engaged in wrong-doing were convicted and went to jail, including the President's closest associates. Nixon himself, who had lied about the affair, resigned in disgrace in August 1974, before he could be impeached by the Senate. He was replaced by Gerald Ford, himself only recently named Vice-President to replace Spiro Agnew, who resigned after pleading no contest to charges of income tax evasion. Gerald Ford offered a, "full, free, and absolute pardon" to Nixon, who returned to his San Clemente, California, estate to write his memoirs. The reputation of the American presidency was certainly tarnished, but the American constitution and the people of the United States had proved themsleves resilient. Gerald Ford in some way appeared to be an unlikely person to become President of the United States. One television commentator asked him if he could "grow into the job." For many people, public confidence in Mr. Ford was shaken when he granted Nixon a presidential pardon, while some of the lesser culprits in the Watergate mess went to prison. Although Ford restored some integrity to the presidency, he was not able to defeat Georgia Governor Jimmy Carter in the election of 1976. Carter, elected by a coalition representing the South, labor, and minorities, was something of a populist. But his reputation too quickly faded, as he proved unable to deal with mounting domestic economic problems and foreign policy crises. Public confidence in Carter as an experienced and decisive head of state eroded. He was defeated in a landslide by Ronald Reagan in the 1980 election, winning only two states and the District of Columbia.

The newly elected president promised to reduce the role of government and balance the federal budget while restoring the country's powerful image in the world and leading the country out of the economic morass. To some people, though, Reagan also seemed an unlikely man for the most crucial job in the world. A former actor, Reagan's election suggested that powerful financial backing and a slick presentation were the most important assets for a would-be president in our age of television.

Whereas in the past incumbent American presidents had a tremendous advantage over challengers in an election, during the sixties and seventies the pattern changed with the defeats of both Mr. Ford and Mr. Carter. The performances of American presidents have become subject to close and almost instantaneous scrutiny by the media. Their speeches are quickly analyzed and graded with the same speed and intensity as the performance of baseball players in the American World Series, or soccer players during the World Cup. Yet the problems recent presidents have had in being reelected also point to diminished public confidence in them; they have lacked the ability to generate public faith that characterized Franklin Roosevelt, Dwight Eisenhower, and John F. Kennedy.

The 1970s saw advances for the rights of women, particularly in the United States. In 1972, the Senate passed the Equal Rights Amendment to the Constitution to end discrimination based upon sex. Yet ten years later the amendment had not been ratified by a sufficient number of states to become law. But there were other changes that altered the legal position of women. In 1973, the Supreme Court legalized abortion during the early stages of pregnancy. More women entered the labor force, including the professions of law, medicine, business, and university teaching, although women continued to be paid lower wages for the same work as men in many occupations. Women running for and winning political office was no longer unusual. In 1974, Ella Grasso of Connecticut became the first woman, who had not succeeded her husband as governor, to be elected governor of a state. Sandra Day O'Connor was appointed by President Reagan as the first woman on the Supreme Court. Women made great strides in athletics, as federal law guaranteed financial support for women's sports in high school and college. Tennis players Billie Jean King and Chris Evert Lloyd became national sports figures. Margaret Thatcher became the first female Prime Minister in England when her conservative party won the 1979 elections. In 1983, Sally Ride became the first American female astronaut to go into space. For millions of women, the gradual shift to being addressed as "Ms." instead of "Miss" or "Mrs"—as a parallel to the address of "Mr." for men— helped enhance their image as a complete person without reference to marital status. All of this was a good beginning. One must never forget the story of Mankind is equally the story of women.

The civil rights movement had been one of the most significant occurrences of the 1960s. During the 1970s, blacks began to attain

political office, particularly as mayors in a number of major American cities, such as Detroit, Los Angeles, and Atlanta. On the
twentieth anniversary of the great "march on Washington" of
August 1963, when Martin Luther King gave his famous "I have a
Dream" speech, few could deny that American blacks had
achieved more advances. But there was still much more to accomplish. Segregation continued in many school systems. The Supreme Court's ruling in the "reverse discrimination" case of Alan
Bakk, a California student, set back court-ordered preference for
minorities in education and business. The civil rights movement
escaped another defeat when the Reagan administration's attempt
to grant tax exemptions to schools that discriminate against blacks
failed. The economic future of young blacks remained bleak, as
they continued to suffer the highest unemployment rate in the
United States, while the government reduced many of the welfare
programs that had helped the poor subsist.

During the 1970s homosexuals began to assert their rights to
fair treatment. Despite a conservative backlash, communities of
"gays" flourished in many cities, particularly New York and San
Fransisco, and found far more acceptance than before, and some
political representation.

Life in the 1970s and early 1980s reflected a combination of
continuity with the past and of change. Symphony orchestras,
opera, and the trumpeted arrival of great artistic exhibitions
brought from Europe found eager audiences in America's largest
cities. But television, radio, recorded music, and the best-seller
book list—all aided by technological improvements—remained
the heart of popular entertainment. Cable television brought
many channels into more and more American homes. No longer
does television reception depend on topography, weather, or the
size and location of an antenna. Some channels began to offer full-
length feature movies twenty-four hours a day. One can push a
button and find round-the-clock news and weather, or sports,
brought from afar by satellite. The development of electronics has
made it possible to record television programs for later viewing and
to rent cassettes of popular movies for showing at any time in
private homes, with popcorn readily available in the nearby

kitchen. FM radio remained popular, particularly stations that emphasized either classical music, usually public radio, or rock and roll. In the late 1970s, the recording industry began to experience some difficulties, largely because of astonishing advances in tape-recording techniques, which seemed on the verge of making the record obsolete. Rock concerts, while less resembling the massive events of the late sixties and early seventies (such as the most famous, in Woodstock, New York, in 1969, attended by hundreds of thousands of people), still were eagerly awaited by the younger generation, their numbers swollen by the grudgingly aging generation of the 1960s who still fill a concert hall or sports stadium to hear groups such as the Rolling Stones and the Who. The fact that the star lead singer of the Stones, Mick Jagger, turned forty in 1983 did not seem to have slowed him or his legions of fans down. Fads like the "Disco-mania" (discotheque music) proved short lived, as nostalgia for the rock and roll music of twenty years earlier survived. One found the same nostalgia in the great success of movies like *American Graffiti*, the story of high school students growing up in the mid-1960s, and *Animal House*, the pranks and pitfalls of college students in the age of innocence before the war in Vietnam.

This nostalgia accompanied the emergence of a new generation of college students who seemed to have abandoned the social activism of the late 1960s. Getting good grades and worrying about careers in a highly competitive age became of paramount importance, this at a time when the quality of American education, particularly in the high schools, was apparently falling, or at least not progressing. Some expressed dismay at the end of idealism expressed by the slogan "Looking out for Number One." Others would argue that, in order to build a better world, one has to be practical.

Yet despite the inevitable aging of the generation of the sixties and the ever-increasing lifespan of mankind, at least in the developed world, much of our culture continues to be centered on youthfulness and the young. Young actresses such as Brooke Shields and Jodie Foster symbolized the cult of youth in successful movies, but in a far more worldly and less innocent way than

Shirley Temple had four decades earlier. Just as "think young" became a maxim for commercialized advertising, "staying young" emerged as common sense for life. Jogging became a national craze in the United States, and many people took the old saying "You are what you eat" seriously and tried to eat healthier foods. So-called natural foods, once associated with hippies who had dropped out from the American scene, now were found in the average household. Scientists made considerable progress in the search for the causes of cancer, that great killer of our century, warning us against the danger of smoking cigarettes and reminding us that certain foods that we had taken for granted for centuries, such as salt and red meat, were not necessarily good for us. Scientists made much less progress in the monumental struggle to find a cure for cancer, despite improvements in detection techniques and enhanced public awareness.

Some years ago, a Russian writer wrote a small book entitled *Will the Soviet Union Survive until 1984?* So far, however, the USSR has proved that it could weather economic problems, repress dissent, and survive surges of nationalism in those countries dependent upon it and within its borders. The Soviet Union showed few signs of change during the years of the leadership of Leonid Brezhnev, who died in 1981. Life for dissidents remained grim. The most famous voice of opposition within the Soviet Union, the writer Alexander Solzhenitsyn, emigrated to the United States as a refugee. The number of Jews leaving Russia for the United States and Israel increased. President Jimmy Carter offered dissidents encouragement in the name of human rights when he sent a letter to the physicist Andrei Sakharov in 1976 pledging to "seek the release of prisoners of conscience."

Although both President Carter and Russian Premier Leonid Brezhnev signed the second Strategic Arms Limitation Treaty (SALT) in 1979, the two super-powers remained bitter enemies. Since then, despite much talk, neither country has seemed serious about reducing its nuclear arsenals, with the Americans placing powerful Pershing missiles in Europe, despite strong anti-nuclear movements in both Europe and the United States. Certainly Soviet actions have not inspired confidence in the West even after

Brezhnev's death. In 1979, the Red Army invaded its neighbor Afghanistan when the Soviet-backed faction faced unyielding opposition in that mountainous, poor country. The Soviets played a role in the repression of the Solidarity Trade Union in Poland and became involved in events in Africa, particularly Angola, Mozambique, and Ethiopia. When the Russians shot down a Korean airliner that strayed over the strategically critical Soviet island of Sakhalin north of Japan in September 1983, taking it for a spy plane, an international uproar followed. We appeared to be on the verge of the return of the "Cold War," particularly as the Red Army began to assert a more forcefully political role in the Soviet Union and the question of leadership within the elite of the Soviet Politboros elderly membership remained unsettled.

During the 1950s and 1960s, Americans, including those who carried out the foreign policy of the United States, tended to lump the Soviet Union and China together as Communist powers hostile to the interests of the free world. After the Vietnam War, in which both the Soviet Union and China aided North Vietnam and the Vietcong, the Western world became more aware of the many historical, territorial, and ideological issues that divided the two powers. By the 1970s, it sometimes seemed that these giant neighbors would be fighting each other rather than the United States.

While the United States and the USSR were so heavily armed that they could destroy each other in much less than an hour, they found that the force of arms was not enough to enforce their wills or win friends throughout the world. The Soviets crushed the spark of liberty, the relative freedom of expression that characterized the "Prague Spring" in Czechoslovakia in 1968. Following their invasion of Afghanistan in 1979, they found themselves bogged down in a war against guerillas determined to fight them to the death.

In 1980, a trade union movement arose in Poland called Solidarity. The support that the Polish people gave to the movement, which opposed the arbitrary decision making of the state in the name of freedom, indicated that other cracks in the Eastern European bloc might occur. The threat of the Soviet army and the imposition of martial law by the Polish authorities could not stamp out the call for greater freedom. Lech Walesa, a worker from Gdańsk, the scene of anti-regime riots in 1970, won the 1983 Nobel Peace Prize for his role in the events there as the lead of Solidarity.

Like the Soviet Union, the United States must take some responsibility for the problems democracy has had in some of the world. In September 1973, the Chilean army, aided and encouraged by the CIA, moved against the popularly elected president, Salvadore Allende, a Marxist. The military government that followed inaugurated a reign of terror, torture, and execution. Ten years later, the United States still backed the dictator General Pinochet in that unhappy country. It also supported other dictatorships in Latin America, such as those in Argentina (although America leaned toward the British during the brief war that England fought against Argentina over the Falkland Islands in 1982) and in Brazil. In Central America, the United States backed oppressive regimes in Guatamala and El Salvador. In Asia, the support of the United States helped lend legitimacy and power to the governments of the Philippines and South Korea, which many of those nations' people saw as repression. After a left-wing revolution ended the dictatorship in Nicaragua, the United States government blamed the Russians and Cubans for that and similar developments in Central America. Such a policy brought criticism from a number of American allies, such as France and our neighbor Mexico.

In October 1983, the United States invaded the tiny Caribbean island of Grenada, (population of 110,000) near the coast of Venezuela. This invasion, although planned earlier, came in response to requests by neighboring islands that the United States remove from power a recently installed leftist faction. Claiming that the United States medical students on the island were in danger, President Reagan cited the presence of Cuban and Soviet advisers and arms of the island as justifying such an invasion. This action, which was widely supported in the United States, brought overwhelming criticism in the United Nations from over one hundred countries, including some of America's closest allies, who deplored the violation of international law. On a smaller and much less bloody scale, the United States intervention recalled for some the

Soviet invasion of Afghanistan, showing that both superpowers were willing to ignore world opinion to accomplish their ends. At the same time, the United States worked openly to overthrow the government of Nicaragua in Central America, as the Soviets engaged in similar activity in Africa. Old Machiavelli, were he still living, might quote the proverb, "The more things change, the more they remain the same."

In Iran, American support could not keep the Shah in power in the face of overwhelming opposition that powerful and wealthy emperor faced. He was driven from power in 1979 and took refuge in the United States and then Egypt before his death. The Iranian revolution brought to power the Ayatollah Khomeini, a religious leader intent on creating a state based on Islamic fundamentalism. Many ordinary Iranians, who hated the feared secret police of the Shah, now had reason to fear the new regime, particularly if they were Communists or Bahais, a religious group.

The close association of the Shah with the United States generated a tremendous hatred of America and Americans in Iran. On a Sunday morning in November 1979, an angry crowd stormed the American Embassy in Tehran and took 150 hostages. The Iranians kept the hostages in bleak conditions for over a year, while the world watched. The United States, despite its power, was unable to secure their release. An attempt to free them by force failed. Finally, they were released after over a year in captivity.

Although at the time it was still the undeclared enemy of the United States in Vietnam, China received a visit from President Nixon in 1972. During the next decade, relations improved dramatically between the two powers. President Carter was the first American chief of state to recognize China officially. Inside China, the Cultural Revolution, begun in 1966, greatly set back the development of the economy. The young "Red Guards" stormed through China in an attempt to "purify" the supposed enemies of Mao and reeducate the intellectuals and other potential enemies by putting them to work in the fields. Mao himself, an increasingly feeble old man, was rarely seen. His wife Jiang Quing and the "Gang of Four" ruthlessly eliminated opposition. Lin Biao, commander of the army, plotted to kill Mao but himself died in a plane crash trying to escape the country after the plot was discovered. He may have been assassinated. A major earthquake in China seemed to augur the fall of the Communist "dynasty," as such natural disasters had during the traditional imperial dynasties signaled the end of God's approval (the mandate of heaven) and the fall of the emperor. Chao En-lai, China's respected leader who had opened the way for better relations with the West, died in January 1976. Mao Tse-tung, Chairman, one of the major figures of our century, passed away in September of the same year.

How long could the madness of the Cultural Revolution go on? Two generals, Ye Jianying and Li Xiannian, led a virtual palace coup, putting the "Gang of Four" under arrest. The old generals brought back into political leadership one victim of the Cultural Revolution, Deng Xiaoping. In 1981, the Chinese Communist party admitted that certain errors had been made. Mao remained a great hero, but one who was human and had made great mistakes. It was left to the new regime to undo much of the damage that had been done during the 1966–76 period. In this they have succeeded remarkably well. China remains a poor country with four out of every five people working in agriculture. When peasants were given more control over the land they worked, production increased. The level of industrial production grew dramatically, with the city of Peking producing ten times more steel than all of China in the early 1940's. China's industrial centers began turning out more consumer goods, some of which could be traded to the West. Lately, commercial advertising has never been seen on Chinese television. The government continued to tackle the enormous problem of overpopulation, its population having more than doubled, to the astonishing figure of one billion since World War II. The current leadership of China wants to maintain good relations with the United States and, at the same time, to improve those with the Soviet Union. Three significant issues still stand in the way of better relations between the United States and China. The United States continues to support and to arm the government of Taiwan, that troubled island occupied by the defeated Nationalist troops who fled Mao's armies in 1949. The successor of

Chiang Kai-shek, Mao's rival for power during the Chinese civil war, still claims to be the legitimate government of China. Furthermore, while the Chinese would like the United States to increase trade with their country, at the same time American manufacturers worry about being flooded with products produced in China at a much lower cost. Finally, the Chinese resent the fact the American government prevents the export to China of particularly sensitive technological equipment that could serve military ends. But, these problems aside, Chinese in major cities are no longer surprised to see American tourists gaping at the wonders of one of Mankind's most fabulous civilizations, one with the potential to contribute as gloriously to our world as did its ancestors who so amazed pioneering European visitors such as Marco Polo and Matteo Ricci centuries ago.

The Middle East became the world's most dangerous hot-spot in the 1970s, adding to tension between the Soviet Union and the United States. A permanent state of unrest between the Arab countries and Israel continued to engulf the entire region. In 1973, six years after the first Arab-Israeli war, Israel's Arab neighbors launched a sudden attack on the day of the Jewish religious holiday of Yom Kippur. After some initial success they were soundly defeated by the superior Israeli army and air force. The support the Western powers, particularly the United States, gave Israel led to the Arab oil embargo, which, as we have already seen, had disastrous consequences for the world economy. Israel and Egypt finally began to discuss possibilities for mutual peace. In 1978, Egyptian President Anwar Sadat and Israeli Prime Minister Menachem Begin signed the Camp David accord. Sadat, who visited Israel in 1977, earned the undying emnity of some Arab states for his part in these difficult negotiations. He was assassinated in 1981. The Camp David accords, in which President Carter had played such a large part, led to the return to Egypt of the Sinai Peninsula by Israel.

But peace in the Middle East has yet to be obtained. The Arab states have refused to acknowledge the existence and legitimacy of the state of Israel, which had been carved out of lands that Jews and Arabs had occupied for several thousand years. The question of the Palestinian people remained unresolved. Some 3.2 million Palestinians remained a people without a land, pawns in the disagreements among the Arab states and second-class citizens in Israel. Several hundred thousand of them were living in terrible conditions in refugee camps on the West Bank and in Jordan. Out of this desperation and poverty emerged the Palestine Liberation Organization. The violent factions of the P.L.O. struck at Israel through terrorism, making Israelis everywhere vulnerable to their bloody attacks.

The tactics of the P.L.O. obscured the fact that something has to be done for the Palestinian people. Israeli expansion on the West Bank, seeking to create the biblical kingdom of Israel, has continued to dislocate them further. The hard-line policies of Premier Begin, who resigned in September 1983, prevented any compromise. Begin, himself a terrorist during the struggle against the British after World War II, ordered an invasion of Lebanon, from whose territory the Palestinian guerilla groups had been able to launch attacks on Israel. In the summer of 1982, the Israelis drove out much of the P.L.O., including its leader, Yassar Arafat. The Israeli presence permitted a shaky victory of the Christian forces over the Moslems in Lebanon, and the massacre of hundreds of Moslems in the Palestinian refugee camps of Sabra and Shatila in Beirut by the Christians. Sadly, while P.L.O. terrorists killed Jews and Israeli bombs rained down on civilians in Beirut, the Palestinian question moved no closer to being solved. At the same time, Lebanon's tragedy continues. That battered land remains sharply divided between Christians and Moslems. Even within these two major religious groups, bitter rivalries remain as small and heavily armed factions compete for power, despite the presence of international peace-keeping forces. In October 1983, enormous bombs shattered the early morning, killing over two hundred United States marines and half as many French troops sent to try to keep the peace. The loss of American life, the most devastating day of casualties suffered by an American military force since the Vietnam War, raised doubts about the role of the United States in the Middle East.

In Europe, the period after 1970 brought the Left to power in the Mediterranean world, while the Right did better in northern Europe. A revolution unseated Portuguese Dictator Salazar. General Franco, who had ruled Spain with an iron fist since the end of the Civil War in 1939, died in November 1975, long after his admired colleagues Adolf Hitler and Benito Mussolini. The personal prestige and determination of King Juan Carlos helped bring about a surprisingly peaceful transition to democracy in that long-troubled country, with the Socialists coming to power in 1982. One would-be coup by army officers failed after they held the Spanish Parliament hostage. France, too, elected a Socialist, François Mitterrand, president in May 1981; he succeeded Valéry Giscard d'Estaing and appeared to be even more anti-Soviet than his supposedly more rightist predecessor. The Gaullists, having lost their hero, de Gaulle, in November 1970 and his successor, Georges Pompidou, several years later, turned increasingly to Jacques Chirac, the mayor of Paris. In Italy, government succeeded government. Terrorism from the extreme left and the extreme right intensified that country's instability. In Greece, a military coup brought George Papadopoulis to power in 1967. In 1973, a student rising preceded another military coup, with an evolution toward a troubled Socialist government, while the United States worried about the fate of its bases in that strategic country.

The Catholic Church went through a period of change. The Vatican II council in 1962 had approved freedom of discussion within the Church. In an effort to bring the faith to everyone, it ruled that the mass no longer had to be said in Latin, but could be in the language of every nation. In 1978, smoke from the traditional Vatican chimney announced astonishing news to the world's 700 million Catholics: the Cardinals had chosen the first non-Italian pope in 455 years, Karol Cardinal Wojtyla of Cracow, Poland. The new pope won great popularity in much of the world, visiting more countries than any of his predecessors and surviving an assassination attempt in 1981. He has followed events in his own country with particular energy and has been a source of support for the men and women of the trade union, Solidarity, against the Communist government.

Africa remains a troubled continent, torn by poverty, hunger, and civil war. Biafra's three-year war for independence from Nigeria ended in 1970, with two million Biafrans dead. A racist regime based upon white supremacy and segregation continues in South Africa.   After a civil war, Rhodesia made a relatively peaceful transition from white minority rule to black majority rule and was renamed Zimbabwe. Libyan-backed forces fought a civil war in Chad against a regime backed by the United States and France, its former colonial power. In Uganda, madman dictator Idi Amin's murderous reign appalled the civilized world, and he was driven away by Tanzanian troops in 1979.

Not all political violence, of course, was directed at its citizens by dictatorships. Political assassination remained a sad sign of the times; terrorism became a way of life for many groups intent on achieving their goals against powerful states. The assassinations of President Kennedy in 1963, his brother Robert in 1968, and Martin Luther King, the great civil rights leader, that same year were followed by attempts on the lives of presidential candidate George

TERRORIST BOMB EXPLOSION

Wallace in 1972 and two attempts to kill President Gerald Ford. Both the Pope and President Reagan survived the bullets of assassins in 1981. And much of the world mourned the murder of former Beatle singer John Lennon, who sang of peace, gunned down in New York City by a crazed man in 1980.

Terrorism emerged as a deadly weapon for violent groups. The Olympic Games, symbol of the possibilities of international cooperation and peaceful competition, were held in Munich, West Germany, in 1972. Eight heavily armed Palestinian terrorists took Israeli athletes as hostages, killing eleven of them as police stormed the building where they were held. The world, shocked by such bloodshed and stunned by the cold-blooded resolve of men to kill innocent people and be killed, saw other such tragedies. In Northern Ireland, violence escalated, beginning in 1969, as the outlawed Catholic Irish Republican Army struck savagely and often at their Protestant Irish and British enemies, demanding that Northern Ireland cease to be part of Great Britain. Protestant groups retaliated in kind. The 1970s witnessed a number of bloody attacks against Jews. Few could forget the horrible sight of bodies lying before a synagogue in Paris in 1980, or in the Jewish quarter in that same city. There were a number of attacks on officials and airlines by Armenians, who were protesting the massacres of their countrymen by Turks before World War I. In Italy the far-left Red Brigades launched a series of bloody attacks against the state. Right-wing terrorists blew up the railroad station in Bologna, killing nearly one hundred people, and were responsible for a murderous explosion at the Munich Oktoberfest in 1980. Terrorists seemed to be able to strike almost everywhere, even near Buckingham Palace in London during a parade. Some terrorist activity could be traced to Libya and the regime of dictator Quadafi. In 1976, the Israelis struck back against terrorism, as commandos rescued 104 hostages who had been flown to Entebbe airport in Uganda. One or two hardened people, willing to die for what they believe is a just cause, could create a mood of fear, sharpening the hatred between enemies, making reasonable solutions to political and international problems even more difficult than ever in our troubled world.

The theme of human resilience is certainly not new to the Story of Mankind. Battered by economic crises and the deterioration of our environment, vulnerable to dictatorship and terrorism, and caught between the power struggle of the two superpowers, the people of our planet can take considerable consolation in knowing that Mankind has outlasted previous dangers. We have seen the revival of several blighted American cities, such as Baltimore and Detroit, and the rebirth of some temporarily destroyed natural resources, such as the Thames River in England and Lake Erie in the United States. Perhaps the gigantic environmental challenges we face can be met by determined action. We should find hope in the massive anti-nuclear-arms movement in Europe and in the ground swell of support for ecological movements in the United States concerned with protecting our environment. We also have in our world the example of many people whose courage, integrity, and energetic commitment to Mankind we can admire: people such as Jacobo Timmermann, the intellectual who stood up to the persecution of Jews and democracy in Argentina; Anwar Sadat, who worked so hard to unite his country, Egypt, and to bring peace to the Middle East; Mother Theresa, the diminutive nun who worked anonymously for years among the desperately poor of Calcutta before winning the Nobel Prize for peace and calling the world's attention to the hungry, the poor, and the forgotten in that vast subcontinent and elsewhere; Gabriel García Márquez, another writer who survived the authoritarian regime in Chile to win the Nobel Prize for literature; playwright Athol Fugard, who emerged from the racially segregated world of South Africa to delight audiences with his plays; and Lech Walesa, who led the Solidarity trade union in Poland in its fight for freedom. These men and women have worked selflessly for a better world. The more difficult the challenges Mankind must face in the future, the more we must work together.

AN ANIMATED CHRONOLOGY
500,000 B.C.—A.D. 2000

800 B.C
CARTHAGE FOUNDED BY THE PHOENICIANS
ROME FOUNDED
THE GREAT HEBREW PROPHETS

700 B.C.
RISE AND FALL OF ASSYRIAN EMPIRE
NINEVEH DESTROYED
GREEK COLONIES ESTABLISHED

600 B.C.
SOLON GIVES THE ATHENIANS THEIR LAWS
BUDDHA IN INDIA
CONFUCIUS IN CHINA

500 B.C.
MARATHON
PERICLES
GOLDEN AGE OF ATHENS
GREEK THEATRE FLOURISHES

400 B.C.
WAR BETWEEN ATHENS AND SPARTA. ATHENS IS DESTROYED
ATHENS REVIVES AS A SEAT OF LEARNING
SOCRATES AND PLATO

300 B.C.
ARISTOTLE
ALEXANDER THE GREAT
HANNIBAL AND THE C.E.F.

200 B.C.
CARTHAGE DESTROYED
GREECE BECOMES A ROMAN PROVINCE
SPQR
ROME MISTRESS OF MEDITERRANEAN SEA.
LAST INDEPENDENT JEWISH KINGDOM OF THE MACCABEES.

100 B.C.
MEDITERRANEAN SEA
POMPEY CONQUERS WESTERN ASIA
CAESAR CONQUERS GAUL
CAESAR IS MURDERED
AUGUST BECOMES EMPEROR

7 A.D.
BIRTH OF CHRIST.
CHRISTIAN DOCTRINES CARRIED TO WESTERN EUROPE
CONQUEST OF ENGLAND

100 A.D.
ROMAN EMPIRE RULES THE WORLD
TRAJAN
HADRIAN
MARCUS AURELIUS
STOIC PHILOSOPHY

200 A.D.
300 A.D.
THE BARBARIANS ATTACK ON THE ROMAN EMPIRE

400 A.D.
SAINT AUGUSTIN. BEGINNING OF THE PAPACY
ROME PLUNDERED BY THE GOTHS.
END OF THE WESTERN PART OF THE ROMAN EMPIRE
SAXONS IN ENGLAND

500 A.D.
600 A.D.
THE DARK AGES
ON THE RUINS OF ROME ARISES THE CHURCH
MOHAMMED

1500 A.D.
COLUMBUS
MAGELLAN
THE AGE OF THE GREAT DISCOVERIES.
REFORMATION
ERASMUS. ZWINGLI. LUTHER. MELANCHTON CALVIN
COUNTER-REFORMATION
LOYOLA AND THE JESUITS
FAILURE OF THE ARMADA
QUEEN ELIZABETH IN ENGLAND
REVOLT OF THE NETHERLANDS AGAINST SPAIN. ABJURATION OF KING PHILIP II
FIRST DEMAND THAT THE SEA BE "FREE TO ALL PEOPLE"

1600 A.D.
EUROPEAN COLONIES IN ALL PARTS OF THE WORLD
RELIGIOUS WARFARE
THIRTY YEARS WAR. GUSTAVUS ADOLPHUS OF SWEDEN
END OF THE RENAISSANCE
BEGINNING OF SCIENCE GALILEO. NEWTON
SHAKESPEARE MOLIERE
REVOLUTION IN ENGLAND. KING CHARLES IS EXECUTED. CROMWELL

1700 A.D.
LOUIS XIV AND WILLIAM OF ORANGE
BALANCE OF POWER.
PRUSSIA BECOMES A WORLD-POWER
RUSSIA BECOMES A WORLD POWER
AMERICAN REVOLUTION
WASHINGTON FRANKLIN HAMILTON JEFFERSON
THE PHILOSOPHERS. SPINOZA DESCARTES DIDEROT VOLTAIRE KANT. GOETHE.
J. S. BACH MOZART.
REVOLUTION IN FRANCE. KING LOUIS XVI IS EXECUTED. FRENCH REPUBLIC

1800 A.D.
RISE AND FALL OF NAPOLEON
HOLY ALLIANCE. AGE OF REACTION
STEAM ENGINE
STEAM BOAT
MODERN MEDICINE
HYGIENE AND SOCIAL STUDIES
SLAVERY ABOLISHED ABRAHAM LINCOLN
RAILROAD
ELECTRICITY
REVOLT OF THE SPANISH COLONIES IN SOUTH AMERICA.
STRUGGLES IN EUROPE FOR NATIONAL INDEPENDENCE.
GERMAN EMPIRE REESTABLISHED.
BEETHOVEN WAGNER

1900 A.D.
COMBUSTION ENGINE PERFECTED
LARGE SCALE PRODUCTION
COMMERCIAL RIVALRY
RIVALRY IN ARMAMENT
WORLD WAR
PUSH-BUTTON AGE
League of Nations United Nations Atomic and Chemical Warfare Space Travel
WORLD WIDE ECONOMIC UNREST
GERMAN AND RUSSIAN EMPIRES COME TO AN END
MANY NEW NATIONALITIES ESTABLISHED.

INDEX